Parties, Politics,
AND THE
Sectional Conflict
IN
Tennessee,
1832–1861

Parties, Politics,
AND THE
Sectional Conflict
IN
Tennessee,
1832–1861

Jonathan M. Atkins

The University of Tennessee Press / Knoxville

Copyright © 1997 by The University of Tennessee Press / Knoxville.
All Rights Reserved.
Cloth: 1st printing, 1997.
Paper: 1st printing, 2012.

Portions of chapter 2 appeared in "The Presidential Candidacy of Hugh Lawson White in Tennessee, 1832–1836," *Journal of Southern History* 58 (Feb. 1992): 27–56.

Portions of chapter 4 appeared in "The Whig Party versus the Spoilsmen in Tennessee," *The Historian* 57 (Winter 1995): 329–40.

LIBRARY OF CONGRESS CATALOGING-IN-PUBLICATION DATA

Atkins, Jonathan M., 1960–
  Parties, politics, and the sectional conflict in Tennessee,
  1832–1861 / Jonathan M. Atkins.—1st ed.
       p.   cm.
  Includes bibliographical references and index.
  ISBN 13: 978-1-57233-844-9
  ISBN 10: 1-57233-844-X
  1. Tennessee—Politics and government—To 1865. 2. Political culture—Tennessee—History—19th century. 3. Political parties—Tennessee—History—19th century. 4. Sectionalism (United States)
  I. Title
  F436.A85 1997
  976.8'04–dc20   96-10028
                                              CIP

For Christie

Contents

Preface xi
Acknowledgments xvii

1. Politics and Republicanism in Jackson's Tennessee — 1
2. The Presidential Candidacy of Hugh Lawson White, 1832–1836 — 26
3. The Creation of Tennessee's Party System, 1837–1839 — 55
4. Federalists and Spoilsmen, Banks and Free Trade: Party Ideologies and Economic Policy — 81
5. The Politics of Relief: Hard Times and Texas, 1839–1845 — 111
6. The Politics of Slavery: Abolitionists, Nullifiers, and Compromise, 1846–1851 — 142
7. The Politics of Union: The Triumph of Democracy, 1852–1857 — 181
8. The Politics of Revolution: Tennessee in the Crisis of Union, 1858–1861 — 215

Appendix A.
Roll-Call Votes Indicating Party Divisions in the Tennessee General Assembly, 1839–1845 — 263

Appendix B.
Roll-Call Votes in the First Extra Session of the Tennessee General Assembly, January 7–February 4, 1861, by Party Affiliation — 270

Appendix C.
Roll-Call Votes in the Second Extra Session of the
Tennessee General Assembly, April 25–July 1,
1861, by Party Affiliation 274

Notes 277

Bibliography 345

Index 359

Illustrations

Figures

1. Mossy Creek Farm, Jefferson County, Tennessee — 12
2. Hugh Lawson White — 38
3. Loading Corn on the Tennessee — 93
4. Gubernatorial Campaign, James K. Polk versus James C. Jones, 1841 or 1843 — 117
5. Slave Auction: Slaves Driven to Market — 154
6. William B. Campbell — 176
7. John Bell — 192
8. James C. Jones — 204
9. Isham G. Harris — 235
10. Swearing in the Flag, East Tennessee — 251

Map

Tennessee Counties Returning Whig and Democratic Majorities in Gubernatorial and Presidential Elections, 1839–1851 — 87

Tables

1. Occupations of Members of Tennessee General Assembly, 1829–1861 — 7
2. Percentage of Slaveowners in Tennessee General Assembly, 1829–1861 — 8
3. Slaves Owned by Members of Tennessee General Assembly, 1829–1861 — 9
4. Median Number of Slaves Owned by Members of Tennessee General Assembly, 1829–1861 — 10
5. Median Number of Slaves Owned by Members of Tennessee General Assembly, 1829–1861, by Grand Division — 10
6. Party Support on Tennessee General Assembly Roll-Call Votes Favoring Amendments to Corporate Charters Stipulating Stockholders' Unlimited Liability, 1839–1844 — 100

7. Party Support on Tennessee General Assembly Roll-Call Votes Favoring Amendments to Corporate Charters Declaring General Assembly's Power to Alter, Amend, or Repeal the Charter, 1839–1842   101
8. Party Support on Tennessee General Assembly Roll-Call Votes in Favor of Ordering Tennessee's Banks Immediately to Resume Specie Payments, 1839–1842   103
9. Party Support on Tennessee General Assembly Roll-Call Votes in Favor of Authorizing Tennessee's Banks to Issue Small Notes, 1839–1848   105
10. Party Votes on Major Economic Legislation, Tennessee General Assembly, 1847–1851   107
11. Results of Tennessee Election for Convention and Delegates, February 9, 1861, by Grand Division   241
12. Results of Tennessee Referendum on Declaration of Independence, Passed by General Assembly, June 8, 1861, by Grand Division   248
13. Results of Tennessee Elections for Governor and for Ratification of the Permanent Constitution of the Confederate States of America, August 1, 1861, by Grand Division   257

Preface

The following words appeared in an editorial in the *Nashville Republican Banner* three days before conflict at Fort Sumter opened the American Civil War:

> Tennessee should weigh carefully her position in these perilous times.... Discarding the extreme views and measure[s] of both sections, she urges conciliation, compromise, and peace. Clinging to the Union as still worthy to be preserved, she would so guard the rights of both sections that neither shall suffer detriment. Contending persistently at all times for the full and undiminished rights of the South, she would secure the[s]e rights in the Union and under a common Constitution. Believing that a separation into two or more Confederacies will be alike disastrous to all sections and interests, she would wield her influence and power constantly to secure a fair adjustment of differences and an amicable reconstruction of the Union.

At the time, this statement appeared to represent the sentiment of the majority of the people in Tennessee. In the presidential election held the preceding November, Tennessee had tried to take a middle course between sectional extremists, by casting its electoral votes for the native-son candidate of the Constitutional Union party, John Bell. Only two months before the conflict in Charleston harbor, a popular referendum solidly rejected the calling of a state convention to consider secession from the Union. The *Republican Banner* stressed that Tennessee's neutrality was conditional on the persistence of peace between North and South. "Devoted as are the Union men of the Border States to the Constitution and the Union, ... " the paper declared, "they will not be expected to sympathize with a sectional administration of the Government, brought into power upon the basis of a war upon Southern Rights." At the same time, the editors warned the leaders of the newly-formed Confederate States of America that "a useless precipitation of hostilities, on their part would still further alienate thousands who, under different circumstances, would have sided with them in a conflict of arms"; upon learning of the attack upon Fort Sumter the paper proclaimed that "a fearful retribution will meet [its] assailants." Within a week, however, the actions of Abraham Lincoln's administration and public pressure within Tennessee forced the *Banner*'s editors to accept disunion. They now watched approvingly as the state declared its independence and joined the Confederacy.[1]

Thus, in the crisis of Union, Tennessee initially pursued a course more moderate than that of the Lower South states, even though it ultimately accepted membership in the southern republic. Despite the similarity of Tennessee's decision to that of the other Upper South border states—Arkansas, North Carolina, and Virginia—Tennessee never endorsed the principle of secession and explained its action as a "revolution." Moreover, the decision for disunion was not a unanimous one. While voters in Middle and West Tennessee overwhelmingly approved separation from the Union, in East Tennessee a substantial majority pledged to remain loyal to the federal government. Historians have long been aware of these facts concerning Tennessee's separation. Surprisingly few, however, have devoted close attention to the sources of Tennessee's strong unionism and its ultimate allegiance to the Confederacy. Those who have studied Tennessee's course during the sectional conflict, while producing useful studies, generally fail to address the deeper issue of why Tennesseans responded to disunion the way they did. Those who have addressed the question of motivation, meanwhile, usually rely upon the experience of other southern states and attribute Tennessee's course to a generic "southern" response.[2]

In recent years, students of nineteenth-century American politics have emphasized the importance of understanding the political cultures of individual states in the federal system of early America. Since disunion was a political action, these scholars note, in each southern state voters understood their decision for separation or Union according to their particular state's unique political heritage and experience. As in most other states, in Tennessee antebellum politics had been dominated by two-party competition between state organizations associated with national Whig and Democratic parties. Like the state's course in the secession crisis, though, the path taken by Tennessee's party system was an unexpected one. Although Tennessee was the home state of the era's "Symbol for an Age,"[3] Andrew Jackson, as well as of two other Democratic presidents, James K. Polk and Andrew Johnson, state party competition in Tennessee ranked among the most evenly matched and heatedly contested in the Union. Moreover, despite the residence of its three successful Democrats, Tennessee's

Whig party was recognized as one of the strongest anti-Democratic organizations in the South. As party competition disintegrated or realigned in most states in the 1850s, Tennessee's party system remained strong. At the same time, Tennessee was proving to be one of the most decidedly pro-Union among the slaveholding states. Given the strength of Tennessee's Unionism, one can understand President Lincoln's faith in Tennessee's loyalty as he worked to preserve the Union during the winter of 1860–61; one can also comprehend his surprise and disappointment when the state chose to join the Confederacy and hence, unwittingly, to become a principal battleground of the war.

Despite the work of several fine historians of antebellum Tennessee politics, many important aspects of that subject have been overlooked or have received only cursory treatment.[4] Most often, previous studies have failed to consider political developments in Tennessee within the context of the state's distinctive political culture. The founding of Tennessee's Whig party, for example, usually is analyzed in terms of the motivations of elite politicians, or is viewed as part of a proslavery states' rights movement. Historians have failed to examine how politicians and slave holders might have persuaded the mass of voters to join them in a "revolt against Jackson," or what effect the economic depression that lasted from the late 1830s through the mid-1840s might have had on politics. Although historians long have emphasized the narrow margin of difference between Tennessee's parties, the nature of party division has yet to be investigated closely in relation to economic circumstances and their effect on state legislation. Little consideration has been given to the importance of voters' established presumptions and attitudes, as expressed through the parties in the 1840s, for the politics of the 1850s, as the national sectional confrontation emerged. Factional division within both parties during the 1850s long has been recognized, but so much attention has been devoted to these quarrels that the questions of why Tennessee's party system survived in the 1850s and why Democrats attained such a preponderant majority at mid-decade have been largely ignored. Finally, few have considered how the political beliefs, assumptions, and expectations that voters learned during their experience in the party system might have shaped Tennesseans' actions in 1860 and 1861.

This study proposes to explore these and other issues by examining anew Tennessee politics from Andrew Jackson's reelection to the presidency in 1832 through Isham G. Harris's reelection as governor in 1861—an election that confirmed the state's decision to cast its lot with the Confederacy. On one level, this work intends to provide a more thorough account of state politics than has previously been available. On another level, it applies to Tennessee the insights that other historians—most notably, J. Mills Thornton, III; Michael F. Holt; Marc W. Kruman; and Lacy K. Ford—have found in their studies of state and national politics in the antebellum era.[5] Previous studies have contended that the dominant theme of Tennessee politics has been either sectional rivalry between the state's three grand divisions or, as has been argued for the South as a whole, the defense of slavery from perceived northern threats.[6] In contrast, this book argues that, in Tennessee, the central concern for voters, as expressed through party competition, was the defense of liberty from the perceived assaults of demagogic politicians who, it was believed, sought to consolidate power into their own hands at the expense of popular rule. In successive elections, throughout the lives of Tennessee's parties, Whig and Democratic leaders reinforced this presumption by consistently portraying the defense of freedom as the fundamental issue in American politics. Although local circumstances often reshaped the popular understanding of the most pressing threats to freedom, and although changing conditions altered the context of political debate, liberty's defense remained a constant concern in the state throughout the antebellum era. Acknowledging the significance of this concern to voters, I believe, contributes greatly to understanding the course of Tennessee politics in the years leading up to the Civil War.

Appeals to the defense of freedom derived from the republican ideology that became a fundamental aspect of American political culture during the Revolutionary era. The past generation of historians found republicanism an analytical tool tremendously useful in the study of politics between the Revolution and the Civil War, but few have applied the concept directly to the study of politics in Tennessee. The most recent study of Tennessee's party system, in fact, is premised upon its author's belief that parties were "essentially electoral machines, not given to notable ideological differences."[7] Some students have recognized the role of democratic appeals in elections, but these appeals usually have been understood in terms of a modern, interest-group style of politics, or as empty rhetoric presented to a gullible, easily manipulated electorate. The general tendency is to portray antebellum Tennessee as an oligarchic society ruled unchallenged by a tightly-knit elite. In this view, party competition represented little more than a power game between "ins" and "outs," while the results of elections had little bearing either upon the state's economic or political development or upon Tennesseeans' attitudes toward the growing national sectional division.

As the following pages show, I believe this portrait of Tennessee's political culture to be inappropriate; and, although its utility recently has been questioned, I believe that republican ideology played a vital role in shaping the course of Tennessee politics.[8] Republicanism, scholars have shown, permeated American culture in the United States' first generation; and, while social and economic change in the first half of the nineteenth century altered the nation's political environment, Americans modified republican principles and built their understanding of the new circumstances upon republican assumptions. Rather than being mere "claptrap" used to manipulate the masses, republican appeals provided the symbols and images with which politicians constructed popular conceptions of the political parties for a potentially active and powerful electorate. These symbols and images often had little basis in reality, but they nevertheless possessed deep cultural meaning and profoundly influenced voter behavior. Moreover, because party appeals were founded upon ideological assumptions concerning economic development, government power, and political rights, the triumph of one party over the other could significantly influence the state's policies as well as its relations in the federal compact.

The degree of acceptance of ideological beliefs no doubt varied among Tennesseans. Nevertheless, the confrontation of party images provided the foundation for political conflict for the antebellum generation. The reconstruction of the conceptions of party ideology presented here, it is argued, offers a better explanation than any presented previously of why Tennessee politics followed the path it did. Specifically, the adaptation of republicanism helps to explain why politicians alienated from Jackson were able to persuade Tennesseans that the president had fallen under the sway of "spoilsmen"; why concern over an economic crisis could be channeled into a party conflict that endured long after the crisis had passed; why Tennessee's parties managed to direct the issue of slavery's expansion into the existing party division; and why, when faced with the choice of union or disunion, the majority remained faithful as long as possible but ultimately saw no alternative but to resist what they perceived to be despotism.

This book's emphasis on ideology and party appeals is not intended to deny the importance of other aspects of state politics. Wherever possible, I have tried to consider the influence of social, economic, and institutional developments, regardless of their relationships to party ideology. Admittedly, several areas of antebellum Tennessee's political culture await further investigation. The contention here is simply that ideology played a vital role in antebellum politics, and that historians must take that role into account if they hope to understand why the *Republican Banner*'s editors and other Tennesseans viewed their politics as a struggle to defend liberty, and why they believed that they had to continue the battle through disunion and war.

Acknowledgments

Like all historians, I owe a tremendous debt to numerous individuals for their assistance and support in the completion of this work. Thanks go first to the staff of the Tennessee State Library and Archives, Nashville, where I undertook the vast majority of my research. The State Library and Archives provided a pleasant environment in which to try to recover nineteenth-century Tennessee, and its personnel proved willing in every instance to facilitate my access to its resources. I also worked on the project at the William L. Clements Library at the University of Michigan, Ann Arbor; the East Tennessee Historical Center in Knoxville; the Jean and Alexander Heard Library at Vanderbilt University; the James D. Hoskins Library, University of Tennessee, Knoxville; the William R. Perkins Library at Duke University; the Southern Historical Collection, University of North Carolina at Chapel Hill; the North Carolina Department of Archives and History, Raleigh; and the Berry College Memorial Library, Mount Berry, Georgia. To the staffs of these institutions goes my appreciation for their assistance.

Several persons, including John M. Belohlavek, Mary A. DeCredico, Donald R. Deskins, Aaron S. Fogleman, Lacy K. Ford, Richard C. Goode, Lawrence F. Kohl, Marc W. Kruman, Kenneth A. Lockridge, Robert Tracy McKenzie, Michael A. Morrison, John W. Quist, John W. Shy, Mitchell Snay, and Harry L. Watson, read and commented on various portions of the manuscript. Daniel Crofts and Major L. Wilson reviewed the manuscript for the University of Tennessee Press, and both provided invaluable comments that have significantly improved the finished product. Stephen R. Grossbart guided me through my brief excursion into the world of statistical methods, while Ralph A. Wooster kindly shared with me the research notes for his study of legislators in the Upper South.

Berry College in Mount Berry, Georgia, supported the completion of this project in a variety of ways. Aside from the awarding of several faculty development grants, the college provided vital assistance through its student work program. I wonder if the work could have been completed without the diligence of three student assistants, Stacey A. McDonald, Sheri Marie Shuck, and Shannon L. Wallace; at least it would have been delayed significantly. Sharon Hall, secretary for the School of Humanities, Arts, and Social Sciences, helped put the finishing touches on the manuscript so that it arrived at the publisher in an acceptable form. Several faculty colleagues, meanwhile, especially John C. Hickman, Peter A. Lawler, E. Dale McConkey, and Chaitram Singh, offered invaluable criticism, counsel, and encouragement. Finally, Berry's students have influenced this work by reminding me constantly of what is important—and what is not—in the study of history.

I am particularly grateful to Meredith Morris-Babb at the University of Tennessee Press for her support and her openness at every stage of the book's production. Meredith's enthusiasm and professionalism, as well as those of everyone else at the press, have made working with the staff there a pleasure and also have insured that the final version of the book will be of the highest quality. My gratitude extends to Mavis Bryant, whose copyediting skills have significantly enhanced the readability of the text.

Two persons, whom I gladly regard as mentors, deserve special mention and thanks. Shaw Livermore has remained enthusiastic about the project since its inception. His musings and reflections forced me to think about this work and its possible implications within the large scheme of American history. His influence, I hope, has prevented it from becoming too parochial. J. Mills Thornton, III, supervised this project as a dissertation and read subsequent chapters upon their completion. His guidance and encouragement revealed a confidence in the subject—and the author—that sustained the work through times when I doubted the value of either. The impact that both Shaw and Mills have had upon me, and for which I am grateful, go far beyond this work.

Douglas and Leslie were not around when I began this project; I can only hope that one day they will be proud to have it as part of their legacy. My greatest debt, and love, cannot be adequately cited in a few brief words. This book's dedication is offered as merely a token of gratitude for what she has meant to me.

ONE

Politics and Republicanism in Jackson's Tennessee

Few voters in Tennessee doubted that Andrew Jackson would be reelected president of the United States in 1832. The old general had received the virtually unanimous support of his home state in his previous two stands for the presidency. Public opinion had warmly approved the measures of his first administration, and as the election of 1832 approached, there appeared to be no serious opposition to the president in Tennessee; hence, the state's voters assumed that their own admiration for the hero equaled the approbation for Jackson throughout the country. "The country is prosperous, and happy, and difficulties with foreign nations, which have long existed, have been favorably and amicably settled," Governor William Carroll assured the president;"what good then[,] it may fairly be asked by every one who loves repose, can result from a change in the Administration?"[1] Confident of Jackson's success and discouraged by heavy rains and cold weather on the election days, only 30 percent of Tennessee's voters bothered to go to the polls; of those voters, 95 percent cast their ballots for the incumbent president. In twenty-six of the state's sixty-two counties, Jackson's tally exceeded 95 percent. Eight counties cast a unanimous vote for the general.

To Tennesseans, Jackson's election meant that the federal government would continue to be administered according to the principles of republicanism. "If his life is spared," wrote Alfred Balch, one of Jackson's political lieutenants, "those who come after us will look to the Era of J[ackso]ns admn. as the Era of sound principles."[2] To Balch, as to most Tennesseans, "sound principles" meant Jeffersonian republican principles. Republicanism signified more to them than merely allegiance to a particular political party, for Tennessee's political culture had developed out of the republican ideology that likewise reigned in the rest of the United States in the first half of the nineteenth century. Republicanism not only formed the basis for Jackson's popularity in Tennessee, but it also shaped Tennessee's political institutions and provided the intellectual framework through which the state's voters viewed their political world.

Republicanism first became entrenched in American political culture during the colonial conflict with Great Britain. Social, economic, and political changes since 1776 had undermined several basic precepts of the republicanism originally embraced by the Revolutionary generation, but several elements of revolutionary republicanism persisted into the antebellum era. Although often vaguely used, the term *republican* still had powerful implications and definite meanings for nineteenth-century Americans. As understood by voters in Tennessee and throughout the United States, republicanism maintained that the American state and federal governments were the only free governments in the world. In the Revolution, the colonial fathers had rejected the tyrannical British monarchy to form a representative government that sought to protect individual liberty. The exact meanings and implications of republican government often might be unclear, but all citizens agreed on a few cardinal tenets: government was to be based upon the consent of the governed; a written constitution represented the people's grant of power to their leaders and provided the framework for government and law; and all citizens were to be regarded as equal before the law, with no special privileges granted to "aristocrats." Adherence to these tenets could ensure the individual liberty of the citizens, for, as Governor Carroll maintained, "the great and fundamental maxim of republicanism" was the belief that "the people have the right to rule."[3]

Republicanism also warned citizens that their liberty was constantly threatened. Powerful forces sought to enslave the people by taking away their freedom. Foreign monarchies, fearful that the American republic's example could influence their own servile populations, might endanger liberty by waging war against the United States, as Britain had done in 1776 and 1812. The greater danger, though, could be found within the Republic, in ambitious, power-hungry individuals who sought to establish themselves as an aristocracy. Such demagogues would gain the favor of the people by assuring them of their respect for popular rights, but, once in office, they would gradually expand their power beyond the limits set by the Constitution until the people found themselves subjected to the will of a despot. "The encroachments of despotism are slow and each successive encroachment is small, until at length the arm of power is so strong that the people can no longer withstand it," warned Andrew Buchanan, a legislator from Warren County:

> The despot does not usurp at once all the powers which he ultimately claims. He establishes his precedents by degrees. He does not directly tell the people, I intend to have my own way, to put men in office according to my sovereign will and pleasure, and for such terms as I in my wisdom may think best. But he very politely offers to save the people the trouble; he is very anxious for their peace; he cannot bear the idea of seeing them agitated and harassed by the ca[r]e of their public concerns; he fears the excitement and discord of political discussion and popular elections; and he, kind, patriotic, prudent soul, would save the people the trouble of looking into their own affairs and intimating their wishes to their public servants. He would anticipate their wishes, and act before they expect him to act or have authorized him to act, so as to prevent their having the dangerous opportunity of consulting on the subject and determining for themselves what ought to be done. Such, sir, are the doctrines of despotism; such is the language of usurpers.[4]

Citizens thus were taught to view their leaders as potential conspirators who might try to expand their power at the expense of the popular will, for only the vigilance of "the people" themselves provided security against despotism. According to republican principles, voters were expected to keep watch on their elected officials, to act when necessary to prevent the misuse of power, and to frustrate potential threats to freedom. As Bedford County's Joseph Kincaid declared in the General Assembly in 1826, "The great safety of the people consists in the check they have on their public servants."[5]

In practice, freedom was a limited commodity in Tennessee. During Jackson's presidency, black slaves accounted for about one-fifth of Tennessee's residents, and the proportion of slaves in the state's population would approach one-fourth on the eve of Civil War.[6] Also, the era's prevailing contention that women depended upon male household heads excluded female Tennesseans from the rights of citizenship.[7] Within the domain of adult white males, though—about 16 percent of the total population—Tennesseans saw themselves as equals, each capable of making independent decisions and exercising properly the prerogatives of freedom. Tennessee was at best a white male republic, but white males were the source of political sovereignty and lived in as democratic and egalitarian a polity as one could find in the antebellum era.

Tennessee's constitutions reflected the republican presumptions of the state's political culture. Its first constitution, written by a convention in 1796, recognized the principle of popular sovereignty to as great a degree as did any state constitution at the time. That constitution did include property qualifications for the governor and members of the legislature; also, to ensure an independent judicial system, it granted to the General Assembly the power to select state attorneys, state judges, and local justices of the peace. Still, all free males over twenty-one who had resided in the state for at least six months were given the right to vote, and since the constitution limited the terms of the governor and every member of the legislature to two years, the electorate had frequent opportunities to elect a new chief executive and an entirely new assembly.[8]

The 1796 constitution had given state judges life terms, and public hostility toward incompetent judges protected by this provision led to the calling of a constitutional convention in 1834.[9] Though convened for the immediate purpose of providing a more efficient judicial system, the convention had full authority to revise or alter any aspect of the state charter; hence that body rewrote the constitution to conform to evolving popular expectations for a democratic republican government. The convention abolished property requirements for office holders, expanded the membership of the General Assembly in order to provide for better representation of the state's population, and changed the constitutional provision for property taxation from an *ad item* to an *ad valorem* basis. Moreover, the revised document granted to the voters the power to select local officials, though judges and state attorneys still were to be chosen by the legislature. Nevertheless, the constitution left the basic frame of government in Tennessee unchanged. When voters ratified the constitution by an overwhelming majority on March 5 and 6, 1835, most seem to have regarded the convention's work more as a revision of the 1796 document than as an entirely new constitution.[10]

The 1834 constitution established, as did its predecessor, a state government characterized by the republican principle that government should be limited and empowered to do only what was deemed necessary to insure the public welfare. The powers granted to the governor, for example, continued to express the revolutionary generation's fear of executive influence and its potential dangers to liberty, for the constitution's limitations on the governor's prerogative made the office's occupant more of a figurehead than an active public servant. Tennessee's citizens expected their governor to execute the law, grant pardons, make appointments to offices that became vacant when the legislature was not in session, call out the militia if the state was in danger, call the legislature into special session when necessary, and do little else. Tennessee's governor had no veto power, and the constitution prohibited any man from holding the office for more than six years in any eight-year period. The executive's only initiative in the operation of the state government was the constitutional requirement that he send a message to the legislature, for this message usually provided the agenda for the assembly's session. In special sessions, in fact, the constitution limited the legislature to acting only upon the business for which the governor had called the assembly together. Despite the limitations on the governor's powers, throughout the antebellum era the governor's office was the most prestigious position the state government could offer. It was, after all, the only office in the state for which Tennessee's entire electorate could cast a ballot.[11]

Politicians knew that, in order to wield power in Tennessee, it was more important to control the legislature than the governor's office. Composed of a senate and a house of representatives—chambers that were distinguished only by their number of members and by the higher minimum age requirement for membership in the senate—Tennessee's General Assembly was the most powerful branch of the state government. Legislators wrote Tennessee's laws without the hindrance of an executive veto; these laws dealt with such crucial topics as the state's banking system and the distribution of public resources for constructing and maintaining internal improvements. Moreover, the legislature could pass resolutions on national issues, resolutions which were considered—by those favoring them, at least—the sentiments of the voters. The assembly devoted a great deal of its time to making appointments to numerous state offices, a task the constitution placed in its hands. Even after the 1834 convention had transferred to the voters the power to elect justices of the peace, the assembly still had the responsibility of selecting all of the state's executive officers, except for the governor, and all of the state's attorneys and judges. Most enticing to the ambitious, the United States Constitution granted to the legislature the power to appoint an individual to the prize most coveted by Tennessee's leaders, the office of United States senator.[12]

The state constitution granted such broad and important powers to the assembly because, according to republican principles, it was considered the body closest to the voters and most representative of the popular will.[13] Still, the constitution and public opinion limited the legislature's prerogatives. Unless called into extra session by the governor, legislators met only once during their terms, in a session beginning in the October after the August elections. Once the assembly convened, the electorate expected it to do its business promptly and at as little cost to taxpayers as possible. If the electorate concluded that its representative in the assembly had failed in his duty, through neglecting public sentiment or through wasting public money, that member could expect little success in future elections. Voters may have expressed only slight interest in public affairs, but they nevertheless recognized that the power of the assembly ultimately depended upon public opinion. Legislators, meanwhile, were conscious that their acts always were under the potential scrutiny of the voters.

Tennessee's voters considered themselves Republicans of the Jeffersonian school. Federalist opposition to the state's admission to the Union had made that party noxious to them, and in every presidential election before 1824, Tennessee cast its electoral votes for the candidate of the Virginia dynasty. Few bothered to participate in presidential elections. Only 50 percent of the electorate turned out at the polls when Jackson won the presidency in 1828, yet that figure exceeded the 27 and 30 percent turnouts registered in the 1824 and 1832 elections. State elections attracted more attention. Even when a candidate ran virtually unopposed, as William Carroll did in most of his contests after 1821, over 60 percent of the voters usually participated in gubernatorial elections. The high turnout in gubernatorial contests probably resulted because, in the August elections, voters also cast ballots for representatives to the state legislature and to Congress, as well as for the chief executive.[14] Despite their inconsistency in exercising the franchise, Tennessee voters apparently recognized themselves as the state's sovereigns and displayed a willingness to assert their authority when necessary.

Many of Tennessee's voters fit the model of Jefferson's "sturdy yeoman." According to the 1840 census, over 90 percent of the state's total working population were employed in agriculture; the 1850 census, which recorded the occupations only of free household heads, showed that 71 percent of these family heads reported their occupations as farmer. Most of these farmers owned their land and lived on farms of less than two hundred improved acres; tenants and laborers, meanwhile, often climbed an "agricultural ladder" toward ownership of their own farms. Tennessee's yeomen, it appears, were self-sufficient in the production of grains and livestock. These farmers practiced a modified subsistence agriculture, in which they produced most of their own necessities and relied upon a neighborhood barter economy to make up for any shortages. Planters in the district west of the lower course of the Tennessee River, and in the Cumberland Basin around Maury and Davidson counties, concentrated on the cultivation of cotton and tobacco for market. For most farmers, participation in a market economy was limited to the sale of surplus food crops and livestock. The extent of a yeoman's participation in this surplus trade depended on the availability of markets, the annual harvest, and the farmers' own inclination to try to produce a surplus for sale. Most seem to have practiced what has been called "safety-first" farm-

Table 1. Occupations of Members of Tennessee General Assembly, 1829-1861 (Percent of Those Whose Occupations Are Known)

Occupation	1829 (%)	1831 (%)	1839 (%)	1841 (%)
Farmer/Planter	35.9	38.3	42.0	39.5
Lawyer	39.6	36.2	29.6	31.4
Merchant	11.3	4.3	6.2	7.0
Farmer-Merchant	5.7	8.5	3.7	3.5
Farmer-Lawyer	1.9	2.1	3.7	3.5
Physician	3.8	6.4	8.6	10.5
Other	1.9	4.2	6.1	4.7
N =	53	48	81	86

Occupation	1849 (%)	1851 (%)	1859 (%)	1861 (%)
Farmer/Planter	42.1	34.0	37.1	30.2
Lawyer	28.4	39.4	35.1	40.6
Merchant	3.2	4.3	4.1	11.5
Farmer-Merchant	6.3	2.1	6.2	5.2
Farmer-Lawyer	7.4	8.5	7.2	2.1
Physician	7.4	7.5	9.3	5.2
Other	5.3	4.3	1.0	5.2
N =	95	94	97	96

Note: N = Number of members of General Assembly whose occupations are known. The 1829 and 1831 General Assemblies each had a total of sixty members; each assembly after 1834 had one hundred.

Source: Robert M. McBride and Dan M. Robison, *Biographical Directory of the Tennessee General Assembly* (Nashville: Tennessee State Library and Archives and the Tennessee Historical Commission, 1975).

ing, in which a farmer geared his annual yields to supply himself and his family before producing for a market.[15]

Few Tennesseans would have been called "planters" according to the modern definition, since in 1850 less than 2 percent of the state's households owned twenty or more slaves.[16] Most planters lived in the state's cotton belt between the Tennessee and Mississippi rivers, although several cotton and tobacco producers in Middle Tennessee also qualified for the title. Despite the scarcity of large slaveholders, Tennessee society still contained a recognizable upper class. Ten percent of Tennessee's households owned about half of the state's real wealth, while 30 percent owned from 70 to 75 percent of Tennessee's landed property.[17] Yeomen, though perhaps envious of the upper strata's good fortune, tended to distrust those with wealth, as they did those too closely tied to commerce. The charge that Edward Ward was the college-educated son of a wealthy Virginia gentleman, for example, contributed to his lopsided defeat in the 1821 gubernatorial election. Some voters refused to consider voting for a lawyer for any office. Throughout the state, rural voters looked upon towns—even the small villages that served as most county seats—as locations more closely connected to the wider world than to their rural surroundings.[18]

Politicians with above-average wealth and intimate connections with commerce nevertheless often succeeded in winning elections. Table 1 shows that, throughout the antebellum era, lawyers and farmers made up a majority of the members of the General Assembly, while merchants, including those who combined mercantile with agricultural activities, usually constituted about 10 to 15 percent of the legislators. The censuses of 1840, 1850, and 1860 each showed that, while fewer than 3 percent of the state's white males listed their occupations as either lawyers or merchants, in antebellum Tennessee members of these groups usually constituted 35 to 50 percent of the state assemblymen.[19]

Voters showed a willingness to be represented not only by non-farmers, but also by men of property. In 1850, only 22 percent of the

Table 2. Percentage of Slaveowners in Tennessee General Assembly, by Year, 1829–1861

Year	Slaveowners %	N
1829	73.2	41
1831	81.1	37
1839	80.1	65
1841	79.4	63
1849	*65.4	78
1851	*79.5	78
1859	*75.0	78
1861	*90.4	73

Notes: * Number of members owning no slaves is estimated.
N = Number of members whose slave ownership could be determined or estimated.

Sources: U.S. Census Office, 1830 Census and 1840 Census, MSS, Schedule 1 (population); 1850 Census and 1860 Census, MSS, Schedule 2 (slave).

Table 3. Number of Slaves Owned by Members of Tennessee General Assembly, 1829-1861

Number of Slaves Owned	1829 %	1831 %	1839 %	1841 %
0	26.8	18.9	20.0	20.6
1-5	26.8	32.4	35.4	38.1
6-10	14.6	13.5	6.2	11.1
11-20	9.8	13.5	23.1	20.6
More than 20	22.0	21.6	15.4	9.5
N =	41	37	65	63

Number of Slaves Owned	1849 %	1851 %	1859 %	1861 %
0	*34.6	*20.5	*25.0	*9.6
1-5	32.1	29.5	22.7	28.8
6-10	11.5	21.8	18.2	28.8
11-20	14.1	14.1	19.3	17.8
More than 20	7.8	14.2	14.8	15.1
N =	78	78	88	73

Notes: * Number of members owning no slaves is estimated.
N = Number of members whose slave ownership could be determined or estimated.

Sources: U.S. Census Office, 1830 Census and 1840 Census, MSS, Schedule 1 (population); 1850 Census and 1860 Census, MSS, Schedule 2 (slave).

state's white families owned slaves, but table 2 shows that a substantial majority of Tennessee's legislators were slaveholders. While table 3 indicates that there were few large planters in the assembly, table 4 nevertheless shows that Tennessee's slave-owning legislators maintained considerable investments in the peculiar institution. The average number of slaves owned among members who held slave property ranged from six to nine. Moreover, these figures probably understate the level of wealth in the assembly. According to table 5, members from East Tennessee were less likely to be slaveholders than their counterparts from elsewhere in the state, and the average number of slaves owned by East Tennesseans who did hold slaves was lower than the average held by the other members of the assembly. While the level of wealth in East Tennessee fell below that of the rest of the state, slavery was not a crucial component of that section's economy, and in that section wealth holders were more likely to divert their invest-

Table 4. Median Number of Slaves Owned by Members of Tennessee General Assembly, 1829-1861

	Data for All Assemblymen		Assemblymen Owning Slaves	
Year	Av. No. Slaves	N	Av. No. Slaves	N
1829	5.0	(41)	8.5	(30)
1831	5.0	(37)	8.0	(30)
1839	4.0	(65)	6.0	(52)
1841	4.0	(62)	6.0	(50)
1849	2.5	(78)	6.0	(51)
1851	5.5	(78)	7.0	(62)
1859	6.0	(88)	9.0	(66)
1861	8.0	(73)	8.0	(66)

Note: N = Members of the General Assembly whose slave ownership is known or can be estimated.

Sources: U.S. Census Office, 1830 Census and 1840 Census, MSS, Schedule 1 (population); 1850 Census and 1860 Census, MSS, Schedule 2 (slave).

Table 5. Median Number of Slaves Owned by Members of Tennessee General Assembly, 1829-1861, by Grand Division

	East		*Middle*		*West*	
Year	Slaves	N	Slaves	N	Slaves	N
1829	3.0	(17)	8.0	(22)	13.0	(2)
1831	4.0	(16)	19.0	(18)	4.0	(3)
1839	1.0	(20)	10.5	(36)	14.0	(9)
1841	0.0	(16)	6.0	(33)	4.0	(13)
1849	0.0	(23)	3.0	(39)	7.5	(16)
1851	4.0	(25)	4.0	(36)	9.0	(17)
1859	1.0	(26)	8.0	(42)	9.5	(20)
1861	2.0	(15)	9.0	(40)	6.5	(18)

Note: Figures in parentheses represent the number of members of the General Assembly whose ownership of slaves could be determined or estimated.

Sources: U.S. Census Office, 1830 Census and 1840 Census, MSS, Schedule 1 (population); 1850 Census and 1860 Census, MSS, Schedule 2 (slave).

ments into other types of property. Still, the number of slaveholders in the legislature indicates that Tennessee's political leaders ranked in the upper echelons of society and controlled a significantly higher proportion of wealth than did the average voter.

The predominance of men of property in Tennessee's politics, especially of landholders in the state's earliest years, has led historians to describe the state's politics as oligarchic.[20] This conclusion, though, understates the degree to which elite dominance depended upon public opinion. In any society, one would expect to find successful candidates having greater wealth than the average voter, since only those with sufficient resources could afford to abandon their vocations temporarily during a campaign and during low-paying service in office. Likewise, a general familiarity with an aspirant among voters throughout an election district—a necessary prerequisite for victory in most contests—usually implied that the candidate had attained a socioeconomic status high enough to attract the notice of the electorate. Politicians who flaunted their wealth before the voters met with little success at the polls. Instead, the winners tended to downplay whatever wealth they did have and stressed to the voters that their own views and sentiments were in line with those of Tennessee's yeomen. Candidates of whatever social rank won elections by convincing the voters that they sought the office in order to serve the public good.

Tennessee's elections rarely centered on debates concerning details of public policy. Instead, the results of a contest turned on the candidates' success in proving to the voters their devotion to the general welfare. When they did address specific issues, aspirants expressed their opinions in terms of how their positions furthered, while that of their opponents endangered, the success of republican government. Once in power, politicians had to confine their actions to those approved by public opinion if they hoped to achieve further political success. Thomas Claiborne, for one, already had considerable experience as a public servant when he stood for the state legislature in 1831. Not only had he served two previous terms in the legislature, but also he had won election to the mayor's office in Nashville and had spent two years in Washington as a member of Congress. His inactivity in the 1831 election, though, opened him to charges that he considered himself too good for the average voter, and he found it necessary to issue a public statement denying accusations that he was "too proud to mix with the common people" and that he had "express[ed] the opinion or wish that none but freeholders should exercise the right of suffrage." Claiborne then proclaimed that he sought the office in order to support judicial reform—because the state's judges "have shown themselves incompetent to the discharge of the duties appertaining to their offices"—rather than for personal aggrandizement. This statement apparently satisfied Davidson County's voters, as Claiborne ultimately won the election with little trouble.[21]

"View of Mossy Creek Farm, Jefferson County, Tennessee, U.S. America." From J. Gray Smith, *A Brief Historical, Statistical, and Descriptive Review of East Tennessee* (1842). Reproduction courtesy of Tennessee State Library and Archives, Nashville.

Governor Carroll, on the other hand, failed to learn this lesson when he ran for another term in 1835. Carroll had served as Tennessee's chief executive for all but two years since 1821. Though he had served three consecutive terms and normally would have been ineligible for reelection in 1835, the governor sought another term on the grounds that the state's new constitution created a new government for Tennessee. The incumbent thus argued that he sought a first term in a newly created position under a new government. Carroll's chief competitor, Newton Cannon, maintained that the 1834 constitution was a revision of the existing government, rather than the creation of a new one; more importantly, the challenger asserted that Carroll's interpretation of his eligibility violated "a great fundamental principle in republican government." Most of Tennessee's voters agreed. The once-popular governor lost by a solid majority to the colorless Cannon, and Carroll never again served in elective office.[22]

More successful at recognizing and gauging the sentiments of the voters were politicians like Miles Vernon, a four-time legislator from Rhea County when, in 1833, he approached the issue of whether to charter the Planters' Bank of Tennessee. Since banks had suspended specie payments during the Panic of 1819, they had been unpopular among yeomen; in the interim, all but one of the state's banks had gone out of business. As a member of the state's House of Representatives, Vernon in 1832 voted in favor of creating the Union Bank, to provide Tennessee with at least one source of credit. Many considered one bank sufficient, and, after winning election to the state senate, Vernon voted against the charter of the Planters' Bank. The vote, a ten-to-ten tie, appeared to kill the charter, but Vernon immediately asked the senate to reconsider the issue. After the senate agreed to Vernon's request, he apparently left the chamber, for, when the charter bill came up again a few minutes later, his absence allowed the bill to pass by a ten-to-nine vote. Vernon thus provided crucial support in securing an expansion of Tennessee's banking facilities, yet he still could stand before his constituents in lower East Tennessee as the friend of the people, working against special interests and monopolies. This duplicity seems to have worked, for he won reelection to the senate before later migrating to Missouri, where he served three terms in that state's senate.[23]

Tennessee's tax structure illustrates how powerful popular sovereignty could be, despite the fact that offices tended to be held by elite politicians. After the ratification of the 1834 constitution, all voters between the ages of twenty-one and fifty paid a poll tax, while landowners paid five cents for every one hundred dollars worth of real estate they owned.[24] Slaves, bank stock, and pleasure carriages were assessed at the same rate as land, and, as a result, the accumulation of property meant the payment of more taxes. In 1844, to compensate for the decline in the state's revenue that accompanied the economic depression following the Panic of 1837, legislators raised the rate on property to seven and one-half cents per hundred dollars of value. However, the lawmakers chiefly sought to raise revenue by taxing the luxuries of the wealthy, which in most cases included themselves; the assembly added pianos, gold and silver watches and plates, and jewelry to the list of taxable property. These taxes adhered to the principle of republican equality, since the same tax rate would apply to all citizens; yet, because of their large estates, the wealthy provided the bulk of the state's revenue: taxes on land, slaves, and luxuries provided almost 90 percent of the state's income, with the remainder provided by the assessment on white polls. The tax structure thus reflected elite deference to the power of the electorate. A legislature that attempted to put a disproportionate share of the burden on yeomen would face certain repudiation at the next election.[25]

Popular sovereignty in Tennessee seldom meant a grassroots desire to control public affairs. Most voters had little experience or interest in the daily business of government. "The honest yeomanry of the country who follow their plow have no motives of interest or ambition to gratify," Carroll noted. "They are content with a faithful administration of public affairs."[26] Once a politician had won the support of Tennessee's electorate, voters, confident that he would promote policies that were in their own best interest, left the details of government in the hands of their chosen representative. Confidence in a politician's republicanism left him free to pursue the objectives for which he had sought election, whether those objectives were to promote his own personal interest; to seek a higher elected or appointed office; or, in some instances, actually to serve the public welfare. Despite the latitude granted the successful politician, though, he knew that ultimately his fate depended upon popular support. That support, in turn, depended upon his ability to maintain his image as the representative of the people's interests and as the defender of republican liberty. Politicians who exceeded the limits of what the people would approve, by appearing to grasp at power or to exercise their own prerogatives rather than obeying the will of the voters, found themselves ostracized by public opinion and defeated at the polls. In spite of the state government's oligarchic features, the electorate ultimately determined both who ruled in Tennessee and how the state actually would be ruled.

One of the most important influences in the state's political life was its separation into clearly defined geographical regions known as the "grand divisions." East and Middle Tennessee had been open for settlement since that state's admission to the Union in 1796, and since that date they had grown into distinct regions with few ties to each other. After 1818, the removal of Native Americans from the land west of the lower course of the Tennessee River added the third grand division, West Tennessee, which likewise saw its interests connected more closely to those of other states than to those of Tennessee's older districts. Only a common association under the same state government united the grand divisions; hence, representatives from the divisions assembled in the legislature with different understandings of the needs of their constituents.

East Tennessee stretched from the Unaka Mountains in the Appalachians, through the eastern Tennessee River Valley, to Marion, Bledsoe, Morgan, and Scott counties on the Cumberland Plateau. The upper eastern end of this region had been the site of Tennessee's first settlements; and when Tennessee entered the Union, the majority of the state's population lived in East Tennessee. By 1810, Middle Tennessee's population exceeded that of the eastern region; by the time of Jackson's presidency, East Tennessee's people numbered fewer than half those in Middle Tennessee. East Tennessee's soil and climate prevented widespread cultivation of the South's primary cash crops, cotton and tobacco; instead, small-scale subsistence farming characterized the division. The mountains surrounding the river valleys contained rocky soil and some of the state's poorest and least populated counties. In the valleys, especially in narrow strips running along the banks of the Tennessee, Holston, French Broad, Nolichucky, and Watauga rivers, the land proved exceptionally favorable for grain cultivation, especially wheat. Ten of Tennessee's twenty leading wheat-producing counties in 1849 and 1859 were located in East Tennessee.[27]

Few farmers profited greatly from wheat production; by the 1830s, East Tennessee already was stigmatized as an impoverished and stagnant region. The mountains surrounding the river valley isolated wheat farmers from ready markets. Aside from the expensive overland trade with Richmond, Baltimore, Philadelphia, and Nashville, the only potential conduit for commerce from the valley counties was the Tennessee River. The Muscle Shoals in northern Alabama, though, prevented convenient shipment of East Tennessee's produce beyond that point. After the War of 1812, cotton planters in northern Alabama did provide a market for East Tennessee's grain and livestock. The arrival of the first steamboat in Knoxville, in 1828, increased trade with that region and stimulated efforts to find a way past the shoals. Nevertheless, as one legislative candidate put it in 1833, East Tennessee was "behind all in those commercial facilities which alone can give to the toil strung nerves of her sons a mete reward for their labors."[28]

West of the Cumberland Mountains, up to the valley where the Tennessee River returns through the state on its way to the Ohio, lay Middle Tennessee, a district characterized as much by its agricultural potential as East Tennessee was by its isolation. Nashville, founded on the banks of the Cumberland River in 1779, lay at the center of a fertile limestone basin that ranged from the north central area of Middle Tennessee to the upper half of what would become Giles and Lincoln counties. Treaties signed with the Chickasaw and Cherokee nations in 1805 and 1806 opened the southern and eastern portions of Middle Tennessee for white settlement, and in the next two decades, migrants, lured by the region's fertility, poured into the district. By 1830,

Middle Tennessee's population approached four hundred thousand persons, over a quarter of them slaves.[29]

Many settlers came to try establishing themselves in the South's burgeoning cotton kingdom, and farmers in the Nashville Basin participated fully in the cotton boom after the War of 1812. Cotton continued to be part of Middle Tennessee's economy throughout the antebellum period.[30] Cotton cultivation, though, never became as deeply entrenched in Middle Tennessee as it did in the Deep South or in West Tennessee. The soil on the Highland Rim, which surrounded the Nashville Basin, kept farmers there from devoting too much attention to cotton. Farmers in the northern half of the division, in the counties bordering Kentucky, found the land there suitable for tobacco cultivation, but most farmers on the rim, like those in the mountains of East Tennessee, found their options limited to the production of grain and livestock. Even in the basin, most yeomen found that their path to success lay in cultivating corn rather than cotton. Twelve Middle Tennessee counties, all but two of them in the basin, produced more than one million bushels of corn in 1849. Even in Maury County, a leading cotton producer, less than 40 percent of the farm units that year produced cotton; of those farms growing cotton, only 11.5 percent grew more than ten bales.[31]

Yeomen in Middle Tennessee could profit from growing food crops because they had relatively easy access to markets. Farmers could load their crops onto flatboats on the Duck and Elk rivers, and these streams then would carry their produce to the Tennessee River and on to the realm of international commerce at New Orleans. Flatboats also dominated the early trade on the Cumberland River, but the Cumberland, unlike the Duck and the Elk, in the 1820s proved navigable by steamboats. The efficiency and volume of the steamboat trade enabled Nashville's commission merchants to extend their sphere of operations throughout Middle Tennessee. By 1830, Nashville was the dominant commercial and political center in the state. Entrepreneurs in Middle Tennessee thus approached the issue of internal improvements with less urgency than did those in East Tennessee, where railroads in particular seemed to offer the region salvation. Still, Nashville's merchants would support improvement projects as a way to consolidate their control of the region's commerce. In the southern portion of the division, many looked to railroads as a way to "deliver us from the wrongs and oppressions of Nashville and make us a free and prosperous people."[32]

Across the Tennessee River from Middle Tennessee lay West Tennessee, or the "Western District." Along the Tennessee ran the river's western valley, a narrow strip with some productive soil but separated from the rest of the division by the western ridge of the Highland Rim. On the other edge of West Tennessee ran the Mississippi bottomlands, an area settlers avoided because of its swamps, frequent floods, and potentially unhealthy climate. Between the two valleys sat the fertile lands of the Gulf Coastal Plain. Here planters found a region perfectly suited to the cultivation of King Cotton. Within a generation of its initial settlement, West Tennessee developed into a region more like the Black Belts of Alabama and Mississippi than like either of Tennessee's older divisions.[33]

During Jackson's presidency, West Tennessee was still a frontier region, though it was passing rapidly through its frontier stage. The district had been closed to white settlement until a treaty with the Chickasaw opened the lands in 1818, but by 1830 West Tennessee's population already exceeded one hundred thousand. Planters in Henry County, the division's most populous county in 1830, concentrated on tobacco production, and in the 1840s corn planters in neighboring Gibson, Carroll, and Weakley counties began to devote more acreage to tobacco, in attempts to enjoy the profits of a money crop. Cotton dominated West Tennessee's best lands, in the southern half of the district. By the 1840s, West Tennessee was no longer a frontier, but a settled and productive region; by the 1850s, Tennessee's southwest corner was the wealthiest and most prosperous area in the state. Here yeoman farmers felt the strongest temptation to abandon the security of safety-first agriculture to gamble for the riches that a cash crop could bring.[34]

Tennesseans recognized the different natures of the state's grand divisions and the effects of their presence on state politics. Sectional differences proved most critical when the legislature attempted to distribute funds for internal improvements. Also, East and Middle Tennessee traditionally had claimed one each of the state's two seats in the Senate—an arrangement that, by the 1840s, became complicated by the growth and prosperity of West Tennessee. In the distribution of state offices and party patronage, politicians at times would appeal to sectional prejudices over party loyalty to try to gain an advantage for their favorite candidates. East Tennessee's representatives in particular played on their constituency's resentment of the other divisions' political and economic prestige and showed a strong preference for men from their own section. In 1851, for example, representatives from the East unified in the General Assembly to elect men from the "mountain district" to some of the state's choicest offices. This unity contributed to the region's loss of a United States senator, though, as

Whig assemblymen from Middle Tennessee, in a caucus for the senatorial election, recalled the easterners' belligerence to justify switching their votes from Washington County's Thomas A. R. Nelson to West Tennessee's James C. Jones.[35]

Slavery exerted an important influence on the political life of voters in antebellum Tennessee. The first settlers in the western North Carolina counties that would become Tennessee brought slaves with them, as permitted under North Carolina law. When North Carolina ceded its western lands to the federal government in 1790, that state stipulated that slaves in that region could not be emancipated without the consent of their owners. Tennessee's first constitution failed to reiterate North Carolina's provision, though the new state's government recognized the institution's legality. Opponents of slavery within Tennessee presented the 1834 convention with several petitions asking that the new document include a plan of gradual emancipation, but the convention refused to consider such a plan on the grounds that it would be "a premature attempt on the part of the benevolent to get rid of the evils of slavery." Instead, by a vote of thirty to twenty-seven, the delegates voted to include in the new constitution the clause prohibiting emancipation without the owner's consent. This convention witnessed the only formal political discussion over whether to end slavery in the state, and the gradual emancipation proposal's rejection met widespread approval. Over the next quarter-century, as slavery's expansion became a crucial national issue, the chances for abolition in Tennessee disappeared, as did the state's few antislavery advocates.[36]

The vast majority of white Tennesseans accepted slavery's existence without question. So widely approved was the institution that few slaveholders saw a need to justify it before their fellow citizens, and when slavery's expansion emerged as a national issue, politicians debated measures for defending slavery without bothering to justify its existence. Most recognized slavery's benefits for agricultural production, probably without questioning its moral implications. The prevailing assumption of black inferiority likewise justified slavery as a means to protect white lives and property from the supposedly brutish blacks.[37] With the emergence of the Abolition movement in the North in the 1830s, white Tennesseans at first displayed little concern over the movement's potential political consequences. They reacted strongly to the abolitionists' threat of encouraging a slave rebellion, however. In 1831, in the aftermath of Nat Turner's rebellion in Virginia,

Tennessee's assembly passed an act that forbid free blacks from migrating into the state and prohibited the manumission of slaves unless an owner provided for the transportation of the freed person to Liberia. The assembly later revised this law to allow newly freed blacks to live in Tennessee if they paid a bond to the state; but in 1854 the legislature increased its pressure, through an act requiring the re-enslavement of blacks who failed to pay their bonds within two months of their emancipation or, in the case of migrants, from the time of their entrance into the state. The 1836 assembly passed a law prescribing penitentiary sentences for up to twenty years for anyone, black or white, found printing or speaking doctrines calculated "to excite discontent, insurrection or rebellion amongst slaves or free persons of color." Three years later, lawmakers made it more difficult for slaves to purchase their freedom by raising to five hundred dollars the penalty on masters who allowed bondsmen to hire themselves out and "act as if they were free persons of color." On the eve of Civil War, the assembly intensely debated a proposal that would have expelled all free blacks from Tennessee.[38]

Lawmakers from East Tennessee tended to divide when voting on legislation regulating slaves and free blacks or resisting the spread of abolitionist propaganda. Representatives from the Middle and Western grand divisions, meanwhile, voted heavily in favor of these laws. Nevertheless, the assembly's votes on slave laws reflected statewide commitment to the institution; representatives from all three grand divisions joined together in their support.[39] Likewise, whites across Tennessee responded quickly to a rumored slave rebellion in Stewart County in late 1856. Although no reliable evidence of an insurrection emerged, several blacks were executed on the presumption that they had organized an uprising. Seventy-five miles away, Gallatin whites took no chance and "hung by lynch law four of those they considered the ring leaders" of the phantom rebellion.[40]

Slaves, however, constituted a smaller proportion of the population in Tennessee than in most other southern states. In 1850, when only 24 percent of Tennessee's inhabitants were slaves, only Arkansas, among the future Confederate states, had a smaller proportional slave population; and that state's proportion passed Tennessee's by 1860. Moreover, in 1850 only 22 percent of Tennessee's white families owned slave property; again, of the states that would leave the Union in 1861, only Arkansas had a smaller ratio.[41] The importance of slavery also varied among the grand divisions. Cotton and tobacco planters needed bound labor for the cultivation of their crops, and successful yeomen could increase their yield by working more acres with the assistance of a slave or two. Hence, slaves made up more than a quarter of Middle Tennessee's population throughout the antebellum era; and by 1860 they accounted for more than a third of West Tennessee's inhabitants. Not counting a few highland counties, the proportion of slaveholders in the white population in Middle Tennessee ranged from 26 to 51 percent. In West Tennessee, by 1860 the proportions ranged from 29 percent to 70 percent. In East Tennessee, where few tried to grow cash crops, slaves never comprised more than 10 percent of the population. Even in the most fertile counties along the Tennessee River Valley, the proportion of slaves seldom exceeded 15 percent. Although in a few East Tennessee counties almost one in five families owned slaves, in most, ownership was restricted to only the most affluent tenth of the white population.[42] While slavery was as firmly entrenched in Middle and West Tennessee as in any southern state, in East Tennessee the institution was accepted, even though slave ownership was available only to the wealthiest elite.

East Tennesseans, in fact, were behind the move to incorporate the gradual emancipation plan into the 1834 constitution. According to the convention committee's majority report, most of the signers of the petitions supporting the proposal lived in Washington and Greene counties; only three East Tennessee delegates voted in favor of the constitution's guarantee of slave property.[43] Yet, even in the East, few advocated emancipation. Elihu Embree briefly published an antislavery newspaper, *The Emancipator*, from Jonesborough in 1820, and a Tennessee Manumission Society that was organized in the eastern division in 1815 survived until the early 1830s. Embree's and the Manumission Society's efforts, however, reflected the personal commitment of a few individuals, rather than widespread antislavery sentiment. While East Tennesseans tolerated these actions, no widespread opposition to the institution developed in the region. Only thirty people attended a public meeting called in Knoxville in 1834 to generate support for a plan for emancipation. The *Knoxville Register* remarked after this meeting that "there is very little feeling on the subject," while, a few years later, the *Jonesborough Whig* assured readers that "so very unpopular is the cause of Abolition" in East Tennessee that the few antislavery citizens in the region "are ashamed to avow their sentiments."[44]

Politicians throughout Tennessee thus faced an electorate committed to the South's peculiar institution, but they also recognized the different nature of the institution in the state's grand divisions. In Middle and West Tennessee, where slaves were numerous and ownership widespread among the upper and upper-middle classes, slave ownership seemed an attainable goal and an essential rung on the ladder of upward mobility. In East Tennessee, where slaves were scarce and ownership reserved to the wealthiest inhabitants, slavery seemed a luxury reserved for the few.

Tennessee's grand divisions and the presence of slavery both played important roles in constructing the state's political culture, and these factors profoundly influenced the course of party competition in the state. During the era of Tennessee's party system, the General Assembly debated several issues important for the state, including internal improvements, banking, and the sale of liquor. Seldom, however, did these subjects become campaign issues for either party, despite the fact that, in the legislature, parties tended to take opposing positions. With a narrow margin of difference between the parties, and with voters closely watching the assembly's actions to see if their particular division received its just due, politicians hesitated to commit their organizations on state questions for fear of alienating potential supporters. Likewise, as voters faced the question of slavery's expansion, the different roles of the institution in the grand divisions kept the parties from adopting a radical pro-South stance. Spokesmen could make more extreme declarations in slave-heavy West Tennessee, but the peripheral position of the institution in East Tennessee made it difficult to unite statewide parties in a "fire-eating," secessionist appeal. As a result, Tennessee's parties tempered their calls for a defense of southern rights with declarations of loyalty to the Union, and Tennessee would become, among the slave states, one of the strongest defenders of Union during the secession crisis.

Tennessee's citizens also viewed both state sectionalism and slavery through the lens of their understanding of republican ideology. Most of the elections in which voters participated involved local candidates seeking to represent a district in the General Assembly or in Congress. Thus voters seldom faced a choice of sectional candidates, but rather had to select between local candidates seeking to prove their devotion to the republican cause. In gubernatorial elections involving a statewide electorate, voters were willing to support a candidate from another division if he seemed faithful to republican principles, rather than vote for a candidate from the voters' home division whose republicanism appeared dubious.[45] Northern attempts to restrict the expansion of slavery, meanwhile, appeared to relegate southern whites to the status of inferior citizens in the republic, because prohibiting slaveholders from taking their slave property to the territories seemed to deny the southerners equal standing with northern property owners. Moreover, southern whites saw slavery as the basis upon which free government existed, since the presence of a black race outside the citizen body, they believed, guaranteed that poorer whites would not become an underclass laboring for the wealthy; thus slavery preserved the freedom and equality of all white citizens.[46]

Perhaps nothing better demonstrates the power of republican assumptions in Tennessee than the popularity of Andrew Jackson. The strength of Jackson's image as a pure republican statesman exceeded even the expectations of the original supporters of his presidential aspirations. The general first emerged as a national figure as commander of the American forces victorious in the Battle of New Orleans in 1815. After the battle, Jackson displayed only a minor interest in Tennessee politics, although he had connections with the political faction first organized by William Blount and later led by Judge John Overton. The financial Panic of 1819 dealt a severe blow to the Blount-Overton faction's prestige in the state, for the suspension of specie payments by the state's banks, which were under Overton's control, created widespread popular resentment against the banks and against Tennessee's incumbent leaders. William Carroll's 1821 election to the governorship over the Blount-Overton faction's candidate, Edward Ward, along with Carroll's advocacy of policies that eventually led to the closing of Tennessee's banks, encouraged Overton and his associates to promote the popular general's presidential nomination as a way to recapture control of the state. The faction's leaders apparently gave little thought to the possibility that Jackson actually might win the 1824 election, but they soon realized that they had tapped into forces beyond their control. Jackson's support spread quickly among voters, not only in Tennessee but throughout the South and West. The general's nomination derailed the candidacy of South Carolina's John C. Calhoun and threatened the prospects of Kentucky's Henry Clay and Georgia's William H. Crawford. Overton and his colleagues themselves subtly attempted to block the progress of the Jackson candidacy, but the groundswell of support for the hero transcended factional politics in Tennessee. By the time of the election, politicians throughout the state—including both Overton and Carroll—had recognized the consequences of open opposition, and they united to advocate Jackson's election.[47]

The general's popularity usually is attributed to his military success and to his identification with the cause of "the people" against special interests. These factors provided the foundation for his image as a republican statesman, a Tennessee farmer who was devoted to public service and who conducted himself according to the tenets of "pure republicanism.""Called by the nation to occupy conspicuous stations," Frederick S. Heiskell, editor of the *Knoxville Register,* explained during Jackson's presidency,

> he has outstripped the anticipations of his most sanguine friends, and amply fulfilled his destiny. As a general, with the decision and intuitive wisdom of Buonaparte, he has been more fortunate, avoided his errors, and conquered the conquerors of Europe; in love of country he rivals Washington; as chief magistrate he adheres to the pure and salutary principles of Jefferson; while in resisting the aggressions of party, and the assaults of power on the constitution, he stands unrivaled and solitary, exhibiting a firmness that never wavers, a courage that never shirks, a decision that meets every exigency, an unexampled patriotism, and a more than Roman magnanimity.[48]

The result of the election of 1824 reinforced this image and directed attention to apparent threats within the Republic itself. Jackson carried almost 98 percent of the vote in Tennessee, and in the national contest he won a plurality of popular and electoral votes. The House of Representatives awarded the presidency instead to the runner-up, John Quincy Adams; then, when Adams appointed House Speaker Henry Clay as Secretary of State, Jackson and his supporters immediately concluded that the people's right to elect the general had been stolen by a "corrupt bargain.""[T]he voice of the people has been disregarded," the *Nashville Republican* proclaimed;" . . . the CLAIMS of the MAN of THE PEOPLE have been overlooked and passed by, by a few vindictive and mercenary politicians."[49]

As they turned immediately to the next election in 1828, Tennesseans now saw national politics as a contest between the people, who were behind Jackson, and "an aristocrat and a federalist" who "got into power by bargain, intrigue and management, and who tries to retain it by the most prodigal and corrupt expenditures of the people's money." Jackson's election alone, it seemed, could rescue control of the government from the enemies of freedom. With only two members dissenting on technicalities, the General Assembly in 1827 nominated Jackson by resolving that the measures of the Adams administration "are injurious to the interests, and dangerous to the liberties of the country," and that "the surest remedy for these evils, now in the power of the people, is the election of Andrew Jackson to the chief magistracy of this union."[50] More than twice as many Tennesseans cast ballots in 1828 as had done so four years earlier, and again they gave Jackson their virtually unanimous support, as the general this time easily defeated the incumbent Adams.

Jackson's rise to the presidency as the defender of the Republic against corrupt and aristocratic demagogues forced politicians in Tennessee to give at least nominal support to the new president, in order to have any chance for success on their own. No aspirant could hope to build a following based upon open opposition to "Old Hickory." Indeed, as Heiskell concluded, "The enemy of Gen. Jackson is now identified with the enemy of free government and free institutions." "No man but a friend to Jackson[']s administration could be elected to office here," wrote William B. Campbell in 1831, "and we have no aspirant of any other politics."[51] Disappointed office seekers or those alienated by the tone of the administration had nowhere else to turn, for a challenge to the president, or known standing as a target of his displeasure, were stigmas nearly impossible to overcome at the polls.[52]

Tennessee voters meanwhile warmly approved the measures of "Old Hickory's" first administration as necessary defenses against the corruption of the federal government. Citizens enthusiastically approved Jackson's decision to move American Indians to the territory west of the Mississippi River, and thousands volunteered to fight when the Seminole tribe in Florida resisted removal. They welcomed—as a step necessary to prevent the consolidation of state powers into the hands of a distant central government—Jackson's veto of the Maysville Turnpike Bill, which authorized federal aid for the construction of a road within the boundaries of a state. They acclaimed his stern rejection of South Carolina's attempt to nullify federal law as a courageous response to a fanatical effort to overthrow the blessings of union. And they hailed his veto of a bill to recharter the Bank of the United States as a victory over a moneyed aristocracy that sought to subvert republican government by using the country's currency to determine the outcome of elections.[53] Tennessee thus followed Jackson into his newly reformed Democratic-Republican party and became a solid component of that party, even to the point of sending to the Baltimore Convention in 1832 a group of delegates who unanimously approved Jackson's choice of Martin Van Buren as his vice-president.[54]

Jackson's overwhelming majority in Tennessee, when he stood for reelection in 1832, thus represented more than a measure of his popularity. Above all, it represented the citizens' adherence to republican principles, as they understood them, and the electorate's approval of the president's interpretation of the policies proper for the preservation of freedom and popular government. They derived this conclusion because their state's political culture revolved around the republican ideals they believed that they had inherited from the Revolutionary generation. Republicanism provided the foundation, not only for support of the president, but also for Tennessee's political institutions and for debates over political issues. Geographically and economically diverse grand divisions separated the state essentially into three distinct societies, but republican assumptions helped to unite voters across the grand divisions, despite their diverse interests. As a southern state, Tennessee also was committed to the maintenance of slavery, and republicanism again helped to unite citizens, despite the varying depths to which slavery was entrenched within the state. While the institution was viewed less as an economic necessity by East Tennessee voters than by their western counterparts, throughout Tennessee slavery provided the basis for social order and for white freedom and equality. During Jackson's presidency, few evinced concern for the future of the institution, but since the hero himself was a substantial slaveowner, those concerned could rest assured that Jackson would tolerate no threat to their property.

With Jackson at the height of his power in Tennessee as he entered his second administration, there seemed little chance that an opposition party could appear in the state. Yet, four years after the president's triumphant reelection in 1832, Tennessee voters rejected his designated successor. By 1839, an opposition party that equaled the strength of Jackson's Democratic party had emerged. This opposition attached itself to the new national Whig party, and the emergence of the Whig party marked Tennessee's entry into the era of the second national party system. The irony of the emergence of the Whig party in Tennessee—the "revolt against Jackson," as it has been called[55]—was that Jackson's opponents built their party upon the same republican themes that had provided the foundation for Jackson's own political strength.

TWO

The Presidential Candidacy of Hugh Lawson White
1832–1836

Soon after the commencement of Jackson's second term as president, conjecture began as to who would succeed him in 1836. Most speculation centered around the new vice-president, Martin Van Buren, who throughout Jackson's first administration had contested with South Carolina's John C. Calhoun for the inside track as heir apparent. Calhoun's prospects were shattered when his role behind the Nullification Crisis became public; at the same time, the New Yorker worked his way into the president's favor until he became Jackson's personal choice to be his successor. Several political leaders in Tennessee thus associated themselves with the vice-president, and they expected little trouble in securing the state's electoral votes for the candidate.[1]

In spite of the efforts of Jackson loyalists, Tennessee's voters rejected Van Buren in 1836, and opposition to the president's chosen successor provided the basis for permanent opposition to the Democratic party in Tennessee. The major events of Jackson's second term—his response to the Nullification Crisis and his "war" against the Second Bank of the United States—played important roles in the development of this opposition. The challenge to Jackson's choice also reflected divisions among political leaders within Tennessee. Advocates of Henry Clay and the National Republican party were few in the state and had little to do with initiating the movement against Van Buren. Instead, the stimulus to the challenge came from those who approved most aspects of Jackson's presidency but disliked the directions being taken by his second administration.

Even before the beginning of his second administration, Jackson found himself forced to respond to South Carolina's attempt to nullify federal law. South Carolina's challenge arose as a protest against the federal government's policy on tariffs. The 1828 act of Congress known popularly as the "Tariff of Abominations" established prohibitively high rates on the import of manufactured goods, as a means of protecting domestic manufacturers from foreign competition. Southerners, however, condemned protection for fear of retaliation against the South's major export crops. John C. Calhoun, who was vice-president during Jackson's first term, argued anonymously in a pamphlet entitled "The South Carolina Exposition and Protest" that a state could, through a specially elected convention, declare a federal law "null and void" within its boundaries, if the convention concluded that the law was unconstitutional. Nullification was necessary, Calhoun maintained, for the protection of a minority's rights against the unbridled will of the majority of the population. The threat that Calhoun's home state might carry out nullification of the Tariff of Abominations encouraged Congress to revise its policy; but, even though the resultant Tariff Act of 1832 lowered rates, the act still upheld the principle of protection. Thus, on November 24, 1832—only weeks after Jackson's reelection—a convention in South Carolina passed an ordinance declaring unconstitutional the tariff laws of both 1828 and 1832.[2]

South Carolina's defiance met a strong reaction from the president. Privately, Jackson denounced nullification as "the wild theory and sophistry of a few ambitious demagogues"; in December, he publicized his official response in a proclamation declaring the doctrine to be "incompatible with the existence of the Union, contradicted expressly by the letter of the Constitution, unauthorized by its spirit, inconsistent with every principle on which it was founded, and destructive of the great object for which it was formed."[3] After arguing against the legitimacy of both nullification and secession, Jackson warned South Carolina that the Constitution required him to execute the laws of the United States and that he would do so, if necessary, by force; at the same time, he condemned the advocates of nullification for using the doctrine to mask their true aim—dissolution of the Union: "Those who told you that you might peaceably prevent their [the laws'] execution deceived you; they could not have been deceived themselves. They know that a forcible opposition could alone prevent the execution of the laws, and they know that such opposition must be repelled. Their object is disunion. But be not deceived by names. Disunion by armed force is *treason*. Are you really ready to incur its guilt?"[4]

After issuing his proclamation, Jackson encouraged Congress to pass a "Force Bill" that would authorize him to use federal troops to invade South Carolina to enforce the law, and in the first few weeks of 1833, armed confrontation between the central government and South Carolina appeared a real possibility. Conflict was averted only by a compromise proposed by Senator Henry Clay of Kentucky. The resultant Compromise Tariff Act of 1833 promised to reduce rates over a period of nine years and ultimately to abandon the principle of protection. Jackson reluctantly and South Carolina eagerly accepted the compromise, although Jackson insisted on the passage of the Force Bill, while South Carolina continued to maintain the legitimacy of nullification—first by repealing formally the ordinance nullifying the tariff laws and then by passing another ordinance declaring the Force Bill to be null and void.[5]

A few politicians quietly dissented from Jackson's rejection of secession, but otherwise Tennesseans gave a virtually unanimous endorsement to the president's condemnation of nullification as disunion and treason. Since most voters depended upon agriculture for their livelihood, they sympathized with South Carolina's opposition to protective tariffs. Protection or retaliation, however, would have only a minimal effect on the state's economy: most farmers continued to practice semisubsistence, safety-first agriculture; Middle Tennessee planters, in fact, were diverting their attention from staple production toward an emphasis on the cultivation of food crops and livestock; and cotton production in West Tennessee, a region just emerging from frontier conditions, did not yet involve enough farmers to constitute a major political or economic interest. While they joined other southerners in criticizing the 1828 and 1832 tariffs, Tennessee voters saw no need for resistance through a constitutionally tenuous and potentially disastrous response like nullification. Instead, through public meetings across the state they expressed their intention to back "the manly firmness of our President" and assist in the suppression of South Carolina's rebellion. "The conduct of the majority in South Carolina to say the least, is very extraordinary," Governor Carroll reported to Jackson, "and however much we might all deplore the necessity of coercing her to do her duty, yet no hesitation should take place in adopting such a course if the emergency requires it." Edmund Dillahunty meanwhile told his friend Robert L. Caruthers that "none desire bloodshed—but there are few who have not made up their minds to stand by the union."[6]

Tennessee's solid support for Jackson during the Nullification Crisis proved most immediately influential in isolating South Carolina and compelling that state to accept compromise. The controversy also played a crucial role in the long-term development of politics in antebellum Tennessee. No widespread faction of nullification sympathizers emerged as a component of state politics, and Jackson's denunciation of the doctrine as treason and disunion, combined with Calhoun's widely known political ambition, effectively branded any politician associated with radical pro-southern positions as a disunionist demagogue—that is, as a politician who threatened disunion as a means to achieve selfish political ends. The image of the Nullifier became a permanent fixture in Tennessee's political culture and later would be used to explain the radical demands of politicians in the Lower South states. In the next generation, advocates of extreme pro-southern policies would find it difficult to receive a hearing in Tennessee because of their presumed association with "the *moral treason* of some of the leading politicians in the South." "The union for which our ancestors battled so long and so bravely should be transmitted unimpaired to our posterity," a public meeting at Elizabethton resolved. "It should not be dissolved by the wild and reckless ambitions of a few designing, selfish, and unprincipled politicians."[7]

The Nullification Crisis also became entangled in the election of one of Tennessee's United States senators. The legislature in 1829 elected Felix Grundy to serve out the term vacated when the president appointed Senator John H. Eaton as his secretary of war. Grundy long had been a supporter of "Old Hickory," but he also was an old friend of Vice-President Calhoun. Grundy maintained his connection with the South Carolinian even through the early stages of the Nullification conflict; Calhoun sent a copy of his "Exposition and Protest" pamphlet for the Tennessean's perusal before its publication, and in 1830 Grundy delivered a speech in the Senate sympathetic to the nullification theory. After Jackson made clear his rejection of the doctrine, Grundy parted company with Calhoun and denied any link with the Nullifiers. His renunciation of nullification in the Senate quickly restored him to the president's favor. In Tennessee, however, Ephraim H. Foster, a Nashville lawyer hoping to further his own political ambitions, saw an opportunity in Grundy's association with Calhoun, as well as in the senator's reputation among many voters as a political opportunist. Since the legislature was not scheduled to meet again until after the expiration of Grundy's term in 1833, Foster in 1831 challenged Grundy's reelection on the grounds that the incumbent was a covert Nullifier who followed Jackson only for political benefit.[8]

Under ordinary circumstances, Foster's challenge might not have received much attention. Grundy was known to be the candidate most in the president's favor. Jackson had openly supported Grundy in his losing 1827 campaign for Congress against John Bell and was known to have favored Grundy's initial election to the Senate in 1829. Moreover, every indication from the administration suggested that Jackson would welcome Grundy's continued service. However, Jackson's effort to secure the resignation of his entire cabinet in the spring and summer of 1831, in an attempt to purge Calhoun's influence in that body, complicated the legislature's decision. The president's action necessitated the resignation of former Senator Eaton, whose recent marriage to social outcast Peggy O'Neale Timberlake had made him a target for criticism of the administration.[9] Eaton published an "Address" defending his conduct and attributing condemnation of his marriage to Jackson's political enemies, principally Calhoun and his allies in the cabinet. Shortly after the opening of the legislative session, Eaton arrived in Nashville to a hero's welcome as a martyr for the administration. Jackson, meanwhile, dropped hints that Eaton's election to the Senate would provide satisfying evidence of popular vindication of his presidency. Eaton never announced himself as a candidate, but several legislators immediately took up his cause. Foster apparently encouraged Eaton's candidacy as a way to divide Grundy's support, and the challenger hoped eventually to draw Eaton's strength to his own claim. With a difficult choice now facing the assembly, the legislature, according to Governor Carroll, was "not disposed to fill the appointment so long before it became vacant," and when the assembly adjourned in December, the question of Grundy's reelection remained undecided.[10]

Jackson insisted that he would not interfere in the election by stating a preference, and he appears genuinely to have been torn between his appreciation of Grundy's loyalty and his desire for vindication through Eaton's election. In fact, however, the president did attempt to influence the outcome. In September 1832, before the opening of a special session of the assembly, the president drafted a memorandum to the members of the legislature, praising Grundy's and Eaton's past services but concluding that "to you the constitution has assigned this duty without any interference on my part, which I have & will continue to avoid." Despite this conclusion, in this note Jackson made it clear that he preferred Eaton as his first choice, although he also indicated that he would find Grundy an acceptable alternative; no mention was made of Foster's name until a token reference appeared in the last sentence. Earlier that summer, Foster had challenged the president to "remove all misapprehension" on his influence in the election, but despite Jackson's reiteration that he "interfere[d] not in State elections," the challenger informed one of his supporters that the president's reply "confirms all you feared, & even more." Foster counseled, "As Genl Jackson will not give his consent, it remains for us to conquest, if we can, without it, and then having gained the proud day, convince him by our acts that we are, as ever heretofore, 'good men & true' to him & our country."[11]

Foster ultimately found Jackson's preference for his rivals too strong to conquer. The 1832 special session did take up the senatorial question, but after a closely deadlocked vote—Foster received the votes of twenty-two members, Grundy twenty, and Eaton eighteen, with a majority required for election—the legislators abandoned the issue. Eaton's departure from Nashville, along with his failure publicly to state his candidacy, appeared to remove him from the contest. His apparent withdrawal allowed Grundy and Foster to attempt to make the 1833 state elections a popular referendum on the Senate issue; they encouraged that year's candidates for the assembly to proclaim a preference for one aspirant or the other. Still, Eaton's supporters managed to keep his name before the electorate enough to allow a sufficient number of uncommitted candidates to be returned to leave the result in doubt. As the assembly prepared to open its session, Eaton returned once again to Nashville. Finally, after the new legislature went through forty-two inconclusive ballots, Eaton—recognizing the potential damage to the president by the continued deadlock—withdrew from the contest. A last-minute effort to unite Grundy's opposition behind Congressman John Bell delayed the final decision, but once the incumbent's supporters proved unmovable, Grundy, Jackson's second choice, won reelection on the fifty-fifth ballot.[12]

While the issue of nullification did not prevent Grundy's reelection, the crisis complicated the contest to such an extent that Jackson's influence—despite his insistence that he would not interfere—became a visible and important factor influencing the outcome. In snubbing Ephraim Foster, the president alienated a rising and powerful local politician, and the Nashville attorney soon became one of the chief instigators of opposition to "Old Hickory" in Tennessee. Likewise, the senatorial election revealed Jackson's inclination to use his popularity to try to force his will in Tennessee politics, even while proclaiming his willingness to leave local matters in local hands. "This interference of the *old chief* I know you will condemn, so do I," William B. Campbell told his uncle in the midst of the contest, "but it is his weak place, and as he, even Jackson, is but a man, we should make the same allowance for him that we make for other individuals."[13] Yet, when Jackson appeared to be interfering to prevent the election to the presidency of another popular Tennessean, most voters would refuse to grant him this allowance. Both Foster's work against Martin Van Buren's campaign and the opposition's charge of Jackson's "dictation" would haunt the president's loyalists during the formation of Tennessee's opposition party.

Notwithstanding the impact of the Nullification Crisis, it was Jackson's "war" against the Second Bank of the United States that became the central event setting the tone of his second term. Likewise, it was the Bank War that primarily encouraged loyal Jacksonians to seek a way to challenge the course of the administration. The Second Bank, chartered by Congress in 1816, since its establishment had become the country's central financial institution. Not only did it serve as the repository for the public treasury, but its power to check over-issues of paper money by state banks had made it, as the regulatory agency for the nation's currency, an integral part of the country's economy.[14] As president, Jackson long had been hostile to the bank, partly because he doubted Congress's power to grant a charter to such an institution, but more importantly because he viewed the bank as the instrument of a "money power." Jackson believed that this "money power," through its control over the currency, sought to subvert the republic by using its wealth to influence the outcome of elections and to make the federal government responsible to the will of an aristocracy rather than to that of the citizens. Convinced that the "money power" had used its influence against him in 1824 and 1828, Jackson again saw the moneyed aristocracy at work when the bank's supporters in Congress forced through a bill in 1832, granting the bank a new charter four years before its original charter expired. Jackson's veto of the bill, on the grounds that "the rich and powerful too often bend the acts of government to their selfish purposes," left open the possibility of the bank's recharter with restricted powers. Once his second term was under way, though, Jackson left no doubt that he intended to destroy the bank.[15]

To accomplish this end, in October 1833 Secretary of the Treasury Roger B. Taney began withdrawing the government's deposits from the bank's vaults. The bank countered this move by calling in loans, in order to reduce the availability of credit and, its directors hoped, direct public hostility toward the president as the reason for its policy. Instead, the panic confirmed in the public mind Jackson's warnings concerning the dangers of the bank's powers. By late summer, 1834, the bank gave up its struggle, relaxed its demands on credit, and began preparing the liquidation of its branches. In the meantime, Jackson had made it clear that he intended the country to have no national bank and that his administration would trust state banks before it would an unconstitutional central "monster bank." He also expressed his hope that the United States eventually could return to the "only constitutional" currency, a "hard money" currency composed exclusively of gold and silver.[16]

Most Tennesseans received with delight Jackson's veto of the bill rechartering the bank. Banks in general had been unpopular among many Tennessee voters since the Panic of 1819 had forced the state's institutions—except for Hugh Lawson White's Bank of the State of Tennessee in Knoxville—to suspend specie payments. A number of farmers and planters, relying on the banks for credit, had suffered when several small banks closed, while the Nashville banks' demand for repayment of loans at the same time that they refused to redeem their own paper in specie convinced many voters that banks were "sources for corruption and aristocracy."[17] All but one state bank and one private bank had closed by 1827; Nashville merchants, with the support of Governor Carroll, thus secured a repeal of the state's tax of $50,000 per year on branches of "foreign" banks and persuaded the Bank of the United States to open a branch in Nashville. By the time of Jackson's veto, the Nashville branch had become enmeshed in Tennessee's economy, but public hostility against banks continued and even intensified when directed toward the national bank.[18]

Jackson's withdrawal of the public deposits from the Second Bank of the United States likewise met with public approval, and the bank's contraction of the currency hardened opposition not only to the existing bank but to any national bank at all. The bank's attempt to restrict credit actually had only a mild effect on Tennessee's commerce. Anticipating the closing of the bank's Nashville branch, the state legislature in 1832 granted a charter to a new state bank, the Union Bank at Nashville. The next year, to increase the state's capital and to provide competition with the Union Bank, the assembly chartered two more banks, the Planters' Bank at Nashville and the Farmers and Merchants Bank of Memphis. These state banks provided currency and capital to fill the void left by the contraction of the Bank of the United States, and abundant harvests in 1833 and 1834, in the words of Tennessee Secretary of State Samuel G. Smith, "afforded a plentiful circulating medium principally in the Sections of the State not engaged in raising cotton or within the immediate influence of the Bank."[19]

The Second Bank's blatant attempt to use its power to coerce the government to grant its recharter, meanwhile, seemed to confirm the contention that it was indeed "the mammoth of aristocracy." Led by James K. Polk and Felix Grundy, the proponents of Jackson's antibank policies fanned the furor against the existing national bank into hostility against any national bank, as a threat to republican liberty. By 1834, opposition to "*a Bank* as well as *the Bank*" had become in Tennessee a test of loyalty to Jackson's administration, and no aspirant for office could offer even a tentative defense of a national bank before the state's voters.[20]

Not all of Jackson's supporters in Tennessee welcomed the destruction of the national bank. Many merchants and commerce-oriented farmers approved the principal measures of "Old Hickory's" administration, and they rejected Henry Clay's "American System" as "hazardous to 'the Constitution and the Union.'" Nevertheless, they believed that some sort of national bank was necessary to regulate issues of paper money by state banks and to provide a reliable currency, which they considered essential to profitable and stable commerce.[21] Because of the president's known hostility to the national bank, and because the Second Bank's early application for a new charter obviously had been intended to excite a sensitive political issue during Jackson's quest for reelection, supporters of a national bank expected the president to veto the bill rechartering the bank. They believed, though, that the veto reflected only an intention either to modify the existing bank or to establish a new, less politically influential institution. "The great object to be attained," according to editor Allen A. Hall, "is a National Bank, divested as much as possible of evils which experience may have shown us to be incident to the present one."[22]

When the Bank War showed that Jackson intended neither "the Bank" nor "a Bank," popular clamor in support of the president's decision crushed the pro-bank Jacksonians' hopes for a more responsible national institution. Moreover, public opinion prevented advocates of a national bank from either supporting the existing national bank or suggesting a new one, without being ostracized from the camp of Jackson's followers. When the minority report of the House Ways and Means Committee, written by Polk, attacked the bank's Nashville branch as founded upon a "vast debt" of "immense risk upon hollow and rotten securities," merchants and like-minded citizens held a public meeting in Nashville on March 28, 1833, to defend the branch and the region's commercial credit. They already realized, however, the impropriety of supporting the existing bank and disavowed any intention to defend a national financial institution.[23] The publisher of the *Nashville National Banner*, W. Hasell Hunt, himself favored a national bank, but by late summer, 1834, the *Banner* was praising the destruction of the bank, while eagerly anticipating a hard-money currency.[24]

Not only were the merchants and farmers who favored a national bank silenced by the Bank War, but politicians who held back from full participation in Jackson's offensive against the Second Bank found themselves wielding less influence with the administration. Those who hoped to advance in either state or federal politics found the road to prominence blocked by the president's preference for the bank's harshest critics. In particular, the Bank War clearly revealed that Jackson considered Senator Felix Grundy and Representative James K. Polk the administration's ablest defenders in Tennessee. Once he had secured reelection, Grundy took a leading role in the cause against the bank, denouncing the institution both in the Senate and on the stump in Tennessee. Polk, meanwhile, had been a leading advocate in the state legislature for Governor Carroll's retrenchment and antibank policies in the 1820s; elected to the House in 1825, the Columbia congressman had worked his way up to the chairmanship of the House Ways and Means Committee and led the assault against the bank in Congress. As a result of their efforts against the bank, Jackson's ties to Polk and Grundy grew closer than those of any other political leader in the state; these links in turn gave Polk and Grundy the influence needed to achieve unquestioned dominance in Tennessee's politics.[25]

Polk's and Grundy's ascendance in Tennessee blocked the aspirations of two politicians in particular—Ephraim H. Foster and John Bell. Both had been regarded as loyal supporters of the administration, but they also had close connections with the commercial interests that saw a need for a national bank. Foster's connections with Nashville's merchant community, and his law partnership with a leading Clay supporter, Francis B. Fogg, encouraged in him a sympathy for some kind of central financial institution. No matter what his bank opinions were, though, Foster's experience in his challenge for Grundy's Senate seat gave him ample reason to oppose the administration. Bell had been elected to Congress in 1827 from Jackson's own district. With his actions in Congress on the tariff and on Indian removal, and by directing through the House Jackson's Force Bill, he had distinguished himself as a steadfast supporter of the administration. Still, his connections with Nashville's wealthy elite—consolidated in 1835, when he married the widow of one of Nashville's richest businessmen and most prominent Clay advocates—caused several administration supporters to doubt his fidelity to the president.[26] The congressman's brother, moreover, served as a director of the Nashville branch of the Bank of the United States, and Jackson and his antibank supporters later charged that Bell himself had borrowed substantially from the national bank.[27]

Aware of the consequences of an open break with the administration, Bell avoided the question of the bank's recharter prior to the Bank War, relying instead on his support for other administration measures as evidence of his loyalty to the president. The congressman voted against the rechartering bill, but he explained in a speech to the House that he did so because the issue should be postponed until closer to the date of the original charter's expiration; he also stated that he thought some "agent or auxiliary" might be necessary to assist the government "in exercising a salutary control over the general currency." Over the next two years, while Polk led the administration forces in Congress in the campaign to destroy the bank, Bell sat silently in the House, making no speeches and avoiding a public commitment on the subject of "a Bank" or "the Bank." Because of this silence, Bell found himself ostracized by the administration and considered by Jackson as secretly aligned with the opposition, although public opinion still viewed him as a faithful administration congressman.[28]

Bell and Foster, along with other Tennesseans favoring a national bank, thus found themselves out of step with Jackson's administration. Only those committed to a hard-money policy seemed in line for presidential preference. Bell snatched a temporary victory from Jackson when he relied upon opposition votes to secure his election as Speaker of the House over Polk, Jackson's known choice. Nevertheless, Bell continued to portray himself as a friend of the administration, and behind the scenes he searched for ways to maintain whatever ties he could to the president.[29] An open alliance with the opposition offered little hope for long-term advancement, for Jackson's popularity still made a break with the president equivalent to political suicide in Tennessee. On the other hand, a challenge to Jackson's chosen successor, Martin Van Buren, offered the opportunity to diminish the dominance of Polk and Grundy in state politics and possibly gain control of national affairs. By supporting the claims of an unquestionably pure Jacksonian, ambitious politicians and bank advocates could affirm their loyalty to Jackson and republican principles; support for such a candidate then could carry into power politicians more sensitive to the importance of a sound currency, while derailing Van Buren and others who were dedicated to Jackson's monetary policies.

By 1834, Bell was working behind the scenes to bring out a presidential candidate to challenge Van Buren. Apparently Bell's first choice was Kentucky's Congressman Richard M. Johnson, for, in the fall of 1834, Bell dropped hints around Nashville about a potential Johnson candidacy, in order to ascertain the Kentuckian's chances. Van Buren's allies later claimed that they had evidence that Bell was encouraging

Johnson to come out as a candidate in favor of a national bank.[30] When Johnson found his own aspirations better served by agreeing to run as Van Buren's vice-presidential nominee, Bell found a willing substitute in Tennessee's Senator Hugh Lawson White. Probably at Bell's instigation, though by East Tennessean James Standifer's arrangement, the Tennessee congressional delegation, with the exception of Polk and Grundy, met in Washington in December 1834 and addressed a formal letter to White, asking him "what would likely be your course, should public opinion seem to require the use of your name as a candidate."[31]

Tennessee voters knew their senator from East Tennessee as a faithful republican and staunch opponent of the Bank of the United States. Not only had White voted against the bill rechartering the bank, but also he had delivered two speeches in the Senate, in reply to Daniel Webster's defense of the bank. These speeches frequently were cited by antibank Tennesseans as "among the ablest arguments delivered in either house of Congress in opposition to the re-chartering of the United States Bank."[32] Suggestions that White would be a popular choice as Jackson's successor had been heard as early as 1833, when several members of the General Assembly, behind closed doors, had advocated a legislative resolution nominating White for the presidency. This move failed, partly because many legislators feared that a nomination at such an early date "might be imprudent," but mainly because White himself discouraged such a nomination; instead, he indicated that he would support the nominee of a Republican party convention. A similar move, promoted by Bell and Foster, to secure a resolution from the next year's constitutional convention failed when Jackson discouraged the nomination. Possibly White by this time would have welcomed a nomination; in any case, by December 1834, White was willing to allow his name to be presented to the public as the candidate of "the people" in opposition to the candidate of a party convention.[33]

Senator White, like Bell and Foster, apparently believed that Jackson had blocked his political aspirations, and in White's case despite his orthodoxy on the bank question. The East Tennessean had indicated an ambition for the White House since Jackson's first presidential nomination, and he seems to have expected to advance to the presidency at the conclusion of "Old Hickory's" terms. White anticipated a position in Jackson's cabinet, but Jackson's choice of fellow Tennessean Eaton as his secretary of war and the necessity of geographical diversity within the cabinet prevented White's appointment to that body. After Eaton resigned the post in 1831, Jackson hoped that White

Hugh Lawson White. From Tennessee Historical Society Picture Collection. Reproduction courtesy of Tennessee State Library and Archives, Nashville.

would take Eaton's place; White, though, knew that the president had indicated an intention to support no man from his cabinet as a presidential candidate, so he declined the offer. Finally, as Jackson's second term progressed, it became clear that the general intended that Van Buren should succeed him. In August 1834, White heard a rumor that Jackson had stated that he would denounce White, if he allowed his name to be suggested. Bell and Foster thus found in White a willing candidate, despite his backers' sympathy for a national bank.[34]

When White received the letter from Tennessee's congressional delegation in December 1834, his reply probably already had been prepared. The congressmen had prepared their address to the senator carefully, in order to avoid any appearance of a nomination or recommendation of the candidate by a congressional caucus—a mode of selecting presidential candidates that Tennessee voters had opposed in 1824 as unrepublican. Instead, their letter simply asked, since White's name "has been frequently mentioned as a suitable person to succeed the present Chief Magistrate," if he intended to allow his name to be considered. This request allowed White to identify his candidacy as one stimulated by popular demand, rather than by the interests of politicians, for in his reply the senator declined seeking the presidency while declaring that "the person who would refuse to accept such an office, if offered by the people of the United States, ought to have a much stronger hold on public opinion than I can ever hope to possess." As a result, White concluded, he could not justify withholding his consent to a candidacy, since public opinion had introduced his name in the first place. White's reply made it clear to potential supporters that he would do nothing to halt the movement in his favor. When the Alabama legislature nominated White in January 1835, the movement to carry the senator to the White House was well under way.[35]

Throughout Tennessee, voters eagerly approved White's candidacy. Political observers quickly recognized that the senator would be the favorite in his home state. In several counties, local leaders arranged and voters attended public meetings to pass resolutions approving White's claims, and Tennessee's newspapers, "with scarcely an exception," began "pressing the claims of White," if they had not already done so.[36]

Much of White's support derived from state pride, especially in the senator's native region of East Tennessee. Still, Tennessee voters did not view their support for White as a respectful but hopeless enthusiasm for a local favorite. The Alabama legislature's nomination persuaded voters to view White's candidacy as a southern and western movement offering the opportunity to advance another Tennessean to the White House.[37] More influential in White's support than his regional ties, as Secretary of State Samuel G. Smith observed, was the senator's "political doctrine," for Tennessee voters knew White as a firm friend of Jackson's presidency and as a faithful adherent to republican principles. White had been "an efficient, sincere, and independent, though not sycophantic, supporter of the most important measures of General Jackson's Administration," the *Republican* proclaimed, "and no man would, we are convinced, *carry out* those measures with more ability, firmness, and discretion."[38]

While presenting White as a Jacksonian candidate, his advocates paid little attention to the question of a national bank. Public speakers avoided the issue, but when it did arise, White's backers either referred to the senator's known opinion of a bank's unconstitutionality or denied the accusation that the Bank of the United States was behind him. The fact that Tennessee's Clay faction had taken up White did not blemish his republicanism, supporters argued. Since there would be no opposition candidate, the contest presented a choice between two republicans, and Tennessee's opposition men would vote for White "because they are convinced that he is an upright man, and a pure statesman, and that he will administer the government with an eye single to the glory and prosperity of the *whole* country."[39] As for the nation's fiscal policy, White supporters—even those who had defended the Bank of the United States until it became a political impossibility—declared their intention to abide by Jackson's antibank policies "until the present system should prove ineffectual."[40]

Some of White's supporters hinted that a central bank might become necessary when Jackson's hard-money scheme did "prove ineffectual," but these insinuations were lost in the White advocates' warnings of another, more pressing issue that overshadowed in importance any dangers presented by a national bank. That issue, Tennessee voters learned, involved Martin Van Buren and the dangers of a "party," for the insistence by the New Yorker's proponents on the importance of party unity presented the voters with the "great question" of "whether the people or mere politicians and demagogues shall rule this mighty republic."[41]

Although Van Buren, among national leaders, never had been a favorite among Tennessee voters, there appears to have been in the state little open hostility to the New Yorker prior to 1835. Voters interpreted the Senate's rejection of Van Buren's appointment as minister to Great Britain in 1832 as an attack upon Jackson's administration, and public opinion widely approved his elevation to the office of vice-president.[42] However, Jackson's arrangement for a convention in Baltimore, to be held on May 20, 1835, for the purpose of nominating a candidate, provided White's supporters with grounds for objecting to Van Buren's advancement to the presidency. Leaders of the Democratic-Republican party presented the Baltimore convention as necessary for selecting the candidate upon whom the party could best unite. White advocates, on the other hand, argued that, since no candidate would be put forward by the administration's opponents, party unity was unnecessary; instead, the Baltimore convention was a "packed jury" of Van Buren supporters that sought to deny Van Buren's Democratic-Republican competitors a fair presentation before the people as presidential candidates. "Instead of giving their great Sanhedrin the title of a *National* Convention," the *Republican* demanded, "let them call it, what it will really be, the VAN BUREN CAUCUS."[43]

The fact that the convention would not nominate White, his supporters claimed, provided the least objection to it. They argued, rather, that the Van Buren men's demand that voters accept the convention's nomination represented an attempt to remove the choice of president from the voters and hence presented a threat to republican government. Behind the insistence on adherence to the convention's nomination, White's advocates contended, was Van Buren's "party," a "well disciplined and vigilant corps" that sought "to lay the privileges and liberties" of the voters "at the feet of office-holders and demagogues."

The party would control the Baltimore convention and insure Van Buren's nomination; then, since the New Yorker's high station in Jackson's administration would allow them to cloak their scheme in the president's popularity, they would attempt to force voters to accept the convention's dictation on the grounds of loyalty to the president and the Democratic-Republican party. Any citizen rejecting the "caucus" nomination would be stigmatized as an enemy of Jackson and his administration. To White's supporters, accepting the Baltimore convention's decision would mean allowing a party, rather than citizens, the privilege of selecting the chief executive.[44]

Association with a party was an acceptable, even an expected, idea among Tennessee's electorate. Most voters considered themselves part of Jefferson's Democratic-Republican party, a party they viewed as based upon principle and composed of the majority of "the people" — citizens with no political ambition but the promotion of the public welfare. Moreover, party division in itself offered no particular threat to the foundation of republican government.[45] The presence of a party presented a serious danger, though, when it was "not founded upon any settled principles" but instead was "composed of men belonging to every political sect, having no common bond of union save that of a wish to place one of themselves in the highest office known to the constitution, for the purpose of having all the honors, offices, and emoluments of the government distributed by him among his followers."[46] Such a collection of demagogues cared little for the public good, acting instead only to further their selfish ambitions. Once in power, the party would deprive citizens of their right to rule themselves by perpetuating the government "in the hands of partizans and favorites," thus making the people subservient to the whims of an aristocracy.[47]

According to White's supporters, Van Buren's party posed such a danger to the republic. By promising them promotions and places in the federal government, the wily vice-president had won the attachment throughout the country of the ambitious politicians who now were promoting his presidential candidacy. These politicians now devoted themselves to the cause of their favorite for the sake of personal gain, regardless of the country's needs and regardless of an aspirant's abilities.[48] James Polk's election over John Bell as Speaker of the House of Representatives in December 1835, White's supporters explained, showed both the power of a party and its potential danger to the republic. Bell had served ably as Speaker, but since he had refused to succumb to the temptations of Van Buren's party, "his sacrifice was early determined upon"; Polk, on the other hand, had aligned himself with the New Yorker's ascendancy, and "warm and violent partizans are to be rewarded, however deficient they may be in the qualifications necessary for the offices to which they may aspire."[49]

The issue of the Baltimore convention, as presented by White's adherents, thus presented the question of whether republican citizens or Van Buren's party would select the next president. By claiming Jackson's preference for Van Buren and arguing that White had been brought out by the president's opposition, Van Buren's supporters were trying to force voters to accept the convention's nomination and subscribe to the dictation of the party. But submission to the convention's decrees, White's advocates countered, would remove the choice of a president—already removed to a degree by the electoral college—further away from the sovereign power of the people. Should Van Buren succeed in the election, the established precedent of a convention would allow the party to select Van Buren's successor and all future presidents; republican citizens then would be deprived of their most fundamental liberty, the freedom of electing their leaders. And, since adherence to republican principles paled in importance beside the party's "life-giving principle," the distribution of offices, once in power Van Buren could pursue any personal whim, whether it was chartering a monster bank or interfering with southern slavery.[50]

The issues of the convention and party dictation resonated deeply with Tennessee's voters. Jackson himself had stood before the electorate in his first try for the presidency as the "anti-caucus" candidate, the candidate of "the people" against William H. Crawford's nomination by a poorly attended meeting of politicians in Washington. "If caucuses and conventions were wrong and anti-republican in 1823," the *Republican* asked, "by what legerdemain are they to be made democratic and correct in 1835?" Leaders of the White movement thus kept the convention issue before Tennessee's voters, casting Van Buren as the "party" candidate in opposition to White, the candidate of the "honest yeomanry." Public speakers, including Bell, admonished voters and statesmen to "guard against the excesses of party," while newspapers backing White constantly reminded voters that their candidate submitted his claims "not to a packed jury, dignified with the name of a *National Convention*—but to the impartial decision of a free and enlightened PEOPLE."[51]

Aside from the salience of the convention issue, the active support of Tennessee's newspapers aided White's cause. The senator's popularity with voters accounted for much of the press's unanimity, though the subtle pro-bank leanings of many White backers probably attracted commercially oriented editors of papers in county-seat villages.[52] No matter what their editors' motivations, Tennessee's newspapers trumpeted White's candidacy before voters and frustrated efforts to stir up popular interest in Van Buren. Supporters of the vice-president's candidacy quickly saw the power of the press in forming public opinion and believed it "necessary to awaken republican and I might say patriotic feelings" among voters, before it would be possible to call public meetings to appoint delegates to the Baltimore convention. Their efforts to awaken such sentiment made little progress, even after the establishment of a few Van Buren newspapers; as a result, Jackson's home state sent no delegates to his party's convention.[53]

White's candidacy received a further boost from state elections for the legislature and governor in the summer of 1835. Candidates for seats in the General Assembly proclaimed their support for the Tennessee senator, in hopes of riding his popularity into the legislature. Also, the new state constitution created several new offices that would be filled by legislative appointment; expecting a pro-White majority in the assembly, aspirants for these offices publicized their support for White's candidacy in order to strengthen their claims with the members of the assembly.[54] In few, if any, of the local elections was support for White or Van Buren made a specific issue, but the candidates' adherence to White and the election to the assembly of a majority committed to the senator—along with the defeat of Governor William Carroll, who had endorsed Van Buren—provided political observers with clear evidence of White's popular support in Tennessee.

The popularity of White's candidacy in Tennessee caught Jackson, Polk, and Grundy by surprise. When White allowed his name to be presented, Jackson and his associates immediately concluded that "men who have apostated from the republican fold for the sake of office," especially Bell, stood behind the senator's candidacy. According to Jackson, these "corrupt office seekers" had convinced White to permit himself "to be prostituted for such wicked purposes in his old age"; now, the president concluded, White was "irrevocably lost to the republican party." In spite of the White supporters' professions of loyalty to Jackson, Van Buren leaders in Tennessee never doubted that the movement for White was part of an opposition plot to divide the Democratic-Republican party and so throw the election to Henry Clay. "[A]t the proper time *Clay* will be in the field," Polk warned, "& the great struggle will be to throw the election into the House."[55]

In spite of White's popularity, Van Buren's backers nevertheless believed that Tennessee's voters could be persuaded to support the New

Yorker's claims. These leaders expected voters to abandon the Tennessee senator once the electorate learned the true nature of the White cause.[56] During the spring and summer of 1835, Van Buren supporters devoted their energy to getting their message to the voters: that Jackson's enemies backed the White movement, that the president preferred Van Buren, and that party unity demanded acceptance of the decision of the Baltimore convention. Governor Carroll, Senator Grundy, and Representative Cave Johnson of Clarksville pledged themselves to abide by the convention's decision, and when that body nominated Van Buren, they immediately came out for the vice-president. Polk, sensing a strong predilection for White in his district, avoided a public declaration on the presidential question until he had secured reelection; in the meantime, he took an active part in the establishment of a Van Buren organ, the *Union*, in Nashville. Jackson himself made it clear to Tennessee voters that he supported Van Buren, writing two letters, addressed to Parson James Gwin and published in Nashville's newspapers, expressing his preference for the convention nominee; later, Jackson franked documents to constituents that indicated Bell's and White's connections to those opposed to the administration.[57]

The message Tennessee's Van Buren leaders sought to convey to the electorate ironically resembled that of the state's White proponents. The vice-president's supporters agreed that a "party" threatened republican government, but they pointed to White's backers as the selfish party of demagogues. Van Buren, they maintained, was the candidate of the majority of the Democratic-Republican party, the party devoted to carrying out the principles of Jackson's presidency. The party behind White, on the other hand, represented no less than the resurgence of the Federalist party, now hiding behind the label "Whig." Although that party had changed its name and methods, it presented a constant threat to the republic by seeking, through the agency of a national bank, to consolidate political power into the hands of the federal government, which a "talented, wealthy and powerful minority" wanted to control. According to Tennessee's Van Buren supporters, Bell and Foster knew that the senator had no chance to win the election, but in exchange for the promise of office, they promoted White in order to help the money power secure its aim of dividing the Republicans. White and his backers were guilty of "abandoning principle & party for office," Jackson explained, in order "to bring into power the opposition, recharter the United States Bank, destroy the republican government & substitute in its stead, a consolidated government under the controle [*sic*] and management of a corrupt, monied monopoly."[58]

Tennessee's Van Buren supporters, then, presented the Baltimore Convention as a meeting necessary to unify the Democratic-Republican party upon one candidate, for unity was essential for the defeat of the schemes of the national bank's party. Denying that the convention was a caucus, they argued that it was instead "a select portion of the *real people,* freshly chosen and instructed by the great body of the *real democracy,* to meet and do their will"; moreover, the convention provided "the most easy, direct, and republican mode of harmonizing personal preferences and nominating a candidate acceptable to all."[59] At first, Van Buren supporters publicly professed admiration for White and a willingness to support the senator if he were the convention's choice, but they admonished voters to sacrifice their local preference and support the favorite of the national majority in order to secure the election, in the electoral college, of a republican president. When White refused to submit to the convention, Van Buren advocates pointed to the December 1834 meeting of the Tennessee delegation as a *"self-appointed caucus,* against the will and wishes of the republican party of the nation." Deriding White as the candidate of the "no-party party," they argued that the "caucus candidate" in fact was White, for he had been brought out by "Bank men and Nullifyers"; Van Buren, meanwhile, was the true candidate of the people, for he had been chosen "by the great body of the republican party of the nation."[60]

In spite of their efforts, Van Buren supporters made little headway against the White movement; and, at the end of the summer canvass, few doubted that White stood in a strong position to carry Tennessee. The predominance of White's newspaper support, along with problems in funding and efficiency in establishing Van Buren papers, made it difficult for Van Buren's cause to receive a widespread hearing. Equally important, White's popularity prevented local politicians from openly supporting the vice-president. Even Jackson's efforts for Van Buren swayed few voters. In fact, Jackson's efforts not only worked against Van Buren but actually diminished "Old Hickory's" reputation as a republican leader by providing evidence for the charge that the president was trying to interfere in a local election. Jackson's weakness—trying to use his popularity to influence a local contest—had been evident yet tolerated in the election for Felix Grundy's Senate seat a few years earlier; but when he exerted himself against White's presidential claims, it suggested to many voters the disappointing possibility that Jackson himself had fallen under the influence of Van Buren's "party."

In particular, Jackson's two Gwin letters appeared to provide concrete evidence that the president was attempting to force Tennessee's voters to accept his chosen successor. The first letter came in response to an editorial in the *Nashville Republican* suggesting that Jackson, if he had a preference in the contest, probably would prefer White; the *Republican* then maintained that, if Jackson did support Van Buren, Tennessee voters, "much as they venerate his name," would "never surrender, *even at his dictation,*" their independence. Jackson's reply made it clear that he intended to support the convention nominee, whoever that might be, and he denounced the *Republican* editor's "appeals in the language of my bitterest enemies, here and elsewhere, to the independence of the people, as a shield against 'MY DICTATION,' which *he* supposes may be attempted." The second Gwin letter appeared in response to the *Republican*'s charge that Jackson's secretary, Andrew J. Donelson, had used the president's frank without Jackson's knowledge in order to send pro-Van Buren and anti-White documents to Tennessee. In his response, Jackson declared that he never "franked any letters or packages for Major Donelson without being informed of their contents." Both letters, in addition, left no doubt that Jackson considered those behind White's candidacy "fractious intriguers, seeking to undermine the course of republicanism, and to defeat the result of the leading measures of my administration."[61]

The editors of Nashville's *Republican* and *National Banner* both expressed their regret at seeing the Gwin letters and proclaimed themselves still loyal to the administration, but throughout the campaign for White, these papers and the senator's supporters kept the Gwin letters before the electorate as examples of the danger presented by "the new corps which is forming under the auspices of Mr. Van Buren."[62] White supporters professed their respect for Jackson and pledged themselves to continue the republican principles of his presidency; nevertheless, they asked voters, "Is it democracy to believe that Genl. Jackson can do no wrong?" As an American citizen, Jackson had a right to his choice between the candidates, but, according to the *Republican*, "when that preference assumes an active and energetic form . . . it becomes a matter of infinite consequence, and may well cause the patriot and the republican to pause, and ask himself, 'where will these things end?'"[63] Even as pure a republican as Jackson could become an unwitting tool for Van Buren's party, for only "by the arts of selfish and corrupt men" could the old hero have been persuaded to pursue such a course. Despite the general's past services, White's supporters concluded, republicanism demanded that Tennessee's voters preserve their freedom to choose their own leaders and maintain the stand that they had "uniformly taken against caucuses, *dictation,* interference in elections, and an unlimited Executive patronage."[64]

Yet, while disapproving Jackson's attempt to appoint his successor, White's supporters emphasized that a White administration would continue the policies of Jackson's presidency. Though they disagreed with Jackson in this instance, White supporters assured voters that they were at one with the republican principles that guided the current administration.[65] This allegiance to Jackson proved the key to obtaining Tennessee's widespread support for White. By portraying their candidate as loyal to the president even while opposing his preferred successor, White's supporters placed the senator in an unassailable position. "If our candidates for Congress had come out in *opposition* to you[,] they would have been swept off as by a tempest," Alfred Balch lamented to Jackson at the close of the 1835 elections. Instead, Balch concluded that "there never was a set of men in such a situation as we in this quarter are":

> We are for the admn. & Van Buren—Those opposed to us say they are for Jackson and the admn. & White a Tennessean who has the wisdom of Solomon & the virtue of an old Roman. When we go before the people, I mean the ignorant who cannot understand this miserable hypocrisy, they say there [*sic*] White men tell us that they love Jackson better than they do themselves and are we to disbelieve them or abandon them merely because they are the friends of a man of our own flesh and blood? When we say Ten. is in fact supporting Webster by sustaining White they unblushingly answer that Webster is no candidate and that they never will vote for him if he is. The matter is then narrowed down to this with many of the voters[:] shall we support Jackson & White or Jackson and Van Buren? White is of our own State and we must vote for him in preference to a foreigner. . . . In other states the opposition say we are against the administration & thus two parties are arrayed against each other. Here, the opposition say we are more for Jackson than you Van Buren men. In this condition of affairs you can easily imagine how hard it is for us to get along.[66]

Balch nevertheless believed it still possible to save his state for Van Buren. If voters could be convinced that White had no possibility of success and that "*throwing* away" the state's electoral votes would open the door for the election of a Whig candidate, they would abandon White for Van Buren in order to insure the success of a Republican. Thus Van Buren leaders continued to denounce White and launched a new offensive in the fall of 1835, confident that they could persuade the electorate to take up the vice-president's cause. Polk came out strongly for Van Buren in a speech at Mooresville, Maury County, and Tennessee supporters of the New Yorker held public dinners to popularize their candidate as Jackson's favorite. Most importantly, they looked to the upcoming session of the state legislature as an opportunity to show Tennessee's voters that their senator, despite his public professions, opposed rather than supported the administration.[67]

Developments outside Tennessee already had encouraged Van Buren's advocates to believe that they could show the electorate that their votes for White would be "thrown away." The contention that the president's opposition would put forward no candidate had provided a major justification for White's supporters' attacks upon the need for party unity. Apparently the strategy behind the White movement had been to rally southern and western Jackson supporters behind the Tennessee senator and to unite them with Whig voters in the North.[68] In January 1835, however, the Massachusetts legislature nominated Daniel Webster, a Whig who strongly favored a national bank; while in Pennsylvania, a state Anti-Masonic convention, apparently with Clay's blessing, nominated William Henry Harrison. Bell attempted to negotiate with Webster's allies to secure their support for White, but the Massachusetts senator refused to withdraw; even worse, Whig papers in the North and West openly stated their desire to divide the electoral vote and throw the election into the House of Representatives, where, Whigs believed, either Harrison or Webster could be elected.[69]

Van Buren's supporters hoped that an offensive in the 1835 session of the state legislature would join national developments in derailing White's candidacy. Popular pressure forced legislators unanimously to support White's reelection to the Senate and resolutions recommending his presidential nomination.[70] The legislators devoted most of their attention, though, to a set of resolutions, written by Grundy and introduced into the state House of Representatives by Sumner County's Josephus C. Guild, instructing Tennessee's United States senators to vote in favor of Thomas Hart Benton's "expunging resolutions." Benton's resolutions would order the secretary of the United States Senate to draw black lines in the Senate journal through a resolution censuring Jackson for his conduct during the Bank War. Clay had forced this resolution of censure through the Senate at the height of the controversy over the bank in 1834; Benton's resolution would have declared the Senate's action in passing the resolution unconstitutional, and it was well known that Jackson wanted "the cruel and wanton injury inflicted on the character of the President" removed from the public record.[71] White had voted against Clay's censure, but he had committed himself against expunging as itself an unconstitutional remedy, since it would alter the constitutionally mandated journal of the Senate. The censure of Jackson could be removed by a Senate order to rescind, reverse, or repeal the censure, White argued, or by passing another resolution declaring it null and void; if it were expunged, "it must be blotted out in fact.... This I think the Senate has no power to do."[72]

The legislature's passage of Guild's resolutions effectively would have ended White's candidacy. Since the senator already had publicly committed himself against expunging, he would have been forced either to resign, to vote against his previous declarations, or to ignore the instructions, each of which would have embarrassed White and revealed the candidate as being at odds with his constituents. Moreover, these resolutions would have marked White as an opponent of what Republicans in Tennessee understand to constitute loyalty to Jackson's principles and would have destroyed the claim that White could be expected to carry on the principles of "Old Hickory's" administration. Even if they failed to secure passage of Guild's resolutions, Van Buren's supporters expected debate on the question to draw a line between Jackson's true followers and those who supported him only for political advantage.[73]

Despite the Van Buren legislators' efforts, they never succeeded in bringing Guild's resolutions before the House for debate. The House came closest to acting upon Guild's resolutions in late January, when Van Buren supporters mustered thirty-six votes in favor of considering the proposal, but the resolutions were still tabled. Three days later, by a substantial majority, that body declined for the last time to take up the resolutions. Pressure from public meetings and the *Union*'s editorials on the "false, illegal and unconstitutional condemnation of Andrew Jackson" placed many legislators in a difficult position, but, as Aaron V. Brown had warned his Van Buren allies, White's position on expunging proved "very plausible" and "shelter[ed] many a vote, against such instructions." Still, the expunging issue did appear to strengthen Van Buren's support in Tennessee; at least, the vice-president's supporters believed that their candidate's prospects had improved over the course of the legislative session.[74]

Nevertheless, at the close of the General Assembly's session, White still maintained a firm hold on Tennessee's voters. Throughout the summer and fall, White's supporters continued to present the message that their candidate was the person most capable of continuing Jackson's principles in administering the federal government. When confronted by the fact that two Whig candidates were in the field, White's backers pointed to the senator's strength in surrounding states and proclaimed his prospects "now better than we have ever deemed them."Yet opposition to "party" and "dictation" remained the chief justification for White's candidacy, as his supporters maintained that "Tennessee will abide by her *principles*, be the result what it may."[75] Probably to emphasize White's image as a candidate brought out by voters, rather than by politicians, the *Banner* urged the selection of a White electoral ticket by public meetings in each electoral district; by mid-August, such assemblies had nominated a complete "Anti-Caucus White Electoral Ticket."[76]

Van Buren's supporters considered holding a state convention to nominate candidates for electors. In the end, perhaps because of the dangers presented by the convention issue, the selection of a Van Buren ticket likewise was left to the discretion of district public meetings. Unlike the messengers of the White movement, the vice-president's supporters also encouraged the appointment of corresponding committees in each district to publicize the district's choice of elector.[77] In spite of their organization, Van Buren supporters were unable over the spring and summer to capitalize on the brief surge of momentum stimulated by the expunging issue. Samuel H. Laughlin's tendency toward inebriation often deprived the *Union* of its editor at a crucial time, and even with Laughlin at the helm, the vice-president's supporters complained that the paper "*is too mild* for the times."[78] Yet, even with an efficient newspaper, Van Buren's backers would have found it difficult to puncture the electorate's attachment to White. The unity of Tennessee's established newspapers behind the senator, and his image as the candidate brought out by the people, made it virtually impossible to dissuade Tennessee's electorate from the notion that, by supporting White, they were supporting the same principles upon which they had earlier supported Jackson.

Jackson himself undertook a final effort to save his home state for Van Buren. The president scheduled a visit to his plantation, the Hermitage, in August 1836, and he took advantage of his travel route through East Tennessee to make it clear to voters that he considered White his political enemy. While in East Tennessee, Jackson denounced the senator as a "red hot federalist"; later, in Lebanon in Wilson County, the old general unequivocally stated that no man could support him and at the same time support White. By the time he reached his plantation, Jackson believed that Tennessee would go for Van Buren.[79] To the electorate, though, Jackson's visit appeared as yet another example of his electioneering and his desire to dictate the choices of Tennessee's voters. "Gen. Jackson has been out and been Electioneering for Van as he intended," John S. Brown reported from Smith County, "but he has done more for *White* than *White* has done for him self." John Young told Polk that, at Knoxville, Jackson "was treated with coldness and disrespect," while at Lebanon "Parson Gwin[']s effigy was hung up and intended for the observation of the President," though the town's postmaster cut down the image prior to Jackson's arrival. "His reception in Tenn. has been not only cool, but *cold*," William Martin explained to William Campbell. "This must be mortifying in the extreme," Martin concluded, "but it has been his own making. For he has made war on all his own friends, who will not go for his choice of a successor."[80]

Leaders of the White movement expressed their regret that Jackson had "permitted himself to be beguiled into this electioneering tour by the parasites of the Vice-President." The contest, the senator's proponents maintained, still pitted White against Van Buren rather than White against Jackson, but if the issue was to be forced on Tennessee's voters, "if they are required to surrender their right of suffrage and to abandon Judge White and his leading friends, or be considered, and denounced as enemies of Gen. Jackson, they will not hesitate a moment—they will act as becomes freemen, who know their rights and are determined to maintain them."[81]

Jackson's visit thus reinforced the conviction among many Tennessee voters that Van Buren's party presented a greater threat to liberty than the prospect of dividing the Democratic-Republican party, for the "party" had persuaded even the venerable old general to degrade himself and his office, in order to serve its selfish purposes. When Jackson cut short his visit to Tennessee and returned to Washington in September, White's supporters concluded that the party's leaders belatedly had realized the popular backlash against the president's electioneering. "[M]any of the best Van Buren men will admit if they are candid, *it was a pity the President made this visit,*" the *Republican* observed.[82]

As the two-year-long campaign for their candidate wound to its close, White supporters in Tennessee confidently expected their state to stand firm for the senator against the evils of "party" and "executive interference." The results of the balloting showed that White's backers had judged well the assumptions and expectations of Tennessee's electorate. Fifty-six percent of the eligible voters went to the polls that November, and while this figure fell far short of the usual turnout in the future elections between Whigs and Democrats, it represented a greater interest in the presidential election than had been shown in

1832. Of those casting ballots in 1836, 58 percent chose the Tennessee senator over the nominee of the Baltimore convention.

Van Buren supporters had especially feared White's popularity in his native East Tennessee. In that region, Van Buren did win Greene, Sullivan, and Washington counties in the state's northeastern corner—three counties that in a few years would be unquestioned Democratic strongholds. Outside these counties, however, White carried almost 78 percent of the votes polled. Only 42 percent of East Tennessee's voters bothered to go to the polls, though, and White's victory depended as much on his strength elsewhere in the state as on the East Tennessee totals. The vice-president ran strongest in Middle Tennessee, especially in James Polk's and Cave Johnson's congressional districts, while White carried most of the counties along the Cumberland River in the northern portion of the Nashville basin, an area deeply enmeshed in the world of commerce and hence, presumably, more attracted by the prospect of a national bank. Van Buren carried twelve Middle Tennessee counties, but White still carried the region by a little more than one thousand votes. In the western district, as in East Tennessee, the vice-president carried only three counties, although he ran strongly in three more. Elsewhere in the district, White again was the favorite by a wide majority.

White's smashing victory in Tennessee had little impact outside his home state. The senator also carried Georgia and ran well in seven other southern and southwestern states, but his twenty-six electoral votes left him a distant third in the electoral college race, behind Van Buren and Harrison. Moreover, whatever hopes Whig leaders or White backers may have had of throwing the contest into the House of Representatives were dashed by the New Yorker's strong showing in the southern states; his 173 electoral votes gave him more than enough to win the presidency. White's triumph in Jackson's state proved an embarrassment and a severe disappointment to the chief magistrate, but the old hero had secured his primary aim. For the next four years, his chosen successor would continue to pursue his policies in the White House.

Although unable to prevent Van Buren's advancement to the presidency, the White movement played a significant role in the development of the Whig party in Tennessee. The images that the supporters of each candidate presented of their cause—as that of the "real people" against either "the party" or "the money power"—would be fleshed out by politicians to describe the Whig and Democratic parties. The economic underpinnings of the two parties also revealed themselves in 1836, as White's followers dropped hints about the necessity of a national bank for a sound currency, while Van Buren's backers stood committed against a bank and leaned toward a hard-money currency. Finally, the voting patterns that emerged in 1836 prefigured those of the party system. Thirty-five of the forty-eight counties that White carried would go for Harrison in 1840, and, while the hardening of party lines strengthened the Democrats, the basic pattern established in the White-Van Buren contest persisted in the era of the party system: most of East and West Tennessee usually voted solidly Whig, while Middle Tennessee consistently returned comfortable Democratic majorities.

The White movement also revealed that Tennessee's antebellum politics would follow a path somewhat different from those of other southern states, particularly in the Lower South. The issues of slavery and states' rights, which several historians have seen as crucial in White's candidacy and in the development of the southern Whig party, in Tennessee played only a small role. Nullification had been repudiated in the state only a few years earlier, and supporters of both White and Van Buren avoided risking the popular association of their champions with radical states'-rights advocates in the Deep South. In West Tennessee's emerging cotton belt, White's supporters did charge more frequently that Van Buren was tied to abolitionists, while the *Nashville Union* devoted a fair amount of space to defending the vice-president from this accusation. Overall, though, the issue seemed a small concern and was overshadowed by the debate over which candidate was the true "man of the people." Tennessee's two leading White papers, the *Nashville Republican* and the *Nashville National Banner*, seldom mentioned the slavery issue, and when they did, it most often followed a recitation of the dangers presented by "the party" and "dictation." Rather than focusing on which party would prove the best defender of the South's peculiar institution, the contest between White and Van Buren debated, as the foundation upon which Tennessee's party system was to be built, the question of which party best defended freedom from the Federalists or spoilsmen.

Perhaps the most important aspect of White's candidacy was that it tarnished Jackson's reputation as a pure republican leader and destroyed the dominance his name once had exercised in Tennessee's political culture. Van Buren's standing in the state relied entirely on his position as Jackson's candidate. "Van Buren seems here, to have no weight, merit or importance of his own," William Campbell noted; "like the moon, his fame & glory are borrowed from an illustrious orb."[83] Yet even the weight of Jackson's name proved unable to carry Tennessee's voters for Van Buren, and the president's efforts for the

New Yorker convinced a majority of voters that republican principles and Jackson's conduct were not always identical. In 1832, Tennessee voters viewed the success of Jackson's administration as inseparable from the persistence of republicanism; in 1836, while Jackson personally was still popular, voters saw themselves as forced to choose between the president and their freedom as electors. In such a choice, these voters showed that their devotion to republican liberty exceeded their admiration for "Old Hickory."

Allen A. Hall, by 1836 the editor of the *National Banner*, perhaps best explained the impact of White's candidacy on Tennessee's political culture. In his response to a statement in the *Washington Globe* that Jackson's name was such a "tower of strength" in Tennessee that it could carry the state even if Jackson were dead, Hall replied that the president's name was indeed a tower of strength, "when used for wise and patriotic purposes—to carry out great national measures, and establish important principles." Moreover,

> it was a tower of strength, when he vetoed the Maysville Road Bill—when he struggled with and overthrew the Bank of the United States—when the policy of removing the Indians west of the Mississippi was established. Above all, it was a tower of strength when the people rallied around it for the purpose of putting down caucus nominations, curtailing the enormous patronage of the Federal Government, and preventing it from being brought into conflict with the freedom of elections. But when used as a rod of terror by political managers, to frighten the citizens of this State out of their constitutional rights, it loses its charm—it is powerless. Gen. Jackson himself, when he comes among the freemen of Tennessee, openly electioneering for Mr. Van Buren, and denouncing with the bitterest imprecations men whom the people delight to honor—interfering with the elective franchise, and bringing the patronage of the Government into conflict with the freedom of elections—under *these* circumstances, even *he* is but a Samson shorn of his locks.[84]

Republican liberty had provided the foundation for Jackson's dominance in Tennessee; republican liberty broke that dominance and likewise would provide the foundation for the second party system in the state. Yet, before White's supporters in Tennessee could align themselves openly with the opponents of "Old Hickory's" administration, voters somehow had to be convinced that the opposition offered better protection for liberty than did "Old Hickory's" Democratic-Republican party. Economic panic and President Van Buren's response to the crisis would provide the evidence necessary for Tennessee Whigs to carry that point.

THREE

The Creation of Tennessee's Party System
1837–1839

As political observers in Tennessee reflected upon the outcome of the presidential election of 1836, they realized that voters recognized both Martin Van Buren and Hugh Lawson White as legitimate republican successors to Andrew Jackson. Consequently, although the New Yorker had not been the preference of a majority of the state's voters, Tennessee's electorate accepted Van Buren's presidency as a republican administration. "Whatever a few politicians may wish, the people are not hostile to V. B. & they will judge his administration by his acts," White supporter James Campbell confessed.[1] Privately, John Bell, Ephraim Foster, and other leaders of the White movement planned to continue their challenge to the New Yorker and to the course of the Democratic-Republican party. Loyalists to Jackson and Van Buren, though, displayed their confidence that Tennessee's voters would support the new president. They believed that the popular sentiment behind the White movement would evaporate if its leaders openly aligned with the national Whig party. "Should Van administer the government upon the principles which he has pledged himself," Samuel Powel wrote from East Tennessee, "I cannot see how those of the Democratic school can consistently oppose the administration."[2]

Almost immediately after Tennessee's voters had cast their ballots in 1836, leaders of both of the state's factions began to look toward the August 1837 state elections. Politicians believed that the election's results would reveal whether Tennessee's course in 1836 had been an aberration on the part of a state basically loyal to Jackson's presidency, or whether it marked the first step in the state's movement toward permanent opposition to Van Buren. Also, although Felix Grundy's term in the Senate would not expire until March 3, 1839, rumors that Bell and Foster both had their eyes on Grundy's seat led many voters to suspect that an anti-Van Buren majority in the next General Assembly would call for an early election for Grundy's successor.[3]

Despite the importance of the upcoming contest, and despite the momentum their cause had gained by their candidate's national victory, the early months of 1837 found Tennessee's pro-Van Buren leaders largely inactive. Simple overconfidence accounted for most of this inertia. White's poor showing in the electoral college, they believed, proved that the senator lacked the national standing of a presidential candidate, and without White at the head of their movement, Bell and Foster would be forced to attempt in Tennessee "what Calhoun & Clay have done in S. Carolina and Kentucky, viz. to make it an opposition state." Such a move would confirm the Van Buren supporters' charge that Jackson's enemies had inspired White's candidacy and would mark Bell and Foster as deserters from republican principles. With this prospect before their rivals, Van Buren men felt little urgency to counter the actions of White's supporters.[4]

In marked contrast to their opponents' apathy, leaders of the White movement immediately launched an offensive to prevent the electorate from developing any sense of loyalty to the New Yorker. Pro-White newspapers continued to attack Van Buren as the head of a party of "anti-republican doctrines" and "despotic and corrupting practices"; at the same time, these newspapers continued to portray White's supporters as "the friends of *Reform,* of *Anti Dictation,* of *Retrenching Presidential Patronage,* and of checking the audacious *interference of Federal Office Holders with Elections.*'" Though White's candidacy had failed, the senator's strong showing among southern Jacksonians convinced his supporters that they could continue their stand against the new president and unite with the national Whigs on the common ground of opposition to "the party," dictation, and interference in the freedom of elections. Unification with the Whigs on these terms, rather than destroying their movement, could establish a coalition that could carry White or a similar candidate to victory over Van Buren in 1840. "The great object now is to prevent any portion of the opposition from falling in with Van's administration," Balie Peyton informed William B. Campbell, "& to produce a general opposition to him upon *principle*[,] *broad & general.*"[5]

The White faction's leaders also recognized their movement's tenuous position in Tennessee. Openly joining with the Whigs too quickly, and on grounds other than resistance to executive power, could ruin the movement's credibility and legitimate Van Buren's claim as the true defender of Jacksonian principles. Success for these men depended upon their own claims as the heirs of Jackson's original principles, and in early 1837, it seemed clear that a Whig party in Tennessee would have to be the party resisting executive power rather than the party of a national bank. Peyton told Campbell in December 1836 that he expected the administration's enemies to unite behind White in 1840, "because his elevation would be the severest rebuke to Executive Patronage." At the same time, Peyton was sure that the national Whig candidates—Clay, Calhoun, Webster, and Harrison—were out of the question, for "the South never can support them."[6]

While politicians were looking to the 1837 elections as a continuation of the 1836 contest, a new concern among Tennessee's voters contributed an additional feature to the state's political landscape. Shortly before the presidential election, merchants throughout the country had begun to complain of pressure on the American money market. The *Memphis Enquirer* reported in November that "the monetary situation of our state was never in so deplorable a condition," and over the next few months the value of paper currency continued to decline as business failures became more frequent. By late April, the *Nashville Union* admitted that "the failures East and South have produced serious embarrassments, and the temporary stoppage of some of our largest dealers in produce and exchange"; at the same time, the *Nashville Republican* reported "a want of confidence in the stability of the banks in this city."[7] The suspension of business by New Orleans's N. and J. Dick Company particularly strained Tennessee's economy, since Nashville's largest cotton trading house, H. R. W. Hill and Company, relied heavily on its business with the New Orleans firm. On May 16, Tennessee's only private bank, Yeatman, Woods and Company, suspended specie payments. New York and Philadelphia's banks already had suspended their specie payments, and when word of the eastern banks' decision reached Nashville, private citizens held a public meeting to recommend that Tennessee's banks follow suit. As a result, the Planters' and Union banks in Nashville suspended on May 25; the next day, the Farmers and Merchants Bank of Memphis did so, too, leaving Tennessee without a specie-paying bank. Thus the Panic of 1837 came to Tennessee, initiating several years of economic hardship.[8]

The panic placed economic issues at the center of political debate. "The people here and else where so far as I have heard are all in a ferment about the monied affairs of this country," Jacob S. Yerger wrote William Campbell in early May; "I do not think it will abate at all during the summer." Yerger's prediction proved correct, for during the summer one candidate noted that "the currency and Bank question seems to have taken full possession of the people."[9] The banks attempted to mitigate the effects of suspension as much as possible by renegotiating loans when they fell due and by limiting their currency issues, while working to increase their specie reserves. Despite these efforts, the consequences of the panic reached deep into the electorate, and John Catron told Polk at the end of the summer that "the State Banks are unpopular, *decidedly* unpopular." Planters and merchants who had built their fortunes on the cotton and tobacco trades saw their estates threatened, as the prices of those staples dropped drastically.[10] Semisubsistence yeomen, the vast majority of the state's voters, stood at the periphery of the market economy, but nevertheless they too suffered in the panic. Production of food crops and local barter economies prevented most from facing absolute destitution, but a decline in the demand for their corn, wheat, and livestock gave farmers little incentive to sell their surplus in hopes of raising their standard of living. Moreover, farmers who had purchased their land, supplies, or slaves on credit confronted the prospect of losing their homes because of an inability to pay their debts.[11]

The absence of a reliable currency was the panic's most immediate disruptive effect. State law prohibited Tennessee's banks from issuing paper money with a face value of less than five dollars; hence, most Tennesseans transacted their daily business using gold or silver coin. When the banks suspended specie payments, widespread hoarding resulted in a shortage of the precious metals. Within a week after suspension, the *Republican* noted that "the 'constitutional currency' is taking unto itself wings and fleeing away, and the greatest inconvenience is felt by every class in the community, by the absence of some medium to answer in its stead the smaller transactions of business men."[12] Yeatman, Woods and Company and the Nashville Bridge Company issued small bills to try to remedy the deficiency, but the most common circulating medium became private notes, written by individuals and backed only by their prospects of future success. Public opinion displayed little confidence in these "shinplasters," especially after the Union and Planters' banks announced that they would not honor the Yeatman, Woods notes. As politicians prepared for the 1837 canvass, voters found the state dominated by a grossly devaluated paper currency and flooded with unstable shinplasters "of denominations from 12 ½ cents to $2 and $3."[13]

Leaders of the White movement wasted no time in attributing the panic to Andrew Jackson and his economic policies. The war against the Bank of the United States, they argued, had destroyed the only agency capable of providing the country with a stable currency. Jackson's subsequent policies encouraged an unprecedented speculative boom and an overabundance of paper money, but then the president arrested this boom by forcing the withdrawal of specie from the state banks that had financed these investments. After the government had removed its deposits from the national bank in 1834, the administration had entrusted the money to seven carefully selected state banks. The Deposit Act of 1836 increased the number of these "pet banks" and distributed the government's surplus revenue to the state governments; the states then immediately deposited their portions into their own state banks. This influx of capital into unregulated and irresponsible local institutions, White supporters claimed, had fueled the speculative frenzy that had raged over the past few years.[14] When Jackson saw the country abandoning his dream of an all-metal currency, he issued a treasury order requiring purchasers of public lands to pay the government in specie. The president expected this order to curb speculation and to increase the amount of metal in circulation, but White supporters immediately denounced the "specie circular" as more evidence of Jackson's "impolitic interferences and continual tinkerings with the currency of the country." By attacking the state banks' specie reserves, the "odious Treasury Circular" had "hastened and swelled the storm" and, together with the destruction of the national bank, had destroyed "the most beautiful system of equalized currency ever built."[15]

White's supporters, moreover, quickly linked the panic to Van Buren and the despotic aims of his "party." The opposition claimed that they welcomed the idea of an exclusively specie currency, but they maintained that such a system was an impossibility because "there never was and we fear never will be, 'hard money' sufficient in this country to answer the enterprise of our citizens." Jackson's attempt to institute a hard-money currency obviously had failed; nevertheless, they argued, once in power Van Buren still sought "to saddle upon us a state of things which if successfully carried out, must inevitably secure the speedy destruction of all most dear to us."[16] "The party" knew that the appeal for a specie currency was "a splendid delusion to captivate the attention of the people, for political effect"; thus they continued to trumpet the cry of "hard money" in order to attain the ultimate goal of maintaining their hold on power. White backers in particular seized upon the advocacy, by a few pro-administration congressmen, of a treasury bank—an institution that would be capitalized by the federal treasury and under the direction of the executive branch—as evidence of "the party's" use of the economic crisis to further its designs. These congressmen claimed that such a bank would ease the transition to a metallic currency, but the opposition charged that the bank would only subjugate the country's money under the direction of the president, increase the executive's patronage, and enable "the party," armed with its new weapon, "to perpetuate itself in power forever."17

Opposition to "the party" as the source of hard times thus facilitated the association of Tennessee's White movement with the national Whig party. The collapse of the economy, the proliferation of devalued currency, and Van Buren's continued adherence to the very policies that presumably had brought on the current crisis all seemed to prove that an ambitious, power-seeking politician occupied the White House. The formation of a Whig party in Tennessee would be presented as part of a coalescing of the administration's enemies throughout the United States, with a unified determination to hurl the demagogue and his minions from power and to restore the purity of constitutional government. Over the summer of 1837, White's supporters increasingly referred to themselves as Whigs, while emphasizing that "the doctrines of the Whigs are the doctrines of our liberal and well-balanced form of Government" and that "upon 'union of action and harmony of sentiment' depend the success of the principles we have labored to establish."18

The panic also exposed a subtle tension within Tennessee's White movement, a tension that would persist in the state's Whig party and that revealed the two dominant impulses behind Tennessee Whiggery. All of the state's Whigs attacked Van Buren's "party" and expressed their belief that some sort of central financial institution would be necessary to restore the nation's prosperity. Commercially oriented Whigs, finding voices in the *Nashville Republican* and the *Memphis Enquirer*, championed a Bank of the United States as Whig policy. Behind their pleas for a national bank lay hints that their preference for a successor to Van Buren was Henry Clay. No candidate openly endorsed Clay during the 1837 canvass, but several Tennesseans proudly declared their support for a United States bank.19 Other Whigs, however, speaking through the *Nashville National Banner* and the *Knoxville Register*, took a more conservative stance. While White supporters found it easy to blame Jackson's policies for the panic, they knew that their 1836 candidate had himself opposed a national bank. Aggressive promotion of Clay and a bank could not only be interpreted as a repudiation of the Tennessee senator—a charge that Van Buren papers already circulated—but could appear to validate the administration supporters' claim that White's candidacy had been part of a plot to divide the Democratic-Republican vote to secure the election of an opposition candidate. Conservative Whigs thus continued their attacks on "the party" and pledged themselves to oppose Van Buren, without proposing specific measures for relief or attaching their cause to any particular candidate.[20]

This tension among Tennessee's Whigs involved differences in inference and means, rather than in the goals of the new party. Whigs agreed that resistance to Van Buren's "party" provided a central justification for their opposition, and as hard times deepened, conservatives came to agree more openly with their pro-bank allies on the need for positive economic legislation. Still, the tension between these two wings would persist for the life of Tennessee's Whig party. The one branch joined with the long-standing national opponents of Andrew Jackson in believing that promoting a sound currency and economic progress provided the Whig party's reason for being. The other branch recognized that, regardless of specific policies, opposition to the demagogic politicians who had seduced Jackson himself away from fidelity to the principles of republicanism remained an explanation for the Whig party's central purpose that would be more acceptable to the mass of voters.

Administration supporters continued to defend Jackson, while arguing that the collapse was the expected consequence of the speculative rage prevailing in the country since 1834. Rather than following a responsible course after the war against the national bank, merchants and bankers instead had pursued a reckless frenzy of "extravagant overtrading and speculation, consequent on over issues of bank paper, and the facilities with which bank accommodations have been obtained." Succumbing to the temptation of easy credit and the lure of wealth, these jobbers, according to the *Union,* had "waded into the flood of mud speculation, beyond the possibility of escape." The current crisis was nothing more than the day of reckoning for the speculators, when they learned the worthlessness of their paper fortunes because they were forced to pay their debts with real money. Those suffering from the panic, then, had brought the catastrophe upon themselves.[21]

Behind the suspension of specie payments, Van Buren backers saw the old Bank of the United States. That bank, still under the direction of Nicholas Biddle, now operated as a state bank with a charter from Pennsylvania, but supporters of the new administration believed that the bank and the Whig party had precipitated the currency crisis as a means of regaining its authority and power in the federal government.[22] Acting in concert with the Bank of England, the Bank of the United States had suspended its own specie payments and forced the country's state banks also to suspend them, in a plot to devalue the nation's currency. Hard times brought on by that suspension would create a popular desire for a new agency to provide a stable medium of exchange, a desire that could be satisfied by granting a new federal charter to the Bank of the United States. Once reestablished in its former position, the bank could continue its work of consolidating political power under its control.[23]

Unfortunately for Tennessee's Van Buren supporters, in 1837 they faced in the electorate what James Walker later described as a "popular desire to have a regular and uniform paper circulation of the same value every where." In May, Van Buren issued a proclamation calling Congress into a special session to deal with the economic crisis; but, since that session would not convene until after the conclusion of the August elections, administration supporters entered the canvass with no common proposal for relief. Rechartering Nicholas Biddle's bank obviously was out of the question. Even so, Levin Coe, a legislative candidate from Fayette County, lamented to Polk that in West Tennessee "very many of our best Administration men have got it into their heads that we must have some sort of National Bank"; moreover, he warned the congressman, "it is even asserted by some that the views of the Administration party have undergone some change."[24] Most pro-administration candidates followed Polk's advice to "wait the administration plan of relief & regulation of the currency," and, when confronted with the panic, they devoted their energies to blaming the Whigs and overtrading for the crisis. Their party's hold on power and the compelling logic of the Whigs' account of the causes of the panic, though, left administration supporters on the defensive in the 1837 summer canvass. Without a policy proposal from the White House, Van Buren supporters could offer no reply when opponents asked in the *Memphis Enquirer* for "some *sensible* and *trusty* Van Buren editor [to] tell us what is the real position they now occupy."[25]

The Panic of 1837 and its consequences moved Tennessee politics a step closer to a party system. By blaming the crisis on their enemies, each of Tennessee's factions became more closely identified in the public mind with the national political conflict between the administration and its opposition. The experience of hard times provided voters with strong evidence that something was awry, and politicians channeled voter dissatisfaction into the belief that political forces threatened not only prosperity, but liberty itself. "[T]hey have been very adroit in attributing all our present difficulties & embarrassments to the measures of the last & the present administrations of the general government," William Rucker told Polk, "and have induced a good many of our party to believe it because, as they think, their pecuniary interests are affected by it." Likewise, John H. Bills complained to the House Speaker that "the general suspension has worked *death* to the cause of free principles. People are slaves to money, and every act has been exercised to induce a belief it is all the fault of the '*Government Experiment.*'"[26]

In the 1837 elections, though, politicians failed to present voters with a clear choice of parties. That year's gubernatorial contest, which could have been used to force a party decision among voters by portraying candidates as representatives of the national political struggle, instead appeared rather uninteresting to the electorate. Strategy and the inability to find suitable candidates encouraged leaders of both the state's factions to avoid party associations in the governor's election. After William Carroll announced his intention not to run, Van Buren's supporters searched desperately for a candidate before finally settling in mid-May on Nashville's postmaster, Robert Armstrong, whose longtime friendship with Jackson and his recent service as commander of Tennessee's troops in the Seminole War in Florida seemed to make him a strong candidate. Yet Armstrong, following a strategy devised by Felix Grundy, stated that, although he supported Van Buren, he "would not be a *party* Governor," and when his circular letter appeared in July he discussed state issues exclusively. Grundy and his associates thought they discerned a growing acceptance of Van Buren's administration among the electorate—an acceptance that would disappear if politicians forced voters once again to choose between White and Van Buren. Should the election become an excited party contest, "a return of the now neutral men who voted for Judge W., would be the consequence, and this throughout the State," John Catron explained to Jackson, "whereas, the present tendency of things, if left unrestrained, will very soon bring a decided majority back to their old principles and friends, and to a support of the administration."[27]

The division within the Whig party further distorted party associations in the gubernatorial contest. Aggressively pro-bank newspapers immediately endorsed the incumbent, Newton Cannon, and emphasized the hardening of party lines in the state. John Bell and Ephraim Foster, on the other hand, searched for a new candidate; in fact, it appears that originally they approached Armstrong about the possibility of his running as the standard-bearer for White's supporters.[28] Though Cannon had supported White, he never had been included among the inner circle of the leadership of the White movement, and his victory in 1835 had depended more upon the electorate's rejection of Carroll's claim of eligibility than Cannon's merits or White's popularity. Also, his apparently incompetent handling of the federal government's call for volunteers to fight in the Seminole War, along with his stringent interpretation of an Internal Improvement Act passed in 1836, had damaged his reputation.[29] After Armstrong agreed to run as the pro-administration candidate, Bell and Foster encouraged retiring Congressman Balie Peyton to challenge Cannon. Peyton delivered several speeches leaving open the possibility of a candidacy, but Bell and Foster abandoned Peyton when he proved unable to unite the opposition forces behind him. Nevertheless, they still refused to acquiesce in Cannon's candidacy and instead made no secret of their intention to vote for the Nashville postmaster.[30]

These pro-White leaders justified their decision on the same principle upon which they originally had backed the senator's presidential candidacy. They refused, they argued, to give up their freedom of choice merely to acquiesce in the demands of a party. Armstrong was not a party candidate, they maintained, and despite his support for Van Buren, his personal opinion should not proscribe him from an office for which he was eminently qualified. "If he were a *mere Van Buren partizan*," the *National Banner* maintained, "then on principle we should feel bound to oppose him," but since Armstrong "had not acted upon that leading principle of the Van Buren party in withholding their support from all men who are not of their party," republican citizens could support the postmaster without yielding their right to the freedom of elections. Conservative Whigs thus tried to strengthen their movement's opposition to Van Buren by countering the assertive pro-bank wing of their movement and emphasizing instead their own objection to the principle of "party" guiding Van Buren's administration. "Did we burst the shackles of *Jacksonism* to put on those of *Whitism,* or *Clayism* or any other *ism* under the sun?" the *Banner* asked, concluding instead that supporting Armstrong on the basis of his qualifications would be more consistent with the principles of the White campaign than would supporting Cannon simply because he had approved the senator's presidential prospects.[31]

When the returns were counted, on the surface it seemed that the Whigs had won an impressive victory. Even without Bell and Foster, Cannon carried 61 percent of the votes cast, easily winning reelection. The ambiguity of party lines prevented an exact numbering, but few doubted that the next legislature would contain a decided Whig majority; moreover, Van Buren's opponents won ten of the state's thirteen congressional seats. Leaders of both factions, however, knew that these triumphs rested upon a tenuous foundation. Armstrong proved to be a weak candidate, for he was little known outside Middle Tennessee and, it turned out, little respected by the volunteers who had served under him. His agreement with Cannon that neither would tour the state also damaged the postmaster's prospects, for, as John W. Childress told Polk, "the people dont know him." "We fail to get up an excitement for Armstrong," John H. Bills noted shortly before the election, "& the people care not for Cannon, but will vote for him because he is in."[32] Because the gubernatorial contest failed to keep national issues before the voters, in elections for legislative seats Whigs were able to use either national or local questions as needed; as the *Union* complained, in counties where White's followers held a majority, "the old White question of 1835 is revived in the temper of proscription," while, in pro-administration counties, "they beg off from the White question, and deceitfully declare that federal politics ought not to be introduced into an election for members of the Assembly."[33]

Even the overwhelming triumph in the congressional elections appeared more as a protest vote against Van Buren than as evidence of a groundswell of support for the Whigs, for as yet the opposition offered no clear alternative to the current administration. Before the next state elections in 1839, though, Whigs would be forced to indicate a preference in the next presidential election, and this move would provide their major challenge. Even before the commencement of the 1837 canvass, Joseph H. Talbot had observed that White's supporters would be "compelled to break ground for Harrison or Clay or Calhoun or Webster," and the mention of any of these candidates, he believed, would prove "fatal" to the cause of the opposition in Tennessee. "Let them go on," Guild assured Polk when he heard of a public meeting discussing Clay's candidacy; "commit themselves," he concluded, "and we have them."[34]

When the General Assembly met in the fall, Tennessee's Whigs found themselves in a vulnerable position and, moreover, troubled by internal divisions. The Whig majority had no trouble bringing on the senatorial election to choose Grundy's successor, though Foster and Bell both lobbied hard for the position before the congressman finally gave way. Administration loyalists charged that the senatorial contest revealed disharmony among Whig leaders. The majority easily passed resolutions instructing Tennessee's senators to oppose Van Buren's Independent Treasury proposal, which was the president's plan to store the public revenue in a public repository and, he hoped, mitigate the consequences of the panic.[35] Whig disunity emerged, though, when Nicholas Darnall of Henderson County introduced into the House a set of resolutions that would instruct Senators Grundy and White to vote in favor of legislation creating a new national bank. "Are not the Whigs of Tennessee for a United States Bank?" Darnall asked. "If not, what are they for?" The *Banner* replied that there was no need to press the bank question, since no bank could come into existence as long as Van Buren was in power, and Whigs avoided even taking up the measure in the House before Darnall finally withdrew his resolutions. Van Buren supporters seized upon these resolutions as evidence of a Whig attempt to distance their cause from Senator White, since the Whigs "now considered [White] almost useless." The *Union,* in fact, argued that Darnall's resolutions had been offered for the purpose of forcing White's resignation, so that he could be replaced in the Senate by Bell.[36]

With their opponents divided and on the defensive on the national bank issue, the legislature's pro-administration members pushed the assembly to provide Tennessee's voters with relief from the panic. By one vote, they failed to bring before the House a bill to order the state's banks to resume specie payments, but they did secure passage of an act suppressing the circulation of change bills, change tickets, paper bills, or bills of credit—a law that they expected would clear Tennessee of its shinplaster currency. More importantly, Andrew L. Martin—one of Tennessee's few Calhoun supporters, who was following the South Carolinian back into Van Buren's camp—and A. O. P. Nicholson transformed a bill sponsored by Giles County Whig Neill S. Brown into a program for economic relief and state development. Brown's original bill would have created a new state bank, under the direction of a state-appointed board of directors and capitalized by the surplus revenue received from the federal government after the passage of the Distribution Act of 1836. Nicholson and Martin added provisions to expand the state's commitment to internal improvements and to use the bank's profits to fund common schools and academies. Because of the internal improvement provision, the final vote on the bill followed geographical rather than party lines, with representatives from Middle Tennessee opposing the bill and East and West Tennesseans favoring it. Privately, though, Van Buren leaders, such as James Walker, expected the new bank to "afford at least temporary relief to the people." This relief, Grundy added, would "commit the State very strongly against a *National Bank,"* because the increase in the state's banking capital "puts down most of the arguments, heretofore used, in favor of a Bank of the U. States, so far, at least as Tennessee is concerned."[37]

Despite the apparent Whig triumph in 1837, popular dissatisfaction with Van Buren and the hard times brought on by the panic by 1838 had not yet hardened sufficiently to create a permanent Whig party in Tennessee. Aside from opposition to the administration, Whig leaders offered no clear alternative candidates or policies. Throughout a large portion of the state, Whigs had tried to keep national issues—the basis of their opposition—out of local politics. The principal Whig leaders had refused to endorse the reelection of an incumbent anti-Van Buren governor, while a division over means had left Whig spokesmen unsure about whether to focus their developing appeal on specific economic policies or on continued ideological resistance to Van Buren's "party." Administration loyalists, meanwhile, still hoped to prevent the formation of a state Whig party by weathering the current storm and luring voters back into supporting the president. For a permanent, institutionalized two-party system to be established in Tennessee, voters needed to have their political concerns directed into loyalty toward one or another clearly identifiable party.

Even before Tennessee's legislature had opened its session in October, voters already had begun to respond to developments that would solidify party allegiances. In September, Congress convened in its special session to deal with the effects of the panic, and in his message to that body, President Van Buren proposed his Independent Treasury system as the administration's response to the currency crisis. By this plan, the federal government would separate itself entirely from the banking system and instead use its own agencies to receive, hold, and disburse public money. The government would accept only gold and silver or the notes from specie-paying banks; then the government's power to demand redemption from the banks would provide, as the old Bank of the United States had done, the regulation necessary to promote confidence in the country's currency. Moreover, by holding its own money, the government no longer would encourage unlimited issues of paper money and reckless speculation by allowing its funds to be used as capital by state banks, and the government's own use of hard money would encourage citizens to move toward Andrew Jackson's original goal, an exclusively specie currency.[38]

A few leaders of Tennessee's administration supporters expressed their disappointment with Van Buren's proposal, believing that the president was "mistaken in supposing *a majority* are friendly to the specie policy as proposed by Gnl. J. and himself."[39] Nevertheless, they pledged, in the words of James Walker, to "stand ready to sink or swim with my political friends," while Polk and Jackson encouraged their associates to stand behind the Independent Treasury. "This issue now palpable should be dwelt upon and enforced," Polk admonished A. O. P. Nicholson. "It is a good one for us. Nothing could tend more to the restoration of a sound currency, than the Independent Treasury scheme, and this our opponents know and therefore they violently resist it."[40] Most importantly, the "subtreasury" provided a positive program upon which administration loyalists could carry their cause against the Whigs, for Van Buren's plan for relief offered an alternative to the Whig's suggested solution of a national bank. "[T]he actual suffering has been great & therefore it is no wonder that many of the timid have gone off in favor of the old Bank," Aaron V. Brown told Grundy. "Shew them now a *better one* & you furnish a *rallying point* to which to flee & become reunited to their former political associates. It was for the want of such a *rallying point,* some decided & definite project of relief[,] that lost Mr. Van Buren so many friends . . . & [they] will stay lost untill something of this sort shall bring them back."[41]

The choice between the subtreasury and a national bank increasingly came to seem the only alternatives, because, over the winter of 1837, Tennessee's Whigs appeared to be moving closer to the presidential aspirations of the champion of the bank, Henry Clay. While not all opposition leaders backed the Kentucky senator with the same intensity, by the end of the summer of 1838 they clearly indicated their preference for Clay over Van Buren. The pro-bank wing of the party had taken a bold stand even before the end of 1837. Edwin H. Ewing suggested Clay as a candidate at a public meeting in Nashville on November 20, and this suggestion was "greeted by the meeting with immense and repeated applause."[42] A few weeks later, the *Memphis Enquirer* formally endorsed Clay. In Nashville, Allen A. Hall secured the merger of the town's two opposition newspapers to form the *Republican Banner.* The new paper followed Bell's conservative course of opposition and withheld open endorsement of any candidate, but four months after the consolidation, Hall's associate editor, Caleb C. Norvell, left the *Banner* to edit the *Nashville Whig,* a paper dedicated to promoting the cause of Clay and a national bank. Yet, while the *Banner* criticized the *Whig* for its bold stand for the Kentuckian, the *Banner* soon agreed that "Mr. Clay is the choice—the decided choice—of the great mass of the American people."[43]

Any doubt about the Whigs' course was eliminated when Hugh L. White effectively removed himself as a candidate. Few now mentioned White as a possible candidate in 1840, and perhaps the senator realized that his lack of national support rendered futile another stand for the presidency. In any case, in a speech at Knoxville on August 1, 1838, White stated that he expected Clay to stand against Van

Buren in the next election, and the senator declared that "for the present incumbent I will never vote, while I entertain the same opinion of him which I now do." Because of Van Buren, White maintained, "our currency is destroyed, and with it the commerce of the country." Thus, despite his past opposition to the Kentuckian, and despite their lingering differences on some issues, White announced that he expected to support Clay in the contest, for the Tennessean found "Mr. Clay greatly preferable to Mr. Van Buren."[44]

Despite different emphases on Clay's worth as a candidate, Whigs throughout Tennessee united in opposition to the administration, using the same reasoning they had employed in rejecting the New Yorker in 1836. Tennesseans, they argued, "never can nor never will vote for Mr. Van Buren under any circumstances," because of both the mode of his elevation and his conduct in office. Now that they had attained control of the executive branch, Van Buren and his party were "constantly seeking by every effort to increase their power and patronage," and the "direct and inevitable tendency" of this encroaching power "is to Monarchy."[45] The subtreasury offered no prospect of relief, Whigs argued, for its insistence that the federal government accept only gold and silver in its transactions ensured only "a sound currency for the use of the Government, or in other words, for the use of Government officers and Government contractors." Instead, the plan only revealed Van Buren's monarchical designs. The location of the control of the national treasury in the hands of the president, the *Republican Banner* warned, would make the public purse "a prey to executive patronage." The subtreasury was nothing more than "an untried expedient to suborn the freemen of the U. States in the exercise of the elective franchise, with their own money."[46]

The success of this subversive "party" and the imminent danger it presented demanded that Van Buren's opponents join together behind an acceptable candidate, to prevent the despot's reelection to office. No matter what past or present disagreements divided the administration's opposition, the present danger required all true Whigs to rise above these disputes in order to preserve republican freedom. "Minor prejudices and partialities must yield to the settled determination of the people to drive the present imbecile and reckless administration from power, and restore the country to its wonted prosperity," the *Nashville Whig* maintained.[47] John Bell, in a speech before Congress, likened the Whig cause to a holy crusade. "There was a time, Mr. Speaker," the congressman explained,

> in the history of modern Europe, when, whatever discord prevailed among the Christian nations which occupied that fair continent—how-

ever bloody and furious the wars which raged between them—the moment it was announced by pilgrim messengers that the Infidel powers of the East were assembled, and advancing their standard to the confines of Christendom, the sacred tocsin was sounded! "The truce of God" was proclaimed, and Christian armies which had lately met in deadly strife, upon many a bloody field, were now seen advancing harmoniously in united columns—a consolidated phalanx—tolling back the tide of war upon the haughty Turk! I will not say, sir, that the parallel is complete. It would be profane to do so; but I will say, that next to the Christian religion, as an instrument for the improvement of the condition of the human race, that which is most precious on earth is in peril. The Constitution of the U.S. is invaded! The janisaries are mustered; the infidel powers advance; already are the outworks carried; they approach the citadel, and nothing but a united effort, and the most determined courage and good conduct, can save it from irretrievable destruction.[48]

Whigs in Congress had called for a national convention to effect this unity of purpose, and Whigs outside Tennessee eventually agreed to meet in a convention at Harrisburg, Pennsylvania, in December 1839. Tennessee's Whigs immediately refused to participate in this body, for, as Bell told Robert Caruthers, the state's opposition leaders recognized that they "cannot with any consistency or propriety advocate a national convention." Van Buren's nomination by the Baltimore Convention in 1835 had provided a central justification for White's challenge to the New Yorker's election, and "it cannot be expected that Tennessee will waive her objections to the caucus or convention system," the *Whig* concluded, "because the proposition in this instance happens to come from the party with which she is proud to be identified." White's candidacy so strenuously had called into question the idea of a national convention that the state's Whig leaders knew that a reversal on the issue would damage their cause; thus they made no effort to send delegates to the Whig gathering.[49]

Even though they refused to participate in the convention, Whigs nevertheless argued that Tennessee's voters could support the Harrisburg Convention's nominee and still preserve their political independence. No doubt, another packed jury would nominate Van Buren, but once the Whig convention nominated Clay or another candidate, the state's electorate could weigh the merits of each nominee and make its choice. Should the Whig candidate prove as offensive as Van Buren, Tennessee voters could reject both candidates. If, on the other hand, the Harrisburg convention did present an acceptable candidate, citizens could support him, despite his association with an unrepublican mode of selection. "The people of Tennessee were per-emptorily

[sic] and dictatorily called upon to support Mr. Van Buren *because* he was the nominee of a National Convention," the *Republican Banner* explained. "If they support Mr. Clay at all it will not be *because* he has been thus nominated, but for the reason, that *in spite* of such a nomination, other important considerations connected with the well being of the country, entitle him to a preference over Mr. Van Buren."[50]

Tennessee's Whigs, then, united in their purpose to elect a Whig president in place of Van Buren. Both wings of the party could accept Clay as a candidate, they argued, because he no longer advocated the most obnoxious features of the American System. Now, Whigs maintained, Clay promised to abide by his compromise tariff of 1833 rather than push for protection; also, instead of direct funding by the federal government, the Kentucky senator favored distribution of the proceeds from the sale of public lands as a means to finance state internal improvements. Clay still promoted a national bank, but that question, the *Republican Banner* maintained, was less important than the issue of removing a corrupt politician from the reins of power. With a responsible leader like Clay in the presidency, "the people can have a Bank if they choose, *but not without a majority of them desire it*"; whereas, if Van Buren remained in office, "they cannot have a Bank, *even should a majority demand it.*" Whether they presented Clay as a statesman or as the lesser of two evils, Whigs throughout the state assured voters that, on the most significant issues, "Mr. Clay is *with* them."[51] Yet Clay Whigs and conservative Whigs both pledged to abandon Clay if necessary and promised the electorate that they would "be found battling with the Whig party, no matter who their candidate may be[,] if the present incumbent of the Presidential Chair is in the field for re-election." The United States could survive without a national bank, the *Banner* observed, "but we must rescue the constitution from the assaults and designs of the 'spoilers.' The country cannot get along and preserve its freedom, unless that is done."[52]

As Van Buren loyalists expected, the open association of Whigs with Henry Clay's presidential prospects produced a strong reaction among Tennessee's voters. Several Whigs sensed a surge of support for the Kentuckian.[53] Administration supporters, on the other hand, believed that Clay's candidacy had stimulated a popular revulsion against the state's opposition leaders, and they tried to fuel this disgust by charging that the attempt "to transfer the White party to Clay in this State" represented the culmination of the opposition's long-standing desire to align Tennessee with the Federalist party. This specter of a President Clay, they believed, was driving White supporters back into the fold of the Democratic-Republican party. As one Democrat, Elihu C. Crisp, bluntly stated, "Henry Clay is a bitter pill for the Whiggs of Tennessee to swallow, and I think that a large Majority of them will gagg at [the] start."[54]

Perhaps no administration supporter recognized the importance of the Whigs' taking up Clay as well as Representative James K. Polk of Columbia. The Speaker of the House had disapproved of Grundy's "temporizing" strategy in 1837, and as soon as the Whigs indicated their support for Clay, he admonished his colleagues that "now is the time for active exertion in the State."[55] Like most Van Buren loyalists, the Columbian expected William Carroll to challenge Newton Cannon for the gubernatorial chair in 1839, especially since Carroll, early in 1838, had indicated an intention to run. The following summer, though, Carroll wavered on his previous determination, and Polk's associates urged the party to find a new candidate.[56] This opening offered Polk the opportunity to take the fate of Tennessee into his own hands. On August 30, 1838, Carroll and Polk both attended a public meeting in Murfreesborough. After Polk's speech, a toast pledged to Carroll the meeting's support in the next gubernatorial contest. The former chief executive thanked the meeting but announced his decision not to seek the office, whereupon a similar toast nominated Polk. To the Whigs' surprise, the House Speaker "accepted the nomination with great cheerfulness," and he declared himself a candidate for the office of governor of Tennessee.[57]

Personal considerations probably influenced Polk to abandon the crucible of political warfare at Washington to pursue the governor's office. Most Americans considered the office of Speaker of the House of Representatives, which Polk had held since 1835, as the third most prestigious position in the federal government, but the Speaker apparently had his eye on higher stations that could be reached more easily from the position of governor. Administration supporters in Tennessee pushed Polk as the next Democratic-Republican vice-presidential candidate in place of Richard M. Johnson, whose open liaison with a slave mistress had made him a political liability. Whig victories in recent state elections indicated a strong possibility of an opposition majority in the next Congress. That majority would gladly elect a Whig as Speaker and thus damage Polk's political standing. A campaign to become governor of Tennessee would allow Polk to retire honorably from the Speaker's chair, while a victory over the administration's enemies in the state would provide the Tennessean with momentum to carry him into the Democratic Convention as the favorite for the party's vice-presidential nomination. Once in office as vice-president, Polk then would hold the strongest claims as Van Buren's own successor to the White House.[58]

Whatever the Speaker's motivation, his candidacy profoundly impacted Tennessee politics, for Polk sought in the canvass to draw a sharp distinction between Jackson's Democratic party and the Whigs. The declaration of his candidacy at Murfreesborough came immediately after he had delivered a speech that "proved the federal party was using the currency question to put down the administration." In his public appearances before returning to Washington for his last session in Congress, he continued to press national issues; then, when his "Address of James K. Polk to the People of Tennessee" appeared in the *Union* in April 1839, the candidate devoted the circular to "subjects of great public importance connected with the administration of the Federal Government."[59] The importance of these national issues, Polk maintained in the "Address" and throughout the campaign, centered on the fact that the present political contest traced its roots back to the Federalist and Republican struggle of the 1790s. Despite their defeat in 1800, the Federalists remained a persistent threat to republican principles, as they were "still contending for the mastery in the government." Jackson's election to the presidency, in fact, had saved the country from the Federalist administration of John Quincy Adams and "brought the ship of State back to the 'Republican tack.'" Throughout these earlier battles, Tennessee had stood firm behind the Republican party, and the candidate pointed to the state's united support for "Old Hickory's" positions on the tariff, internal improvements, the public debt, Indian removal, and the Bank of the United States as evidence of Tennessee's steadfast devotion to republican principles.[60]

Now, Polk argued, a portion of his former political allies had broken away from the Democratic-Republican party. These apostates had attached themselves to the opposition, which was "headed and led on by Clay and Adams and Webster and Harrison, and embodies in its ranks the federalists of the Northern States." They knew that Tennesseans had been "steady and unwavering in the support of Democratic principles," but they nevertheless sought to use the economic crisis to persuade the state's voters to follow them into the support of the Federalists. Polk reminded voters that they had backed White for the presidency in 1836 as "the friend of Gen. Jackson." "And what do you see and hear now?" he continued. "The very men who pressed Judge White upon you as the man best fitted to carry out the measures of Gen. Jackson now advise you to abandon the principles which you and your fathers have cherished, to espouse the principles of Federalism, and throw yourselves into the arms of that party. They counsel you to abandon the principles and party of Jefferson and Madison and Jackson, to adopt the principles of Hamilton and Adams and Clay, and to aid in electing Mr. Clay, the second Hamilton, to the Presidency of the United States."[61]

Clay and the Federal Bank party, Polk maintained, still stood behind the American System, whose tenets, as all could see, were identical to Hamilton's plan to consolidate political power in the federal government. No matter what Whigs might say concerning their devotion to the Constitution, their central purpose was nothing less than to form "a strong government, far removed from popular control ... and to create other influences than the will of the people to control the action of their public functionaries." Van Buren's administration, on the other hand, offered the Independent Treasury, a republican measure that proposed, not to increase the power of the executive, but to have the government "keep its money in its own Treasury, where it can at all times, in peace and in war, be commanded for the public uses." Since the plan ultimately left the fate of the nation's treasury under the control of officers responsible to the electorate, Polk concluded, it evinced Van Buren's dedication to the principles of the Democratic party.[62]

Polk's strategy, as revealed by his "Address," called for Tennessee's administration loyalists to "push on the reaction" to the Whigs' association with the presidential prospects of Henry Clay. The Van Buren supporters' standard-bearer sought in the gubernatorial election to demand the voters' decision on the outcome of the contest between Republicans and Federalists. Polk himself oversaw the fielding of candidates for the legislature and for Congress, as he encouraged local leaders to run candidates who were not only personally popular but also unquestionably committed to Jackson and Van Buren. At the same time, the *Nashville Union* admonished voters to "make each and every candidate for their suffrages at the approaching election unmask himself upon the stump" and force politicians to address "the only true issue: 'Clay or Van Buren?'"[63] Unlike in the muddled 1837 contest, the significance of the election of 1839 was made clear to Tennessee's voters: according to Polk, those behind him remained loyal to the Democratic party of Andrew Jackson, while those opposed to his candidacy supported the Federalists. With Whigs already committed in their opposition to Van Buren's "party," Tennessee's voters for the first time would face a clear choice between Democrats and Whigs.

The Democratic offensive hit the Whigs at a time when they were uncertain both about the proper way to present Clay to Tennessee's voters and about Cannon's desirability as a candidate. The *Nashville Whig* and the party's pro-bank wing, immediately after Polk's declaration of his candidacy, endorsed Cannon and accepted the Democratic challenge to wage the campaign upon "the broad issue of POLK, VAN BUREN, and the SUB-TREASURY, against CANNON, CLAY and a NATIONAL BANK."[64] Conservative Whigs, though they denounced Polk as "the mere *instrument* of the Federal Government," again hesitated to back Cannon's reelection. When Hugh L. White attempted to resign from the Senate in November 1838, on grounds of ill health, Democratic leaders believed that the move actually revealed an attempt to force Cannon from the field by making White an available candidate. Cannon's response to White's resignation suggests that the governor also suspected such a challenge, for he refused White's letter and asked the senator to give his health time to recover before the next session of Congress convened. This move destroyed any claim White might have had to seek the governor's chair, and with Cannon again clearly determined to stand for reelection, conservative Whigs this time endorsed the incumbent and gave him their full support.[65]

With the Whigs finally united behind Cannon, they accepted Polk's challenge to fight the campaign upon national issues. In a speech at Murfreesborough in April 1839, Cannon declared that he had no wish to discuss federal politics, since "they do not properly belong to, and ought not to be introduced into a canvass of this kind." Because his opponent "seems to confine himself to such an issue," though, the governor showed that he would not hesitate to address national affairs, and he declared his preference for Clay over Van Buren. While Cannon's own "Address," published in the next month, made no mention of the Kentucky senator, the incumbent did pledge his support for "a National Bank, founded on proper principles and regulated by Congress, as calculated to preserve and secure to the people of the whole Union, a sound and convenient circulating medium of uniform and established value." Moreover, in the paper Cannon stated his opposition to "the annual expenditure of nearly forty millions under Mr. Van Buren"; to the subtreasury, the expunging resolutions, and increased executive patronage; and "to the Administration of the General Government on party principles, and to the influence of the Federal Government on State elections."[66] Whig newspapers, meanwhile, rejected Polk's charge that the Whigs were Federalists; instead, they claimed that they stood on the original republican principles upon which they had supported Jackson in 1828 and that Jackson and the "spoils party" had departed from those principles. The subtreasury plan in particular revealed that Van Buren's "party" were the true Federalists, for, as the *Republican Banner* warned, "their objects will in the end make manifest not only their *Federalism,* but their *Monarchism.*"⁶⁷

Polk's candidacy in itself, Whigs argued, showed the selfish designs of the spoils party. Polk's agreement with Cannon on state issues indicated that the incumbent had performed his duties well; the Democrat's only grievance against the governor, Whigs maintained, was simply the incumbent's refusal to conform to the "party's" decrees on national policy. This attempt to cast aside a faithful public servant simply because of a difference of opinion once again represented the administration's attempt to interfere in a local election; thus, Whigs concluded, "the interests of Mr. Van Buren, in the Colonel's [Polk's] estimation, are of far more importance than those of the State." When several Democratic papers suggested Polk ultimately as a vice-presidential candidate, Whigs seized upon this point as further evidence that Polk had no interest in serving as governor of Tennessee; the Speaker, they charged, obviously was using the governor's office merely as a means to advance his own selfish ambitions.⁶⁸

In contrast to the 1837 canvass, in 1839 both candidates took their party's causes directly to the voters. Almost immediately after the announcement of his candidacy, Polk began a speaking tour at public meetings in Middle and West Tennessee. In the spring, the two candidates shared the stump on several occasions, before Cannon, probably recognizing his inability to compete with Polk's dynamic campaign style, abandoned the joint canvass.⁶⁹ Throughout the summer, national issues took center stage as campaign appearances followed a usual pattern: Polk's speeches continually defended Van Buren and denounced the "Federalist" attempt to transfer the state to Clay, while Cannon always expressed his inability "to appreciate that intimate connexion between State and Federal politics which his opponent is so anxious to impress upon the people" before condemning "the hypocritical cant about Federalism, and Democracy" and discussing "the necessity of a change of men in the general government."⁷⁰ The question of who would serve as the next governor of Tennessee proved a secondary concern. Instead, politicians and voters both believed that the state's position in the 1840 presidential election provided the 1839 contest's primary significance. "The Governor's office is but the die," the *Tennessee Whig* proclaimed. "The Presidency is the Stake." Likewise, John Bell told the Kentucky senator, "The real question now before the people of this state is will they take Henry Clay 'to rule over them' and as the vote shall be in August next so will it be in 1840."⁷¹

Polk's energetic electioneering provided Democrats with an advantage over their opponents, for, as James Campbell wrote, "Polk has ten times the activity of Cannon, & is traversing the state like a missionary, making speeches."[72] Local factors also bolstered the Democrats' efforts. Cannon's strict interpretation of the 1838 Bank and Internal Improvement Act led the governor to continue to deny state aid to several companies in East and West Tennessee. As a result, many East Tennesseans agreed with the *Knoxville Argus*'s charge that Cannon was "the Governor of ONLY A PART OF THE STATE," while a West Tennessee correspondent assured Polk that the governor's construction of the law "has rendered him odious with every man who desires to see the Improvements of the state progress."[73] The same act also gave the governor the power to appoint the new state bank's board of directors. A supplemental act authorized the directors to locate branches throughout the state, and when the board announced its decision on branch locations in the spring of 1838, voters in regions without a branch expressed their outrage at the board's leaving several areas without banking facilities. A convention of citizens at Sparta petitioned Cannon to call a special session of the General Assembly to change the board and its decision. Cannon refused, but, as James Walker observed, the controversy over the branches left the incumbent with "no hole for him to creep out of." If he called a special session "to correct the blunders of *his own directory,* it will be a palpable acknowledgment of his own incompetence." On the other hand, if he failed to convene the legislature, it would be "looked upon as a defiance of popular opinion."[74]

Yet the strongest current in the Democrat's favor was that, by the summer of 1839, it appeared that the monetary crisis had ended. New York's banks resumed paying specie on May 10, 1838, but by that date Tennessee's banks already had determined, if conditions continued favorable, to resume their own specie payments on January 1, 1839. Public confidence in the banks' stability increased, for, according to the *Republican Banner*, on the day that they did resume, the demand for specie was "very inconsiderable." Two weeks later, the *Union* predicted the disappearance of shinplasters, because, with the reappearance of small coins in the economy, "all pretence for the circulation of individual change tickets has ceased." Also, in 1839 Tennesseans enjoyed the finest harvest they had seen in several years. These improving economic conditions removed the urgency of Whig pleas for a national bank; moreover, recovery without the aid of the federal government lent credence to the Democrats' argument that the causes and consequences of the panic went beyond the reach of the administration's authority. "The seasons of panic are over," the *Union* proclaimed less than a week before the election; "the crops are coming in plentiful, the husbandman is glad, and all are preparing to act purely UPON PRINCIPLE."[75]

The results of the August elections showed that Polk's energetic campaigning, Cannon's apparent incompetence, and brightening economic prospects had combined to give the Democrats the victory. The former House Speaker narrowly won the gubernatorial election, carrying 51 percent of the votes cast. The bulk of the victor's strength came from Middle Tennessee, where he carried 54 percent of the votes. While Cannon carried West Tennessee easily, the challenger managed to break even with the incumbent in East Tennessee, as Polk lost that division by only three hundred votes. The electorate also returned to the state legislature a comfortable Democratic majority, fifty-six to forty-four, and administration supporters recovered from their devastating defeat in the 1837 congressional elections, winning six of the state's thirteen seats in the national legislature.

Democrats rejoiced at these results. The electorate clearly had rejected Whig attempts to transfer Tennessee to Henry Clay, they believed, and they were convinced that their state had been redeemed from the control of the Federalists. "Tennessee is truly the '*Keystone of the Arch* of the *Republican Party*!'" Alexander Anderson proclaimed in his congratulatory letter to Polk, while Jackson assured Francis Preston Blair that "Tennessee is again safe in the republican fold."[76]

The immediate results of the contest proved less significant than its long-term effects. The prospect of influencing the country's political and economic future, and intense electioneering, brought about 89 percent of the state's voters to the polls, a figure higher than in any previous election and second only to the proportion voting the next year in the presidential election (when the highest turnout rate in Tennessee's history was recorded). State elections occasionally had attracted widespread participation before 1839, but that year marked the beginning of a period of consistently high voter turnout in a series of state and national elections centering upon questions of federal politics. More importantly, the 1839 conflict institutionalized party politics among Tennessee's voters, for, over the next two decades, citizens continued to identify with the party they had chosen in the gubernatorial contest. The overwhelming majority of Tennessee voters, once they made a decision between the two parties as represented by Polk and Cannon, stood by that decision until the crisis of secession.[77]

Voters adhered to their choices because they believed that a crucial issue was at stake. The experience of the panic deepened the political division in Tennessee. No longer did the rivalry within the state appear to voters to be a struggle within Jackson's Democratic party. Now it seemed a battle over conflicting principles—one that would determine the future of republican government. Association with either Whigs or Democrats provided a voter with an explanation for the hard times that had overtaken him for the past few years. It also gave him a way to take action—to take matters into his own hands, by enlisting in a crusade that would both bring relief to the country and defend the sovereign people by driving out of power the apostates from the principles of republicanism. The next generation of Tennessee voters would understand participation in party politics as necessary for the defense of freedom; that understanding would provide for them an explanation of political affairs in the state and nation and a justification for their political actions.

Yet the creation of parties involved more than elite manipulation of the electorate's conspiratorial fears. Resistance to potential despotism had been a component of Tennessee's political culture since the state's foundation. Most of Tennessee's semisubsistence yeomen remained at the edge of the state's expanding market-oriented commercial economy; but the prosperity of the early 1830s, followed by the financial Panic of 1837—the second panic within twenty years—displayed to Tennesseans both the potential promise and the possible consequences of participation in that economy. The Whigs' acceptance of Henry Clay as their presidential candidate ultimately combined the conservatives' explanation of the threat to the republic with the pro-bank wing's positive economic policies. At the same time, the offensive campaign of Polk and the Democrats reminded the electorate of the union of strict construction, limited government, and opposition to the Federalists'"money power." As a result of the 1839 canvass, the parties merged the voters' understanding of the dangers facing republican government with the hopes and fears aroused by changes in Tennessee's economy. For both Whigs and Democrats, the defense of freedom now would involve not only preventing demagogues from gaining power, but also elevating to power those statesmen who would enact the proper government actions for the welfare of all.

Concern for the state's and for one's own material prospects were thus channeled into an ideological confrontation over which party best defended republican freedom from its enemies. After he had cast his vote for Newton Cannon, George W. House recorded in his journal that, in the election, "freemen are called upon at the Ballot Box to say whether or not the present Corrupt Dynasty of federal usurpation of power—shall still rule." A year later, Jeremiah G. Harris reminded the *Union*'s readers that he designated the Democrats' opposition as "Federalists" because "it is a term that is full of meaning—it is the type of anti-republican principles—[and] it bears fitness and propriety as applied to modern Whiggery." And both House and Harris claimed for their parties what William G. Brownlow attributed to the Whig national convention in 1839. Their cause, Brownlow maintained, was involved not merely in a struggle to attain office, but in "a combat for *liberty* against *oppression*."[78]

Polk's election in 1839 was an unusual one among the contests between Whigs and Democrats in Tennessee only in that it presented a rare Democratic triumph in the party system's early years. Whig dominance in Tennessee in the 1840s derived much of its strength from the return of hard times, the severity of which exceeded that of the bleak summer of the Panic of 1837. The dearth of money, though, only reminded voters that the battle between Whigs and Democrats would determine the future, not only of their pocketbooks, but of their liberty.

FOUR

Federalists and Spoilsmen, Banks and Free Trade
Party Ideologies and Economic Policy

The two-party system that crystallized in Tennessee in the 1839 state elections proved over the next two decades to be, among the state political divisions in the Union, one of the most evenly split and most durable. Until 1856, never more than a 3-percent margin separated the parties, except in two statewide elections. In the General Assembly, Whigs and Democrats alternated control of the legislature until, in the 1849-50 session, each party controlled fifty seats in the hundred-member body. While northern and Lower South states saw the party systems in their regions disintegrate and realign in the 1850s, Tennessee was one of the few border states to experience continued competition between two parties, with virtually the same constituencies, through the presidential election of 1860.

So evenly divided was Tennessee's electorate that members of both parties believed that the majority of voters in the state adhered to their cause. Politicians considered a full turnout of the party's supporters the surest guarantee for victory, and to encourage such a turnout Whigs and Democrats organized committees in each county and in each civil district within the county, all under the guidance of a central committee in Nashville, to broadcast their parties' messages as well as to oversee attendance at the polls by the party faithful. So convinced were party leaders that they represented a majority of the electorate that, when defeated in a contest, they often attributed the result to their opponent's superior organization.[1]

Ironically, the Whig and Democratic organizations presented similar messages to the electorate, for both parties constructed their crusades for liberty upon interpretations of republican ideology. Both parties, for instance, maintained that, unlike the factional rivalries of the first forty years of Tennessee politics, party competition involved a contest between "great and vital principles," upon which depended the perpetuation of the country. Both, too, claimed to represent the continuation of Thomas Jefferson's original Democratic-Republican party and argued that the success of Jeffersonian republicanism depended upon the triumph of their principles. Finally, Whigs and Democrats each proclaimed that they represented the "real people" against demagogic politicians seeking to establish a despotism in the United States. Party apologists admitted that many "honest hearted men" voted for their opponents, but these citizens, they explained, had been misled into giving their support to "*designing and treacherous* LEADERS, who are under the evil instigation of human passion and human crime" and who sought "the overthrow of the Republic." Activists in both parties worked to "give forth true information and sound republican doctrine" in political campaigns, in order to convince electors that their own party, and not that of their opponents, provided the true defense of republican liberty.[2]

As they had in 1839, Tennessee's Democrats continued to denounce their political opponents as "Federalists" who "looked upon the mass as an ignorant herd incapable of self government." Tracing the origins of the parties' competition to the era of the founding fathers, Democrats maintained that a party composed of the rich and powerful had always "feared the turbulence of popular violence, and apprehended anarchy[,] inefficiency and weakness, if the people were invested with supreme power and governed themselves." To undermine the popular sovereignty established by the Constitution, this "money power" sought to consolidate political authority under the control of the federal government; ultimately, as Charles Faxon, editor of the *Clarksville Jeffersonian,* warned, it "would endeavor to bring us to the footstool of an aristocracy of wealth, and subvert the very principles of our government."[3]

Citizens earlier had banded together behind Jefferson and Jackson to defeat the efforts of the money power, when it attempted to enhance government authority as Federalists and, through the Bank of the United States, as National Republicans. Now, as Knox County Democrats proclaimed, "Federalism has changed its odious name to whig," and that party, despite its claim of fidelity to popular rule, revealed its true nature by advocating the same measures—a national bank and a protective tariff—as had the "master-spirit and soul" of Federalism, Alexander Hamilton. Now, too, Federalism had gained a foothold in Tennessee. The state's electorate had stood united behind the Democratic-Republican party until the money power had used promises of office to lure ambitious politicians away from Jackson's fold. These demagogues were working feverishly to lure Tennesseans away from republican principles, first by promoting Hugh White's presidential candidacy against the national party's nominee, and then by openly espousing in Tennessee the cause of the Whigs.[4] To Democrats, the issues between their party and the Whigs all narrowed down to the "great question" of whether "the people" should "continue to govern themselves" or whether they should "be governed by priviliged [sic] corporations."[5]

Democrats viewed their own party as "made up of the real people" and pledged to the protection of "the cherished principles of the authors and founders of our Republican system." The defense of popular sovereignty provided the foundation of the party's maintenance of these "cherished principles." It was "a fundamental axiom in the creed of democracy," the Democratic state convention declared in 1843, "that man is capable of self-government"; thus the party dedicated itself to "resist all encroachments" on self-government "and to expose all insidious attempts to undermine it or to control the exercise of it by the power of moneyed monopolies."[6] To counter such intrusions on popular rule, Democrats advocated a narrow and strict interpretation of both the state and federal constitutions, for limits upon the sphere of government authority ultimately would leave political power in the hands of the citizens. A "latitudinarian construction of the Constitution," on the other hand, would, in effect, provide the money power with the means to accomplish "the utter destruction of our sheet-anchor and free[dom]" by allowing the Federalists to expand their power at the expense of popular rule. Democrats promised to apply strict construction most rigidly to the federal government, for the national administration's distance from the citizens and the extent of its potential power posed greater threats to liberty than did the state governments. Citizens' proximity to their local institutions, party members believed, gave them greater control over operations at the state capitol than they had over the distant and obscure dealings in Washington.[7]

Hence Democrats promised to uphold the distinction between federal and state authority. Upon entering the governor's office, James K. Polk declared that he would use whatever power was available to defend the state from "every encroachment of the Federal Government on its rights." While protecting Tennessee from the danger presented by federal power, Polk also admonished state governments "to confine themselves in their own action to the exercise of powers clearly reserved to them." Those powers of any government authority, Democrats argued, should be wielded only to insure "equal and exact justice to all, [and] favors to none."[8] The money power, along with smaller combinations of ambitious individuals, sought to use government authority to enrich itself by gaining special privileges that would be recognized by law. Yet these privileges, according to Democrats, ran "contrary to justice and to the genius of our government" and would permit a "favored few" to "aggrandize themselves and their dependents [at] the sacrifice of popular liberty, honest industry and every thing calculated to make us a great and happy nation." Rather than the promotion of such privileges, Democrats instead professed their devotion to the principle of "equal rights" and claimed for their guiding precept Andrew Jackson's belief that the "blessings of government, like the dews of Heaven, should fall alike upon the high and low, the rich and poor."[9]

Democrats in Tennessee thus proclaimed their opposition to the dispensation of privileges and promised to use government authority primarily for the purpose of insuring an impartial distribution of these "blessings of government." In state legislation, party members opposed laws that they believed would benefit one segment of citizens at the expense of another and endeavored to restrict the powers granted in corporate charters. Likewise, in national affairs the party placed great faith in the presidential veto power—a "great and sacred conservative power" that was "eminently calculated to prevent the growth of aristocracy"—to void any unjust and inequitable acts that might slip through Congress. Yet only the triumph of the Democratic party could best insure the perpetuation of liberty, for that party alone promised to sustain a limited republican government that would stay out of the way of the citizens' maintenance of their own freedom.[10]

Whigs rejected charges that they represented a resurgent Federalist party and that their proposals benefited a few at the expense of the many. Instead, Tennessee's Whig party presented itself as the party defending the people from the "spoils party," which Whigs claimed to oppose not simply because it was a party of politicians, but because it was a coalition based upon demagoguery and greed, instead of upon principle. The *Republican Banner* defined the "spoils party" as a collection of office-hungry politicians "bound and banded together by the Spoils, fighting to retain the Spoils, and playing the arrant demagogue and hypocrite for the sake of the Spoils." These opportunists, Whigs asserted, had abandoned whatever principles they may have had, solely for the purpose of attaining the perquisites of government office.[11]

According to the Whigs, the spoils party had come together during

Jackson's second term as president, and, led by Van Buren, had persuaded the old hero to abandon republican principles and exercise presidential power as a tyrant. Van Buren's administration continued to encourage the consolidation of power in the executive branch; by enhancing presidential power, Whigs argued, the spoilsmen believed they could best insure their hold on public office, since their tenure would depend upon the decision of one man rather than upon the popular will. And, Whigs warned, the Democrats would continue to exalt executive prerogative until they had succeeded in their goal of establishing a national despotism, a system that would insure the spoils party's hold on their offices but also would leave citizens "without any other will than that which eminates [sic] from authority." Rather than being a party of "the people," Whigs concluded, the Democratic party was the party that ultimately sought "to concentrate all power in the hands of ONE MAN, and that man, the President of the United States."[12]

Even with the spoils party out of power, Democrats still presented a menace to republican government, for, in their attempts to win elections, the spoilsmen excited voters against the order and stability established by the federal Constitution. These doctrines, which Democrats promoted under the banner of "equal rights," Whigs interpreted as "locofocoism"—radical, leveling, and disorganizing policies that would tear down the Constitution's restrictions against unlimited mob rule. Democratic candidates championed these principles merely to flatter the people, but, if not arrested in time, "locofoco" doctrines would "eventually overturn all order and good government, and establish a wild democracy."[13] Unless the "mad spirit" of the Democrats be restrained "by the good sense of the people," the *Nashville Whig* warned, "we fear that the assertions of the enemies of republican institutions, that the people are incapable of self-government, will be fearfully realised."[14]

Whigs saw it as their duty to defend citizens from the dangers presented by the spoilsmen and locofocoism by upholding what they believed to be pure republican principles. These principles, they asserted, were nothing less than the principles upon which Andrew Jackson had been elected to the presidency in 1828. In that election, the *Republican Banner* recalled, "Old Hickory" had promised that "he would retrench expenditures and reform abuses" in the federal government, that he would serve only one term, that he would not appoint members of Congress to office, and that "the patronage of the Government should not be brought into conflict with the freedom of elections."[15] The general's attempt to dictate his successor to Tennessee voters and his handling of the nation's monetary affairs had revealed his apostasy from republicanism; hence, Whigs claimed, despite their past loyalty to the president, they parted company with him and chose instead to remain loyal to his original principles. These principles had always respected the balance among the executive, legislative, and judicial branches of the federal government, and since locofocoism sought to achieve its ends through the exaltation of the presidency, Whigs dedicated their party to opposing executive usurpation as the best way to preserve "the prosperity of the country and the permanence of our institutions."[16]

Central to the Whigs' appeal in Tennessee were promises to limit presidential patronage and to reduce the expenditures of the federal government—by which abuses, they argued, a corrupt executive bought political support. Specifically, Whigs proposed a constitutional amendment to limit an individual's service to one term in the presidency, a restriction that would, they expected, compel the incumbent to devote his energy to public service rather than to seeking means to continue himself in office. Moreover, Whigs advocated the abrogation of the presidential veto, since it subjected the acts of the people's representatives to "the *arbitrary* will of one man."[17] To a lesser extent, Whigs also supported a law to prevent federal office holders from campaigning for party candidates or aiding aspirants in any other way—or, as the Whigs' expressed their position, to prevent office holders from "interfering" in elections. This law would preserve the purity and freedom of the electoral process, according to Caleb Norvell, editor of the *Nashville Whig*, because it would "effectually secure the elective franchise against the interference of Federal patronage, and the officious intermeddling of Executive officers in our local and Presidential elections."[18]

Both of Tennessee's parties based their appeals for votes upon similar, though sharply contrasting, interpretations of the forces menacing republican government. As we have seen, however, the parties formed during a period of economic distress, and they waged their most heated warfare after renewed suspension of specie payments by the state's banks brought on several years of hard times. While warning voters of the dangers presented by "Federalists" and "Spoilsmen," party spokesmen at the same time linked these threats to freedom to the causes of economic disruption; hard times, they maintained, provided clear proof of their opponents' despotic designs. The parties' economic appeals thus deepened voters' acceptance of the ideological understanding of party competition. The success of the voters' chosen parties, they believed, not only would provide the most effec-

Federalists and Spoilsmen, Banks and Free Trade 87

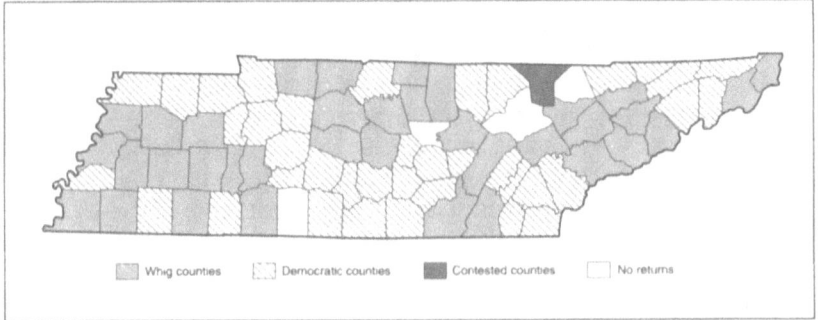

Tennessee Counties Returning Whig and Democratic Majorities in Gubernatorial and Presidential Elections, 1839-1851

tive defense of their freedom, but also would insure that they would be governed by statesmen who would advocate the proper use of government power for the promotion of the electorate's material well-being.

The geographical distribution of the parties' strength in Tennessee indicates the importance of their economic creeds to voters. Depicting those counties that consistently returned Whig and Democratic majorities in the elections of 1839-51, the map included here shows that support for both parties cut across the state's Grand Divisions.[19] Contemporaries considered East Tennessee a Whig stronghold, as voters in the region usually turned out solidly for that party's candidates. Much of Whig predominance appears attributable to the legacy of the presidential candidacy of Hugh Lawson White, the Knoxville native who defended republican principles when Andrew Jackson attempted to dictate the presidential succession.[20] Yet Whigs gained their strongest support in East Tennessee from the counties surrounding Knoxville, the region's center of trade, and in the area around Chattanooga, the proposed terminus of Georgia's Western and Atlantic Railroad and later an important junction for the southern railroad network. Democrats, meanwhile, dominated the counties in upper East Tennessee and in the southeastern corner of the state. These mountainous regions were distant from the political and economic dominance of Knoxville, and many farmers in these counties found themselves separated from the world of market production by the mountain's rocky soil or by natural barriers to trade.

Similar patterns suggesting a correlation between party affiliation and commercial orientation appear in Middle and West Tennessee as well. Whigs claimed majorities in the counties in the northern half of

Middle Tennessee that ran along the Cumberland River, an area characterized by the rich soil of the Cumberland Basin and centered on the state's political and commercial capital, Nashville. In West Tennessee, the Democrats' more vocal position in defense of slavery probably strengthened that party in the state's cotton belt. Still, Whigs also dominated most of West Tennessee, a region where the production of staple crops for trade provided the central economic activity. Democrats in Middle and West Tennessee relied for their support on counties more remote from those centers of trade, and on areas less directed toward market production. James K. Polk's long-standing popularity in his congressional district did give the Democrats a few of the counties of the prosperous Nashville Basin; the southern portion of Middle Tennessee also expressed a deep resentment against a "Nashville Regency," a Whig merchant elite that dominated the state's trade "with a power as unlimited and irresistible as an absolute despot." The "strong hold of LocoFocoism," though, proved to be the counties running along the Highland Rim and in West Tennessee along the Kentucky state line. These were areas of mountainous terrain and varying—though generally poor—soil quality, as well as regions located away from the influence of their Grand Division's centers of trade.[21]

Party affiliation, of course, cannot be reduced to a simple formula, and whatever statewide patterns may have emerged were subject to qualifications. Political division occurred within each county, and local heritage and conditions, along with the quality of local leadership, profoundly shaped a county's political culture.[22] Nevertheless, it is significant to note the tendencies revealed by the election returns. Within counties, Whigs usually drew strong support from towns and county seats, while Democrats gained their heaviest majorities in civil districts distant from these market centers—areas, as John W. Childress told Polk, that were "not under the control of merchants & Banks."[23] Throughout the state, moreover, voters in regions close to commercial centers and geared toward agricultural production for the market proved more receptive to Whig denunciations of "locofocoism" and to that party's arguments concerning the blessings of a stable currency provided by a national bank. Farmers in counties removed from commercial centers, while willing to sell their surplus and depend upon the market for goods not provided by home production, instead listened to Democratic warnings of the danger presented by the "money power" and by an active federal government.

Economic considerations came to the forefront of politics within a week after Polk's inauguration as governor in October 1839, as the state's banks once again suspended specie payments. This renewed suspension followed similar actions by eastern banks in consequence of monetary pressure that eventually destroyed the remnant of Nicholas Biddle's national bank, the Bank of the United States of Pennsylvania. As they had after the 1837 panic, Tennessee's banks followed suspension with attempts to curtail the amount of their currency in circulation, while increasing their specie reserves.[24] This time, though, suspension lasted almost three years and appeared to affect the electorate more deeply than it had in the late 1830s. The most pressing concern became the shortage of money. The banks' policy proved successful in maintaining the solvency of those institutions, but, along with the hoarding of specie, the curtailing of note issues drastically reduced the state's money supply. For a while, the notes issued by Alabama banks remedied at least part of the deficiency in East Tennessee and in the southern counties of Middle Tennessee, but the abolition of the Bank of Alabama in 1842 likewise left those notes "at an enormous discount below our own depreciated bank paper—and all scarce at that."[25]

While money became harder to find, the values of property and prices in Tennessee declined significantly. The total value of taxable property in Tennessee declined approximately sixteen million dollars between 1837 and 1844. Over the same period, the average value of the two most important types of property, land and slaves, fell to almost 75 and 70 percent, respectively, of their 1836 levels, before the effects of the panic finally leveled off in 1845. By the latter year, the price of land had dropped to almost three dollars an acre, a dollar less than an acre's worth a decade earlier. During the same period, slave prices fell from about six hundred dollars per slave to nearly four hundred. Cotton prices had begun to recover from their 1837 collapse, but in 1839 they again declined and remained at levels far below those of the prosperous mid-1830s. Tennessee cotton sold at 14.5 to 16.5 cents per pound on the New Orleans market in 1836, but in 1843 a pound could be purchased in Memphis or Nashville for as low as 3 to 5 cents. Unlike the situation in the earlier crisis, hard times also affected the price of surplus crops produced for sale by yeoman farmers. In Nashville, corn prices fell from $1.25 per bushel in 1836 to 40 cents per bushel in 1842. During these same years, the price of a bushel of corn in Memphis fell from 87.5 cents to 37 cents, while pork prices in that city dropped from $22.50 per barrel in 1836 to as low as $6.00 in 1843.[26]

With money scarce and little hope of profits from their crops, debtors particularly suffered from the crisis, for, with no money to pay off their loans, they faced foreclosure and the loss of their property to their creditors. As a consequence of these conditions, "hard times" dominated popular discussion in the early 1840s.[27] The most desperate complaints came during the summer of 1842. Tennessee's banks resumed specie payments during July of that year, but shortly before that month, the state experienced a particularly severe decline in prices. Thomas L. Bransford, a merchant living in Gainesboro, Jackson County, in June described the bleak conditions in his county to his friend and congressman, William Campbell:

> The times are really distressing, the pecuniary embarrassment of the people and the sacrifices of property, are greater than I have ever seen before. Although I was only a boy, I well remember the vexation of 1819 & '20, it was not as bad as the present. The Tobacco, corn, pork, sheep & other produce taken to market this Spring, has brought nothing in return; in some instances it has not paid the cost of transportations. The loss sustained by shippers, from this County, is not less than sixty thousand dollars. The merchants make no collections, there is no money in circulation. Nearly all who went down the river with such produce as we are in the habit of sending, of which you know corn, Beef & Pork constitutes a considerable portion, are broken and can pay nothing.... As to ourselves we owe but little and are hard run to pay that. A large number of persons in this County who were thought to be perfectly solvent 12 months since will be broken up. In Overton and Fentress [counties] the times are Still worse. The Execution law in these two Counties is virtually suspended for want of bidders.... Confidence between man & man is entirely lost, *and we are in an awfully bad condition*. I assure you my friend that I have not given a worse colouring to things here than they deserve, in deed the description falls far short of the reality.[28]

In the midst of these bleak conditions, the defense of freedom and the promotion of economic prosperity came to be seen as one and the same goal. The depression presented a calamitous, defining moment for antebellum Tennesseans. The shortage of money and the dwindling of trade, if they did not threaten an individual's survival, at least threatened to devastate his wealth and raised the specter of persistent poverty. As a result, hard times etched the Democratic and Whig ideologies more deeply in the minds of voters. Party leaders provided an explanation for one's misfortune by attributing the causes of the depression to the designs of their enemies. At the same time, party affiliation offered a means for voters to work for recovery, for the contest between parties demanded that electors choose between contrasting policy proposals—one viewed as likely to produce prosperity and freedom and another seen as leading to destitution and tyranny. In this atmosphere, party competition appeared more than a mere game or entertainment; rather, it seemed a struggle for one's personal future as well as for that of the republic.

According to Tennessee's Democrats, the depression had come about because the "avarice and over-reaching of speculation" again had brought irresponsible merchants and speculators to the verge of bankruptcy, and the encouragement of this extravagance by the state's banks had forced them to suspend specie payments when the speculators had extended themselves beyond their means.[29] As in 1837, in 1839 the "money power" and its desire to recharter a national bank stood behind the collapse of the nation's currency. The "desperation of the Federal or Whig party" in recent elections had compelled the money power to use its control over the country's credit system to impose a general suspension in order to revive the Whigs' political prospects. By creating this new crisis, Democrats maintained, this potential aristocracy sought to create a popular revulsion against Van Buren's administration and so "induce the people to cry out for a National Bank, as a panacea for existing evils."[30]

Democrats rejected outright Whig claims that a new national bank could remedy the economic troubles. Instead, they proposed that "the remedy for our pecuniary distresses" could be found only "in a rigid economy and industry, and by ceasing to deal in excessive bank credits." The problems in the money market affected only speculators and "jobbers in the stock markets of eastern cities," Democrats maintained; the real, laboring people of the country, on the other hand, could provide for their needs by their own honest industry, and they required no assistance from the government to achieve prosperity. Even as prices and property values continued to fall, Democrats remained firm in their belief that "our only relief will be found in industry and economy," rather than in assistance that would expand the authority of the federal government.[31]

Throughout the crisis, Democrats asserted that their party's primary objective, its "sacred duty," remained its dedication to "a stern and rigid adherence to the letter of the Constitution." A Bank of the United States might provide citizens with temporary relief, but it still was an unconstitutional and dangerous measure. Prosperity would return with good harvests and with wise management on the part of citizens, but the ultimate consequence of a national bank would be the abrogation of republican government and the establishment of a moneyed aristocracy.[32] With strict construction at the heart of the Democratic appeal, Van Buren's Independent Treasury proposal became the "cardinal measure" of the party in Tennessee, for the system would encourage citizens to work their way out of the crisis while providing a constitutional means to care for the public revenue. The establishment of the "subtreasury" would mark "the divorce of the government from the Banks" and remove the government's fiscal affairs from the nation's economy; at the same time, the program's stipulation that federal transactions utilize only specie or notes from specie-paying banks would ensure a "*steady* and *uniform*" currency with which citizens could conduct their private business. This "total and entire separation of the Government in its fiscal operations from the faithless banks, . . . " the *Union* explained, "can alone establish the basis of permanent prosperity."[33]

Beyond public unity behind the subtreasury proposal, Democrats appeared unsure and divided over the proper economic policies that the party should promote. Radical Democrats advocated an exclusively gold and silver currency and the eventual elimination of all banks. Polk, in his message to the state legislature, recommended policies that would promote a mixed currency, which would provide paper money for transactions involving large sums and specie for smaller, routine purchases. His friends James Walker, John Catron, and Cave Johnson, meanwhile, advocated some sort of treasury bank, controlled by Congress, to issue paper money backed by the federal government's revenue. These and other moderate Democrats saw state banks as useful institutions; not only could they ensure the existence of necessary banking capital, but the power to create them fell within a state legislature's authority, and their nearness to the citizens provided a watch upon their operations.[34] Despite these differences, opposition to the "money power" and faith in the propriety of a strict construction of the Constitution united Tennessee's Democrats. This evil kept Democrats together, for party members of all shades of opinion on the financial question abhorred most of all the specter of "the tyranny of a Monied Oligarchy."[35] Party members feared that the money power would use the poor economic conditions to expand its influence; thus they believed that the government's principal obligation was to thwart this potential aristocracy and prevent it from establishing a despotism. To Democrats, the responsibility of preserving a limited republican government took precedence over providing immediate financial relief; they would maintain their fidelity to strict con- struction and let irresponsible speculators suffer rather than accept the potentially disastrous solution of rechartering a national bank.

As they had during the late 1830s, Whigs continued to attribute the currency's instability to the fiscal policies of Jackson's and Van Buren's administrations. The refusal to recharter the Bank of the United States

"Loading Corn, on the Tennessee." From *Harper's New Monthly Magazine* (1858). Reproduction courtesy of Tennessee State Library and Archives, Nashville.

had proven the most detrimental action, Whigs explained, for, prior to Jackson's veto, the national bank had provided the people with a strong, stable, and uniform currency.[36] Persistent Democratic opposition to a national bank and promulgation of ruinous policies, Whigs maintained, not only kept the economy in its depressed condition but also provided evidence of the Locofoco party's sinister designs. According to Whigs, their opponents continued to advocate a hard-money currency merely "with a view of deluding the people, and exciting their prejudices against a National Bank," even though they knew that the lack of available gold and silver rendered the idea of an exclusively specie currency "a complete humbug." The Independent Treasury, too,

Whigs described as nothing more than part of the spoils party's plan to consolidate power under executive authority, for, if enacted into law, the plan would "keep the public monies in the hands of an unprincipled set of office-holders, appointed by the President, and by him retained in office, to do his dirty work."[37]

Aside from the Democratic policies' implications for the stability of republican government, Whigs charged that their opponents' proposals would fail to provide the people with any sort of relief from the consequences of the panic. While for Democrats this duty fell outside the realm of government authority, for Whigs the promotion of the general good stood at the center of their own conception of the proper use of government power. In both their criticism of Democratic measures and their defense of their own party's policies, Whigs evinced a conviction that government had a responsibility to encourage, within constitutional bounds, the well-being of the population. Quoting Andrew Jackson himself, the *Republican Banner* bluntly reminded voters in 1840 that "the object of a free Government is the good of the people." A few years later, Columbia jurist Edmund Dillahunty urged his friend Robert L. Caruthers, then a member of Congress, to support measures that expressed "the *parental* care that government should always manifest towards their own subjects or citizens." Whigs agreed with Democrats that government actions must abide by the federal constitution; in fact, Whigs maintained that their opposition to the enhancement of presidential power proved that they were more loyal to that document than were their opponents. Nevertheless, unlike the Democrats' reliance upon the principle of strict construction, Caleb Norvell explained that, "if the general government can exercise no powers, but such as are *expressly*, or in so many words, granted by the constitution, measures the most important and essential to the 'general welfare' would have to be abandoned."[38]

Whigs promised to use the power of government to institute policies that the party believed "essential to the prosperity of the country and the permanence of our institutions." Most immediately, with the nation's currency in shambles, the country's economic condition became "a subject to which the attention of Congress, as the guardian of the public weal, should be specifically directed."[39] A new national bank, on the other hand, would provide the crucial remedy for the citizen's economic ills, and throughout the depression, conservative Whigs joined together with the party's pro-bank wing to place a bank at the center of the Whig appeal. The country's experience with the first two Banks of the United States, Whigs maintained, showed that such a central agency was "no longer an experiment"; instead, a national bank had proven "entirely adequate to the regulation of the Currency" as well as "an incomparable agent in the transaction of public and private pecuniary affairs."[40]

The promise of a national bank became the central tenet of the Whigs' appeal because, they argued, it was the only remedy that could provide the nation with the reliable currency necessary to restore prosperity. State banks could prove helpful in providing capital, Whigs admitted, but without the assistance of a central regulating agency they could do little toward alleviating the prevalent hard times. A national bank's "extended means" and "wider limits" would empower it to prevent overissues of notes by state institutions and restore confidence in the paper in circulation. This restoration of a sound currency—the "spur to every species of enterprise and energy," since it provided "the hope of adequate reward that sweetens labor"— would provide the basis for recovery from the depression, and the gradual expansion of the money supply that would result from returning prosperity, as well as from the national bank's own capital, would elevate all segments of society.[41]

Throughout the early 1840s, Whigs claimed that the question of a national bank or the subtreasury furnished the "great issue" dividing the parties in Tennessee. Beginning in late 1841, they began to promote a revision of the nation's tariff policy as an equally important measure in providing economic relief. In the 1820s and 1830s, Tennessee's electorate had opposed a high tariff, since the proposition that protective duties favored northern manufacturing at the expense of southern agriculture had been a key tenet held by Jackson's Democratic-Republican party. Whigs and Democrats both had accepted the issue as "permanently and satisfactorily settled" by the compromise tariff of 1833, which had been passed in the midst of the Nullification controversy.[42] As hard times deepened, though, Whigs discerned among voters growing support for an increase in tariff rates as a means to encourage recovery. Only one of the state's Whig congressmen voted in favor of the Tariff Act of 1842. Nevertheless, Whig newspapers already had begun to publish arguments in favor of tariff revision, as the issue joined the national bank at the center of the Whig appeal. By early 1843, the *Jonesborough Whig* could claim that "a Tariff for revenue, and the protection of home industry, cannot be opposed but at the expense of the popularity of its opponent."[43]

Whigs denied that they advocated a tariff only for protection, and in private, party leaders expressed a concern that the aggressive promotion of the principle by northeastern Whigs would damage the party in the state. Instead, Tennessee's Whigs maintained, as did Ephraim Foster, that they had "ever been in favor of that *protection* which the necessary wants of the public treasury and discriminating imposts can easily and constitutionally ensure." The depleted condition of the national treasury demanded an increase in duties in order to provide the federal government with money. "A Tariff for revenue, or *direct taxation,* must be resorted to," James C. Jones explained concerning the 1842 tariff during his campaign for reelection as governor, "and the Whigs chose the former." Yet a modest increase in tariff rates would provide "incidental" protection for American industry, a type of protection that not only was clearly within the bounds of the Constitution but also represented, like a national bank, a positive action on the part of the government to stimulate the return of prosperity to the economy. In the long run, incidental protection would end the country's "degradation of foreign vassalage" by "enabling our manufacturers to enter into competition with foreign establishments." Eventually the United States would be able to end its dependence on Britain and France for manufactured products; national self-dependence would promote "the continued well-being and advancement of the laboring classes of the entire Nation," and southern farmers in particular would enjoy the "home market" for their agricultural produce, a market that would be created by the nation's expanding manufacturing sector.[44]

Democrats rejected the Whigs' justification of incidental protection and charged that their opponents revealed their Federalism by advocating an unconstitutional tariff that would only aid northern manufacturers. Party spokesmen, like Whigs, accepted a tariff in itself as a legitimate means for the government to raise revenue, but Democrats maintained that the Tariff Act of 1842 intended to discriminate against foreign goods in order to grant preferential treatment to northern capitalists at the expense of southern agriculturists. Cotton and tobacco planters and yeoman farmers alike not only would be forced to buy necessary goods from these "northern aristocrats" at whatever price the manufacturers demanded, but also they would suffer from foreign retaliation against southern staples.[45] Consistent with their belief in the limited sphere of governmental authority, Democrats proposed to set duties on foreign goods according to the principles of "free trade." Low rates on imports would in no way interrupt the normal flow of trade, and the revenue received from the duties on this unrestricted commerce, when combined with the proceeds from the sale of public lands, would provide revenue adequate "to carry on the government upon a system of the most rigid frugality and economy—and no more." Moreover, by keeping government within the bounds of its legitimate authority, free trade would prevent the government's fiscal affairs from interfering in the nation's economy—an interference that, despite Whig claims, would provide no relief for Tennessee's electorate. Protection would augment yeoman farmers' difficulties, because the increased prices on manufactured goods would, in effect, place "an indirect tax upon the producers of the South." Likewise, while a protective tariff might promote a "home market," retaliation by other nations would close the more extensive markets abroad and leave farmers with restricted outlets for their surplus.[46]

The Democratic policy, on the other hand, would provide the government with the necessary means to perform its operations in a limited and constitutional manner while providing no special advantages that would "enrich one class of citizens at the expense of all others." Like the Independent Treasury, free trade would provide the necessary conditions to allow farmers to rely upon themselves for the restoration of prosperity. "The farmers have asked for nothing that was not right, and they should submit to nothing that was wrong," the *Clarksville Jeffersonian* concluded. "They ask for no legislative protection, though it might enrich them; and they should not submit to any that will injure them."[47]

These policy positions regarding the American economy, the proper use of government power, and the demagogic menace to republican government played a crucial role in establishing the identities of the Democratic and Whig parties in Tennessee. Even after economic recovery in the late 1840s made the currency issue less salient in political warfare, both parties continued loyal to the policy programs outlined during hard times. Democrats took credit for recovery by attributing the return of prosperity to the Polk administration's re-establishment of the Independent Treasury and reduction of tariff rates, while Whigs, in the 1851 state convention's "Address," expressed their conviction that, despite the current affluence, "the country has been subjected to great inconvenience and loss in not adopting their opinions in relation to a sound, uniform currency." J. M. Sturtevant, superintendent of the state's school for the blind, in 1853 revealed the fundamental importance of economic concerns in the parties' identities, when he reported to the General Assembly that the "moral atmosphere of the school forbids lying"; dishonesty, he explained, was considered, "in the estimation of the scholars, worse than Free Trade to Whigs, or a National Bank to Democrats."[48]

Since both parties attributed the cause and solution of the monetary collapse to sources outside the state, debate between the parties over economic policy and relief focused upon the role of the central government. National issues, in fact, dominated electoral contests in Tennessee throughout the history of its party system. James K. Polk's conscious determination in 1839 to force the electorate to take sides in the confrontation between "Jeffersonian Republicans" and "Henry Clay Federalists" so entrenched the conception of party warfare in the state as part of a nationwide struggle between a republican people and the country's demagogic enemies that the contest for freedom remained the dominant issue as long as Tennessee's Whigs and Democrats competed. State issues could serve only as auxiliary concerns in the larger battle over the future of the American republic.

Others factors also worked to keep local issues at the periphery of the party conflict. The narrow margin of difference between Democrats and Whigs made candidates reluctant to add state policy to their party appeals. Convinced that their cause would prevail if they simply insured a full turnout of their associates at the polls, party leaders viewed local concerns, particularly in a state where party competition overlay a sectional rivalry among three distinct Grand Divisions, as questions upon which taking a definite position could easily lose as much support for candidates as it could gain. While standard-bearers for both parties routinely promised to improve the public education system and to encourage a general system of internal improvements, and while legislators argued over the consequences of granting licenses to "tippling houses" where patrons could purchase and consume liquor on the premises, Whig and Democratic leaders remained uncommitted on these issues and encouraged voters to let fidelity to their party outweigh dissension on local matters. In the early 1840s, the most important factor keeping national concerns at the center of party debate was the contention that the national government's policy had been the cause of the economic crisis and that only a change in policy could provide relief for citizens of all states.[49]

While national concerns provided the focus of political debate, in the General Assembly the parties battled over several important policy issues. In the early 1840s, pressure from constituents compelled lawmakers to consider and enact measures designed to alleviate the effects of hard times. Appeals for relief culminated at the 1842 extra session of the assembly. Whig Governor James C. Jones called the session primarily for the purpose of reapportioning the state's congressional and legislative districts, but after the particularly sharp decline in prices and property values over the summer, a member of the House of Representatives noted that his colleagues "see[m] to regard the subject of *relief*, with more interest than any other."[50] Democrats in the Senate defeated a Whig-backed bill to authorize the state banks to issue "post notes," which would be redeemable only eighteen months or two years after their issue. Also, although the House passed a bill to reduce from three to two the annual terms of circuit courts, where creditors sued debtors for payment on their loans, the bill failed in the Senate by five votes. Before the extra session ended, though, the assembly not only passed a law staying executions against property for eight months, but also authorized the state banks to issue small bills, amended the law for the redemption of real property to facilitate the recovery of land sold for the payment of debt, and abolished the law requiring imprisonment for debt.[51]

These measures passed the assembly with bipartisan support, but during most sessions, questions that involved Tennessee's long-term economic development occupied the legislators more often than did the issue of relief. One of the most important subjects was state aid for the construction of turnpikes, bridges, railroads, and other internal improvements. Since the 1834 constitution included a statement encouraging the assembly to provide for a "well regulated system of internal improvement," neither Whigs nor Democrats challenged either the legitimacy of state aid or the legislators' authority to grant charters to corporations for the construction of transportation lines. Democrats did oppose *federal* aid to projects as unconstitutional, because the assumption of that power by Congress "tends to consolidation with its numerous evils"; and in state policy Democratic legislators usually favored limiting state aid in order to keep the public debt low and to avoid "a burthensome course of taxation." In 1842, for instance, Senate Democrats voted to strike a preamble, renouncing the principle of repudiation, out of a Whig resolution pledging the state's intention to honor its debt.[52] Most votes on internal improvement legislation followed sectional lines. Middle Tennessee already benefited from the series of rivers linking the region to the world of commerce, while representatives from the other Grand Divisions favored state aid for the construction of lines that would facilitate their regions' trade links. East and West Tennesseans provided the votes for the passage of an act in 1835 that authorized the governor to subscribe for stock in internal improvement corporations, and for the 1838 act extending state aid. Likewise, Whigs and Democrats from Middle Tennessee joined together in 1840 to support the repeal of the provisions for state aid. Whether favoring state aid or not, members of both parties accepted the need for corporations to accumulate sufficient capital

Table 6. Party Support on Tennessee General Assembly Roll-Call Votes Favoring Amendments to Corporate Charters Stipulating Stockholders' Unlimited Liability, 1839-1844

Session	Number of Votes	*House* Percent Democratic	Percent Whig	Index of Disagreement
1839-40	2	80.3	7.3	73.0
1841-42	4	85.9	15.0	70.9
1843-44	4	89.3	20.1	69.2

Session	Number of Votes	*Senate* Percent Democratic	Percent Whig	Index of Disagreement
1839-40	8	68.0	5.6	62.4
1841-42	2	75.0	4.8	70.2
1843-44	1	100.0	0.0	100.0

Sources: *House Journal* (1839-40), 238-39, 400; (1841-42), 268-69, 470-71, 617-18, 643-44; (1843-44), 371, 482, 503, 508. *Senate Journal* (1839-40), 116, 307, 308, 316, 317, 365, 385, 468-69; (1841-42), 368, 550; (1843-44), 138-39, 158.

for the construction of improvement projects. Throughout the era, Whigs and Democrats both bought stock in chartered companies and served on the boards of directors of corporations. Several Democrats, especially from East Tennessee, became prominent advocates of state aid for the construction of railroads.[53]

Despite individual Democrats' activities with corporations, the party revealed a distrust toward the powers granted by corporate charters. The Bank of the United States, after all, had been a chartered corporation, and the potential wealth and economic leverage that might be accumulated by even the smallest corporate body could prove a threat to popular government. "It seems to us," the *Republican Banner* complained, "that ever since the Old Hero run a tilt against the Bank of United States, the imaginations of his friends are continually haunted by 'bank monsters,' and 'chartered monopolies.'"[54] To limit the possibility that a state corporation could develop into such a "monster," Democratic assemblymen proposed to amend bills granting charters to include restrictions that would hold stockholders individually liable for all debts incurred by the corporation, and that would reserve to the General Assembly the power to alter, amend, or repeal the charter at any time in the future, if the legislature considered it in the best interest of the public welfare to do so.

Table 7. Party Support on Tennessee General Assembly Roll-Call Votes Favoring Amendments to Corporate Charters Declaring General Assembly's Power to Alter, Amend, or Repeal the Charter, 1839-1842

Session	House			
	Number of Votes	Percent Democratic	Percent Whig	Index of Disagreement
1839-40	5	81.8	16.7	65.1
1841-42	5	79.3	10.0	69.3

Session	Senate			
	Number of Votes	Percent Democratic	Percent Whig	Index of Disagreement
1839-40	4	60.4	2.6	57.8
1841-42	9	81.3	4.0	77.3

Sources: *House Journal* (1839-40), 221, 399-400, 514-51, 597-98, 627-28; (1841-42), 101-2, 471-72, 625-26, 643-44, 688. *Senate Journal* (1839-40), 307, 365, 393-94, 477; (1841-42), 158, 213, 217, 371, 549, 554-55, 610-11, 664, 675.

Democrats emphasized the necessity of these restrictions for subordinating corporations to popular control, but Whigs saw the potential consequences of unlimited liability and legislative control as deterring investors and so impeding the state's economic development. The experience of other states and of Europe, the *Nashville Whig* explained, had shown that the inclusion of these restrictions in charters had "done much to impair public credit, and create distrust in every act where corporations are concerned." Whigs could point to Tennessee's own experience to justify their position, for an unlimited liability provision in the 1832 act chartering the Union Bank had so discouraged purchase of the bank's stock that the legislature had to pass a new charter, without the restriction, in 1833 before the bank could secure enough capital to begin its operations. Tables 6 and 7, compiled from roll-call votes recorded on proposed amendments to bills granting charters, show that the votes on provisions for individual liability and for legislative power over charters generally followed party lines, with Democrats strongly favoring these amendments and Whigs united against their passage. The few Democrats usually willing to tolerate corporations without these restrictions frequently caused the amendments' defeat, for only two of the eight corporate charters granted by the Democratic-controlled 1839 assembly included unlimited liability provisions or declarations of the legislature's power over the charter. Nevertheless, until the eve of the party system's demise, Democrats could be found in the state legislature attempting to attach individual liability and legislative control amendments to newly created corporation charters.[55]

Tennessee's state banking system also became a point of contention between the two parties. As with the internal improvement issue, the parties accepted the existence of the three banks that had been chartered in the early 1830s, and during the years of depression, Democrats gave no indication of hostility toward the idea of state banks. Several Democrats, in fact, became prominent supporters of the 1838 bill that created a new state bank. To the Democrats' dismay, the state bank failed to divert attention from the demand for a national bank. Over the next three decades, mismanagement led to frequent calls for its abolition, although the bank remained in business until 1869. Moreover, control of the bank often became a political issue between Whigs and Democrats, as both parties accused their opponents of corruption, while packing the bank's board of directors with party loyalists whenever they gained control of the state government.[56] Nevertheless, Tennessee's Democratic party never called for the elimination of the state's chartered banks, and the conduct of both parties indicated their agreement that the state needed some form of banking capital.

The banks' suspension of specie payments as a consequence of the depression, however, became a crucial issue between Whigs and Democrats. The acts that incorporated the three state banks forbade them from suspending specie payments and outlined forfeiture proceedings in case the legislature concluded that they had violated their charters. Democrats called for the assembly to use this threat of forfeiture to compel the banks to end the suspension. The banks, Democrats argued, were enjoying the full benefit of their corporate privileges at the expense of the public good, for, by suspending, they had "exempted themselves from the performance of their duties, to the great detriment of the public at large." During the 1837-38 session of the assembly, Whigs managed to defeat a bill, sponsored by pro-Van Buren legislators, that would order the banks to resume specie payments. The crisis atmosphere of the panic, Whigs argued, necessitated a "conservative" policy toward the banks. "The times are such," the *Republican Banner* maintained, "as to call for the utmost leniency towards every public institution which has been engulphed in the common ruin of the currency and business of the country." Resumption of specie payments in 1838 temporarily ended the debate over legislative action, but the renewed suspension of October 1839 rekindled the issue.

Table 8. Party Support on Tennessee General Assembly Roll-Call Votes in Favor of Ordering Tennessee's Banks Immediately to Resume Specie Payments, 1839-1842

| | House | | | |
Session	Number of Votes	Percent Democratic	Percent Whig	Index of Disagreement
1839-40	13	86.9	14.9	72.0
1841-42	12	97.6	19.2	78.4

| | Senate | | | |
Session	Number of Votes	Percent Democratic	Percent Whig	Index of Disagreement
1839-40	8	71.9	18.1	53.8
1841-42	5	79.4	20.0	59.4

Sources: *House Journal* (1839-40), 99-100, 107, 139-40, 144, 255-56, 263, 315-16, 475, 530-31, 591-92; (1841-42), 542-44, 550-53, 555-56, 819-20, 912-15, 941-42. *Senate Journal* (1839-40), 74, 84, 305, 320-21, 331, 449-50, 466-67; (1841-42), 465, 540, 618-20, 688.

Democrats again threatened to forfeit the banks' charters if suspension continued, while Whigs again defended the banks by arguing that, without a national bank, it would be pointless to expect relief from "the feeble and rickety operations of State Banks."[57]

The Democrats' 1839 victory gave them the opportunity to implement their policy, and in his message to the legislature, Governor Polk admonished the assembly that the banks "should be required at an early day to be fixed by law" to resume their specie payments. Democratic leaders, though, as well as Whigs, realized that the immediate consequences of ordering resumption would work against the party's majority; as a result, Democrats hesitated to carry through Polk's proposal. Whigs chided their opponents either to order the banks to resume or to declare unequivocally that the legislature would leave the banks in control of their own policies, so that the institutions could proceed with supplying credit for marketing the fall harvest. "Until some definite action be taken by the Legislature," the *Banner* charged, "it is impossible for the Banks to know what to do." Yet Democrats recognized their adversaries' plea as a mere electoral ploy to embarrass their party; they easily voted down Whig resolutions renouncing the legislature's intention to order resumption. Most Democrats then supported resolutions ordering resumption, but a small contingent of Democrats broke with their party to prevent the resolutions from passing (see table 8).[58]

Two years later, with a Whig majority in the assembly and with the continuation of hard times intensifying party hostility, Democrats renewed their efforts to order resumption. In January 1842, they forced through the House of Representatives, with the aid of a few Whigs, a new series of resolutions that declared the banks' charters already forfeited; ordered them to resume specie payments by July 1, 1842; and authorized the state's attorney general to file proceedings for writs of *scire facias* against the banks if they failed to comply with the order. By this time, however, the banks' curtailment of their currency in circulation had reached the point at which they could safely resume paying specie; even the *Nashville Whig* encouraged the assembly to "let the banks be put to the test." It appears, too, that the parties already had worked out some sort of arrangement on the resolutions before they came up for consideration in the Senate, for in that body three Democrats joined a majority of the Whigs to move the deadline for resumption to January 1, 1843, although most Whigs still voted against the passage of the resolutions. House Democrats, before giving their approval, altered the Senate's changes only by requiring Tennessee's banks to resume within twenty days after resumption by the banks of Kentucky and Louisiana, if those banks did so before January 1. This stipulation probably encouraged the banks to go ahead with resumption, for, in early July, Tennessee's banks announced that they would end their own suspension of specie payments by August 1. Even before that date, the *Republican Banner* reported that in Nashville the banks "have now been paying specie on all amounts for several days."[59]

Whigs took the initiative on other measures that would expand the state's available capital. In 1843, the party's majority chartered a new Bank of East Tennessee, a venture that lasted only a few years.[60] Also, as a means of increasing the state's money supply, Whigs advocated removing from the charters of the state's banks the restrictions prohibiting them from issuing bills with a face value of less than five dollars. Suspension again had stimulated the hoarding of specie and the proliferation of private notes and shinplasters. "Small notes" issued by the state banks, Whigs believed, would provide a sound local currency to drive out the unstable private notes and "afford relief *at the expense or sacrifice of nobody.*" An issue of small notes, Whigs contended, would expand the amount of money in circulation and provide a medium for payment of debts. Moreover, although backed by the banks' specie reserves, the notes' small face values would discourage holders from

Table 9. Party Support on Tennessee General Assembly Roll-Call Votes in Favor of Authorizing Tennessee's Banks to Issue Small Notes, 1839-1848

| | | House | | |
Session	Number of Votes	Percent Democratic	Percent Whig	Index of Disagreement
1839-40	3	20.5	82.6	62.1
1841-42	3	22.5	97.2	74.7
1842	2	14.2	85.5	71.2
1843-44	2	11.1	85.3	74.2
1847-48	3	15.8	86.9	71.1

| | | Senate | | |
Session	Number of Votes	Percent Democratic	Percent Whig	Index of Disagreement
1841-42	2	52.0	95.8	43.8
1842	4	30.2	85.7	55.5
1843-44	2	25.0	96.2	71.2
1847-48	1	44.4	66.7	22.3

Sources: *House Journal* (1839-40), 222, 487, 558-59; (1841-42), 65, 282-83, 711-12; (1842), 98-99; (1843-44), 178-79, 185; (1847-48), 929, 996, 997. *Senate Journal* (1841-42), 499-500; (1842), 38-39, 43, 80-81; (1843-44), 437-38; (1847-48), 493.

bothering to present them to the banks in exchange for specie; at the same time, knowledge that the banks could redeem these small notes would prevent them from circulating at a discount.[61]

Democrats, already suspicious of paper money, opposed the Whigs' small-note proposals by arguing that these bills would propagate the use of the "inferior" medium of exchange to the detriment of hard money, the currency "possessing intrinsic value." Governor Polk recommended that the legislature increase the level of the restriction of note issues on the stock banks to that of the Bank of Tennessee, the charter of which contained a provision raising the level of the smallest denomination it could issue from five to ten dollars after January 1, 1841. "If all the channels of circulation below ten or twenty dollars were left to be supplied by gold and silver coin, leaving the Banks to issue and circulate their notes in these denominations," the governor stated, "it cannot be doubted that there would be a sounder and more stable state of currency than exists."[62]

The majority party in the 1839 legislature failed to act on Polk's suggestion, but in this and subsequent sessions, Whig unity remained strong in roll-call votes on the small-note issue. With their own majority in the 1841-42 General Assembly, Whigs passed a bill authorizing the state bank to issue notes with a face value as low as one dollar. Then, in the 1842 extra session, the assembly passed another Whig-sponsored small-note act, this one permitting all Tennessee banks to issue one-dollar notes until January 1, 1845. With an eight-seat majority in 1843, Whigs easily defeated their opponents' attempts to set the minimum value of notes issued by the Bank of East Tennessee at five or ten dollars, and, even after the need for relief had disappeared, the party continued to advocate a currency utilizing bills of small denominations. The Democrats' victory in 1845 meant that the next legislative session would do nothing to revive small notes after the 1842 act had expired, but when the Whigs returned to power in 1847, the majority party passed a law allowing the Bank of Tennessee again to issue notes worth one dollar (see table 9).[63]

Whigs expanded their proposals for government assistance for economic development as the economy recovered from the depression in the mid-1840s. Beginning in the 1847 session, Whigs revived demands for state aid for internal improvement companies, particularly for those involved in the construction of railroads. The party's control of the Senate in 1850 allowed it to pass a new internal improvements bill providing for financial assistance for railroad companies. Democratic votes killed the bill in the House, but Whigs continued their support for state aid, while advocating other measures to create a favorable environment for business investment, including general incorporation and bankruptcy laws and a reduction of the state's tax on merchants. The party displayed its most unified stand on a proposal to create a free banking system, which would increase the state's banking capital by allowing the establishment of banks without a charter, once its organizers had posted bonds with the state government for its note issues.[64]

Democrats, for their part, attempted to make a party issue of a proposal for a constitutional amendment that would permit the selection of state judges and attorneys general by popular election; but Whigs, sensing widespread support for the proposal, themselves backed the amendment while continuing their push for state assistance to economic growth.[65] The state's prolonged prosperity persuaded enough Democrats to join most Whigs in the 1851-52 session to secure the passage of an internal improvement act that provided capital for the construction of about twelve hundred miles of track over the next decade. In that session, too, a sufficient number of Democrats joined

Federalists and Spoilsmen, Banks and Free Trade

Table 10. Party Votes on Major Economic Legislation, Tennessee General Assembly, 1847-1851

A. *Votes Authorizing Elections for County And Municipal Subscriptions for Stock in Internal Improvement Corporations*

| | | House | | |
Session	Number of Votes	Percent Democratic	Percent Whig	Index of Disagreement
1847-1848	1	33.3	94.7	61.4
1851-1852	1	43.3	75.0	31.7

| | | Senate | | |
Session	Number of Votes	Percent Democratic	Percent Whig	Index of Disagreement
1847-1848	1	11.1	36.4	25.3
1851-1852	1	28.6	66.7	38.1

B. *Votes Establishing a Free Banking System*

| | | House | | |
Session	Number of Votes	Percent Democratic	Percent Whig	Index of Disagreement
1847-1848	2	3.6	54.9	51.3
1849-1850	4	14.1	89.6	75.5
1851-1852	3	30.9	75.0	44.1

| | | Senate | | |
Session	Number of Votes	Percent Democratic	Percent Whig	Index of Disagreement
1847-1848	1	41.7	92.3	50.6
1851-1852	3	51.7	66.7	15.0

Sources: *House Journal* (1847-48), 510, 915, 1044; (1849-50), 171, 768, 810, 816; (1851-52), 389, 444, 446. *Senate Journal* (1847-48), 445-46, 587; (1851-52), 469, 470, 474, 608-9.

Whigs to pass an act authorizing county and municipal governments to hold popular elections on whether local governments could subscribe for railroad stock, and an act creating a free banking system that allowed for the rapid expansion of the state's capital (see table 10).[66]

On several other questions, division more often than agreement characterized the Whigs' and Democrats' courses in the assembly. The issues upon which they divided further indicate their divergent positions on the state government's role in the long-term development of the economy.[67] Democrats in the assembly most often supported legislation that would limit the state's authority and proposed to exert its power only against what they saw as the dispensation of unfair advantage to a select few. These principles were exemplified in their consistent support for regulation of corporations and their aversion to creating a state debt that might lead to oppressive taxation. Whigs, on the other hand, showed their willingness not only to expand the state debt during hard times, but also to increase the rate of the property tax to insure a revenue sufficient to allow the state to meet its obligations. In general, that party revealed no hesitancy to sanction legislation that would use Tennessee's resources to promote the state's economic development.

As in their national platforms, in state politics Tennessee's Whigs and Democrats presented different measures for relief from hard times and advocated divergent propositions regarding the state's economic future. Like the national party, Tennessee's Whigs wanted to use the power of the state government to further the material well-being of its citizens. While willing to accept some state assistance, Tennessee's Democrats, like the Democratic party nationwide, promised to use government authority primarily to check the misuse of its power by those seeking special privileges; beyond this duty, the party strove to restrict the action of government in order to allow industrious citizens to control their own destinies.

National rather than state issues dominated political debate in Tennessee's electoral contests throughout the era of the party system. Even in the 1850s, when state issues either sustained or provoked shifts in party alignments in other states, Whig and Democratic leaders continued to keep local concerns out of the political arena in Tennessee.[68] Moreover, the approval of the constitutional amendment providing for the popular election of judges and attorneys general, along with the legislature's passage in 1852 of the Free Banking and the Internal Improvement acts, removed from consideration the major questions that might have provided powerful statewide local issues for the parties. With the margin of difference between the parties still minuscule, party leaders continued to avoid reference to potentially disruptive local issues, anyway. Not until 1859, when Whigs—then campaigning under the name "Opposition"—challenged incumbent Governor Isham G. Harris on a platform pledging to recharter the Union and Planters' banks, did a party center its canvass upon a state issue. By that time, however, Democrats had established such a preponderant majority that the Opposition had little to lose by relying upon a local issue.

Although Tennessee's parties offered no clear alternatives on state programs, voters for the most part retained confidence in their chosen parties until the crisis of secession. National issues, after all, had provided the focal point of confrontation since the beginning of the state's party system, and as the question of slavery's expansion came to the forefront of national politics, party spokesmen in Tennessee channeled the issue into the long-established ideological confrontation between the state's Whigs and Democrats.

Throughout the antebellum era, however, the parties' constituencies, their understanding of government power, and their actions on state policy indicated that underlying the parties' conceptions of the proper defense of freedom were contrasting responses to the expansion of commerce prevailing throughout Jacksonian America. This "Market Revolution," as it usually is called, presented both an opportunity for material prosperity and a challenge to the customs and the stability of a rural, communally organized society that traditionally had practiced subsistence-oriented, "safety-first" agriculture.[69] In Tennessee, as elsewhere in the United States, Whigs encouraged the expansion of the market as the harbinger of material progress for all and became, as one historian concludes, "unabashed champions of enterprise and the bourgeois/middle class ethic."[70] Democrats presented a more ambiguous response. Enticed by the temptations of "progress," they nevertheless perceived that the triumph of commerce could result in prosperity for a few and poverty for the many, while it abrogated freedom by consolidating political and economic power in the hands of a distant "moneyed aristocracy." Their party would encourage economic development only if legislation contained some type of assurance that governmental action would respect equal opportunity, preserve the rights of individuals, and give no exclusive benefits to special interests with close ties to either the state capital or the District of Columbia.

While an economic and cultural transformation provided the foundation for Tennessee's party division, party adherents understood the political confrontation as a struggle to protect voters' liberty, for the parties interpreted a depression's sources and remedies according to the republican ideals that long had prevailed in the state's political culture. Whig and Democratic voters went to the polls convinced that they could best preserve their freedom by electing men who would uphold the pure republican principles of their own party over the demagogues and aristocrats leading their opponents. These voters also recognized that the triumph of one party over the other could determine their own material conditions for years to come.

FIVE

The Politics of Relief:
Hard Times and Texas
1839–1845

With party loyalties established among voters by 1839, the following six years witnessed the most heated party competition, the most intense electioneering, and the most widespread participation of any period in Tennessee's history. That period began and ended with Democratic majorities in the General Assembly, but most of the early 1840s found the party struggling to recover from a series of defeats. Renewed suspension of specie payments, worsening economic conditions, and the promise of relief offered by proposals for a new national bank contributed to successive Whig victories and placed the Whig party in a strong position. The question of the immediate annexation of Texas revived the Democrats' prospects, and, although the party failed to carry Tennessee for James K. Polk in 1844, the momentum stimulated by the Texas issue allowed the Democrats to regain control of the state government in the next year.

The issue of economic recovery dominated political discussion in the early 1840s. Expansion also made its appearance in politics during these years. Despite the prominence of territorial issues over the next two decades, the expansion question first gained visibility as a component of the conflict over the best policies for securing relief from hard times. At the center of the parties' dispute, though, remained the battle over which party truly represented "the people" against demagogues and potential aristocrats. Whether a national bank, the election of United States senators, or Texas annexation formed the chief point of contention, party spokesmen directed discussion of these issues into the established party ideologies. The primary focus of party competition through these years remained a battle between "the people" and either Federalists or the spoils party.

Ultimately, depression politics proved most disastrous for Democrats. In the aftermath of their victory in 1839, Democrats began their preparations for the 1840 presidential election with confidence. Although Martin Van Buren had failed to carry Tennessee in 1836, Democrats believed that in a direct contest between Van Buren and his "Federalist" opponents, without the distraction of Hugh L. White's candidacy, Tennessee voters gladly would return the incumbent to power. Within a week after voters had cast their ballots in 1839, Democratic newspapers endorsed Van Buren's reelection.[1] After the state's banks' renewed suspension of specie payments in October 1839, indicating that hard times had not yet subsided, Democrats counted on the expected vice-presidential nomination of the state party's champion, James K. Polk, to carry the ticket in Tennessee. Prior to the convening of the General Assembly in October, party leaders encouraged supporters to hold local public meetings expressing popular support for a Van Buren–Polk ticket. Two days after Polk's inauguration as Tennessee's governor, Samuel H. Laughlin introduced into the state senate resolutions recommending Van Buren's and Polk's election as president and vice-president. These resolutions quickly received the approval of the Democratic majority in both branches of the state legislature.[2]

Confident in the strength of their party's position, the Democratic majority then proceeded toward its goal of "redeeming" Tennessee from "Federal Whiggery." Central to achieving this goal was ensuring, in the national government, proper representation of the electorate's presumed Democratic sentiments. For six weeks, the assembly's session was dominated by debate over a series of resolutions instructing the state's two United States senators, Hugh L. White and Ephraim H. Foster, to "support in good faith," according to the resolution's final form, "the leading measures and policy as brought forward and advocated by the present President of the United States." Party leaders expected these resolutions to coerce the two Whig senators to resign, for, during the 1839 campaign, Foster had indicated that he would resign in the event of a Democratic victory. Foster's resignation in particular would have satisfied one of the state's most prominent Democrats, Felix Grundy. Aside from the legacy of Foster's challenge for Grundy's seat in 1831, Whigs had tried to force Grundy's own resignation from the Senate in 1837, both by electing Foster to succeed him with two years left in Grundy's term, and by passing their own resolutions instructing Grundy to oppose Van Buren's Independent Treasury proposal. Yet, even if neither Foster nor White resigned, they would be compelled to support Van Buren's administration or else face public condemnation for violating the people's will as expressed through their representatives.³ Fulfilling the Democrats' expectations, both senators resigned, with White charging that "those who can vote such a Resolution have more *confidence in the President than a Papist has in his Pope.*" Whigs throughout the state decried the instructing resolutions as means by which the state's senators had been "CONVERTED INTO PALACE SLAVES."⁴ The Democratic majority nevertheless jumped at the chance to fill the seats with reliable Democrats, and they completed their "redemption" of Tennessee by electing Grundy and Knoxville's Alexander O. Anderson in place of Foster and White.

While Democrats worked to consolidate their party's hold on the state, Whigs already had initiated their preparations to recover the state in the presidential election. Whig leaders attributed their loss in 1839 to their failure to challenge Polk's aggressive campaign, but the narrow Democratic majority convinced party members that an energetic effort could carry Tennessee for the Whig candidate.⁵ Almost immediately after the tabulation of the votes in 1839, John Bell arranged a meeting of Whig leaders throughout the state to plan for the 1840 canvass. Throughout the fall, Whigs held county meetings to appoint "vigilance committees" to direct local electioneering efforts. In both Nashville and Knoxville, Whigs appointed committees to visit Kentucky and invite the expected Whig presidential nominee, Henry Clay, to visit Tennessee.⁶

The national convention's nomination of Ohio's William Henry Harrison instead of Clay temporarily stunned Tennessee's Whigs, but party leaders quickly recovered and honored their pledge to accept the convention's choice.⁷ The "struggle for principle" facilitated the shift of support from Clay to Harrison; since Van Buren's election, Whigs had emphasized the need for unity among all opponents of the administration, so as to secure the goal of casting the "spoils party" from power. The prominent measures of the administration—particularly the subtreasury, a plot by which Van Buren intended to achieve "the permanent establishment of his control over the money of the nation"; and Secretary of War Joel R. Poinsett's proposal to place state militia under national control, which Whigs interpreted as a plot to establish a "standing army"—proved to Whigs that Van Buren and his minions had moved to consolidate their hold on power by establishing a national despotism.⁸

Thus Whigs in 1840 rallied behind the cry of "The Union of the Whigs for the sake of the Union" and pledged to "march up in solid phalanx to the rescue of the Constitution under the banner of the distinguished citizen of Ohio." Harrison, while not the state party's first choice, nevertheless proved acceptable as a candidate because he was, as the *Nashville Whig* maintained, "emphatically *one of the people,* and independent of all party consideration."⁹ To emphasize the centrality of their opposition to the "spoils party," Whig conventions in Knoxville and Nashville, called to select candidates for presidential electors, both unanimously chose the state's recently deposed senators, White and Foster, as the party's two at-large electors. If the president could secure so much power in a state legislature that he could order its representatives to give blind obedience to his will, Whigs argued, "what is more wanting, so far as the legislature is concerned, to make Mr. Van Buren King?"¹⁰

With the "spoils party" cast from office, Whigs promised to "carry out those great measures of national policy, the execution of which we deem of vital importance to the perpetuity and healthful action of our cherished institutions." Whigs seldom specified these "great measures," but few voters could doubt that they would aim at relieving the electorate of the effects of the nation's economic misfortunes.¹¹ Harrison's election, according to Whigs, offered the hope of relief, for with self-serving office holders out of power, responsible statesmen once again would guide the country's economic prospects. Pro-bank Whigs openly avowed that a Whig victory would lead to the creation of a new national bank; conservative Whigs left the issue open, but they did acknowledge that their candidate stood pledged "to abide by the *wishes of the people,* and to sanction a National Bank, if through a majority of their representatives, they so will it." Yet both wings of Tennessee's Whig party came together behind the promise that Harrison's election could only improve the nation's economic condition. As the *Nashville Whig* quoted one of the town's "oldest merchants," Whigs portrayed "but one gleam of hope for the future—the triumph of Old Tippecanoe over the reckless authors of our ruin."¹²

While Whigs rallied behind Harrison, Democrats watched their own party's prospects in the coming contest evaporate, despite the confidence they had gained in recent state elections. The return of hard times once again forced Van Buren's supporters to defend their party's fiscal policies and gave their opponents a powerful advantage. To add to the Democrats' chagrin, the incumbent vice-president, Richard M. Johnson, refused to step aside in favor of Polk, and, as a result, the national convention adjourned after nominating Van Buren, without naming either aspirant as his running mate. Polk immediately withdrew his name from consideration for the office in a public letter to Grundy, for the governor already had told Cave Johnson that he would not consent "to play the part, which Judge White did in the Presidential election of 1836," by allowing his name to be run only in states where it could attract votes. The *Nashville Union* and the *Knoxville Argus* continued to run Polk's name on their mastheads as their vice-presidential candidate until July, but long before that month, it had become clear to Democrats that they only could stand behind Van Buren and the party's claim to represent true Democratic-Republican principles.[13]

Unlike the previous presidential election, in which Hugh L. White and Van Buren both had stood as "members of the Jackson party," Democrats argued that the 1840 contest represented "the first time that Tennesseans are called upon to desert their long cherished principles." Harrison's past record proved that the Whig candidate was a Federalist, Democrats charged, for not only had he supported the administrations of John and John Quincy Adams, but as a congressman he had voted in favor of a protective tariff and federally-funded internal improvements. Moreover, as a member of the Ohio legislature, Harrison voted in favor of a bill "TO SELL FREE WHITE AMERICANS" into slavery, as Democrats interpreted a proposed law to hire out prison labor.[14] As for the nation's economic maladies, Democrats again explained that the "money power" had brought on a suspension of specie payments in an attempt to induce voters "to barter the liberties of their country for the few ephemeral advantages to be derived from a National Bank." This time, too, the Federalists sought to aid their schemes through a popular campaign that appealed to "the lowest order of intellect" and by stimulating "a feeling of 'enthusiasm,'" as Van Buren loyalists described the frequent campaign rallies sponsored by their opponents. Equally ominous, Democrats maintained, was the alliance that Whigs had forged with northern abolitionists, for it showed that the Federalists would even threaten the South's security in order to secure Harrison's election.[15]

Charges of Harrison's "Federalism" and "Abolitionism" could do little to counter the Whigs' offensive against Van Buren and his "party," especially when the hope of recovery offered by Harrison's election carried the Whig appeal. With leaders of both parties portraying the election as vital to the existence of the republic, a higher proportion of voters than in any other election in state history went to the polls in November. When the votes had been counted, the electorate learned that it had given Harrison a majority of more than twelve thousand votes, as the Ohio challenger carried Tennessee on his way to defeating the incumbent in the national election. "We are to have a Federal administration," Democrats lamented, and they blamed the

Whigs' aggressive popular campaigning for stirring up an enthusiasm that permitted "unprecedented frauds upon the elective franchise" and deceived the "honest yeomanry" of the country. Privately, party leaders acknowledged that the return of hard times had severely weakened their cause. "Whilst we could only point them to their workshops & cotton-fields with the aid of economy for relief," A. O. P. Nicholson told Polk, "our opponents presented them the more alluring prospect of abounding cash from a National Bank."[16]

The Whigs' stand against "the party," aided by the "alluring prospect" of relief, likewise carried them to victory in the state elections of 1841. During the presidential canvass, Polk had declared himself a candidate for reelection as governor, a declaration primarily designed to justify his speaking efforts on behalf of the Democratic presidential nominee, and to dispel notions that he was actively campaigning for the vice-presidency. With Foster anxious to return to the Senate, and with Bell rumored about to receive a cabinet appointment from the new president, no Whig appeared to have the prominence to challenge the Democratic incumbent, so a state convention, held at Murfreesborough, nominated to stand against Polk a political novice, James C. Jones of Wilson County. Aside from taking a leading role in organizing Wilson County's White supporters in 1836, the thirty-one-year-old Jones's public service was limited to one term in the state legislature and a canvass as a Harrison elector in 1840.[17] Yet Whigs recognized in Jones, whose six-foot, one-inch, 125-pound frame earned him the nickname "Lean Jimmy," a master of popular campaigning who could match Polk's own dynamic campaign style. "Majr. Jones is one of the best stump speakers in our State, or almost any where else & he will beat Polk at his favorite game," William Campbell predicted to his uncle.[18]

Polk again had planned an energetic, offensive campaign like the one he had waged against Newton Cannon in 1839, and Democrats believed that, behind such a campaign, they could maintain their ascendancy. Jones, however, launched his own offensive that checked Polk's efforts, and the challenger forced the incumbent to devote his energy on the stump to defending his political consistency. Jones produced evidence, from Polk's past writings and speeches, indicating that the governor himself once had been "the warm advocate of Internal Improvements by the General Government" and that he had opposed the subtreasury until "the party" demanded that all office-seekers support the measure. Whig newspapers, meanwhile, reminded voters that "a subservient party Legislature" had forced White and Foster out of the Senate and had "filled their places with their own parti-

"Gubernatorial Campaign, 1841 or 1843, between James K. Polk and James C. Jones." Tennessee Historical Society Picture Collection. Reproduction courtesy of Tennessee State Library and Archives, Nashville.

zans," and they derided the governor for denigrating "his high place and duties" during the 1840 presidential canvass to "become a party missionary and stump orator." While Whigs attacked Polk as a demagogue, Jones centered his own campaign upon the need for a national bank and his support for the national party's proposal to distribute to the states the proceeds from the sales of public lands.[19]

The governor defended his actions while in office and proclaimed his political consistency against Jones's charges, while continuing to stand behind the subtreasury as the only "constitutional treasury." The incumbent based his own campaign upon his conviction that the early developments of the new administration proved that the nation had entered "The Third Reign of Federalism." Democrats expected Harrison's call, immediately after his inauguration, for an extra session of Congress to work to their advantage, for, as Jackson explained, the expense of this "unnecessary" session would "open the eyes of the deluded people & prostrate the Whiggs who have been crying out retrenchment & reform." Polk contrasted Harrison's call for the session with his own refusal to burden the state with a session of the state legislature merely to elect senators for the session, and the incumbent maintained that the new president's cabinet appointments, especially his appointment of Daniel Webster as secretary of state, provided conclusive proof that "the power of the General Government has in truth passed into the hands of the Federal party."[20]

Polk's campaign did manage to reduce the margin between the parties from the Democrats' devastating defeat in 1840 to about three thousand votes. Nevertheless, the Democratic champion lost in his bid for reelection. Although Polk's party managed to retain a one-seat majority in the state senate, the Whigs won a three-seat advantage in the house of representatives, an advantage that would leave the Whigs in control of a joint session of the General Assembly. Despite Jones's narrow margin of victory, these results, along with the party's control of eight of the state's thirteen congressional seats, permitted Whig leaders to proclaim that the state elections had "triumphantly demonstrate[d] the continued ascendancy of Whig principles in TENNESSEE."[21]

Developments in Washington overshadowed the state canvass in 1841. Tennessee's Whigs interpreted Harrison's election as a public mandate in favor of the creation of a new national bank, and throughout the state, voters expected the establishment of a new central institution to take priority at the extra session of Congress.[22] Whigs mourned when they learned that Harrison had died on April 4, but they expected no change in policy with the accession of Vice-President John Tyler, for Tyler, they believed, "likewise inherits the political principles of the late President." This confidence appeared justified as Tyler signed into law Whig-sponsored bills to repeal the subtreasury, to distribute the proceeds from the sales of public lands, and to create a national system of bankruptcy. Yet, three weeks after they had cast their ballots in the state elections, Tennessee's citizens received the news that Tyler had vetoed a bill to charter a bank. By the middle of September, they also had learned of the president's second veto of a similar bill; of the resignation of all members of the cabinet, except Webster, to protest the vetoes; and of the meeting of Whigs in Congress that passed resolutions effectively expelling Tyler from the Whig party.[23]

Tyler's vetoes shocked Tennessee's Whigs. Party members wasted no time in joining together to castigate the president for his action. A

Whig meeting in Gallatin, Sumner County, condemned the vetoes as acts "contrary to the will of the people," while similar meetings in Murfreesborough and Franklin included in their proceedings hanging the president in effigy. Tyler had denied "the great body of the American People, the prime measure for their peculiar relief, demanded at his hands," the *Nashville Whig* concluded; "we see not, indeed, *how* or *when*, he can atone for such enormous wrong." Beyond Tyler's denial of relief to a suffering people, Whigs decried the president's actions as violating their party's fundamental creed of restricting executive power in order to allow the popular will to determine public policy. Whigs thus resoundingly approved the cabinet's resignation and the national party's renunciation of the president. Tyler had proven "a TRAITOR to the party which had brought him into power," William G. Brownlow charged; by his actions, he had "forfeited all claims to the future support and confidence of that party."[24]

In response to Tyler's apostasy, Whigs immediately revived their efforts to elevate Kentucky's Henry Clay to the presidency. Brownlow's *Jonesborough Whig* endorsed Clay in September 1841, even before news of Tyler's second veto of a bank bill had reached the state. After the sharp decline in prices and property values in the first half of 1842, the *Nashville Whig* and the *Republican Banner* both proclaimed the Kentuckian, as the *Banner* stated, "the great favorite of those of whose virtuous principles he has been so bold, so faithful, so powerful and so true an advocate."[25] As they had in 1840, Whigs promoted their presidential favorite as a virtuous republican statesman who would respect the people's will and the constitutional restrictions on executive power. This time, the promise to charter a national bank moved to the center of the party's appeal. With the party faithful furious at Tyler's course as president, and with the depression deepening and no prospect of recovery in sight, the banner of Clay and a bank provided a powerful rallying point for Tennessee's Whigs. "Let HENRY CLAY once appear on the track," the *Jonesborough Whig* maintained, "and let the issue be made of Bank or no Bank, a sound currency or no currency, and the battle will be easily won."[26]

While Whigs repudiated Tyler and identified their party with Clay's presidential candidacy, Democrats praised the president for his actions against the establishment of a national bank. Although opposed to him on most issues, the *Nashville Union* declared that on this issue Tyler had proven "true to his trust; faithful to the Constitution; and faithful to his professions." The paper then called the president "the instrument we doubt not in the hands of a wise Providence of rescuing a betrayed and insulted people from this monstrous mare—this nurturing mother of an embryo nobility."²⁷ With hard times continuing, and with Whigs attaching themselves to Clay, Democrats believed that political currents in the state were shifting in their party's favor. Even before Harrison's inauguration, Democrats had begun to criticize the Whigs for failing to provide relief. "The people were not asked to wait until Harrison should be inaugurated, but were told that as soon as it became positively certain that he would be elected, confidence would dawn on the 'mercantile community,' and ease and plenty on all," the *Knoxville Argus* chided. "Now, indeed, the people are told that they must wait a year or two before the promised era of good times can arrive!"²⁸

Moreover, Democrats interpreted the Whigs' actions since their victory as aiding the Democracy's cause. The course of the extra session of Congress, Democrats maintained, vindicated their prediction that the costly session would "*prove a failure.*" Party spokesmen reminded voters that the Whig champion Clay had supported the Bankrupt Act passed at that session. This act had received widespread public condemnation in Tennessee, for even the Whig Francis B. Fogg recognized it as a law that would "not only relieve the honest and unfortunate debtor, but a far more numerous class of debtors who have neither been honest or unfortunate."²⁹ Most important, the Whigs' popular campaigning no longer obscured their promotion of a bank. Democrats expected those citizens who had followed Hugh White into the Whig party to repudiate their Federalist allies, because in the next election—for the first time—"*the question will have a fair hearing, and the people will have a fair hearing*, and the end will doubtless be the will of the people."³⁰

Whatever chances Democrats may have had of recapturing Tennessee in the 1843 state elections suffered a severe blow from the party's course in the "Immortal Thirteen" controversy during the 1841-42 legislative session. The death of Felix Grundy in December 1840 and the expiration of Alexander Anderson's term on March 3, 1841, left vacant the state's two seats in the United States Senate, seats that had been subjects of bitter contention between the parties since Whigs had tried to force Grundy's resignation in the 1837-38 legislature. Since the 1841 elections had given them a two-seat majority in a joint session of the assembly, Whigs expected to have no trouble electing two members of their own party to fill these seats, notwithstanding John Bell's arrival in Nashville at the opening of the session after his resignation as Tyler's secretary of war. Bell had been Ephraim Foster's chief rival for dominance in Tennessee's Whig party and for a seat in the Senate since Foster had won the party's support as Grundy's successor; now Bell came to Nashville looking for a way to secure his own election to one of the two vacancies. Nevertheless, the Whig members of the assembly met early in the session and agreed to unite behind Foster and McMinn County's Spencer Jarnigan, who had replaced Hugh White on the Harrison electoral ticket after White's death in April 1840. The desire to vindicate Foster for the resignation that had been forced on him by the Democrats' instructing resolutions gave him the strongest claims on a seat, while Jarnigan's residence in East Tennessee would preserve the state's traditional balance in the Senate seats between East and Middle Tennessee.[31]

Unknown to Whigs, the assembly's Democrats planned to use their thirteen-to-twelve advantage in the state senate to frustrate the election of Whig senators. In every previous election since Tennessee's admission to the Union in 1796, the legislature had chosen senators in a joint session of the assembly's two branches, in which session a majority vote determined the victorious candidate. With their party in a minority in a joint session, Democrats now claimed that this mode of electing senators violated both federal and state constitutions. The Constitution of the United States directed that state legislatures choose senators, and since Tennessee's legislature consisted of two independent bodies, Democrats argued that the legislature's choice of senators must meet the approval of both the house and the senate in their independent capacities.[32] Thus, when Whigs in the senate introduced resolutions to meet with the house to elect U.S. senators, the "Immortal Thirteen" Democrats defeated the resolutions on the basis of their newly-developed interpretation of the Constitution. When Democratic Speaker of the Senate Samuel Turney temporarily deserted his party and voted to pass the Whig resolutions, the remaining twelve prevented a quorum in the joint session by refusing to attend. Instead, these Democratic senators remained in the Senate Hall and sent to Turney a message informing him that they were "ready to transact any constitutional business pending before this branch of the General Assembly."[33]

The key to the state party's strategy lay less in its claim to have discovered the correct interpretation of the Constitution than in the charge that the Whigs were attempting to force their party's choice of senators upon the assembly, regardless of the popular will. Shortly after the assembly's session opened, the Immortal Thirteen drew up a list of questions, or "interrogatories," and sent them to potential senatorial candidates in both parties. Most of these interrogatories involved the leading policy issues dividing the parties, and they concluded by asking whether the candidate accepted the General

Assembly's right to instruct senators and whether a senator had a "duty, when instructed, to obey or resign." Foster and Jarnigan refused to reply, with Foster declaring in a public statement that his enemies possessed "neither power to deter, nor wealth nor honors enough to purchase me." Democrats in turn now claimed that the Thirteen's insistence on constitutional purity prevented the Whigs from sending to the Senate "dumb," or "mum," candidates who refused to submit their political principles for public consideration.[34]

The Thirteen apparently believed that, through their stand upon constitutional principles, they could direct public outrage toward their opponents for their seemingly highhanded intention to choose senators regardless of the citizenry's will. With public opinion in their favor, Democrats not only could prevent Foster's and Jarnigan's election, but instead elevate at least one, and possibly two, Democrats into the vacant Senate seats. Although Whigs already held a solid eight-seat majority in the national Senate, the additional Democratic votes could play a significant role in Congress's deliberations on federal policy. If, in the end, Whig senators were elected, the Thirteen's determination only to accept candidates who had answered the interrogatories meant that the senators would be publicly committed to the legislature's right of instruction, insuring that a future Democratic Assembly could compel them to vote for Democratic measures in Congress or resign. And if the Thirteen's stand prevented the election of any senators at the current session, the Whigs' refusal to compromise on their "dumb candidates" convinced Democrats that public condemnation would fall upon their opponents.[35] "Our whole object," state house member William H. Polk told his brother, the former governor,

> is, to place them in the position of refusing to elect State officers, necessary and essential, to the proper administration of our State Government, because we prevent them from placing in the Senate men who stand *Mum,* virtually controverting and denying the right of the people to know the opinions and political *views* of their public servants. They will stand in the *indefensable* [sic] attitude, of having clog[g]ed the wheels, and prevented the necessary opperation [sic] of our State Government, because we would not passively surrender up the *rights* of the people, by *permitting* the election of Foster and Jarnigan. If we can succeed in placing them in this light before the country our conquest will be easy.[36]

Despite Polk's optimism, the strategy behind the Thirteen's stand backfired. Privately, Foster and Bell offered to negotiate some sort of arrangement with the Democrats. Publicly, Whigs remained firm in their determination to elect Foster and Jarnigan, and they treated the interrogatories as an insult.[37] Whigs could afford to refuse to compromise, for, aside from Democrats, few in the electorate apparently found plausible the party's argument concerning the unconstitutionality of the election of senators by a joint session of the assembly. Precedent had established the authority of a joint session, Whigs argued, and "if the precedent had not been acceptable to the People, perfectly so, why did not the Convention of 1834 take some action on the subject?"[38] Rather than their opponents, Democrats soon found themselves under attack—for blocking the election of senators and for selfishly preventing the execution of the popular will.

As the session progressed, Democrats realized their party's tenuous position. In January, ex-Governor Polk admonished Democratic legislators to permit the election of at least one senator. The Thirteen, however, not only had launched their offensive upon a weak position, but also they had left their party at a point from which an honorable retreat appeared impossible. "[M]ost of the 'immortal thirteen,' for weeks before the adjournment, were in unspeakable travail," Foster told Robert Caruthers. "They saw the error of their way, & would have been glad to retrace their steps, but that a retrograde march would have damned them with *double* infamy."[39]

Democrats tried to shift the burden of the legislature's inability to elect senators back upon their opponents. As early as December, the Thirteen offered a compromise by passing, in the state senate, resolutions electing Democratic Congressman Hopkins L. Turney and Thomas Brown, an East Tennessee Whig who had answered the interrogatories. Then, on the final day of the session, the senate considered a resolution to allow each party to select one senator, though dissent among the Thirteen themselves defeated this proposal's passage. In the house, the Whig majority, recognizing that the weight of public opinion lay in its favor, refused to concur in the resolutions electing Brown and Turney and displayed no inclination to compromise. When the assembly adjourned in early February, Tennessee's two seats in the United States Senate remained vacant. The state would remain unrepresented in the Senate for the next two years, and popular sentiment blamed the assembly's failure to provide senators on the Immortal Thirteen. "[T]here is now, here, a deep feeling of dissatisfaction among the people generally, at the conduct of the democratic members of our legislature in not electing senators," James Campbell, a Whig member of the state senate, told his nephew. "The Whigs loudly condemn, & the democrats do not pretend to justify. If we cant succeed now with the people of Tennessee we may give up the ship."[40]

Even if Democrats had not stumbled into the "Immortal Thirteen" fiasco, it remains doubtful whether they could have recovered the state in the next elections. Notwithstanding party leaders' confidence in the potential of the issues provided by Congress's extra session in 1841, Democrats still suffered from the stigma of being, as the Whigs alleged, the party responsible for the collapse of the economy. The party appeared to offer no solution to the deepening depression, and the Thirteen's gamble saddled Democrats with the additional image of politicians fighting desperately for their political survival. Over the summer of 1842, Democrats challenged Whigs to a general resignation from the legislature to let the electorate pronounce judgment on the senatorial question, but Whigs instead continued to remind citizens, in the words of the *Republican Banner,* that "the present hard times . . . are the result of a continuation of *the Democratic policy."* Although Democrats charged that the Whigs had failed to provide the prosperity they had promised in 1840, Whigs merely pointed to Tyler's vetoes of the party's central proposal for restoring confidence in the currency as the chief factor preventing recovery.[41] As long as hard times continued, and as long as they offered nothing to counter the Whigs' promise of relief, Democrats could have little hope to carry Tennessee.

As a result, Whigs had little trouble retaining their hold on the state in the 1843 elections. Polk again faced "Lean Jimmy" Jones for the governor's chair, and the Democratic challenger entered the canvass convinced that his prospects were "better than they have ever been: better decidedly than they were in 1839." Polk expected Jones's proclamation that he favored "*Henry Clay, first,* and last, and all the time" to produce among voters a reaction in the Democrats' favor. To encourage this result, the challenger continued to denounce the claims of the constitutionality of a national bank, while he accused the Whigs of promoting a protective tariff. As in 1841, though, Jones forced Polk to defend his political record, this time producing evidence that the Democratic champion in 1832 had voted in Congress in favor of tariff rates higher than those established by the Whig Tariff of 1842. Throughout the state, meanwhile, Whigs reminded voters that the Thirteen had denied Tennessee its right to representation in the Senate, and Whig candidates continued to attribute the prevailing hard times to their opponents. "A National Bank or no National Bank is the issue," the *Jonesborough Whig* proclaimed as it admonished Whig candidates to "meet Locofocoism fairly upon the grand question of the Currency."[42] Despite the Democrats' attempt to "make a distinction between White Whigs & Clay Whigs,"[43] Jones increased his margin of victory over Polk to thirty-eight hundred votes in his reelection to the executive office. Democrats did capture six of Tennessee's eleven congressional seats, according to the state's new apportionment, but the Whigs carried both branches of the General Assembly and secured an eight-seat majority in a joint session, a majority that quickly put to rest the "Immortal Thirteen" controversy by electing Foster and Jarnigan to the Senate.

Whigs interpreted their triumph in 1843 as a popular endorsement of their stand for Henry Clay. In the legislature, the party's majority repealed the resolutions, passed by the General Assembly in 1827, that condemned Clay for his presumed role in a "corrupt bargain" with John Quincy Adams. While party leaders encouraged local organizers to keep up the fervor for Clay and a bank, they also, for the first time, prepared to send a delegation to the party's national convention. Rather than attempt to force a candidate upon an unwilling electorate, the 1844 Whig convention would merely ratify the nomination of Clay,"whose nomination has already been made by the PEOPLE!!"The convention's most important duty, however, now required Tennessee's representation, for it would also select a vice-presidential candidate upon whom all Whigs could agree. "Had Tennessee been represented in the Convention that nominated Gen. Harrison, the *Ass* who now disgraces the vacated chair of the lamented Harrison, would not be there!" Brownlow's *Jonesborough Whig* reminded readers.[44] Thus Whigs in each of the Grand Divisions held conventions to select delegates to the party's national meeting. At the national convention and on the stump, Tennessee's Whigs endorsed the convention's nomination of Clay and New Jersey's Theodore Frelinghuysen as the party's national ticket.[45]

Democrats, too, recognized the significance of the result of the 1843 elections. Despite Polk's explanation to Martin Van Buren that "local causes" and "questions of state policy" had determined the result, Polk and the other party leaders knew that questions of federal policy indeed had played a central role in the canvass. "[E. G.] Eastman agreed with me that the *bank question* was the great cause," Samuel H. Laughlin noted in his diary after he had discussed the recent defeat with other prominent Democrats. "Gov. Polk thought it was this, and the divisions among our friends in local elections, that beat us," Laughlin added. The *Knoxville Argus* confessed that "the result of our recent elections show that the bank question, although absolutely dead almost every where else, is yet alive here." Although Polk admonished his colleagues to "keep their armour on, and to fight for principle," Democrats realized that, without an issue to counter the Whigs' promise of financial relief, their prospects in the coming presidential election were bleak.⁴⁶ As the parties neared the commencement of the 1844 campaign, there seemed little doubt that the home state of Andrew Jackson would cast its electoral votes resoundingly for Jackson's antithesis, Henry Clay.

A large part of the Democratic despondency derived from the party's lack of an attractive presidential candidate upon whom to unite. Although President Tyler attempted to gain the favor of Tennessee's Democrats through the exercise of his patronage, it appeared that the state party again would take up Martin Van Buren as its candidate. Polk, notwithstanding his recent defeat, still desired the vice-presidency, and as the election approached, he concluded that his aspirations would be best served by attaching himself to Van Buren's prospects. After observing the maneuvering of the leading presidential contenders, by the fall of 1843 the former governor considered it "settled that *Mr. Van-Buren* will be the nominee for the Presidency." With the New Yorker heading the ticket, Polk observed, "the candidate for the Vice Presidency must come from the West, and from a slave-holding state." Despite Van Buren's lack of popularity in Tennessee, most party leaders approved Polk's efforts to line up the state behind the New Yorker. As in 1840, Democrats rested their slim hope of carrying Tennessee upon the possibility that the Tennessean's name on the national ticket could rally enough support for the party, despite Van Buren's nomination.⁴⁷

A significant portion of the state party expressed disgust at the prospect of another Van Buren candidacy, for they believed it impossible to gain support for the New Yorker in a state that already twice had rejected his claims. "[T]here is one thing Certain to my minde and that is, that the State cannot be carried for Mr Vanburen," Greeneville's Andrew Johnson wrote to Robert B. Reynolds, while even Polk's close political confidante, Representative Aaron V. Brown, warned that Van Buren "wants availability. It always was and will be an uphill business to sustain him in Tennessee especially."⁴⁸ Brown and a few others indicated a willingness to take up John C. Calhoun, but most dissatisfied Democrats followed the lead of Andrew Johnson and A. O. P. Nicholson and advocated the nomination of Michigan's Lewis Cass as the state party's favorite. Nicholson apparently hoped to push the presidential claims of his friend Cass as a means by which to replace Polk as the most prominent Democrat in Tennessee. When the state party convention met in November 1843 to select delegates to the national party convention, several members, under Nicholson's direction, encouraged the nomination of Cass and Polk as the state party's candidates. This move failed to gain Cass the nomination, as Polk and his associates had already determined to promote only a promise by the state party to support the nominee of the national convention. The challenge from Cass's supporters, though, left the impression that Polk's leadership of the party in Tennessee had suffered a severe blow.[49]

Polk tried to remedy the damage to his position by explaining to Van Buren that the convention could have nominated the New Yorker but that the pro-Van Buren delegates "thought it prudent under the circumstances, to abstain from the attempt." Had these delegates attempted to nominate Van Buren, the Tennessean explained, "there would be some division and probably an excited discussion, which it was feared would have a tendency to weaken us in the State." Likewise, the state party's central committee prepared an address to party leaders in other states repeating this explanation, although division within the committee itself gave the address a noncommittal tone that prevented its being sent outside Tennessee. Such assurances hardly could have concealed the growing dissension within Tennessee's Democratic party. Notwithstanding the state convention's unanimous nomination of Polk for the vice-presidency, his failure to secure Van Buren's nomination suggests that the former governor's influence in the party was slipping. Several delegates headed to the Baltimore convention ready to abandon Polk's claims if necessary to secure a more suitable presidential nominee than Van Buren.[50]

By the time that Tennessee's delegation departed for Baltimore, Polk himself had come to doubt the wisdom of Van Buren's nomination. Ironically, the former governor's doubts coincided with the state party's conviction that the prospects of their cause were reviving. This shift occurred as the immediate annexation of the Republic of Texas emerged as a political issue. Since Texas had won its independence from Mexico in 1836, Tennessee's electorate, by a large margin, had favored statehood for that republic. The support had been indicated by the General Assembly's overwhelming approval in both 1838 and 1842 of resolutions calling for Texas's annexation to the United States. The Texas question remained outside the political arena until early 1844, when President Tyler announced that his administration was negotiating a treaty with the Lone Star Republic for its annexation. Democratic leaders surmised that the president intended to use popular support for the treaty to build a new political party that would back the incumbent's reelection, and at first they expected to gain little from the issue.[51] As they perceived the popularity of the issue and as they sensed Henry Clay's probable opposition to annexation, however, Democrats adopted the Texas issue as their own. From retirement at the Hermitage, Andrew Jackson issued a public letter declaring his support for Texas's admission, and in early April the *Union* concluded that immediate annexation would become "a question in the pending Presidential election of the most momentous consequence." Concerning that question, the paper assured readers, "the democracy will take the side of re-uniting our dismembered territory and of once more bringing under our glorious stars and stripes our brethren of Texas."[52]

As Democrats expected, Clay committed himself against annexation in a public letter written from Raleigh, North Carolina. Democratic hopes for revival almost were derailed the day after the Raleigh letter arrived in Nashville, for that day's late mail brought a public letter from Van Buren announcing that he also opposed annexation. Van Buren loyalists attempted to justify to the electorate their support for the New Yorker despite his position in his letter.[53] Privately, even the most adamant Van Buren supporters knew that their favorite's position on the Texas issue killed whatever prospects he might have had of carrying Tennessee. "On Saturday we had a most glorious meeting, ... but behold that night comes V.B.'s letter & leaves us no ground to stand on," Leonard P. Cheatham relayed to Polk from Nashville; while Robert Armstrong concluded that, if the national convention nominated Van Buren, "we are whipt in the South & West, and nothing will save us except the nomination of a Texas man for that section." Even Polk now admitted that "it will be utterly hopeless to carry the vote of this State for any man who is opposed to immediate annexation." "I have stood by *Mr. V. B.* and will stand by him as long as there is hope," Polk told Cave Johnson, "but I now despair of his election— even if he be nominated."[54]

Democrats thus rejoiced when they learned that the deadlocked convention at Baltimore had bypassed all the leading aspirants and instead had nominated Polk himself as the party's presidential nominee, with Pennsylvania's George M. Dallas as the vice-presidential candidate. Polk had known that the convention might consider his name for the presidency; although he still focused his hopes upon the vice-presidential nomination, he had authorized Cave Johnson and Gideon J. Pillow to negotiate for the first position on the ticket if those two saw the opportunity present itself at the convention.[55] For most Democrats, news of the nomination came as a welcome surprise, and the candidacy of the state party's champion unified the recently fragmenting organization.

Nicholson, his recent rival for dominance in the state party, admitted to Andrew Johnson that he had "never before seen the democracy waked up as it is now and I cannot doubt our success." Nicholson's own course signified the suppression of division in Tennessee's Democrats, for at the Davidson County public meeting called to ratify the ticket, Nicholson declared "'Polk and Dallas—Texas and Democracy,' as the sign by which we cannot fail to conquer."[56]

Democrats expected "state pride" in Polk to strengthen their cause, but they never let voters forget that the presidential election chiefly involved the continuing struggle between republican citizens and "Federalists." While reviving charges of Clay's perfidy in the "corrupt bargain," party spokesmen reminded voters that a Whig victory, aside from its implications for Texas's annexation, would result in the creation of a new national bank and in the burden of a protective tariff.[57] Still, the popularity of the prospect of immediate annexation provided the driving force behind the Democratic campaign. Democrats presented the annexation issue as the logical extension of the party's battle against Federalism. Indeed, according to the *Union*, "opposition to the admission of Texas into the Union is only a new manifestation of the old spirit which dictated the alien and sedition laws of old John Adams's time."[58] Most importantly, the Federalists opposed annexation as a way to attack the institution of slavery in the southern states. The threat to slavery, Democrats maintained, revealed their opponents' complicity in a deeper plot that threatened the independence and perpetuation of the American republic.

In fact, Democrats explained, the true enemy of Texas's admission to the Union was Great Britain, which saw in Texas a means to gain a foothold in the Southwest in order to undermine American independence. "[T]he question of the annexation of Texas," Alexander O. Anderson declared, "is one of British supremacy, or American liberty."[59] According to Democrats, abolitionists in England and America had conspired to bring about "the forcible abolition of slavery in Texas and the United States or the dissolution of this Union," and this conspiracy "is known to the English Government" and "has its countenance—its encouragement and cooperation." Aside from its resentment toward the young republic for its successful rebellion from the English monarch's rule, Britain recognized in the United States its "great rival upon the land and upon the sea,—in commerce and in manufactories." The young republic thus stood as the "only nation in the world" which could check Britain's "*arbitrary will* among the nations of the earth." Under the guise of humanitarianism, the British government encouraged the Abolitionist conspiracy and opposed the annexation of Texas to the United States, on the grounds that the move would expand the institution of slavery. Britain knew that, without the aid of the United States, the Lone Star Republic would be forced to turn to Britain for assistance through a commercial alliance—an alliance that would lead to Texas's own subjugation as a British colony. "Entangle yourselves by a treaty with England, and remember the fate of India," Gideon Pillow warned Texans, "or protect your own commerce and interests, by excluding British goods or dregs from your port, and she will remonstrate at the mouth of the cannon."[60]

Once Britain had established its authority in Texas, it would abolish slavery in that region and encourage abolitionists to continue their activities in the United States. The presence of a refuge for escaped slaves so close to the country's southern border would destabilize the institution and threaten the South's internal security. The prime object of British policy, however, was not abolition, but the dissolution of the Union of states, a dissolution that inevitably would occur as the southern states experienced civil discord and as the abolitionists aggressively pursued their policy of rule or ruin. "What a dark cloud will at once hang over the prospect of all our southern states," Andrew J. Donelson predicted, in the event of Clay's election. "Great Britain will forthwith resume her projects for the abolition of slavery, and with the aid of Webster & Adams will consider that her game is ensured."[61] As Pillow explained, Britain's apparent concern for the fate of slaves merely covered that power's true "game":

> England knows she dare not attack us openly.—She knows that while these mighty States are *united,* the world cannot conquer us. She herself has *twice tried it,* and upon the plains of New Orleans we taught her a *lesson* which she will not soon forget. But actuated by her *implacable hate,* and her *never dying hostility,* she has seized hold of the abolition excitement, and hopes by fanning the flames of domestic discord, by carefully concealing her hidden purpose, and cloaking her rights under *assumed* humanity for the slaves of Texas, she trusts to effect a dismemberment of this Union, and thus accomplish what she dare not attempt openly. This is the great purpose of her heart, her real design. She cares nothing about the African slave....
>
> She knows that in our *Union,* consists our *strength* and *national greatness.* She knows that if she could dismember this Union, she would prostrate her great rival, and that she could then dictate laws to the world.[62]

Clay opposed annexation to gain the support of the abolitionists,

Democrats maintained, and thereby the Whigs ultimately aided Britain in its schemes against the republic. Even without the prospect of abolitionist aid, Polk's supporters charged, Whigs would oppose Texas's admission, for the geographical expansion of American territory would undermine the Federalists' own expectation regarding the disintegration of popular government. According to Democrats, Whigs knew that, if they could confine the nation's rapidly growing population within the country's current boundaries, the declining availability of land upon which citizens could establish homesteads eventually would force the population to become dependent upon a wealthy ruling class for their livelihoods. Large landholders, the *Jeffersonian* later explained, opposed expansion "under the belief that they can sell their estates in small parcels and at high prices, or force those who are too poor to purchase, to become renters, like the laborers of England." Alexander Anderson warned that, if a yeoman were forced "to remain forever within the sound of the spindle and the loom of his rich neighbor, [the] monopolist manufacturer," the farmer would be left with "no hope but that he must work at *his* [the manufacturer's] wheel, and ply *his* baton, and his children after him, for longer generations than his simple mind can count." With this prospect before the yeoman, Anderson concluded, "hope dies within him, . . . and his whole existence resolves itself into a question of bread and clothing."[63]

Annexation, on the other hand, would delay this bleak prospect by adding to the United States a vast territory waiting for settlement under the guidance of American institutions. Most immediately, this additional land would provide an opportunity for relief for yeomen suffering from the current depression, for those who had fallen on hard times now would have the opportunity to work their way into prosperity by attempting to establish a new homestead in Texas. In the long run, the process of settling Texas, and any other territory that might become available, would ensure the perpetuity of the population of free, self-reliant, independent citizens necessary for the success of republican government. "We do not want to condense closely, for a long, long time, our population, as if we were raising Princes, Nobles, and nabobs of wealth," Alexander Anderson explained. Instead, the former senator proclaimed,

> give to the poor—to the laborers—the honest husbandman—the promise of improving his condition, land upon which he fells his own forest trees, plants his own orchard, and builds his own cabin, and, with his improved fortunes, you will improve his virtues, increase his stake in

society, and make him a good citizen and a brave soldier....A hardy population, honest, industrious and virtuous, spread over a large surface—the larger the better, if they are all the same—never can be corrupted.... In such a country, the poorest man, with his axe daily upon his shoulder, or following his plough, is sensible that his child is probably born to a higher destiny than his own. The Far-West has already multiplied such examples, and in a country such as Texas, it is certain, if we held it, the thousands and thousands who would go there, and might have land for settling it, the number of the fortunate would be increased in proportion to its very superior advantages.[64]

According to Democrats, then, the question of annexation involved, not simply the future of slavery, but the security of the United States and the perpetuation of republican government. "The democratic party regard the question of annexing Texas as a national one, and they favor the acquisition of that territory because they believe it necessary to strengthen the Union, and to secure us peace, harmony and increased prosperity," the *Union* declared, admonishing "our countrymen ALL, and all who desire to see our institutions flourish, our Union, perpetuated, and the principle of popular sovereignty prevail," to "look well to the signs of the times." Unless the nation acted quickly, Democrats warned, the nation never again would have the chance to add Texas to the Union, for the present offered probably the last opportunity to acquire the Lone Star Republic. Since their rebellion against Mexico, the people of Texas had established a *de facto* and *de jure* independent state, and they had expressed their desire to join the United States. Opposition within the Union, particularly after the Senate rejected Tyler's treaty of annexation on June 8, along with "the alarm created in Texas by the dangerous intrigues of England," had led Texas's citizenry to doubt the sincerity of the American public's desire for annexation. A victory for the Democratic ticket would show the people of Texas that the American electorate favored immediate annexation. The new administration, backed by the popular mandate, could then carry out the measure, negate Britain's designs in the Southwest, and insure the continuation of American freedom.[65]

The issue of the immediate annexation of Texas provided Democrats with a powerful issue with which to counter the Whigs' promise of relief through a national bank. With their opponents revived, and with the depression having reached its nadir more than two years before the presidential election, Whigs found themselves scrambling to maintain the momentum that had carried them through the last three elections.

Most Whigs appear to have favored Texas' admission, as is shown by the party's unanimous support, in the 1843-44 session of the legislature, of resolutions approving annexation. When the question first emerged as a political issue, party leaders recognized it, as had Democrats, as a maneuver by President Tyler to break up the party system and to enhance his own political fortunes. "Foster here is for it—but thinks it a humbug of the Captain's [Tyler's]," Aaron Brown noted; while the *Republican Banner* commented that, "favorable as we are to the admission of Texas into the Union, . . . we have no hesitation at all in condemning the course which Mr. Tyler has pursued in regard to the measure itself." As Democrats adopted the annexation issue, a few Whigs, such as James Campbell, recognized the popularity of the issue and urged their compatriots to match their opponents' zeal in calling for annexation, even if advocating annexation required abandoning Clay as the party's presidential candidate.[66] Most party leaders, seeing Democratic support for Texas merely as a ruse to revive that party's fortunes and sensing that their own standard-bearer intended to oppose the measure, continued to portray the Texas question as one outside the realm of party politics. "It is a subject upon which both parties are divided," the *Nashville Whig* commented, "so they might just as well abandon the scheme and be content to fight the battle on other grounds."[67]

Whigs endorsed Clay's opposition to Texas's admission when the candidate's Raleigh letter arrived in Nashville. Through most of the campaign, though, Whigs in Tennessee made few references to Clay's stand against annexation; by the end of June, in fact, the *Whig* assured readers favorable to Texas's admission that "under his auspices annexation will be accomplished, whenever it can be done without violating the faith of treaties, or impairing the national honor."[68] Whigs chiefly portrayed the Texas question as one too delicate to become entangled in party debates. Immediate annexation would lead to a war with Mexico and to "divisions and dissensions" within the United States itself; while Texas's admission might be desirable, it would require careful consideration by citizens and a statesmanlike course by American leaders, to execute the measure peacefully. As attractive a policy as annexation might appear, Whigs maintained, "the possession of the fertile plains of Texas will not compensate for the loss of national honor, and the danger to the integrity of the Union."[69]

In the present contest, Whigs argued, Democrats called for immediate annexation only to stir up excitement among voters and to obscure the "true issues" from public consideration. "Aware the people never will sustain their Anti-Tariff, Anti-Bank, [and] Anti-Distribution" positions, Brownlow declared, "they have let go the whole, and seized upon *Texas,* as the last and only hope of doing battle in the cause of dying Democracy!" According to Whigs, the central issue in the campaign remained the Whig party's stand against demagogic, office-seeking politicians, for the Democrats' promotion of the Texas issue revealed once again that "the party" would stop at nothing, no matter what the consequences, in its quest for power. In taking up the issue, these so-called Democrats "appealed to the prejudices and sympathies of the people, rather than to their reason and judgement," and when Van Buren failed to follow Andrew Jackson's direction and opposed annexation, "the party" cast its favorite aside and replaced him with Polk, whose "chief merit," the *Whig* claimed, "consists in being a partizan politician of the rankest order."[70] Echoing the arguments used in 1836 against Jackson's "dictation," the *Banner* maintained that Polk's nomination proved that these demagogues had "surrendered themselves unconditionally, without a single reserve, to the guidance and direction of the *Chief of the Hermitage.*" "The Head of the Party having thrown aside Mr. Van Buren," the paper explained, "the followers abandon him, and by way of making atonement for having persevered in striving for his nomination so long, and of manifesting due submission, they select the person who equalled the cast-off favorite in unscrupulous devotion to the Chief, and, next to him, was the Chief's most cherished partisan and courtier, and who now possesses the additional recommendation to favor of having followed directly in the footsteps while the discarded sycophant had somehow got off the track!"[71]

According to Whigs, "the party," despite its rejection by the electorate in 1840, sought to regain power behind Tennessee's most ambitious demagogue by riding the popularity of the Texas issue. Once back in office, these self-serving politicians intended to renew their attempt to perpetuate their hold on power at the expense of the public welfare and of constitutional government. Notwithstanding their professed concern, Democrats cared little about the national security of the United States or about the people of Texas, Whigs maintained. As the *Republican Banner* asked, if Texas's admission truly were the Democrats' goal, "why discard Mr. TYLER, who has done all he could to bring about immediate annexation?"[72] Instead, "the party" took up this sensitive question merely for the advantages it supposedly would bring them in the presidential canvass:

> The advancement of the personal fortunes of Mr. Polk, and the additional consequence which his immediate followers in this state hope to derive from it, have much more influence with them, than any thoughts about 'the lone star.' With a view to those primary objects of

regard, indeed, they would be glad to make 'Texas' the issue;—that is, they would rejoice to exclude from any consideration in the present contest, the Administration of the Government by Locofocoism for so many years past;—to keep out of view all its corruptions and abuses;—all the usurpations of the Executive, all the base subserviency of his followers;—all its Jacobin principles;—all its pestiferous measures;—all the violations it made upon the Constitution, all the accumulated mischiefs it brought upon the country. Most especially would they desire to divert the attentions of the people from *the share* which JAMES K. POLK bore, (not indeed as a leader, for he never had the capacity or influence to *direct*, but as an unscrupulous agent and instrument[)] in sustaining and giving effect, so far as in him lay, to every one of the long train of ruinous and anti-republican doctrines and acts which, during the ascendancy of Locofocoism, led to so many grevious [*sic*] disorders and disasters.[73]

Whigs thus remained confident that they could carry Tennessee for Clay, despite the popularity of the Texas issue, for the nomination of Polk reinforced their position as the champions of the citizenry's liberty against "partizan politicians." Twice, the state's electorate had rejected Polk when he stood for the governor's office, and Whigs reminded voters that they had opposed the candidate then because, during his one term as governor, "he did nothing to promote the interests of the People of Tennessee"; instead, the *Banner* noted, "he prostituted the influence of his high office to the accomplishment of his own personal, self-seeking, and vainly ambitious objects."[74] Polk's supporters now tried to stimulate "state pride" to secure backing for the candidate, but William Campbell noted that "state pride cannot be excited for Polk,—he is too small, too feeble,—has no decided characteristics whatever—& it is too plain a case that he is to be carried along by the strength of his party & the favor of the hero of New Orleans." State pride might be introduced into a canvass between candidates of similar qualifications, the *Nashville Whig* admitted, but in cases such as the present, when one candidate's claims so heavily outweighed the other's, "it ought to have no influence whatever; the *pride of country,* the *whole country,* should always predominate over the selfish and contracted principles of *pride of State."*[75]

Whigs also tried to turn the Texas issue against their opponents. By seizing upon resolutions calling for "Texas or Disunion," which resolutions had been passed at meetings of Polk supporters in South Carolina and Alabama, they charged that Democrats had allied themselves with Nullifiers and Disunionists. These radicals had remained out of public favor since Andrew Jackson had thwarted their attempt to nullify a federal law within South Carolina, but the Texas issue, Whigs maintained, revived their hopes of gaining power by dissolving the Union of states. Their "grand object," according to Thomas L. Bransford, was "the acquisition of territory with a view to the dissolution of the Union, and the foundation of a Southern confederacy." The *Nashville Whig* explained that this confederacy would come "at the cost of our present Union and with the loss of 'the North Eastern States,' with which, we are insultingly told, we ought to have less sympathy than with Texas!"[76] Democrats promoted annexation to gain the Nullifiers' support in the election, but, by stirring up popular enthusiasm on the issue, they aided these radicals in their ultimate goal of disunion. Polk himself might be among those "ready to subscribe to the doctrine" of the Nullifiers, Whigs suggested; but, in any case, a Democratic mass meeting (scheduled to be held in Nashville) actually, Whigs claimed, would become a party convention designed "to make the DISSOLUTION OF THE UNION an issue with the Annexation Question." That convention's purpose, according to the *Republican Banner*, would be to give effect "to the declaration that the issue before the South should be 'Texas or Disunion.'"[77]

Tennessee's Whigs pledged their party to the integrity of the Union, with or without Texas, and called upon the electorate to repudiate their opponents' bargaining with disunionists by casting their ballots for Clay. "We are against disunion, let the proposition come from what quarter it may—whether from the north or the south, the east or the west," the *Nashville Whig* proclaimed; "we can conceive no motive that can ever justify the discussion." Reminding the electorate of the state's united stand against nullification in 1832, the *Banner* assured readers that "such principles can never take roots in the soil of Tennessee, distinguished as this State has always been for loyalty to the Constitution and the Union."[78] Polk enjoyed more support in "the hot beds of Democracy in the South" than he did in his home state, Whigs claimed, and Democrats relied upon the support of these Disunionists to carry them in the election. "[W]ithout Mr. Calhoun and his followers [they] can do nothing in the South," the *Banner* asserted; but in Tennessee, Democrats "dare not avow openly any more than they dare repudiate publicly their association with the Nullifiers and Disunionists." Clay, on the other hand, was renowned for his defense of the Union; he enjoyed widespread support in the North, not because of any alliance with abolitionists, but for the same reason that southern voters could approve the Whig candidate: because he was "the friend of the whole country—a statesman whose views comprehend the true and permanent interest in every quarter of the Union."[79]

Democrats recognized that the charge of "disunion," if not quickly countered, could severely damage their cause. Party leaders worked to dispel any notion that the August 15 mass meeting in any way resembled a sectional convention. "The idea of a Southern Convention or sectional meeting to be held at Nashville or elsewhere *must not for a moment be entertained*," Polk directed from Columbia, and the *Union* called upon Democrats throughout the country to attend the meeting to "prove to the world, that democracy, whether assembled in the North or the South, at New York or Nashville, is still the same in its deep and enduring devotion to the permanency and perpetuity of the Union."[80] Polk's supporters also tried to deflect the Whig charges back upon their opponents. The *Knoxville Argus* reminded voters that the Federalist and Abolitionist Whig John Quincy Adams himself had declared in Congress that he "would go for the abolition of slavery if it DISSOLVED THE UNION, and drenched the whole south in blood." The *Union* meanwhile complained that, according to Whigs, if southerners "dare express a sentiment of freedom, and remonstrate against injustice and oppression—then they are disunionists, nullifiers, and traitors!" Such accusations provided clear evidence, the paper concluded, that "the Whigs are banded with the Northern federalists to make the North everything, and the South nothing—to make the North the master, and the South the slave."[81]

Nevertheless, the center of the Democrats' appeal remained the importance of the immediate annexation of Texas for American security and for the perpetuation of republican government. Whigs, meanwhile, continued to portray a national bank as the election's crucial issue, denouncing the Texas question as a "vile humbug" and, especially in East Tennessee, circulating charges that Polk's grandfather had been a Tory during the American Revolution.[82] Party lines remained firm in the November election, and Whigs carried Tennessee, despite Polk's victory in the national contest and despite the energetic offensive by Tennessee's Democrats. "*The Coons have cheated you out of Tennessee,*" Julius W. Blackwell charged to Polk, but most Democrats claimed the slim margin of defeat as a success for their party. "Under all the circumstances, the result in Tennessee may well be claimed a decided triumph to democracy," the *Union* concluded, noting that the 1844 result "points to a triumph in our next contest in Tennessee which will be decisive and complete."[83] Throughout the state, political observers recognized the result in Tennessee as a virtual draw. Polk's supporters had reduced the Whigs' margin of victory from Jones's 3,800-vote advantage in 1843 to less than 250 votes. Whigs, although stunned by Clay's defeat in the national contest, proclaimed the state result a vindication of the party's principles, because, with Jackson and Polk both residing in Tennessee, "in no State in the Union, have the Whig party had to contend against odds more fearful." Still, Whigs knew that they narrowly had averted defeat against a powerful challenge. "In truth," the *Republican Banner* admitted even before its editor knew how close the result would be, "it is wonderful that, with the weight of the TEXAS QUESTION thrown in since the election of Governor Jones last year, the Whigs have been able to come so near their majority of August 1843."[84]

Clay's loss left Tennessee's Whigs demoralized. Ephraim Foster, with his Senate term scheduled to expire on March 3, 1845, tried to rally the state party by altering its position on annexation. On January 13, 1845, Senator Foster and Representative Milton Brown, a Whig from Jackson, Madison County, introduced into their respective chambers in Congress identical resolutions outlining a plan for Texas's annexation. The senator then arranged for his nomination as the party's candidate for Tennessee's governor, and in the canvass, while continuing the call for a national bank, Foster maintained that the Whigs always had favored annexation and only opposed Tyler's plan to carry the measure into effect.[85] The Whig leader's offensive failed to revive the party, as several party newspapers condemned Foster's and Brown's resolutions as repudiations of the Whigs' position in the presidential campaign. Moreover, Foster's vote against the final passage of the joint resolution annexing Texas, on the grounds that the plan failed to establish any provision for the institution of slavery in the newly acquired lands, opened him to Democratic charges of inconsistency. Democrats, meanwhile, backed the gubernatorial nomination of Polk's associate, Aaron V. Brown, admonishing voters to "ratify the choice of the Union" and to "turn the scale in favor of the new administration," while party spokesmen reminded the electorate that Democrats had called for annexation from its first appearance as an issue. Instead of a candidate like Foster, who had balked at every opportunity actually to acquire Texas, the *Memphis Appeal* proclaimed, "give us such advocates of annexation as A. V. Brown, Stanton, and others, who have stood up for Texas all the time."[86]

After six years of continuous excitement, Tennessee's electorate had grown weary of politics. While prices and property values remained depressed, the resumption of specie payments by the state's banks in 1842 had stabilized the state's currency and had allayed the sense of crisis that had characterized the contests of the early 1840s.

Also, the defeat of the champion of a national bank left Whigs with little hope that the government again would charter a central financial institution. "The Whigs are not only quiet, but passionless," John Catron noted early in the 1845 canvass. "In the election to come on in Augt. less interest is felt, than I had thought possible." Democratic leaders sensed that a low turnout would aid their cause, and they did little to excite a party animosity that might encourage their opponents to go to the polls. Whig newspapers tried to stimulate action among the party faithful, but with sparse results. At the election's conclusion, a correspondent for the *Nashville Whig* noted that "neither party turned out well, but the Democrats went to the polls better than the Whigs."[87] Foster's totals fell off more than three thousand votes from Clay's tally in 1844, as Brown defeated the former senator; by carrying both chambers in the legislature, Democrats captured a four-seat majority in the next session of Tennessee's General Assembly.

As they had in 1839, Democrats in 1845 proclaimed that they had "redeemed" their state from "Federalist" domination. After that year's passive campaign, many Democratic loyalists expressed their belief that the era of party competition had come to an end. "The war of the conspirators upon republican principles in Tennessee is over," David Craighead assured the new president, while William Hunter told Polk that he hoped "that by the next Presidential election that their [*sic*] will be but one common feeling amongst us all and that will be who shall best serve his country."[88]

These predictions of the twilight of the party system proved premature. In the next state elections Whigs would rebound from their lethargy and regain control of the state government, and party competition would continue along the same lines as it had in the early 1840s. In those past years as in the following ones, Democrats and Whigs battled in the name of "the people" as defenders of republican principles. Whether arguing over the economic depression or the "Immortal Thirteen," the parties justified their positions in terms of their own republicanism, viewed both as pure and as opposed to the apostasy of their adversaries. When Tennessee's Democrats revived their fortunes behind the issue of the immediate annexation of Texas, both parties interpreted the question according to their different understandings of the conflict—as a struggle either for freedom against a Federalist-Abolitionist conspiracy, or against the same coalition of demagogic politicians who had bewitched Andrew Jackson during his presidency.

Still, the emergence of the Texas issue marked the beginning of a change in the environment within which Tennessee's two parties competed. In the early 1840s, the depth of the depression and the demand for relief had placed economic policy issues at the forefront of political debate. The Whigs' offer of a program for recovery had given that party a slim but firm hold on the state; Democrats, meanwhile, presented Texas annexation as a means by which their party could offer a measure of relief. With the economy having stabilized somewhat after the depression had reached its lowest point in 1842, however, economic questions—so crucial to the establishment of the Whig and Democratic identities—had begun, by 1844, to lose their power as campaign issues. Party identification among the mass of voters remained strong, but without the trauma of hard times, politicians had to find new ways to mobilize the faithful and convert the few uncommitted. The popularity of annexation convinced Democrats that in territorial expansion they had found a winning appeal. Whigs, by finally accepting annexation, hoped to neutralize the expansion issue while seeking a cause of their own. The rival parties continued to provide each other with enemies to battle in the crusade for liberty, but once the politics of relief had run its course, it would be difficult for party leaders to rally the ranks without clearly recognizable issues that the latter deemed worth fighting for.

The war with Mexico would provide Whigs with the issue they needed for the revival of their prospects. This war also would bring the issue of slavery's expansion to the forefront of national politics and force Tennessee's parties, for the first time, to address a sectional confrontation between North and South as a major political issue. The debate over annexation highlighted an aspect of Tennessee's political culture that profoundly shaped the parties through this confrontation and for the remainder of the antebellum era. Whigs found the chief antidote to the popularity of annexation in the argument that the move would endanger the Union of states as well as republican liberty. Democrats scrambled to defend themselves against this charge by assuring voters that, instead, annexation was necessary for the survival of both of these cherished objects. What emerged most clearly in the parties' clash over Texas, then, was the importance of each party's demonstrating its commitment to the integrity of the Union. Although Andrew Jackson died in June 1845, party battles over expansion and sectional conflict showed that his legacy lived on in Tennessee politics. So strongly had that hero's denunciation of nullification in 1832 associated extreme measures in defense of southern interests with "disunion" that, more than a decade later, Whig and Democratic politicians still found the charge a potent political weapon. Once the controversy over Texas had displayed its power, the argument as to which party best defended liberty and Union would remain a prominent component of Tennessee politics, until voters believed themselves forced to choose between the two values.

SIX

The Politics of Slavery: Abolitionists, Nullifiers, and Compromise
1846–1851

In the late 1840s, the hard times that had provided the focus for political conflict in Tennessee since 1837 finally gave way to economic recovery. The resumption of specie payments by the state's banks in 1842 once again provided Tennesseans with a stable circulating medium. Then, beginning late in 1846, crop failures in Europe stimulated the demand for the grains produced by the state's farmers. "The cries of starving Ireland have opened the corncribs of the remotest tributaries of the great 'inland sea' of the West," Abraham Caruthers noted in 1847, as Tennessee's economy entered a period of prosperity that persisted with few setbacks until the Civil War.[1] Corn and wheat prices rose throughout the 1850s, while the value of land and slaves in the state increased 27 and 32 percent, respectively, between 1846 and 1852, before soaring in the final few years before war. "[O]ur country is advancing rapidly in bettering the condition of all classes," Adam Ferguson noted as early as 1846. A year later, William Brownlow confirmed that "the present is a glorious time for the farmer."[2]

Debates over the sources of hard times and over proposals for relief had played a crucial role in the creation of Tennessee's party system. As foreshadowed in the debate over Texas, however, the return of prosperity eased the anxieties aroused by economic policy issues. Without the fear of a crisis stimulating interest, both parties suffered a mild erosion in party unity. Whig and Democratic leaders complained that too many of their politicians appeared willing to deal with their opponents to advance their own or their followers' claims in the distribution of state offices. In the General Assembly, legislators more often than before indicated their intention to sacrifice party concerns to further their Grand Division's interests in the election of United States senators or in receiving state aid for the completion of internal improvement projects.[3] A declining popular zeal for politics displayed itself most forcefully in the absence of the enthusiasm characterizing the parties' competition in the early 1840s. Turnout rates remained high, averaging about 83 percent in the contests between 1847 and 1851, but party leaders observed that politics appeared a less crucial concern to voters than it had in the past.[4]

The declining sense of urgency most severely affected Democrats. James K. Polk's election to the presidency removed from Tennessee the principal leader who had managed to keep the party unified during its misfortunes earlier in the decade. The new president's distribution of patronage did little to promote harmony within the state party. Not only did his appointments to positions outside Tennessee remove from party leadership the experienced and influential managers whose prominence might have mitigated the strains on party unity, but also Polk alienated several influential Democrats—most notably, Andrew Johnson and George W. Jones—by ignoring their recommendations for appointments.[5] Within state government, the new General Assembly's Democratic members, flushed with victory in the aftermath of their triumph in 1845, quickly divided among themselves in their competition to secure state offices for their favorite candidates. In the most significant of these maneuvers, Hopkins L. Turney, a former congressman from Franklin County, lured Whig support in his quest for the vacant United States Senate seat, when he accused Polk of interfering in the election. Polk actually had indicated no preference in the contest, but Turney charged that the president had expressed an opinion in favor of A. O. P. Nicholson; the legislature's Whigs echoed the congressman's criticism of executive "dictation" and joined six Democrats to provide the necessary votes to elect Turney to the Senate.[6]

Despite internal quarrels, Democrats remained confident that their ascendancy would persist. The nation's improving economic fortunes provided one key to Democratic optimism. Party leaders praised, as the source of the nation's prosperity, the Polk administration's repeal of the Whig tariff of 1842 and its support for the "free-trade" tariff of 1846.[7] Likewise, Democrats maintained, the administration's settlement of the dispute with Great Britain over the occupation of the Oregon territory, by dividing the territory at 49° latitude, marked another Democratic success. The state party had joined the national party in calling for the United States to assert its claim to all of Oregon through 54°40' latitude, but the Whig Senate's refusal to pass stern resolutions notifying Britain of the American intention to occupy that region, the *Nashville Union* explained, "rendered it impossible for the President to maintain our title successfully beyond the 49th parallel." Under these circumstances, Democrats argued, the president's firm stand against Britain had achieved the best result possible.[8]

The Mexican War became the leading political topic in Tennessee after citizens learned in May 1846 of the clash between American and Mexican troops in the Southwest. On this issue, Democrats considered their position particularly strong. Thousands of the state's citizens rushed to volunteer for military service when President Polk announced that "American blood" had been "shed on American soil" in a region that Democrats claimed was part of the recently annexed state of Texas. Party spokesmen immediately pronounced the war a patriotic cause necessary for the vindication of offended American honor. According to Democrats, the Mexican army had provoked the conflict when it attacked the American force defending the nation's southwestern border; it was "now the duty of our government to inflict upon Mexico the chastisement she has so richly deserved."[9] Furthermore, Democrats explained, aside from administering justice to the aggressor, the war offered another opportunity to "extend the area of freedom," for the northern half of Mexico would provide an adequate indemnity for that nation's responsibility for inaugurating the conflict. Party leaders denied that the United States had engaged in a war of conquest. Nevertheless, as the American army of invasion moved deeper into Mexico, the *Nashville Union* demanded that the nation occupy the California and New Mexico territories for "the same reasons [that] operated in the acquisition of Texas, which were strengthened by the well known intrigues of Great Britain." The cession of these territories, the paper added, would "extend the blessings of comfortable subsistence, of the largest liberty of speech and of action, and all the advantages of good government, to a greatly increased number of the human family."[10]

By linking the war to the prospect of territorial expansion, and by equating the administration's policies in conducting the military campaign with American patriotism, Democrats expected popular support for the war to translate into success for their party at the polls. When Whigs questioned the administration's explanation of the source of the conflict, Democrats maintained that their opponents' treason provided conclusive evidence that Whiggery embodied Federalism.[11] To the Democrats' dismay, this strategy failed to rally new voters to their cause. The Whigs' rush to support the war effort negated the

Democratic charge that they gave "aid and comfort" to the nation's enemies. Whigs as well as Democrats hurried to volunteer for service when news of the conflict reached the state, while Whig papers proclaimed their party's willingness to exert its energy to hasten an American victory. "We do not mean to stop now to enquire fully whether the administration has performed its duty in the circumstances in which we have been placed with Mexico," the *Republican Banner* assured readers; "Under these circumstances the United States MUST FIGHT HER." In the current crisis, the *Banner* explained, Whigs were "even willing to forget that JAMES K. POLK is President, and to stand by him as their Chief Magistrate . . . when war is raging upon their borders."[12]

Whigs, in fact, reaped the political benefits from the war that the Democrats had expected. From the war's commencement, Whigs reminded citizens that their party had predicted the conflict in the event of the annexation of Texas. While Whigs continued to call for a vigorous prosecution of the invasion of Mexico, at the same time they concluded that responsibility for the war rested solely on the shoulders of President Polk. The Democratic executive, Whigs argued, had ordered the American army into "a war-like position" in a territory claimed by both nations. This belligerent move represented an attempt "to bully the authorities of Mexico into a cession of California, the most valuable part of the Republic[,] to the United States," an event by which Polk expected to win for himself "unfading laurels." When Mexicans chose "to fight rather than be robbed of their land and home," Polk instead found that he had plunged the nation into a war of conquest.[13] The war had been "begun without any definite cause, justified on very questionable grounds, and prosecuted without any apparent decision or concert," a Whig meeting in Stewart County contended, and throughout the war Whigs perceived that in Tennessee the "universal sentiment" was "one of disgust for Polk, as a weak ambitious demagogue."[14]

According to Whigs, "the President's war" revealed once again that the country faced the danger of a Democratic executive seeking to expand his power in order to subvert republican government and promote the interests of "party" politicians. The president's responsibility in the origin and conduct of the war, Whigs charged, provided overwhelming evidence that, "by the aid of the power and patronage of office in his gift, he is more formidable than the head of the British monarchy." Whigs particularly condemned the president's military appointments; not only did Polk appoint Democrats almost exclusively to positions of command, but also he had taken over the authority previously reserved to army and volunteer companies to select "every officer in the army, who is now in command, from the General-in-Chief, down to the corporal, almost."[15] Moreover, by erecting civil governments—without the consent of the people—in Mexican territories occupied by the American armies, and by requiring inhabitants to swear their allegiance to the United States, Polk had "exercised absolute, and in this republic unheard of power—not delegated to him by the constitution." Whigs thus distinguished their support for the military effort from their condemnation of an administration that not only had entangled the country in an unnecessary war, but also had threatened to extend executive power to limits unprecedented in the history of the American republic. "[U]nless this expansion of Executive power is rebuked," the *Memphis Enquirer* warned, the American government would become "the worst of all despotisms—a REPRESENTATIVE DESPOTISM."[16]

As a contrast to Polk's "tyranny," in the spring of 1847, Whigs began to advocate the claims of war hero Zachary Taylor as Polk's successor in the presidency. Taylor commanded the army that Polk had ordered into the disputed territory, and he had guided his troops to several military victories since the initial clash. Since a great deal of the general's popularity emanated from his success on the battlefield, Whig approval of his presidential prospects affirmed the party's support of the war effort. At the same time, Whigs portrayed the general as a patriotic statesman who would "administer the government upon high and elevated principles—above party intrigues and party ends." Unlike the "experiments upon the prosperity of the country for the benefit of heathen demagogues" that had characterized Locofoco administrations, a Taylor presidency would "regard constitutional restrictions by administering the government as it was administered by the Father of his Country." Taylor's Allison letter, issued in April 1848, listed restriction of the veto power and respect for the people's will, "as expressed through their representatives in Congress," among the candidate's fundamental political principles. According to Whigs, Taylor's election would symbolize "the rescue of the Government from the grasp of Demagogues and Spoilers," for, with the general in office, the republic would be guided by "an independent chief magistrate" who would return the government to "its original principles" and permit "the will of the people, instead of the will of the President, [to] prevail in the councils of the nation."[17]

By advocating the pure republican Taylor as their candidate, Whigs shifted the state party's emphasis away from economic policy issues and back to the promotion of the "simple, honest, old-fashioned republicanism of Thomas Jefferson," upon which the party had coalesced in the late 1830s. The contrast between Polk's "tyranny" and Taylor's "statesmanship" gave the Whigs a strong issue with which to recover from the demoralization prevalent in its ranks after Henry Clay's loss in 1844.[18] Advocacy of Taylor's candidacy also signified the return of John Bell to the forefront of Tennessee's Whig party. Ephraim H. Foster's vacillations on the Texas issue and his unsuccessful canvass for governor in 1845 had weakened his position as the state's most prominent Whig. In his public refusal to run for governor again in 1847, he further damaged his standing by referring to "the destructive rivalries" within his own party "by which I was soon unfortunately surrounded" as a cause of his previous defeat.[19] Bell, meanwhile, early established himself as one of the state's most forceful advocates of Taylor's presidential claims. The party's gubernatorial nominee, Pulaski's Neill S. Brown, followed Bell's lead in the 1847 election by attaching his own candidacy to Taylor's stand for the presidency. The results of the state elections revealed the strength of the general's appeal. In a contest that centered on Polk's responsibility for the war and upon Taylor's claims to the presidency, Whig candidate Brown defeated incumbent Aaron V. Brown by about one thousand votes.[20]

Along with their gubernatorial victory, Whigs regained control of the state government in 1847, as the party won a majority of fifty-two to forty-eight in the General Assembly. Bell himself held one of the seats, as one of Davidson County's members in the House of Representatives, and from this seat Bell maneuvered for support, while East and West Tennessee Whigs deadlocked for forty-eight ballots in an election for United States senator. On the forty-ninth ballot, Bell emerged as the party's compromise candidate, and Whigs sent him to the Senate as Spencer Jarnigan's successor.[21] With Bell back in Washington, the Whig majority completed its business by passing resolutions nominating Taylor for the presidency. Though the party's "Old Clay Guard," led principally by former Governor James C. Jones, tried to rally support in the spring of 1848 for another nomination for the Kentucky statesman, Tennessee's Whig party stood virtually united behind the general's candidacy. The movement for Clay did compel the party to send a delegation to the Whig national convention. Two strong Taylor newspapers, the *Nashville Whig* and the *Memphis Eagle,* had considered a convention "wholly unnecessary," as they preferred their candidate's nomination to come from "the people themselves, in their own honest primary assemblies." Nevertheless, Taylor supporters dominated Tennessee's delegation to the convention, as the state cast a unanimous vote for the general.[22] With their candidate receiving the national party's endorsement, Bell and his ally, Representative Meredith P. Gentry, maintained the most influential positions as leaders of Tennessee's Whig party, and when the general entered the White House, his two allies in Tennessee controlled the new president's appointments to federal offices in the state.[23]

From the earliest mention of the possibility of a Taylor candidacy, Democrats realized its potential damage to their cause. Party leaders recognized the Whig roots of the movement, even though Taylor's backers promoted him as a "no-party" candidate, but the general's popularity compelled them to admit the possibility of their supporting his candidacy. Democratic editors, Daniel Graham told Polk, "to prevent the *Stampede* from overwhelming them, have many of them joined the chase" for Taylor's claims. During his campaign for reelection, Governor Aaron V. Brown found it necessary to state his willingness to endorse the general for the presidency, "*provided* he could be run as a great national candidate, and not identified with either party."[24] Still, the Whig triumph in the state elections stunned Democrats and indicated the momentum that their opponents had gained by identifying their party with Taylor's prospects. Party leaders publicly attributed the result to their own overconfidence and their failure to establish a state central committee to direct the campaign, but Alfred Balch informed Polk that "the annunciation of Taylor as a candidate for the Presidency was one of the chief causes of our late defeat."[25]

Even as they professed a willingness to support Taylor as a "great national candidate," Democrats derided Whigs for "trying to hide beneath the shadow of Gen. Taylor's fame." Their opponents' "real purpose" in promoting the general's claims revealed that the democracy's long-standing enemies were still at work, for the party's old Federal opponents now attempted to ride the general's fame back into power. "The present Taylor party is the successor and representative of the old federal party," the *Union* proclaimed, while the *Clarksville Jeffersonian* explained that "if they should ever by accident obtain the power in this country we should witness the resurrection of that old exploded humbug, the National Bank, as well as every other of their aristocratical and anti-democratic principles."[26]

With the parties' offering divergent explanations for Taylor's candidacy, the presidential election of 1848 in Tennessee presented a continuation of the conflict between "Federalists" and "Spoilsmen." Despite their early professions for Taylor, Democrats always expressed their intention to back their national party convention's nominee. Most doubted that the incumbent Polk would be that nominee. Though the president had promised at the outset of his administration to serve only one term, a handful of backers in Washington promoted a movement to draft him for a second nomination. In Tennessee's party, "a majority which was secretly dissatisfied with the dispensation of the patronage here," again led by A. O. P. Nicholson and Andrew Johnson, worked instead to commit the state behind Lewis Cass's claims for the nomination. The state convention declined to express a preference for any candidate, but Cass's supporters won a majority of seats in the delegation to the national convention. When that body nominated the Michigan senator, Democrats united behind "Lewis Cass and our declared principles, against Zachary Taylor and no principles." Throughout the campaign, Democrats defended Polk's administration as the source of the nation's newfound prosperity and justified the Mexican War as a vindication of national honor, but at the heart of the party's appeal remained its stand for the voters' liberty against the Federal Whigs' ambitious scheming in their attempt to return to power.[27]

Democratic unity behind the colorless Cass could do little to diminish popular sentiment in favor of Taylor. Whigs derided their opponents' candidate as himself a former Federalist and as a demagogic politician who was "preparing himself to act the President of a *party*, if elected." Taylor, on the other hand, stood upon the Whigs' core principles when he affirmed the need to restrict the use of the veto power and the president's duty to execute "the will of the people" rather than the will of a "party." Throughout the campaign, Whigs devoted less attention to criticizing Democratic principles than to promoting Taylor's position as the candidate of "the people."[28] Because of Taylor's refusal to issue a direct statement promising a national bank and protective tariff, a few prominent Whigs, including William G. Brownlow and Knoxville's Joseph Williams, refused to vote for the general. Their abstentions had little effect upon the state party's enthusiasm. Taylor easily carried Tennessee by over six thousand votes on his way to winning the national election.[29]

The institution of slavery played a more prominent role in the 1848 presidential election than it had in previous contests in Tennessee. Spokesmen for both parties, though more often Democrats, ritually charged that their competitors maintained covert ties with the northern abolitionists who sought to destabilize slavery in the southern states. At the same time, party leaders condemned their rivals for irresponsibly dragging the potentially explosive issue into the political arena.[30] Warnings about an Abolitionist alliance with a party were used most prominently by Democrats during the 1840 presidential campaign—in which the Whig candidate soundly defeated a Democratic incumbent. Party leaders, it seems, most often turned to the slavery issue in desperation, when facing certain defeat. Concern for slavery's protection received more attention in the Democrats' demand for Texas in 1844, but warnings of a British-Abolitionist conspiracy virtually disappeared once annexation had been secured. Aside from James K. Polk's allegations of Whig-Abolitionist ties in his campaigns for governor, slavery received virtually no mention in Tennessee's state elections before 1849. Likewise, when Pennsylvania Congressman David Wilmot proposed in the House of Representatives to amend a war appropriations bill with a provision to exclude slavery from any territory acquired from Mexico as a result of the war, the event received little notice in Tennessee. Although Wilmot first offered his proviso in August 1846, Nashville and Memphis newspapers made no comment on the proposal until early 1847. In that year's summer canvass, candidates largely ignored the proviso.[31]

The Senate's ratification of the Treaty of Guadalupe-Hidalgo in February 1848 not only ended the war with Mexico, but also brought the Wilmot Proviso to the forefront of political discussion. In that treaty, Mexico ceded California and the New Mexico territory to the United States, with no provision concerning slavery's status in those regions. With the responsibility for organizing territorial governments in the new lands now devolving upon Congress, the Wilmot Proviso no longer appeared "a mere abstraction without any view to its immediate practical application"; now it stood as a possible measure of policy to be established in the new territories—a policy that seemed to endanger the right of Tennessee's slaveholders (and its nonslaveholders who dreamed of acquiring slaves as they improved their standard of living) to reside in "a territory won by common valor, and paid for out of the common treasury of the nation."[32]

The attempt to prevent slavery's expansion transformed political debate on the institution from vague warnings of a conspiracy to eradicate slavery into an actual threat to political rights associated with slavery's existence. On the one hand, the exclusion of slavery from the newly acquired territories seemed insulting to southern citizens. First, by denying slaveholders any share in the new land, Congress would "deprive the South of the rights promised by the guarantees of the constitution." Second, the exclusion of a southern institution would mark southerners as inferior citizens in the republic, as it would place the southern states "in a position of subordinate dependencies instead of their true position of equal and co-ordinate sovereignties in one great national compact." "The determination to have no more slave States," the Memphis Whig Robertson Topp wrote, "is in plain English saying to the slave States—we feel degraded with our present connection—we will have no more."[33] Few could doubt, moreover, that abolitionists would intensify their efforts—now with national sanction—if southerners failed to resist prohibition of slavery's expansion.

With the territorial issue now before the country, Democratic charges that their opponents had "sold the South for the promise of Massachusetts abolitionists to vote for their candidate for President" took on greater significance in 1848 than they had in previous elections. The Whig vice-presidential candidate, Millard Fillmore, who openly had voiced antislavery sentiments in 1838, symbolized the alliance between Federalism and Abolitionism, Democrats maintained. The Whig presidential nominee, however, was equally unacceptable to southerners. General Taylor's vow to restrain his use of the veto power, they explained, removed the South's principal defense against the Wilmot Proviso or any other act of Congress that infringed upon southern rights. Party spokesmen pointed to the northern Whigs' interpretation of Taylor's position on the veto as proof that he would not oppose the Wilmot Proviso if it passed Congress. Despite the candidate's southern roots, Taylor revealed clearly in a letter to a northern newspaper, the *Cincinnati Signal*, that he himself harbored antislavery sentiments. Southern Whig support for Taylor thus constituted merely one more example of ambitious politicians betraying their constituents' interests. "Anxious to gain all factions, willing, at the risk of infringing upon the Constitution, to obtain the aid of northern fanatics, aye, perilling their very institutions," the Democratic State Central Committee warned, "the southern whigs have calmly submitted to allow the canvass to commence without any understanding either on the part of their candidates, or the Northern wing of whiggery, upon this vital question."[34]

While attacking Whig sincerity in defending slavery, Democrats portrayed themselves as the party loyal to southern rights, both within the Union and in the new territories. Their candidate, Lewis Cass, they noted, had promised to veto the Wilmot Proviso if it passed in Congress. In a widely published letter to his friend A. O. P. Nicholson, the Democratic nominee proposed to determine slavery's status in the Mexican cession by adhering to "the cardinal principle of democracy, to wit, the leaving of the whole subject of slavery to the States in which it exists, and to the people of the territories after they have organized themselves into states." This doctrine of "nonintervention" by the federal government, or "popular sovereignty," to Democrats represented "the doctrine of the Constitution of the United States." Also, nonintervention offered the prospect of preserving southern rights in the new region, while providing a settlement to northern and southern claims to the area, in accord with fundamental beliefs that "the people of the Territories and States have the capacity to govern themselves" and that "the Union itself will best be preserved by a cautious abstinence by the general government from all exercise of despotic power." Individual northern Democrats personally might dislike slavery, party spokesmen admitted, but the vast majority of the northern wing of the party stood behind Cass in its determination to respect the compromises on slavery affirmed in the federal Constitution. "Remember, citizen-voter of the South," the *Nashville Union* admonished, "the No[r]thern Democracy is with you upon the free soil question, however much they may be opposed to slavery in the abstract—while every northern whig, without a single exception, is against you."³⁵

Democrats devoted increasing attention to slavery as the election approached. Whigs, though, managed to deflect their opponents' accusations by casting doubt on the Democrats' own credibility in the defense of southern rights. Wilmot himself, Whigs noted, was a Democrat, and the Democratic members of Tennessee's congressional delegation had approved the principle of the proviso when they voted in favor of the bill creating the Oregon territory, a bill that included an express prohibition of slavery in that region.³⁶ Moreover, the presidential nomination of the Democrats' former standard-bearer, Martin Van Buren, by the explicitly antislavery Free Soil Party, showed the danger of trusting another "northern man with southern principles." Lewis Cass might assert his fidelity to southern interests, but Whigs noted that the Democratic nominee hailed from "the far Northwest, in the very hotbed of Abolitionism itself"; accordingly, they proclaimed, prior to his nomination, Cass had expressed his approval of the Wilmot Proviso. Whatever his professions now, the *Republican Banner* concluded, "he is too late a convert to be trusted."³⁷

Whigs insisted that they alone stood as the true friends of southern rights. According to Whigs, Democrats revealed their infidelity to their section in their support for Polk's despotic war of conquest, for that war had agitated the question of slavery's extension in the first place. Party spokesmen reminded voters that the Whigs had condemned Polk's war and had opposed the acquisition of new territory, primarily because expansion would involve "the revival of this slavery question—a question of so much moment, as to swallow up all others."[38] Now that the issue had been provoked, Whigs asserted, only their own party's candidates could provide the leadership necessary to guide the country to a peaceful solution. Whatever that solution might be, southern voters could trust Taylor to insure that it would respect their rights. Whigs dismissed as "perfectly ridiculous" Democratic charges that Taylor would approve the Wilmot Proviso, claiming that their opponents misrepresented his position in the *Signal* letter. The candidate's position as the owner of the large number of slaves who worked on his plantation in Louisiana, in fact, guaranteed that the general would approve a solution to the territorial question only if it preserved southern interests. Taylor, then, stood before the nation as "the only candidate upon whom the South can rely." The Whig candidate not only was "a Southern man in principle," but also he was the only aspirant who would conduct himself in office "with enlarged patriotism enough to look to the interest of the whole country."[39]

Assurances of Taylor's affiliations with the South satisfied Whigs, and the prominent role of the slavery issue in the election had little effect in altering party lines in Tennessee. Elsewhere in the South, several politicians viewed Taylor's election, along with several concurrent proposals from northern members of Congress to act against slavery, as the portentous opening of a renewed assault upon southern rights. Led by South Carolina's Senator John C. Calhoun, these politicians called for a meeting of all southern members of Congress in December 1848 to present a unified sectional front against any congressional attempt either to prevent slavery's extension into the territories or to restrict the institution in the southern states. Only 48 of the 121 southern members of Congress signed the final version of the "Address of the Southern Delegates in Congress to their Constituents," and most of those who did approve it were Democrats from Lower South states; few southern Whigs displayed much interest in what they considered a Democratic maneuver to undermine the new Whig administration even before the inauguration of the party's victorious candidate. Despite the meager support for their efforts, Calhoun and his backers nevertheless issued the "Address" as a call for southerners to "be united among yourselves, on this great and vital question."[40]

Only two Tennesseans in Congress, Senator Hopkins L. Turney and Memphis Representative Frederick P. Stanton, signed Calhoun's "Address." Most Whig and Democratic newspapers in the state offered only an uninterested response to the call for united southern action.[41] A portion of the state's Democratic party, however, led by former Governor Aaron V. Brown, followed Calhoun's lead and sought to bring

"Slave Auction: Slaves Driven to Market." Abbey Aldrich Rockefeller Folk Art Center, Colonial Williamsburg Foundation, Williamsburg, Virginia. Reproduced courtesy Tennessee State Library and Archives.

the plea for southern unity to the forefront of Tennessee politics. As governor, Brown had assumed the mantle of party leadership after Polk's election to the presidency. After losing in his stand for reelection in 1847, Governor Brown vowed to avenge his defeat. Following Zachary Taylor's relatively easy victory in Tennessee, Calhoun's call for an aggressive stand upon slavery probably appeared to Brown the most promising avenue for the Democratic party's return to power. A large slaveholder himself, Brown as a congressman always had been partial to Calhoun's strong southern-rights position, even when most Tennessee Democrats had avoided too close a connection with the leader of South Carolina's Nullifiers. The intensity of discussions of slavery in West Tennessee during the 1848 campaign suggested that an appeal based upon defense of the institution might enjoy a natural constituency in the Grand Division with the heaviest slave population.[42] With the public uninspired by the old economic issues, and with Taylor's election showing that the Whigs had capitalized upon the political benefits to be derived from the war, the question of slavery's extension into the territories must have seemed to Brown and his associates their party's strongest issue.

Encouraged by Brown and driven by E. G. Eastman and Henry Van Pelt—editors, respectively, of the *Nashville Union* and the *Memphis Appeal*—Democrats, by the opening of the 1849 canvass, had placed the defense of southern rights at the center of the party's creed. While the *Union* and the *Appeal* warned voters of the imminent threat to southern liberty, party leaders resolved the claims of rival aspirants for the gubernatorial nomination by settling upon William Trousdale of Gallatin, Sumner County. Trousdale had distinguished himself in military service in the War of 1812 and the Seminole War, as well as in the recent conflict with Mexico; and Democrats expected the "Veteran of Three Wars" to capture some of the military euphoria that had aided the Whigs in Taylor's election.[43] Yet the state Democratic convention signaled that the defense of southern rights would provide the foundation of Trousdale's campaign. After nominating their candidate, the convention approved a platform that included a resolution declaring that, if the Wilmot Proviso should pass Congress, Tennessee's Democrats would resist its enforcement, "by the adoption, at all hazards and to the last extremity[,] of such measures as will vindicate our constitutional rights."[44]

Behind Trousdale, Democrats warned the electorate of the peril presented by the unresolved problem of slavery's status in the territories. The responsibility for agitating the dispute over slavery's extension, Democrats maintained, rested upon the intrigues of northern abolitionists, for these perpetual allies of the Federal Whigs sought to deny southerners their fundamental rights by prohibiting them from taking slaves into lands acquired by a national military effort. The Wilmot Proviso, Trousdale explained, represented only the first in "a system of measures which must terminate, if persisted in, in the entire abolition of slavery in the United States." Forced abolition would result in far more devastating consequences than the mere deprivation of citizens' property rights. While a few of the abolitionists "honestly and conscientiously oppose slavery, because they regard it as a great moral evil," the Abolitionist movement itself worked to achieve the ends of northern manufacturing capitalists, who viewed slavery as the cause both of high prices of cotton and high wages of white laborers in the South. The abolition of slavery would reduce the level of wages in the South to that of northern wages, giving capitalists the control over the nation's labor that they desired. At the same time, the decline of southern wages would bring about "the other grand desideratum," the reduction in the price of cotton, their chief raw material. "They calculate, therefore," the *Union* concluded, "to secure the same results by the abolition of slavery, which they enjoyed under the system of protection and National Bank."[45]

The question of slavery's extension, according to Democrats, ultimately involved the future of southern society within the American republic. Aside from "the horrible consequences of having to turn the slaves loose amongst us," abolition promised to degrade the standard of living of all southern citizens, slaveholders or nonslaveholders, merely to promote the interests of northern manufacturers. Moreover, the abolitionists' scheme threatened to abrogate southerners' republican freedom; the plan to compel the eradication of slavery would remove from the prerogative of the citizenry the right to determine the institution's status within their home states and place that prerogative in the hands of the northern aristocrats.[46] As Eastman explained in the *Union*, in the Democratic party's stand against abolitionist aggression, the party opposed the long-standing enemies to the voters' freedom:

> Those peculiar friends of the colored man were blind to his oppression, so long as they were permitted to get labor and raw material at their own prices. . . . But so soon as the National Bank was prostrated and protective duties were abolished, and new territory was added to the Union, they were moved with a holy horror for slavery, and commenced agitating the necessity of its abolition. As earnest and zealous as they appear to be in their denunciations of slavery, we have not a doubt but that they would readily agree to cease the agitation of the subject, and permit slavery to go to New Mexico and California, if the

South would consent to the restoration of the protective policy, and especially if along with that policy they could have another National Bank. If we would agree to bow our necks to their yoke, and submit to their exactions as in times past, they would cheerfully consent to let us make as much cotton as possible with our slaves.—But as we refuse to be slaves to northern capitalists, they seek to punish us by rendering the African slaves useless to us. They would again drive us into vassalage to them, as an escape from the evils which they threaten to bring on us by the abolition of slavery.[47]

The abolitionists had gained political influence because office-seeking politicians, particularly northern Whigs, had promised to disregard the Constitution's compromises on slavery in order to gain the fanatics' endorsement. Southern Whigs had contributed to the antislavery plot, Democrats charged, for they had given northern voters the impression that southerners themselves were divided on the necessity to defend the institution. Most recently, southern backing for Zachary Taylor, "with a full knowledge that he was sustained in the free States upon the belief that he was committed to their views on the slavery question," seemed to indicate a willingness among southern voters to tolerate the Wilmot Proviso.[48] Northern Democrats, in their support for Cass, had reaffirmed their willingness to leave slavery in southern hands, but with the Abolitionist candidate gaining strong support in the South, as the *Union* had asked during that contest, "How can the south long expect the north to stand by her when her own citizens betray her?"[49]

Democrats called for the unity of all southerners in defense of their rights, as the only solution to the present crisis facing the region. "A union of all parties at the South can alone save the rights of the South," the *Union* declared, "and on the safety of those rights the Union depends." Tennessee's party, in its recent convention, had stated its conviction that Congress had "no control directly or indirectly, mediately or immediately, over the institution of slavery," and it had resolved to defend southern rights "at all hazards and to the last extremity" if Congress passed the Wilmot Proviso. Trousdale's election, and a Democratic majority in the General Assembly, would send the clear warning to the North that Tennessee's citizens "never will consent to submit to the dictation and aggressions of northern abolitionism[,] come in what form it may." With this popular mandate, the Democratic majority in Tennessee could work in concert with other slave states to adopt measures that would present to the North a united front on the slavery issue. Northern Democrats, convinced that the South stood as one in defense of the institution, would once more adhere to the compromises of the Constitution. If northern Whigs and their southern allies did manage somehow to pass the Wilmot Proviso into law, with the Democratic party in power, Tennessee would find itself ready to take action with the rest of the South to counter the assault on southern liberty. "We have it in our power to arrest the encroachments on our rights, and to save our glorious Union," Nashville's *Union* concluded. "We have but to stand together, in one solid column, resolved with firmness, but yet with moderation, to act with one mind and one purpose."[50]

While calling for resistance, Democrats denied that they in any way sought to promote a dissolution of the Union of states. As for resistance to the "last extremity," the *Union* and the *Appeal* proposed that southern merchants agree to trade only with that region's ports. Should the South adopt this policy of "commercial nonintercourse," the *Union* maintained, "the slavery question would be yielded by northern fanatics in less than one month, and we should forever afterwards enjoy uninterrupted peace upon this question."[51] The final decision on any measure of resistance would result from the common decision of all of the slave states, and Democrats assured voters that any policy the South approved would ensure southern rights within the present Union. Still, party spokesmen warned the electorate that disunion would occur if southerners failed to stand now against northern aggression. "The Union is dissolved when the Constitution is broken, and the rights of a minority trampled upon," Eastman declared. "We will resist the threatened violation. And should the Constitution be broken and the Union thereby dissolved, the South will be free from responsibility in the matter." Southern citizens would have little interest in preserving a federal compact that failed to guarantee their fundamental rights, but the abolitionists' scheming promised to transform the Constitution into such a worthless agreement. It became the duty of all southern citizens to preserve the integrity of the Union by resisting the attempted dictation of the northern oppressors; should that resistance fail, southerners would have no alternative but to take action according to "THE LAW OF SELF-PRESERVATION."[52]

The campaign for southern unity covered dissension within the Democratic party itself. Several Democrats indicated their concern that the Brown wing's emphasis upon the slavery issue might work against the party. The state convention voted down an "incendiary" resolution, proposed by Levin H. Coe of Memphis, calling for commercial nonintercourse as Democratic policy, but that body also defeated Andrew Ewing's motion to strike the "last extremity" resolution from the party platform after Coe's defense of the necessity of the assertion. Throughout the election, important Democratic newspapers like the *Clarksville Jeffersonian* and the *Nashville American*, while endorsing Trousdale's position on the slavery question, portrayed the defense of southern rights as only a portion of the Democratic creed, rather than treating it as the all-consuming issue, as the *Union* and the *Appeal* did.[53] Cave Johnson and James K. Polk, before the retired president's death on June 15, confided to each other their belief that the party relied too heavily on the Wilmot Proviso issue, while Representative Andrew Johnson encouraged E. G. Eastman to balance the party's "high ground upon the slavery question" with its support for more populist issues, such as the popular election of judges and a homestead law.[54] Despite these doubts, the Southern Rights advocates' forceful presentation of the slavery issue permitted them to seize the initiative within the party, and Democrats united behind Trousdale's determination to defend southern liberty.

As they nominated the incumbent, Neill S. Brown, for another term as governor, Whigs welcomed the Democrats' insistence on centering the canvass on the slavery issue. The 1848 presidential election had encouraged Whigs to believe that their party enjoyed an advantage on the territorial question. In the 1849 campaign, party spokesmen relied upon the same arguments that they had articulated in the previous year's contest. First, southern rights would face no threat, had not Polk and the Democrats demagogically determined to "extend the area of freedom" before providing for slavery's status in the Mexican cession. Second, northern Democrats provided the main force behind the Free Soil movement. And third, President Polk had "surrendered the question of the constitutionality of the Wilmot Proviso" by signing into law the bill establishing the Oregon territory.[55] Since Democrats had brought about the current predicament facing the South, Whigs charged, their present claim to stand as the sole defenders of southern rights displayed "the very madness of party." It was clear to Whigs that Democrats had latched onto the slavery issue merely to stir up an excitement upon which they could return to power. "[T]he action of that party in all this has, and must[,] result most disastrously for the South, . . ." the *Republican Banner* concluded, "and now, after having led them to the brink of this pitfall, they call upon the people, South, to trust their lead, further to extricate them from their dangerous position."[56]

Once the campaign opened, Whigs devoted most of their attention to the charge that the Democrats' call for resistance to the "last extremity" promoted an eventual dissolution of the Union. At this time, Whigs claimed to see no particularly dire threat to the South; the Wilmot Proviso had not passed Congress, Whigs reminded voters, and even if it did, they could rely upon "the old Louisiana Planter they have elected" to adopt the proper response to the measure. In any case, the geographical conditions of the Mexican cession left it doubtful whether slavery ever could persist in that territory, as the region was ill-suited for the plantation agriculture necessary to make slavery economically viable.[57] The "last extremity" declaration instead revealed conclusively to Whigs that Tennessee's Democrats had surrendered their fortunes to John C. Calhoun and South Carolina's Nullifiers, for they followed the South Carolinian's lead in attempting to use the slavery issue to achieve the Nullifiers' "vain and hopeless idea" of electing Calhoun, "their desperate leader," to the presidency. These demagogues, Whigs proclaimed, had endeavored to return to prominence in the United States government since their treasonous attempt to nullify law, and they threatened to destroy the republic and form their own government if they failed to gain positions of power. Democrats not only endorsed these schemes by echoing the Nullifiers' hysteria on the dangers presented by the Wilmot Proviso, but also they encouraged the sentiment for disunion among the electorate and presented that prospect as a possible alternative at a time when no unusual danger to southern rights presented itself. "The slavery question, as presented by the democratic party, connects itself with dangers much more terrible than abolitionism," Edmund Dillahunty told George W. Gordon. "No man should ever be tolerated as a public leader who can seriously talk about the dissolution of our union as a *remedy* for existing evils—for evils that exist on paper and [in] the lively imagination of fanatics and heated partisans."[58]

In contrast to the Democrats' "last extremity" declaration, Whigs portrayed themselves as the party pledged to defend the Union from its extremist enemies in the South as well as in the North. Governor Neill S. Brown set the tone for the campaign in his speech accepting the Whig convention's nomination when he declared, as the *Republican Banner* paraphrased, that "he '*was for the Union* AT ALL HAZARDS.' For the South, so long as he could be consistently with the preservation of the Union, but for the Union at all events." Whigs promised to uphold southern rights and to support some sort of arrangement with the North to resolve the current dispute over slavery in the territories, but they refused to consider disunion as an option. Should the Wilmot Proviso pass Congress, Brown observed, citizens could expect President Taylor to veto it. Even if the president failed to issue a veto, the Constitution itself provided a remedy from the oppression of unconstitutional laws. A challenge in the federal courts still could force a review of congressional laws, after all; and Whigs expected the Supreme Court to declare unconstitutional the proviso or any measure that violated southern rights. With this avenue still available to southern citizens, there appeared no necessity in the present controversy to discuss breaking up "this glorious confederacy, built up, and cemented together by the blood of Patriots." If the territorial issue ever did imperil the federal compact, Whigs asserted, they echoed Brown's declaration that he "would not give one foot of ground on Bunker Hill, or Saratoga, or Yorktown, for all the land west of the Rio Grande, though all its hills were studded with gold, and all its valleys tilled with slaves." Despite Trousdale's ravings about the "false" issue of an abolitionist threat, Whigs behind Neill Brown maintained that they presented to voters "the true issue: Disregard fanaticism, Northern and Southern, and submit to law and order."[59]

With slavery's status in the territories as yet undetermined, however, the slavery issue worked against the Whigs. In West Tennessee, a group of Whigs in the Tenth Congressional District—the district with the heaviest concentration of slaves in the state—objected to their party's emphasis on Union at the expense of a united defense of southern rights. Even before the opening of the canvass, Whig meetings in Memphis and in Somerville, Fayette County, passed, "after a hard struggle between the two wings of the party there," a series of resolutions expressing the intention to support no candidate "who is not pledged against all of these aggressions upon Southern rights, and willing to co-operate in any measures of redress that the people of the southern States may seem fit to adopt." After Brown's nomination, the *Memphis Enquirer* expressed its support for the Whig candidate but also announced its intention to "continue our demonstrations in behalf of Southern rights as freely as if we had a whig candidate for Governor who came fully up to our scribe." At the district Whig convention in Somerville, called to select a candidate to challenge Representative Frederick P. Stanton, the so-called "Calhoun Whigs" failed to win the convention's approval of resolutions calling for a strong defense of southern rights, but a few weeks later, these Whigs met together with Southern Rights Democrats at Raleigh, Shelby County, to pass resolutions approving a convention of the southern states, "should a measure so odious, unjust and unconstitutional as the Wilmot Proviso become a law." Finally, six weeks before election day, Robertson Topp, Memphis's most prominent Whig and a leading contender in 1847 for the Senate seat eventually won by John Bell, published in the *Enquirer* a letter condemning northern assaults upon slavery and concluding that "nothing short of a prompt, decided, and united stand, with the South standing up as one man, can resist this abolition avalanche which threatens to overwhelm them [southern citizens], and with them the union."[60]

Brown's professions of devotion to the Union aroused little enthusiasm among these Whigs. The nominee further damaged his standing among voters when he admitted on the stump that, if the Supreme Court ruled in favor of the Wilmot Proviso's constitutionality, "he would have to yield, he would suppose." Democrats immediately seized on this concession and derided Brown as the "submissionist" candidate, and they charged that the Whig nominee also advocated submission should Congress pass a law abolishing slavery in the states where it already existed.[61] With Brown forced to defend his loyalty to the South, Trousdale defeated the Whig incumbent in the August election by about fourteen hundred votes. The Whigs also lost their hold on the General Assembly, as each party won fifty of the legislature's one hundred seats.

Aside from the slavery question, several factors worked against the Whigs. Party leaders warned of "an amount of supineness amongst our friends that *may* & *will* be fatal to our hopes if not obviated"; and, at the election's conclusion, several attributed the result to the usual apathy that weakens a party in power. Also, Brown's popularity in East Tennessee suffered when, in the 1847 General Assembly, he failed to promote a bill to provide the funds necessary to revive work on railroad projects in that Grand Division.[62] Nevertheless, the uncertainty surrounding slavery's future in the territories encouraged Trousdale's strong defense of southern rights, while rendering suspicious a Whig position that easily could be confused with "submission" to northern demands. In Middle Tennessee, the Whig tally fell by more than three thousand votes from their turnout in 1848, and in West Tennessee the party received almost twelve hundred fewer votes than in the previous year. The *Union* denounced the Whigs' excuse of voter apathy for these declines and argued that Whig slaveholders had "condemned the position of Governor Brown on the slavery question"; only "the strength of old party attachments kept them from voting at all." Likewise, Eastman claimed that three of the four Whigs elected to Congress that year approved Trousdale's call for resistance on the slavery question, leaving Meredith P. Gentry as "the only Tennessee representative left to countenance John Bell in his abandonment of the rights of Tennessee slave-holders."[63]

Democrats immediately proclaimed Trousdale's victory a popular mandate in favor of a determined and united southern stand against abolitionist attacks. Over the next two years, though, Tennessee's electorate would reconsider the issues presented to it in 1849. California's application for admission to the Union as a free state compelled politicians throughout the country to search for a settlement that permanently would resolve northern and southern disputes over the future of slavery in the United States. In Tennessee, concern over a national settlement was joined at the center of state politics by the question of whether the state should participate in a convention of southern states—called in October 1849 by a bipartisan convention in Mississippi—to consider a unified southern position on the slavery issue. Tennessee's political leaders knew that the state's response to the proposed convention could influence its result significantly, for the Mississippi call specified that the convention should gather in June 1850 in Tennessee's capital, Nashville.[64]

Prominent newspapers of both Tennessee parties at first expressed approval of the proposed convention, but by late February 1850 the issue had become a "party question."[65] Driven once again by its Southern Rights wing, Democrats boldly advocated Tennessee's participation. According to Democrats, California's application for statehood proved that southern citizens could not rely upon President Taylor to defend their rights. Taylor in fact had precipitated the crisis, they charged, when he sent an agent to California to arrange for the composition of a state constitution that prohibited slavery. By this "rank usurpation of power" and "criminal dereliction of his official duty," the president intended to bring California and New Mexico into the Union as free states, thus attaining an abolitionist goal, without the Whigs' having to face the political consequences of approving the Wilmot Proviso. With a "cordon of free states" surrounding the South about to become a reality, the proposed Nashville Convention provided "the only hope of our salvation," for it offered the prospect of presenting to the North the united defense of southern rights necessary to impel northern Democrats to adhere to the constitutional provisions protecting slavery.[66] "A firm and united stand," the *Jeffersonian* stated when it concluded that Whig opposition had undermined the convention's primary purpose,

> by the people of all the Southern States, in favor of their constitutional rights, with those rights defined and declared by official representatives, in the proposed convention, would have impressed the people of the North with the conviction that we knew our rights

and were determined to maintain them. Northern Demagogues would have trembled before the spectacle of an outraged and insulted people, meeting in convention to devise schemes of mutual protection, and the effect would have been most salutary upon the future legislation of Congress.[67]

Encouraged by their recent victory, Democrats expected the electorate to rally behind the Nashville Convention as the logical sequel to the party's bold stand for southern rights. Several developments in 1850, however, transformed the convention from the Democrats' standard into their most damaging liability. Most significantly, the Congress that convened in December 1849 hesitated to adopt Taylor's plan to create new states out of the Mexican cession. Instead, northern and southern leaders both appeared willing to accept some sort of equitable settlement of the territorial issue.[68] Hope of a sectional agreement was strengthened when Henry Clay introduced into the Senate his plan for a compromise to end the controversy over California statehood, resolve the conflict over slavery's status in the remainder of the territory acquired from Mexico, and permanently remove the question of slavery from national politics. Whig and moderate Democratic newspapers in Tennessee immediately expressed their approval of the proposed adjustment and promised to support "any compromise which will settle the questions at issue *honorably to the South.*" After a Senate committee of thirteen reported a bill containing the provisions of Clay's compromise, popular sentiment in the state for the arrangement appeared overwhelming. "I think the people here without distinction of party are in favour of the compromise," Jacob McGavock wrote from Nashville a few days before the opening of the convention. A few weeks later, William B. Campbell reported from Sparta, White County, that "the Whig party in this State with a large portion of the Democratic party are warm for the Compromise of Mr. Clay['s] committee."[69]

While the prospect of compromise appeared to remove the need for a southern convention, Whigs reiterated their warnings concerning their opponents' association with treason. The Nashville Convention, they charged, marked the first step toward the Nullifiers' ultimate goal of dissolving the Union. A meeting of the southern states might have been beneficial, the *Republican Banner* admitted when explaining the paper's previous approval of the convention, but over the winter of 1850 it had become clear to Whigs that Calhoun and his associates had promoted the movement for the meeting. "[T]hat which might have been the medicine to the body politic in the hands of discreet men," the *Banner* concluded,"is likely to become a deadly potion in the practice of those *avowing their purposes to* DESTROY IT." The convention would become such a "deadly potion" to the Union because "the old Nullifiers," frustrated finally in their efforts to gain prominence in the federal government, would become "the prime workers" at the gathering. Claiming to speak with the authority of "the people" of the South, these designing politicians intended to use the convention to scatter the "seeds of political disaffection" and to broadcast "the disorganizing doctrines promulgated by a portion if not a majority of its members and advocates." Disunion, the *Nashville True Whig* concluded, would be "its certain, inevitable tendency." "Who doubts," the *Memphis Eagle* added,"but that it will be proposed to nominate a sectional candidate, upon sectional issues, for the presidency, or to form a Southern confederacy!" The Nashville Convention, according to Whigs, confirmed their predictions that extremists in both North and South presented a threat to the perpetuation of the Union.[70] As William G. Brownlow explained in his new *Knoxville Whig*, the prospect of a Southern Convention revealed that the agitations of the Nullifiers constituted a more immediate danger than did the antislavery rumblings of a small clique of northern fanatics:

> These *Southern Burrs*, with mischievous industry and criminal pertinacity, have been for years exciting hostile feelings, and fomenting the most deadly strife, between the North and South; and now that they have lashed the waves of the Union into an angry rage, they need but a second *Hartford* Convention at Nashville, to enable them to ride on these waves, into offices of honor and profit! This dangerous agitation, which now menaces our glorious Union, they have kept alive, by applying all the meanes [sic] which unscrupulous minds could suggest. Disappointed ambition, for despicable party purposes, had called this foul convention at Nashville, in the vain hope of being able to uproot the greatest government on earth.[71]

While denouncing Democratic calls for Tennessee's representation at the Convention, Whigs bolstered their image as the "great conservative party of union" by declaring their willingness "to join our fellow-citizens in any action which will aid in exercising a right influence in Washington." Fanaticism "must be put down, trodden down, crushed down, North and South," the *Eagle* proclaimed;"it is the food of demagogues, the incendiary spark of fanatics, the sharpened weapon of madness" that "talks treason to the Union."[72] Party spokesmen reminded citizens that the Constitution provided "redress, *without* destroying the government," in case a northern majority in Congress passed an unconstitutional law that violated southern rights. Nevertheless, Whigs argued, southerners faced no danger from such a law as long as "the conservative spirit" which had "always been the glory of the Union" prevailed over the perturbations of Abolitionists and Nullifiers. As in 1849, Whigs in 1850 refused to "speculate on the value of the Union as it is"; instead, they would trust the prevalent sentiment in favor of compromise to carry through a just and equitable settlement. "There must be men enough in the country of both parties," the *Republican Banner* assured readers, "who have a *national* pride in the magnificent fabric of free government bequeathed to us by the Fathers of the Revolution, to join hands in its preservation."[73]

By spring, Democrats found themselves forced to devote most of their attention to refuting the charge that disunionists sponsored the Nashville Convention. After the aggressive stand the party had taken in defense of southern rights and its energetic endorsement at the original call for the convention, William Cooper explained to J. Knox Walker, Tennessee's Democrats could not "back out from their position at the false and treacherous cry of the Whigs. . . . *That* would irretrievably ruin us in Tennessee for 'years and years,' for, it would be a direct admission that the design of the Convention was disunion." When Cooper wrote this letter, he and other Democratic leaders already recognized the difficult position in which their advocacy of the convention had placed them. The meeting would "prove a failure so far as Tennessee is concerned," Cooper concluded, for he saw "certainly no enthusiasm, and scarcely any interest, felt by the people here for the Convention."[74] Even before the convention opened—and even before Congress had taken direct action on the committee of thirteen's compromise bill—Democrats watched the momentum they had gained from their 1849 victory evaporate because of their association with the unpopular and presumably treasonous southern assembly. While Democrats found it difficult to inspire their followers to attend public meetings in support of the convention, Whigs and moderate Democrats had no trouble arranging bipartisan "union meetings" expressing popular approval of the proposed compromise.[75]

The Democrats' difficulties in arranging a delegation to represent Tennessee reflected lack of popular interest in the convention and created the impression that the party was forcing the meeting on voters despite the public will. In the General Assembly, the Democratic-controlled house of representatives passed a resolution endorsing the convention and authorizing Governor Trousdale to appoint delegates, but the Whig Senate refused to consider the proposal. Instead, the Senate passed its own resolution renouncing the legislators' responsibility to "aid in organizing a southern convention." Unable to gain official sanction for a delegation, Democrats then attempted to arrange bipartisan county meetings to choose representatives.[76] By the first of May, only the Democratic strongholds of Cannon and Lincoln counties had called meetings and appointed delegates successfully. In a Maury County meeting, a sufficient number of Whigs attended to vote down pro-convention resolutions, a vote that forced Democrats to hold a separate meeting in order to approve any choice of delegates. Finally, in May, several counties managed to arouse enough interest to appoint 101 members to the state delegation. These meetings occurred mostly in predominantly Democratic counties in Middle Tennessee and appear largely to have been dominated by members of that party. "We do not believe," the *Eagle* noted, "that at any meeting, in the whole space of West Tennessee, even in the most heavily populated counties, more than forty citizens have participated." Davidson County's Whigs, meanwhile, forced Democrats to hold a rump meeting like the one in Maury County before the host city itself could approve any delegates.[77] Democrats now found themselves associated with an assembly that appeared not only seditious but also unrepresentative. The convention's proponents had taken steps "to *mis*represent the great masses who stand at a distance frowning upon their anti-republican movements," the *Republican Banner* charged. "Their case is to be commisserated, truly: for there is no possible way of patching up their defeat—no way of justifying their broad departure from the first principles of republicanism."[78]

The nine-day session of the Nashville Convention in June did little to improve the Democrats' position. As Whigs had warned and Democrats had feared, radical "Fire-Eaters" from the Lower South played a prominent role in the proceedings. "This Convention has satisfied me, that South Carolina and Georgia are, already, decidedly, and almost unanimously, in favor of a dissolution of this Union, and the formation of a Southern Confederacy," concluded William Cooper, who, with Eastman, served as one of the convention's secretaries. William H. Polk attempted to counter the Fire-Eaters' extremism by proposing a resolution stating the South's willingness to approve the committee of thirteen's compromise bill, "provided it was amended or modified so as to meet the views of our Southern Senators." The convention paid little attention to Polk's motion. Instead, it passed resolutions calling for a division of the Mexican cession and proclaiming as the South's "extreme concession" an extension to the Pacific Ocean of the Missouri Compromise line of 36°30´—the line that had protected slavery south of that meridian in the Louisiana Territory. In addition, the convention endorsed an aggressive "Address" denouncing the proposed compromise and insisting upon the extension of the Missouri Compromise line as a northern renunciation of "the insufferable pretension of restricting and preventing the extension of the South, whilst they should extend indefinitely." Tennessee's delegates joined the representatives of the eight other states participating in the convention to cast a unanimous vote in favor of the committee's "Address," but the host state's representatives appeared far from satisfied with the result. The two Tennessee members of the committee on resolutions, Aaron V. Brown and A. O. P. Nicholson, both objected to the committee's report and issued statements after the convention's conclusion explaining their opposition. Most of Tennessee's delegates would have voted against the "Address," Cooper told David R. Arnell, "but for a clause inserted for their benefit, which stated, in effect, that some of the members of the Convention dissented from portions of the address, and the reasoning by which these portions were attempted to be sustained."[79]

Tennessee's reluctant approval of the "Address" appeared to secure the Fire-Eaters' goal of presenting a united southern front in defense of southern rights. In Tennessee, the "ultra" tone of the convention's "Address" seemed to confirm Whig charges that the convention actually encouraged a dissolution of the Union.[80] The convention, Whigs concluded, had issued an "ultimatum" in its demand for the application of the Missouri Compromise line to the Mexican cession. Democrats maintained that the convention's "extreme concession" showed that southern citizens were "not only prepared to acquiesce in the Missouri line, but in any other plan of adjustment which might substantially secure to the south the rights asserted in the resolutions." This explanation failed to assure skeptics, especially after South Carolina's Robert Barnwell Rhett, the author of the "Address" and the presumed leader of the Fire-Eaters after Calhoun's death in March, delivered a revealing speech in Charleston upon his return from Nashville. In it, Rhett openly declared that a dissolution of the Union offered the "one course left for the peace and salvation of the South." South Carolina's new senator specifically included Tennessee's Democrats among his compatriots, for he assured his audience that "in five days" Tennessee's moderate delegation had been "brought into line" behind the convention's declarations. "One thing is now clear," the *Banner* observed. "The men who are led by Mr. Rhett are the enemies of the Union—are bent upon its *destruction!*"[81]

The convention's "Address" and the "Rhett Manifesto" brought into open view the division among Democratic leaders concerning the proper emphasis to place on the slavery issue. Nothing more clearly indicated this rupture than the *Nashville Union*'s dismissal of its "ultra" editor, E. G. Eastman, in July. Former Congressman Harvey M. Watterson, who had purchased the paper in 1849, referred to the *Union*'s need to trim expenses as the reason for Eastman's removal, as Watterson himself took over the editorial reins. Under Watterson's direction, the paper came out strongly in favor of Clay's compromise and maintained that congressional nonintervention—the doctrine upon which Democrats had supported Lewis Cass in 1848—represented the party's true position on slavery's status in any new territory. At the same time, Watterson argued against the constitutionality and efficacy of the proposal to extend the Missouri Compromise line.[82] Few now could deny that the slavery issue had driven a wedge through Tennessee's Democratic party. Those adhering to the *Union*'s and the *Clarksville Jeffersonian*'s position promoted the compromise, advocated nonintervention, and encouraged the state party to emphasize its stand on traditional Democratic principles rather than the slavery issue. Southern Rights advocates, meanwhile, followed the *Nashville American* and the *Memphis Appeal* in endorsing the Nashville Convention's "Address" and in keeping the defense of southern liberty at the center of the Democratic creed. The *American*, in fact, hired Eastman as its associate editor, and from his new office, Eastman continued to insist that the South "must be united upon some ultimatum" while pointing to "the resolutions of the late Southern Convention" as his platform.[83]

The Unionist Democrats' assertion of their preference for compromise came at a critical time. On July 31, the Senate essentially defeated the committee of thirteen's compromise bill, leaving behind no evident solution to the conflict over slavery. Whigs joined Unionist Democrats to assure the electorate that the defeat of the bill provided no cause for desperate measures. "The people," the *Republican Banner* maintained, would repudiate "the accursed demagogues whose highest ambition appears to be notoriety and a love of office" and compel politicians to produce some settlement that would preserve the integrity of the Union.[84] Events in Congress soon vindicated the paper's faith in the ultimate triumph of popular devotion to the Union. Senator Stephen A. Douglas of Illinois divided the committee's compromise proposals into five separate bills; by late September, each of these bills had passed both the Senate and the House and had received the signature of new President Millard Fillmore, who succeeded Taylor after the general's death on July 9. The votes of Tennessee's congressional delegation allowed both parties to claim a share in achieving final passage of the Compromise of 1850. Three Democrats and one Whig voted against the bill admitting California to the Union as a free state, while Gentry proved the only Tennessean willing to accept abolition of the slave trade in the District of Columbia. Otherwise, Tennessee's congressmen voted virtually unanimously in favor of the bills establishing the New Mexico and Utah territories according to the principle of nonintervention, settling Texas's border dispute with New Mexico, and strengthening the country's law providing for the return of fugitive slaves.[85]

Despite their party's support in Congress for the compromise, the Unionist Democrats' acclamation of the settlement failed to free the state party from the burden of the "disunionist" label. Southern Rights newspapers denounced the compromise and refused to accept it as a final adjustment. "Shall Tennessee acquiesce in the passage of the several bills in Congress? So far as we are concerned, we answer emphatically, NO!" Eastman proclaimed in the *American,* and he announced that he and his allies would "stand upon the platform of the Southern Convention" and "endeavour to maintain our foot hold even though its last timbers are cut down by the treachery of those who professed to be its staunchest supporters."[86] As the Democrats' two wings squabbled through the fall, Whigs praised the compromise as "a peaceful and honorable adjustment of a controversy which threatened disruption and disaster to the south as well as to the north." At the same time, Whig papers reminded citizens that "the advocates of Disunion and Secession in South Carolina and Georgia are still at their work." The "masses of both parties" in Tennessee would sustain the compromise, Whigs maintained; "every one must see that with the people of this State, the merest squinting at *Rhettism* is done." Nevertheless, the Nashville Convention had planned a second session six weeks after Congress adjourned; and, at that session, according to Whigs, the Fire-Eaters intended to designate Tennessee's capital as "the spot for unfurling the standard of Disunion!" "Let the people press this question home to every candidate for public favor—every organ of popular sentiment in Tennessee," the *Nashville True Whig* proclaimed. "*Union* or *Disunion* is now the plain issue before the country."[87]

The second session of the Nashville Convention proved a mere shadow of the earlier meeting. Only fifty-nine delegates attended, none of whom had been appointed by the authority of the six states represented. Still, the convention's action in the November session resulted in the last of a series of embarrassments suffered by Tennessee's Democratic party that year. Most of the state's fourteen-member delegation promoted Gideon J. Pillow's resolutions expressing an intent to support the Compromise of 1850, "on the express condition that the North shall faithfully carry it out on her part," while warning the North of dire consequences, should that section's leaders attempt yet again to agitate the slavery question. The majority of the convention delegates—dominated, the *Union* noted, by those "who are *classically* styled 'Fire-eaters'"—again ignored Tennessee's proposal and instead approved another radical declaration, this time denouncing the compromise and acknowledging the right of a state to secede from the Union. Tennessee produced the lone dissenting vote against the "Address," but the statement's severe tone again appeared to confirm the charge that the convention all along had been the project of disunionists.[88]

The convention's confusing termination increased the Democrats' dismay. After the assembly had completed its vote on its resolutions, Andrew J. Donelson requested a reconsideration of the vote and asked permission to speak at the convention. Because Tennessee had voted against the passage of the resolutions, and because the delegates had been given an opportunity to speak earlier in the session, the president of the body ruled Donelson's propositions out of order. Donelson, backed from the gallery by the "vociferous applause of those who were opposed to the resolutions which were adopted," attempted to address the convention nonetheless; but, as he began his oration, the session quickly was adjourned. Southern Rights Democrats in Tennessee denounced Donelson's course as "disreputable to Nashville"; it had been "understood by all" that the convention intended to adjourn when it did, Eastman explained, for "the church in which it was held was wanted for a funeral." The session's abrupt ending, though, further exacerbated the rift among Democrats, as Unionists condemned the convention for muzzling a Tennessean's dissent from the Fire-Eaters' direction. With a portion of the Democrats themselves now decrying the Nashville Convention as unrepresentative, the November session above all reinforced the Whigs' portrayal of the gathering as the means by which a clique of politicians sought to attain its designs, regardless of the popular will. "Although that Convention was ostensibly assembled for the purpose of consultation as to the steps which were most suitable to avert the dangers which menaced our Union," Donelson asserted at a bipartisan pro-Union meeting held a week after his disruption of the convention's conclusion, "yet its resolutions were adopted by a process which gagged the mouths of all the delegates, except such as represented what may now be termed the *secession* party of the South."[89]

Democrats emerged from the crisis of 1850 embarrassed by their association with the Nashville Convention and openly divided over the Compromise of 1850. Still, the narrow margin of difference in previous elections between Whigs and Democrats left Democratic leaders optimistic about the prospect of carrying the state in the 1851 elections. The possibility of victory encouraged the party's Unionist and Southern Rights wings to preserve at least a semblance of harmony. Governor Trousdale's personal popularity likewise promoted party unity, as the incumbent faced no opposition when the state Democratic convention unanimously nominated him for a second term. From his position as president of the convention, Aaron Brown apparently controlled its deliberations; but the state's leading Southern Rights advocate attempted to promote unity behind Trousdale, by composing a platform affirming that Democrats would abide by the Compromise of 1850, notwithstanding their belief that its provisions "fall short of that measure of justice to which the South, in our opinion[,] are [sic] fairly entitled." At the same time, the convention's declaration warned northerners that any tampering with the compromise, or any other future agitation against southern rights, would be considered "a breach of plighted faith and a violation of the constitution so palpable and willful, as well to justify the Southern States to resort to any and every means of self-preservation, which their peace, safety, and honor might demand."[90]

The Democratic platform thus sought to mask the party's division by assuring voters that Democrats held the same ground upon the slavery issue as they had in previous contests. Brown's platform, "in the most distinct and emphatic manner," reaffirmed "the principles and sentiments set forth in the resolutions of the last Democratic Convention held at Nashville in 1849," Democrats insisted; Watterson's *Union* explained that the state party's 1849 platform had become "the platform of the Union party at the South."[91] Though the Compromise of 1850 had quieted agitation over slavery, Democrats maintained that the South needed to proclaim once again its support for a national party dedicated to the defense of southern liberty, for Abolitionism had become "more prevailing and more powerful than it has ever been" in the North. Popular obstruction of the enforcement of the new fugitive slave law—the South's principal gain from the compromise—indicated the abolitionists' intention to persist in their assault on southern rights. "We would not disturb the compromise," the *American* insisted, "but we cannot shut our eyes to what is daily going on around us." Northern opposition to the return of runaway slaves provided clear evidence of that section's goal "not only to repeal, or what is the same thing, to essentially modify the fugitive slave law, but to drive through other bills which are designed to extirpate slavery from this whole continent."The national Democratic party, the *Jeffersonian* added,"in all its State Conventions, *without exception*," had acknowledged "the constitutional rights of the South to protection of her peculiar institution of slavery," and Tennessee's endorsement of the party's stand would aid the South's natural allies in the North in their efforts to put down the abolitionist Whigs.[92]

With slavery's status in the territories now settled, aggressive calls for the defense of southern rights seemed less urgent than they had two years earlier. Moreover, since some of the Lower South states were planning conventions to consider secession, another aggressive campaign centered upon the slavery issue could leave Democrats open to further charges of promoting disunion.[93] Nevertheless, on the stump Trousdale devoted the greater part of his energy to condemning the specific measures of the Compromise of 1850, explicitly stating his belief that "the South had derived little benefit" from its provisions, before he gave any indication of his party's intention to comply with the agreement. At the same time, Southern Rights papers continued their denunciations of the settlement's offensive features.[94] Unionist Democrats emphasized the party's willingness to uphold the settlement and reminded voters that Trousdale did not favor disunion. Still, the harsh declarations of the party standard-bearer, along with the grudging acquiescence of the Southern Rights wing, created the image of a party dissatisfied with the compromise and eager to agitate further public excitement over the future of slavery. As one Clarksville Whig told his party's gubernatorial nominee, it was "evident that the Democratic party with Genl. Trousdale at their head would have all been opposed to the Compromise and in favor of ultra southern rights if it were not for fear of the direful condemnation of their whole party by the overwhelming public opinion favoring the compromise."[95]

Despite the party's unification behind Trousdale, the division exposed in 1850 plagued Democrats throughout the 1851 canvass. The rift between Unionist and Southern Rights Democrats reached into the party's lower ranks, as rival Democratic candidates competed for seats in the legislature.The most influential leaders from both wings, Aaron Brown and A. O. P. Nicholson, encouraged many of the candidates; both aspired to be chosen by the General Assembly to fill the United States Senate seat vacated by the expiration of Hopkins L.Turney's term. Still, while the exact number of contests among Democrats is not known, in several of the races, candidates identified themselves as either "Compromise" or "Southern Rights" Democrats. The *Union* and the *American* both lamented the presence of "too many candidates" in the field and encouraged rivals somehow to settle their conflicting claims. These admonitions did little to restore party unity, however. Even in the strongly Democratic First and Sixth Congressional districts, appeals for harmony were unable to prevent challenges for congressional as well as legislative seats. In upper East Tennessee's First Congressional District, Landon C. Haynes stood against the incumbent Unionist congressman, Andrew Johnson; while in Middle Tennessee's Sixth District, several Democrats persuaded James H. Thomas to seek reelection against front-runner William H. Polk, because of Polk's association with the moderate Tennessee platform at the Nashville Convention.[96]

With Democrats divided, Whigs presented to the electorate a united front centered upon the party's image as the "great conservative party of the Union, ever toiling to save the country from the *radical extremes* of democracy, in *every crisis.*" Party leaders persuaded William B. Campbell, one of the most popular Tennesseans since he had distinguished himself at the Battle of Monterrey in 1846, to accept the Whig nomination for governor. After the state convention nominated the former congressman, it approved a platform declaring the Compromise of 1850 "the best which, under the circumstances, could have been adopted" and "a *final settlement* . . . of the dangerous and exciting subjects which they embraced."[97] Throughout the summer, Campbell, Meredith Gentry, and Thomas A. R. Nelson—who spoke in place of Campbell when the candidate fell ill in June—lauded the compromise as "a triumph of wisdom and of patriotism over the mischievous purposes of designing politicians at the north and at the south." Party newspapers endorsed their candidate's promise to support Millard Fillmore's election to the presidency in 1852, because his administration had "bent all its energies and power to preserve the Constitution, and to promote the peace, prosperity and happiness of the people." "Bad men in the North, and ambitious men in the South" still worked to destroy "the Union of our fathers," and Whigs reminded voters that their opponents had approved the Nashville Convention, where "the doctrines of Secession and Disunion were both *boldly taught.*"[98]

Each of the two parties contended that the success of the Compromise of 1850 depended upon its own victory. Democrats attempted to justify their call for continued southern unity by arguing that such a stand was necessary to compel the North to honor the adjustment. Not only did northerners persist in their obstruction of the fugitive slave law, but also the presence in the White House of the "malignant abolitionist" Fillmore symbolized the permanent danger facing southern institutions. Even if Fillmore did prove true to the South, Democrats warned, northern Whigs already had indicated their plan to replace Fillmore with the abolitionists' ally, Winfield Scott, as their presidential candidate. Likewise, southern Whigs persisted in their assistance to the abolitionists by advocating "submission" to the compromise, even to the extent of accepting a repeal of the fugitive slave law.[99] Trousdale's reelection would sustain the compromise by marking the electorate's repudiation of submission and its declaration to the North that southerners remained united in defense of their rights."The *real issue* between parties here in Tennessee," the *Union* explained,

> as we have already stated, is not which party *acquiesces* in the compromise now that it has been passed as a final adjustment, and which party refuses so to *acquiesce*. —There is *no issue* of that character, for both parties announce their *acquiescence*. The *real issue* is, as we have stated, *which party is for firmly and sternly holding the north to abide by and maintain in good faith the whole compromise as it stands, under penalty of the worst,* if Northern aggression shall proceed to violate it and break it up under plea of *modifying* it. *That* is the real issue.[100]

Despite the Democrats' explanations, the 1851 elections became in essence a referendum on the value of the Compromise of 1850. Denunciations of the compromise by Southern Rights advocates did little to reassure voters of the Democrats' fidelity to the agreement. Trousdale's censure of the compromise's specific measures,Whigs argued, showed that the governor "should be watched as at heart a *Disunionist*" who "sympathizes with those who are believed to be plotting disunion." A Democratic victory in the state would "stimulate South Carolina to hope that she can make her last desperate and fatal movement in reliance upon the sympathy and support of Tennessee," while northerners would view the election of a candidate threatening further disturbance of the slavery issue as evidence that "the South does not regard the Compromise as a final settlement." Campbell's election, on the other hand, would signify the state's approval of the settlement and its repudiation of the Union's enemies in both North and South."The true issue, therefore, is the Compromise or Disunion," the *Knoxville Whig* concluded; "carry out the Compromise measures

William B. Campbell, by Washington B. Cooper, c. 1852. Tennessee Historical Society Picture Collection. Reproduction courtesy of Tennessee State Library and Archives, Nashville.

and preserve the Union, or set them all aside, renew the slavery discussion, and dissolve the Union."[101]

The results of the election indicated that Tennessee's voters were willing to accept the compromise and put discussions of slavery's future behind them. Democrats improved their strength among West Tennessee's rapidly growing population, and the party retained its three-seat advantage over Whigs in the state's congressional delegation. Nevertheless, the return to the polls of Middle Tennessee Whigs, along with a particularly heavy turnout of party members in East Tennessee, countered Democratic gains in the West and elected Campbell to the governor's office by a margin of almost two thousand votes. More importantly, Whigs won their greatest victories in the elections to the General Assembly. The "conservative party of Union" won a ten-seat majority in that body, and it would control both chambers in a legislature that not only would elect a United States Senator but also would redraw the state's legislative and congressional districts. With this resounding triumph, Whigs interpreted the outcome as a vindication of the party's endorsement of the Compromise of 1850. "[T]he people of Tennessee have roused themselves and come to the rescue of the friends of the Union," the *Banner* proclaimed; while the victorious Campbell assured his uncle that "Tennessee may be put down as sound on the Union question[,] for the Compromise & for Mr. Fillmore or a sound Union man for the next Presidency."[102]

Democrats again attributed their defeat to their lack of organization, but they also recognized that their cause had been damaged by the

Southern Rights advocates' presumed association with Fire-Eaters in the Lower South. In Middle Tennessee, the *Bolivar Democrat* noted, "the cry of 'Glorious Union' made the nerves of some timid Democrats tremble, and caused them to be lukewarm in Trousdale's election."[103] Whigs acknowledged, too, that "our opponents being *divided in opinion among themselves*" proved "a great advantage" in their efforts. The multiple candidacies of Democrats in legislative races appear to have given the Whigs their tremendous advantage in the General Assembly. Still, the outcome of the contests between rival Democrats emphasized popular repudiation of agitation on the slavery issue. Unionist Democrats Andrew Johnson and William H. Polk defeated challengers in their races for Congress. In what perhaps was the state's most revealing contest, in Franklin County the "Compromise Democrat," Jesse Arledge, won election to the state house of representatives, defeating the Tennessean who had been the state's most outspoken advocate of southern rights in Congress, former Senator Hopkins L. Turney.[104]

Whigs emerged from the Crisis of 1850 in their strongest position since the formation of the party system in Tennessee. At the same time, Democrats entered the new decade divided and weakened by being linked with southern "disunionists." Most significantly, Tennessee's party system emerged from the crisis intact. In several southern states, Whigs joined with Democrats favoring the Compromise of 1850 to form a "Union party" that opposed a "Southern Rights" party composed chiefly of a remnant of Democrats.[105] Some of Tennessee's Whig leaders proposed the formation of a Union party, but this suggestion received little consideration from the leading spokesman of either of the state's extant organizations.[106] The leaders of both Whigs and Democrats saw no need to try to gain power by promoting a realignment of parties. The narrow margin of difference between the existing parties encouraged politicians to trust a full mobilization of their compatriots to ensure victory at the polls, notwithstanding the stress exerted on the party system by the conflict over slavery's extension.

Nor did voters see much reason for new political organizations. Both parties responded to the conflict over the defense of slavery according to their established conceptions of power and their ideological understandings of the American polity. Democrats and Whigs agreed that the federal government had no authority over slavery's status within individual states. When confronted with the question of the institution's expansion into the new territories, Democrats grounded their opposition to congressional power to prohibit slavery in these regions upon their belief in a strict construction of the Constitution. Southern Rights Democrats conceded to Washington the power to guarantee slavery's existence in the territories, but only because they believed it necessary to insure southerners equal access to those lands; Unionist Democrats, meanwhile, upheld the principle of congressional nonintervention on slavery as the only true Democratic doctrine.[107] Whigs, likewise, never accepted the premise of congressional power to enact the Wilmot Proviso, but they nevertheless expressed faith in the ability of the federal government to provide an equitable settlement to the conflict over the territories. This faith transcended simple policy to encompass a reverence for the federal Constitution that perceived the Union not merely as a means to protect personal interests, but as a familial bond among all citizens of the nation. Thus Whigs declared their willingness to trust the Constitution's provisions and a national tribunal's decision, should an oppressive law somehow slip through Congress. Moreover, Whigs declared, if necessary they preferred to give up the territories acquired from Mexico rather than disturb the harmony of the Union as it existed. Most important, throughout 1850, both parties maintained their positions as defenders of the citizenry's liberty against the manipulations of demagogic politicians. Democrats continued their stand against abolitionists and their Federal, Whig, and southern submissionist allies. At the same time, Whigs capitalized upon their position as the friends of liberty and Union who challenged their opponents' aid to the nation's long-standing enemies, South Carolina's Nullifiers.

Tennessee's voters entered the 1850s with their party loyalties reaffirmed, despite the fact that the old economic issues virtually had disappeared and new concerns had arisen concerning slavery's expansion. "I love the Whig party," Edwin H. Ewing told William Campbell in February 1851, "because I believe [that] in it & it alone are to be found the conservative principles upon which our Government is to stand, if stand it may. Its Tariff, its Banks, & its *measures of the time* may pass away; but its deep law-abiding, order-loving, Constitution-supporting principle remains." Three months later, the *Clarksville Jeffersonian* reminded readers that there always had been "two parties in this country, holding the most antagonistic opinions in regard to the powers conferred upon Congress by the constitution." "The Whig party have ever been in favor of a latitudinous construction of the constitution," the *Jeffersonian* continued, while the Democrats had "ever been in favor of a strict construction of the constitution."[108]

The conflict over slavery's expansion reinforced in Tennessee the political strength of sentiment in favor of preserving the Union of states. Arguments in favor of defending southern rights to the "last extremity," including a dissolution of the Union, gained the favor of a portion of the state's Democratic leadership, and Southern Rights newspapers openly accepted the doctrine of state secession as a legitimate constitutional principle. The 1851 elections, though, indicated that Tennessee's politicians could expect only difficulty if they attempted to ride the hobby of secession. Most likely, the proportion of slaves in the population in a given locality strongly influenced the degree of concern over slavery's future evinced there; perceived threats to slavery undoubtedly appeared more frightening in an economy heavily dependent upon slave labor, as in West Tennessee, than they did in areas with few slaves, such as the counties along the Cumberland Plateau, dividing East and Middle Tennessee. Still, across the state, voters associated southern "ultraism" with Calhoun and the "kingdom of South Carolina." Since Andrew Jackson's damnation of nullification, in Tennessee's political culture, Calhoun's followers had been viewed as a collection of frustrated demagogues who presented as great a threat to republican freedom as did northern abolitionists. "The object of the Secession party is to establish a 'SOUTHERN CONFEDERACY.' They want a government of their own," the *Winchester Independent*, a Unionist Democratic paper, stated in 1851. Should that party succeed in its goal, "we will see the end of ORDER and LIBERTY and then will commence the reign of KINGS and TYRANTS in the country, for the liberty of which Washington fought, and patriots bled and perished."[109]

Yet the parties' debate over slavery also revealed the limits of Tennessee's Unionism. Although they owed their triumph in 1851 to their bold stand for the Compromise and the Union, Whigs always agreed with their opponents that any northern attempt to repeal or restrain the fugitive slave law could only be regarded as a breach of faith. Moreover, while rejecting the southern rights advocates' justification of secession as a constitutional principle, Whigs and Unionist Democrats agreed that republicanism provided an ultimate remedy from an unquestionably oppressive government: the same redress to which the founding fathers had been driven, the right of revolution. Whigs would not "dissolve the Union upon a *doubtful* question of constitutionality," the *Banner* reminded readers; nevertheless, the *Banner* seconded the *American*'s contention that "'the people may, if they choose, throw off any government when it becomes oppressive and intolerable, and erect a better in its stead.' They believe this is their right, but they regard it as '*the right of revolution,*' and [it] should not be exercised but in the *last resort.*"[110] Notwithstanding the electorate's devotion to the Union, Whigs joined Democrats in leaving open the possibility of dissolution while sending the message to the North that further abolitionist aggression would not be tolerated.

In the aftermath of the 1851 state elections, few Democrats or Whigs probably expected that Tennessee would ever face the need to resort to either secession or revolution, at least as a consequence of the slavery issue. The Whigs' triumph announced the state citizenry's willingness to consider the Compromise of 1850 the final settlement of that issue; similar results in other state elections, along with the failure of secession movements in the Lower South, appeared to preclude further agitation on the future of the institution in the United States. A short ten years later, after a decade of further strife over slavery, Tennessee indeed would take the step of revolution. Until that revolution, as throughout Tennessee's antebellum political existence, the question of who truly defended the citizens' freedom continued to provide the central issue of state politics.

SEVEN

The Politics of Union: The Triumph of Democracy
1852–1857

The Whig victory in the 1851 elections marked the zenith of that party's strength in Tennessee. Taking advantage of their ten-seat majority in the General Assembly, Whigs tried to use their success to guarantee the party's continued dominance. Former Governor James C. Jones, one of the state's most popular figures, was selected to fill the vacancy in the United States Senate created by the expiration of Hopkins L. Turney's term. Then, the majority easily passed two bills, written and sponsored by Clarksville's Gustavus A. Henry, that gerrymandered the state so that Whigs would control the General Assembly and congressional delegation for the remainder of the decade. Most satisfying was the fact that reapportionment deprived of their seats three popular Democratic congressmen, Frederick P. Stanton, Isham G. Harris, and Andrew Johnson.[1] Democrats condemned the "Henrymander" as "morally and politically *dishonest*" and charged that the Whig redistricting plan defied "the commonest principles of justice and fair dealing." Whigs publicly denied any intention to injustice while privately congratulating themselves on the obliteration of their enemies. "If the Whigs act as they ought to act," Alexander Williams told Thomas A. R. Nelson, "they now have the power, to kill Locofocoism for 10 years to come, if they do not do it they ought to be demolished and no longer called Whigs."[2]

By early 1852, Whigs appeared to have entrenched themselves in power in Tennessee for at least the next decade. The party's hold seemed confirmed when, in that year's presidential election, Tennessee stood as one of only four states to cast its electoral votes for the unpopular Whig nominee, General Winfield Scott. Within a year after the presidential election, however, Whigs lost control of the governorship, never to regain it. In the next presidential contest, Democrats would establish their own dominance in the state to a degree far greater than that ever enjoyed by Whigs. The dissolution of the national Whig party after Scott's defeat and the reemergence of the slavery issue in national politics contributed to the state Whigs' demise, but local developments also contributed to the shift in the parties' strength. Democrats successfully distanced themselves from "Nullifiers" in the Lower South and reassured voters of their own devotion to the Union, thus reviving their support. Factional division meanwhile prevented Whig leaders from uniting upon a solution to the dilemma presented by the demise of the national party. Still, new conditions and new alliances did not alter the parties' roles as defenders of the voters' freedom. Amid the sectional controversy, for both parties the defense of the Union increasingly appeared to provide their most crucial method of protecting republican institutions.

Democrats entered the 1850s in a weak position. Party leadership remained divided into Southern Rights and Unionist factions, and competition between these factions increasingly reflected a personal rivalry between Aaron V. Brown and A. O. P. Nicholson. Among voters, Democrats still suffered from the stigma of association with the southern "disunionists" who had opposed the Compromise of 1850. The loss in the 1851 contest sobered party leaders into recognizing the need to reconcile their differences in order to recapture the state government.[3] Rivalry persisted, though, as leading Democrats tried to maneuver the state party behind their chosen candidates in the upcoming presidential election. A contingent of Unionists, led by Andrew Ewing, William H. Polk, and J. Knox Walker, attempted to unite the factions behind Stephen A. Douglas of Illinois, by linking the champion of the Compromise of 1850 to the vice-presidential aspirations of Brown's close associates, Gideon J. Pillow and William Trousdale.[4] Brown and Nicholson both indicated interest in the Douglas movement, but ultimately both pursued their own candidates. Nicholson refused to abandon his personal friend, Lewis Cass, while Cave Johnson persuaded Brown to back Pennsylvania's James Buchanan. Consequently, the state party convention held in January 1852 endorsed no candidates for either spot on the national ticket. The factions compromised by sending to the national convention a delegation evenly divided between Cass and Buchanan.[5]

Democrats united behind the national ticket when the divided convention nominated New Hampshire's Franklin Pierce. Pierce, Tennessee's once-contentious party now proclaimed, clearly was a candidate "thoroughly with the South in her feelings," one who "ever respected her constitutional rights." Confidence in Pierce's chances to carry Tennessee abounded when the Whig national convention bypassed the favorite of the southern wing, Millard Fillmore, in favor of General Winfield Scott, who Democrats maintained was the standard-bearer of northern Whig "Free-Soil" abolitionists.[6] By late summer, Democratic leaders believed that a full turnout of voters would guarantee victory in Tennessee, and they began speculating on which faction would benefit from the patronage of a Pierce administration.[7]

Despite this optimism, the 1852 presidential canvass became a virtual replay of the preceding year's gubernatorial election. Democrats again centered their appeals upon the "finality" of the Compromise of 1850 and promoted Pierce, as they had Trousdale, because "the most vital interests of the South are at stake in this contest." It was true that some Democrats had opposed the compromise while it was being debated, party spokesmen admitted, but now that the agreement had become law, the *Union* explained, party members agreed "that these measures shall be regarded as a *definite settlement of the slavery question.*"[8] Although the Whig platform also pledged support for the compromise, Democrats warned that the northern wing of the party planned to subvert the compact by repealing the fugitive slave law. Scott himself refused to state in writing his support for the compromise, and his election, Democrats charged, "would be the placing of this Government in the hands of those free-soilers, who openly proclaim, in advance, that they 'defy, execrate, [and] spit upon the [Whig] platform.'"[9] Should Scott somehow triumph, they maintained, the compromise would be repudiated, and "in the South, the ultimate effects will be to make disunion—now a proscribed idea—the ruling sentiment."[10]

The Democrats' presumed association with the extreme advocates of southern rights allowed Whigs once again to charge that their opponents ultimately sought the dissolution of the Union. Free-Soilers stood behind the Democratic candidate, Whigs argued, for Pierce clearly was "a northern man with northern feelings," and southern disunionists joined them in supporting the northerner as part of their plan to use the slavery question to destroy the Union. "All the discordant elements of the country . . . seem to have coalesced, in a desperate struggle for power," the *Republican Banner* wrote, denouncing Pierce's supporters. "[T]his contest has brought about a singular union of extremes,—of men North and South, who were recently in open hostility—freesoilers and pro-slavery men—

Union men and disunionists—secessionists and anti-secessionists—compromise men and anti-compromise men."[11] Democrats again found themselves in a defensive position, forced to defend themselves from charges of "ultraism." "[W]e do not believe," the *American* proclaimed, "that the craziest man among us has the slightest fear that any effort will be made in the South to disturb the compromise," while Cave Johnson denounced disunion charges as "slander."[12] Nevertheless, as Democrats warned voters that the greatest danger facing the country came from northern Abolitionists, Whigs continued to point to an alliance between Free-Soilers and Nullifiers as most threatening to the Union's future.

The result of the November election stunned and embarrassed Democrats. Pierce won a landslide victory in the national race, in which Scott won the electoral votes of only four states. One of those states, though, was Tennessee; even though the state's Whigs themselves expressed little enthusiasm for their candidate, enough Whigs went to the polls to give their candidate a majority of thirteen hundred votes. Democratic leaders attributed the result to the electorate's fondness for military heroes, but in fact, as in 1851, the Democrats' reputed association with sectional extremists had weakened their cause. Cave Johnson admitted that the northerner Pierce was perceived as "an abolitionist at heart & only going with us now for effect to get their votes," while Whigs pointed to Pierce's support from "a singular combination of extremes,—of men North and South, who were recently in open hostility," as the reason for Scott's majority.[13] Scott's devastating loss nationally allowed party leaders to console themselves with the belief that the national Whig party had been irreparably damaged. Still, the loss of the state showed the party that it had gained little from the national triumph and that its position remained as weak as it had been when it entered the canvass.

The result of the 1852 election revealed the plight of Tennessee's Democratic party. National victory alone could not insure the success of the state party. Factional rivalries continued to distract the party leadership. At the same time, Democrats had not recovered from their gamble to defend southern rights "to the last extremity." That promise, and their support of the Nashville Convention in 1850, had allowed Whigs to associate the Democrats with the "ultra" movement in the Lower South; the Democrats' division over the Compromise of 1850 failed to satisfy its followers that their party was not somehow involved in a movement for disunion—despite Democratic pleas that "there is no disunion party out of South Carolina."[14] Democrats could share in the national party's success only if they could present a united front that managed to distance the state party from the designs of the Nullifiers. Somehow, the party needed to be revived in a manner that would assure voters that the Democrats equaled, if they did not excel, their opponents in devotion to the Union.

In early 1853, the party took some crucial steps toward recovery. In May, Nashville's two Democratic newspapers merged to form a new party organ, the *Union and American*, with a toned-down, less "ultra" E. G. Eastman as senior editor.[15] The party's leadership now could speak with a single voice, and the existence of one Democratic paper at the state capital at least would give the appearance of unity.

A more significant development already had occurred the previous month. At the state convention in Nashville, six names had been placed before a nominating caucus as potential candidates for governor. The clear choice of a majority of delegates was East Tennessee's displaced congressman, Andrew Johnson. Johnson, a Unionist during the Crisis of 1850, already had earned the particular disfavor of Brown's faction, both because of his opposition to some important measures during Polk's administration and because of his reputation as a maverick who advocated "radical and extreme" democratic doctrines. Southern Righters tried to block Johnson's nomination by uniting the caucus either behind their own favorite, Isham G. Harris, or behind Unionists A. O. P. Nicholson or Andrew Ewing. These moves failed when Harris proved unable to garner the necessary support and when Nicholson and Ewing refused to stand in Johnson's way. With no other alternative, Southern Righters reluctantly accepted Johnson's candidacy, and the state convention ended up unanimously nominating the East Tennessean as the Democratic standard-bearer.[16]

Contrary to the expectations of Brown and his associates, Andrew Johnson's gubernatorial candidacy proved the vital component in the Democrats' recuperation. Johnson's nomination moved the state party away from the sectional issue and back toward its traditional image as the opponent of an ever-present Federalist "money power." Democrats never had abandoned that appeal completely during the crisis over slavery's expansion.[17] Declarations about defending southern rights to the "last extremity," though, had distracted party leaders from this focus; questions concerning the party's support of the Compromise of 1850 had led its traditional constituency to wonder whether the party still represented yeoman farmers and artisans or if it had become an instrument of disunionist slaveholders. A candidate such as Johnson, however, seemed far removed from any connection with the latter group. His rise from humble circumstances (he once had been an illiterate tailor's apprentice) to become a member of Congress highlighted the party's role as the defender of equal opportunity for all citizens, while his own political career had been built upon attacks against "aristocrats" who sought to exploit the nation's laboring people. Whigs found "a 'sheep skin' . . . much better evidence of merit and qualification, than a life spent in honest toil, and constant effort at self-improvement," Democrats charged, while trumpeting Johnson's reputation "not only as a sound democratic statesman, but as the friend and advocate of the rights of the laboring man." Behind Johnson, Democrats could reassure the party's rank and file that it had not abandoned its primary purpose; it still stood for the defense of the voters' freedom against their enemies, whether those enemies were Federalists or Abolitionists.[18]

Johnson had loyally supported the state party as it committed itself to the "last extremity" doctrine, but at the same time he had encouraged his comrades to stress instead issues that would advance the power of the humble citizen, such as his own pet hobby of a proposal to grant a homestead to occupants of public lands. Once the 1853 canvass opened, the candidate himself went beyond the Democratic platform to center his campaign upon a homestead law and upon constitutional amendments providing for, first, the popular election of the president and senators; and, second, elections and term limitations for justices on the federal Supreme Court. Southern Rights newspapers made it clear that these proposals were Johnson's personal opinions and not party doctrine; still, perhaps recognizing Johnson's prescience concerning too heavy a reliance on the defense of southern rights, both factions endorsed Johnson as the "MECHANIC STATESMAN," while pointing to his advocacy of expanding the power of the people as proof that he was the "successor to the principles of JEFFERSON and JACKSON."[19]

The Whigs' nomination of Gustavus A. Henry as Johnson's opponent aided the Democrats' revival. The author of the Whig gerrymander at the last legislative session, Henry had been a popular Whig speaker during the 1840s and had run for elector in four presidential contests. Yet, while living in his native Kentucky, Henry had voted for John Quincy Adams against Andrew Jackson in 1828, and as a member of the Kentucky legislature in 1832, Henry had voted against a bill giving mechanics a lien for payment on completed work.[20] These actions, along with having a victim of the "Henrymander" as his rival in the governor's race, allowed Johnson and the Democrats easily to portray the 1853 contest as part of the long-standing struggle against those seeking to remove power from the sovereign people. "No two men have ever been opposing candidates for the office of governor of Tennessee, who so well illustrate in their own conduct the antagonistic principles in our Government which have been struggling against each other since the days of JOHN ADAMS, as our present candidates," Eastman's *Union and American* proclaimed. "A strong government . . . was the darling theory of the ancient federalists, as it is of Maj. HENRY. A Government of the People, was the theory of JEFFERSON, as it was of JACKSON, and as it is of JOHNSON."[21]

Henry and his comrades attacked Johnson as a radical and dangerous demagogue whose constitutional changes would threaten social stability. Not only had the Democratic nominee been one of the masterminds of the "Immortal Thirteen" fiasco a decade earlier, Whigs charged, but his proposal in 1842 to apportion the legislature on the basis of the state's white population—with no consideration of slave property—represented an innovation that "cannot fail to be hailed with joy by every Abolitionist in the Union." Johnson, they maintained, also intended to eliminate using three-fifths of the slave population as the basis for the southern states' representation in Congress. The Democrat's proposals for popular election of Supreme Court justices likewise would assist abolitionists, Nashville's *True Whig* argued; with the admission of additional free states to the Union, northern voters "would elect a majority of the Judges—and it is a part of their sectional education as non-slaveholders, to wage increasing warfare upon the peculiar institutions of the South." At the same time, Whigs tried to appeal to Democrats who disagreed with Johnson's demand for constitutional amendments by warning of the potential excesses that would result from the candidate's "pure democracy."[22] Despite these charges, Whigs found it difficult to counter the East Tennessean's popularity, and throughout the campaign they found it necessary to join attacks upon Johnson with references to the domination of Pierce's cabinet by "freesoilers, secessionists and disunionists." Such charges were unable to diminish the enthusiasm for the Mechanic Statesman.[23] When the votes were tallied, the "Henrymander" left the Whigs with a fourteen-seat majority in the assembly, but Democrats managed to win a thirteen-to-twelve advantage in the senate. Across the state, Johnson defeated Henry for governor and received over 7,500 more votes than Pierce had nine months earlier.[24]

Johnson's inaugural address put the capstone on his party's return to its original appeal. In this speech, the new governor equated self-government with Christianity and declared that the Democratic party had "undertaken the *political redemption of man*." "Democracy progressive corresponds also to the Church Militant: both fighting against error—one in the moral, the other in the political field," Johnson declared, concluding that "Democracy is a ladder, corresponding in politics, to the one spiritual which Jacob saw in his vision; one up which all, in proportion to their merit, many ascend." Johnson's association of Democracy with Christianity was deplored by Whigs as evidence of his unsuitability for public office. They failed, however, to see the significance of this speech, for its central theme clearly echoed James Polk's inaugural address in 1839 and among Democrats reinforced their understanding of the history of parties in the country. Party division, Johnson recalled, went back to the federal Constitutional Convention and involved "the advocates of a popular form of government, vesting the sovereign power in the mass of the people, and those who stood opposed to it."[25] With a Mechanic Statesman waging war against potential aristocrats, and with Johnson casting that battle as the party's central mission and its holy purpose, the 1853 campaign ultimately restored the confidence of the Democrats' constituents that their party represented real people rather than southern disunionists. Democrats would not abandon their commitment to southern rights, but after 1853, those rights would be treated as auxiliary to the party's central appeal, rather than as its defining issue. For voters, support for the Democratic party would provide the best way to protect both slavery and Union, but until either appeared seriously threatened, Democrats would emphasize their work for the "political redemption of man." And nowhere among Democrats, in 1853 or afterward, was any more discussion heard about defending southern rights "to the last extremity."

While Democrats recovered from factional strife, Whigs suffered their own dissension, stemming from a direct challenge to the preeminence of John Bell. The senior senator had stood as Tennessee's dominant Whig since his election in 1847 in the wake of his early advocacy of Zachary Taylor's presidential claims. Taylor's election placed Bell in control of appointments to federal offices in the state, and he preserved that power after the president's death, by ingratiating himself with Millard Fillmore's administration.

The return to public office of James C. Jones, though, disrupted Bell's leadership of the party. The popular "Lean Jimmy" had announced his retirement from politics at the conclusion of his second term as governor in 1845, but since that time, he had been far from inactive. A disciple of Henry Clay, Jones devoted much of his energy to promoting internal improvements in the state. In 1850, he had moved to Memphis to take over the presidency of the Memphis and

Charleston Railroad Company. For the most part, Jones had maintained a low profile in political affairs—his leadership of the 1848 movement to commit the state party to Henry Clay over Zachary Taylor for the presidential nomination had been his most visible activity—while building a solid political base among Whigs in the cotton counties of West Tennessee and entrepreneurial Clay Whigs throughout the state. This political engineering paid off in 1851, when he emerged as the winning candidate to serve as the state's new United States senator.

As the assembly's session opened, the leading senatorial candidate had been Bell's favorite, East Tennessee's Thomas A. R. Nelson. Nelson expected the seat as a reward for filling in for William B. Campbell after an illness took Campbell out of the gubernatorial canvass temporarily. Several other aspirants, including Ephraim H. Foster, former Congressman Milton Brown, Gustavus A. Henry, and John Netherland, joined Jones in challenging Nelson's claims. Campbell, annoyed by Nelson's attempt "to ride on my popularity" into the Senate, refused to endorse any candidate.[26] After several contentious sessions, a Whig caucus came within one vote of approving Nelson's election, but on the final ballot, three East Tennessee representatives—"particular friends of Gov. Campbell," the *American* noted—abandoned Nelson for Jones and gave the West Tennessean the caucus nomination. The assembly ratified the caucus's selection, and the amateur poet Nelson wrote a bitter satire implying that Campbell was responsible for his defeat. Democratic newspapers obtained copies of Nelson's poem, but, even before its publication embarrassed Campbell, Whig leaders faced the condemnation of East Tennesseans who charged that their sectional interests had been betrayed.[27]

Whig leaders saw less danger in sectional rivalry than in the emergence of Jones as a political wild card. T. Nixon Van Dyke of Athens told Campbell that several East Tennesseans had assured him that "the Whigs there have a warmer feeling for Jones than Nelson, and that Nelson will receive cold comfort there if he attempts to array a party against Jones." Henry acknowledged to Nelson that Jones "is a potent man & possesses a wonderful popularity" and added with a touch of irony, "I am of the opinion we both underrate him."[28] Jones quickly showed that he intended to use his seat to hunt for bigger game.

At this time it was uncertain who the Whigs' 1852 presidential nominee would be. The Tennessee party strongly favored the incumbent, Millard Fillmore; with the signer of the Compromise of 1850 measures at the head of the ticket, Whigs were sure that they could continue their stand as the party of Union against the advocates of disunion. Fillmore's nomination was uncertain, though, because northern Whigs had expressed a preference for General Winfield Scott. In Tennessee, Whigs recognized Scott as the weaker candidate, because of his reputed association with abolitionists.[29] Throughout the spring, Whigs tried to enhance Fillmore's standing by praising the president in newspapers and county meetings, so as to show the candidate's strength in the state.[30]

Before departing for Washington, Jones attached his own aspirations to Fillmore's popularity by arranging for the state convention in February to endorse Fillmore's candidacy while recommending Jones himself as the party's vice-presidential nominee—with his recent rivals for the Senate, Henry and Nelson, at the head of the state's electoral ticket.[31] Upon reaching the capital, however, Jones and his lieutenant, Representative William Cullom of Carthage, immediately began working to promote Scott's nomination.[32] Perhaps, as some of his opponents feared, the new senator hoped to place himself in a position in which a convention deadlocked over Fillmore and Scott would select him as a suitable compromise candidate. Whatever hopes he may have had for a place on the national ticket were dashed when Jones treated Washington politicians like the voting masses, particularly in his first speech in the Senate. "He raved and ranted more than I ever saw him rave and rant on the stump," Gentry wrote of this speech. "Senators were disappointed and some of them disgusted."[33] Still, Jones's maneuvering proved decisive. At the party's national convention in June, Tennessee's delegation cast a unanimous vote for Fillmore on the first forty-six ballots; but on the next ballot, Jones persuaded three other members of the delegation to join him in voting for Scott. This switch helped to break the convention's deadlock and paved the way for the general's ultimate nomination. Jones in fact was given the honor of announcing to the convention that Scott had written a letter endorsing the convention's platform. This move was intended to satisfy southern Whigs concerning Scott's acceptance of the Compromise of 1850, since the platform declared the agreement's "finality"; but its largest impact was to demonstrate that the Tennessean's crucial support had placed him in the company of the party's national leadership. The way was now open to Jones for a possible cabinet position in a Scott administration; at a minimum, as Bell realized, Jones would be "apt to command the patronage of Ten. if Scott is elected." That power would lift Jones past Bell into position as the state's dominant Whig.[34]

Scott's nomination received a cold reception in Tennessee. In itself, the candidate's ambiguity on the Compromise of 1850 was distasteful enough, but Whig leaders found particularly offensive Jones's role in securing the general's nomination—a fact that Democrats refused to let voters forget.[35] Most members of the party swallowed the convention's decision, acquiescing in Scott's candidacy while emphasizing the platform's declaration that the Compromise of 1850 was final. Bell's associates, meanwhile, displayed little enthusiasm for the nominee, and some of his closest associates rebelled against the national party's choice. Brownlow's *Knoxville Whig* condemned Scott's nomination and attempted to get up an electoral ticket for Daniel Webster. Representative Christopher Williams and Representative Meredith Gentry—Bell's closest allies in Washington—openly repudiated the Whig nominee, with Gentry proclaiming in Congress that Scott "could not receive the vote of a single Southern State—not one." One of the party's leading managers in Nashville, Dr. Boyd McNairy, announced in the *American* that he would vote for Pierce, because the men behind Scott "are as corrupt as the influences which support him are dangerous to the South and the union." Bell himself used ill health as an excuse to avoid campaigning for Scott until about three weeks before election day—and then, Bell confessed, he was "forced to do [it] by my friends."[36] Jones and Cullom traversed the state assuring voters of Scott's fidelity to the Compromise of 1850, despite the absence of a written pledge from the candidate.[37] Nevertheless, Whigs remained generally apathetic concerning the election. Long before the ballots were cast, it was clear to observers that Jones's gamble had backfired.[38]

Party loyalty among most Whigs combined with Democratic disaffection to save the state for Scott. When the votes were counted, the Whig nominee beat Pierce by a majority of seventeen hundred votes. While Whigs consoled themselves after Scott's national loss with the evidence that their state was a "citadel of Whig strength," the low turnout reminded party leaders that neither candidate had inspired voters. As Brownlow noted, Whig voters "went to the ballot-box cursing the nomination and those who procured it, saying that they would go for their party. The Whigs of Tennessee voted for *their party*—not for *Scott.*"[39] The results, too, left the state party's future uncertain. Scott's devastating loss revealed the weakness of the national party, while embarrassing Tennessee's Whigs. Jones's maneuvering, meanwhile, had created a bitter division within the state party's upper echelons.

This division persisted long after the presidential election. Gentry's and Williams's refusal to accept Scott damaged their standing among Whigs, to the extent that both were forced to decline running for reelection to Congress in 1853.[40] Bell would go before the next legisla-

John Bell. Library Collection, Tennessee State Library and Archives, Nashville. Reproduction courtesy of Tennessee State Library and Archives.

ture seeking reelection to the Senate, so when Governor Campbell announced his intention to retire, Bell's associates persuaded Henry, who would be one of the senator's strongest competitors and whose service for the Scott ticket had won him the backing of Jones's followers, to run as Campbell's successor. This attempt to get Henry out of Bell's way failed when the Democratic party, rejuvenated behind Andrew Johnson, defeated Henry.[41] Henry and an embittered Nelson both challenged Bell's reelection, and the depth of the Whigs' division became manifest when Jones threw his influence behind Henry. Hard politicking and the support of ten Democratic legislators ultimately secured Bell's reelection.[42] Still, only two years after its greatest victory, Tennessee's Whig party found itself not only severely divided, but on the defensive against a revived Democratic party and associated nationally with a disintegrating organization. No doubt Bell himself was aware of the irony that his own reelection had depended upon an artificial Whig majority in the legislature, a majority created by the manipulation of legislative districts that had been arranged by his recent rival, Gustavus A. Henry.

Tennessee's Whig party thus already was in a fragile condition when Stephen A. Douglas introduced the Kansas-Nebraska Act into the United States Senate. Douglas, chairman of the Senate's Committee on Territories, originally presented a bill that would establish a territorial government in the unorganized northern portion of the Louisiana Territory. To secure southern support for his bill, Douglas had to agree to provisions that would organize two territories, with the status of slavery to be decided by popular sovereignty. The implication was that the division of the territory would result in the creation of one free and one slave state. These provisions rekindled the sectional conflict over slavery, because the application of popular sovereignty to the Louisiana Territory necessarily repealed the 1820 Missouri Compromise, which had prohibited slavery in that region north of 36°30′ latitude. After five stormy months of debate, Congress passed the bill, and President Pierce signed it into law in May 1854. Throughout the country, public argument over the act continued. In Nashville, the *Republican Banner* noted, "the question has produced on the public mind here about as much of a rifle [*sic*] as a buck shot, if dropped from the bridge, would produce on the smooth surface of the Cumberland river."[43] For the rest of the decade, the Kansas-Nebraska Act and the virtual civil war in "bleeding Kansas" became focal points of the sectional confrontation.

Democrats in Tennessee quickly endorsed Douglas's bill as a laudable measure backed by the national party. Kansas-Nebraska would mark an important step toward guaranteeing southern rights, they maintained. "It may be that slavery will never go to the new territories," the *Union and American* observed. "But it has a chance, and the south is thus saved from unconstitutional proscription and insult by Congress."[44] Consistent with the recent emphasis on their party's traditional appeal, Democrats presented the bill as a defense of the South by the triumph of democratic principles. The provision to apply popular sovereignty to a territory, the *Memphis Appeal* noted, was based "upon the principles of the compromise of 1850, which has received the unanimous approval of nearly all the States of the Union." Repeal of the Missouri Compromise restriction merely removed an unconstitutional decree from the nation's laws, since, by the 1820 act, Congress had assumed the unwarranted power to interfere with property rights in the territories; nonintervention, on the other hand, would recognize the Democratic ideal of allowing the citizens of a region to determine the fate of slavery in the states created out of the territories. "It is an important bill," the *Clarksville Jeffersonian* argued, "and a great republican principle is involved in the decision of the question—whether the people shall decide for themselves the question of their domestic institutions, or whether Congress shall have the power to decide for them— whether, in brief, the people are or are not capable of self-government."[45] Northern Democrats' support for the repeal of the Missouri restriction, moreover, reflected their devotion to a strict construction of the Constitution and so emphasized their respect for southern rights and the nationality of the Democratic party.[46]

For Whigs, Kansas-Nebraska brought the party's division into plain view before the electorate. Bell saw in the issue an opportunity to revive the Whigs in Tennessee. After remaining silent on the bill for several weeks, he finally announced his opposition to it in a speech in March; ultimately he became the only southern senator to vote against it. The bill abrogated the nation's treaty obligations to Indians in the territory, Bell argued, but the senator justified his course primarily on the ground that repeal of the Missouri Compromise was unnecessary. In a second speech delivered in May, Bell argued that the bill would only reopen national agitation on the slavery issue; rather than a vital southern interest, Kansas-Nebraska was merely a tool for promoting a dissolution of the Union. "[T]he tendency of this bill is to stimulate the formation of a sectional party organization, . . ." the senator declared; "I regard that as the last and most fatal evil which can befall this country, except the dissolution of the Union; and that last and greatest calamity to the country, the success of such a movement would infallibly bring about."[47] Most Whig papers endorsed the senator's opposition. They reinforced his argument by noting that there was no demand among Tennessee's citizens for a repeal of the Missouri Compromise and that the measure's provision for "squatter sovereignty" would allow territorial legislatures to prohibit slavery long before the organization of a state government.[48] Yet the focus of the Whigs' attacks coincided with Bell's presentation of the question as part of a disunionist plot. Behind Bell, Whigs would reinvigorate their own party by reviving the appeal that had brought them victory in 1851—that is, as the party of the Union-loving people standing against the politicians who would sacrifice the Union for their own selfish fortunes.[49]

Bell's opposition to Kansas-Nebraska, however, failed to rally the entire state party behind him. Even before Bell announced his position, Senator Jones came out in favor of the bill as a measure necessary for preserving southern equality.[50] A few Whig papers, including the influential *Nashville True Whig* and the *Knoxville Register,* likewise supported the act and endorsed Jones's approval. "Northern men, in effect, ask us if we are willing to co-operate with them in establishing a great national principle, the sheet-anchor of all hope of peace and permanent security upon the slavery question," the *True Whig* proclaimed. "For one, we answer affirmatively." Ultimately, two Tennessee Whigs in the House of Representatives joined Jones in voting for the bill.[51] With the state party's congressional delegation divided on the Kansas-Nebraska question,

Whigs were unable to present a united front on the issue; instead, they were forced to present the bill as "a question about which public men might honestly differ, without compromising their positions or principles, as Whigs."[52] The factional confrontation between Tennessee's two senators now not only was obvious to voters, but also had impeded the party's ability to present a unified position on a crucial issue. As a result, Whigs emerged from the Kansas-Nebraska debate without an issue around which to rally and with even less optimism concerning their party's future.

The Whigs' quandary coincided with a sense of confusion prevailing throughout the country following the demise of the second party system. For Democrats, the political consequences of the Kansas-Nebraska Act became acutely clear when the 1854 elections in northern states resulted disastrously for the party; Democrats lost sixty-six of the ninety-one northern seats the party had held in Congress. For Whigs, Kansas-Nebraska drove the final nail in the coffin of their own party's northern wing, which had been in the process of disintegrating since the party's poor showing in 1852.

In the northwestern states, the void left by the Whigs' disappearance had been filled by "anti-Nebraska" coalitions that, by 1855, had organized into a new "Republican" party—a party particularly frightening to southerners because it appealed only for northern support and proclaimed opposition to slavery's expansion into the territories as its central principle. "[N]o Southern man, no national or Union man no matter where he may be located, can have any sympathy for or affiliation with a party coming before the country on an issue of purely sectional character, and which looks to divide the nation into two great sectional parties and to a result fatal to the present happy fraternity of States, . . . " the Athens *Post* proclaimed. "The country might survive the rule of the democratic party under another Presidential term, but the Union would not endure under the Black Republicans a twelve month."[53]

In the Northeast, meanwhile, "Black Republican" growth was challenged by a growing nativist movement that pointed to the recently swelling immigrant population as the source of the nation's troubles. Democrats ridiculed nativists as "Know-Nothings," because members of the "Order of the Star-Spangled Banner," the movement's initial organization, had pledged to maintain the secrecy of the order's deliberations and to deny any knowledge of its proceedings. Meeting in secret, Know-Nothings selected candidates to support in elections, and, despite its clandestine origins, the "American" movement in 1855 became the Democrats' primary opponent in the East.⁵⁴ While Tennessee's Democrats trumpeted the death of Whiggery, their own party still faced major challenges in the national arena. These national developments threatened to reshape politics in the state as well.

The antislavery creed of the "Black Republicans" prevented Tennessee's Whigs from associating with that party. The American movement, on the other hand, offered a new issue and a new national organization with which to revive the party. Americanism's potential appeal became apparent in late 1854 and early 1855, when Democrats began to win local offices in the traditional Whig strongholds of Nashville, Memphis, and Clarksville. These elections showed that the Know-Nothing movement had reached Tennessee, for the victors had defeated regular Democratic candidates with Whig votes but had not been presented to voters until shortly before their elections.⁵⁵ After these elections, local American "councils" sprouted rapidly throughout the state. J. J. F. Billings reported to Bell in December 1854 that "the Know-nothings are strong here . . . and if they continue to increase as they have done, they can easily elect their candidate for the Presidency." Brownlow gave the senator a similar report in January 1855, noting that "the *Know Nothings* now have 150 councils in this State, and are increasing rapidly." By the time Tennessee's Americans held a state council meeting in October, the number of local councils had increased to 675.⁵⁶

While estranged Democrats benefited most immediately from Know-Nothing political support, Whigs—especially those following John Bell's lead—were the ones who recognized nativism's potential and quickly became its most prominent advocates. The upper echelons of Whiggery maintained an identity separate from the movement. Bell himself never joined an American order, and major Whig newspapers denied that they had become Know-Nothing organs. Nevertheless, Bell declared that he felt "at heart as true to the great and leading principles of the party, as I could be, were I formally initiated into one of its councils," while the party's newspapers indicated their approval by defending nativism from its critics.⁵⁷ Politicians associated with Bell, meanwhile, took over the direction of the statewide movement. Former Governor William B. Campbell became president of the state council, while two of Bell's warmest adherents, William G. Brownlow and Neill S. Brown, became Tennessee's leading spokesmen for Americanism.⁵⁸ The movement also offered Whigs who had followed Jones in the Scott gamble in 1852 a graceful way to return to a party under Bell's leadership. W. N. Bilbo had been described as a "warm friend of

Governor Jones" in 1852, but in 1856 he became editor and eventually proprietor of the state's American organ, the *Nashville Gazette*. Likewise, Congressman Felix K. Zollicoffer, who had been one of Jones's chief lieutenants, announced his conversion to Americanism and in June 1855 joined Bilbo, Brown, Brownlow, and Campbell as a delegate to the national American party convention in Philadelphia.[59]

Following Bell's lead, Americanism provided an outlet for Whigs to continue their opposition to the state's Democrats and to justify their cause as part of a national movement. In presenting their case to voters, Americans echoed the national party, attacking foreign immigrants and Roman Catholics as threats to the security of the republic. Although there were relatively few immigrants in Tennessee, Americans explained, the recent flood of foreigners to the United States and their ability to become citizens after living in the country for only five years filled the nation with a population not only ignorant of the responsibilities of republican government but also one easily manipulated by demagogic politicians. For southerners, these voters presented a particular concern, because, as Zollicoffer argued, the states with the largest foreign populations "are the hottest of all the hot beds of abolition fanaticism in the Union." Abolitionists would send immigrant voters to the new territories to populate the region with antislavery votes and use "squatter sovereignty"—the right of settlers to make laws before the organization of a state government—to prohibit slavery from existing in the territories.[60]

More ominous, Americans maintained, was the Catholic Church's sponsorship of the recent influx of immigrants. That church's hierarchical structure permitted the Pope and his minions to rule in the most oppressive of the world's absolute despotisms, and their lust for even more power had made Catholicism the enemy of freedom everywhere. The freedom enjoyed in the American republic presented a particular annoyance to the Roman despots, and the prevalence of Catholics among recent immigrants revealed that the papacy had launched a plan to destroy the republic by filling it with voters loyal to the papacy rather than to the republic. To thwart this plot, Americans promised to support legislation to "prevent the shipment to our shores of all foreign criminals and paupers" and to restrain their political influence by lengthening the period of residence required in the country before naturalization. Americans thus called upon voters to defend their freedom from the schemes of the Pope by supporting the party that promised to insure that "AMERICANS SHALL GOVERN AMERICA."[61]

The American movement also capitalized on the electorate's dissatisfaction with politicians in the traditional parties. Since the return of economic prosperity had removed the sense of urgency that had propelled party politics in the previous generation, the absence of a dominant issue and the open competition for place among leaders of both parties had encouraged the popular view that "the lust of conquest has extinguished political honesty, and made any professions of patriotism a subject of jest or of suspicion."[62] Despite the Whigs' prominence in the movement, Americans portrayed their organization as a new party altogether, one that would purify politics by rejecting the manipulations of politicians and allowing the voice of the people to direct public affairs. As a lure to Democrats, Americans admitted that "the Whig banner is no longer unfurled to the breeze" and insisted that "the question is no longer Whig or Democrat but whether Americans or Foreign Catholics shall rule America." The American party, the *Knoxville Whig* explained, "are [sic] a great and patriotic party, composed of men of all parties, who seek to restore the government to its original purity and simplicity—to put down bad men and demagogues[;] and hence these hangers-on, and designing men of both parties, oppose them." The *Nashville Gazette* agreed: "The sole object of the American party is, in short phrase, *the purification of the ballot box*, to preserve immaculate that palladium on which depends our liberties."[63]

The promotion of several Democrats for office seemed to give credence to the Americans' claim to represent a new organization, composed of members of both old parties, that sought the purification of politics. Democratic converts appear to have been disturbed by the trend of "Progressive Democracy" indicated by Andrew Johnson's emergence as leader of the state party. The distinction between "the old line Democracy of Jackson and Polk, and the 'progressive,' disorganizing, destructive, 'Red Republican' Democracy of Andrew Johnson, is clear and well-defined," the *True Whig* observed, "and independent, conservative, old-line Democrats, all over the State, cannot fail to vindicate their own consistency and self-respect . . . in *repudiating the lead* of such a monstrous HERETIC as the present Governor of Tennessee."[64]

The most important conversion was that of Andrew Jackson's nephew and private secretary, Andrew J. Donelson. Donelson had taken over in 1851 as editor of the *Washington Union*, but his editorial career proved financially disastrous and politically frustrating. He quickly learned that he had no influence among national Democratic leaders, and the Democratic majority in Congress denied him the nation's public printing business. He resigned his post for political retirement in 1852, but in 1855 he announced his allegiance to Americanism and soon became one of the leading proponents of the movement in Tennessee. In several speeches, the old hero's kinsman defended the Americans' anti-foreign principles, while condemning his former comrades as "a nullification party."[65] "Mr. Pierce and the new-school Democrats have surrendered to the nullifiers," Donelson proclaimed. "Nullification in the South is the highest passport to public favor, and stretches out its hand to nullification in the North for succor and aid. Can a sound Jackson man, or a Clay Whig, witness the fraternization without agreeing to bury their former differences on minor questions, and make one united effort to rid the country of such a systematic attack on the body politic? It is the object of the American party to accomplish this."[66]

As Donelson's sentiment indicates, despite Democratic conversions, the American appeal in Tennessee ultimately represented a continuation of Whiggery. The new party merely merged its anti-foreignism with the argument that Whigs had relied upon since 1835: that the demagogic politicians leading the Democratic party presented a threat to the voters' freedom. Most immigrants voted Democratic, Whigs charged, a fact that aided the spoils party's hold on power. Not only had immigrant votes cost Henry Clay the presidency in 1844 by swinging New York and Pennsylvania for James K. Polk, but in Tennessee, Irish railroad workers provided the party with a "floating vote" to use when needed. Also, with the introduction of sectional issues into national politics, the surge of recent immigrants would give the party of Free-Soilers and Nullifiers additional weight in the crucial coming national election. Now, Whig-Americans explained, Democrats had committed their greatest offense against republican liberty, for Catholic support for Democratic candidates provided clear evidence that the "spoilsmen" had entered into a corrupt bargain with the papacy in its efforts to subvert the republic. "Can any one doubt that the Democratic party is in league with all the dangerous elements that have disturbed and are continuing to disturb our once peaceful and happy country, and that they stickle at nothing when votes are at stake?" Thomas A. R. Nelson asked.[67] Likewise, Brownlow proclaimed that

> there never was a time known, since the dark days of the Revolution, when the civil and religious liberties of this country were so much endangered as at the present time. The danger we are threatened with [derives] from *Foreign influence,* and the rapid strides of *Romanism,* to which we may add *Native treachery,* connived at, as they are, by certain leading demagogues of the country, and a powerful and influential political party, falsely called *Democrats,* who seek the Foreign and

Catholic vote, and are willing to obtain it at the expense of Liberty, and the sacrifice of the Protestant Religion!⁶⁸

The Americans' identity with Whiggery became even clearer when American leaders turned to the sectional conflict, for the new party's position on the slavery issue proved identical to that presented by the Whigs before their division over the Kansas-Nebraska question. Disunionist politicians now stood on the verge of achieving their goal, Americans insisted; abolitionists had found an access to power in the "Black Republican" party, while southern nullifiers had come to dominate the Democrats. The American party's mission, Nashville's *True Whig* explained, "is to strangle sectionalism, by whatever name it may be called, at the North or at the South, and to foster the heart-warm, profound, all-pervading American sentiment, which recognizes the preservation of the Federal Union upon the basis of the Constitution, as a paramount duty." As for the slavery issue itself, the party promised, as the state platform stated, to "ignore the agitation of all questions, of whatever character, based upon geographical distinctions or sectional interest." No further policy statement was necessary, for, with the party devoted to the principle that "Americans must rule America" in power, citizens could be assured that the nation would lie in the hands of leaders pledged to "maintain and defend the CONSTITUTION as it stands, the UNION as it exists, and the RIGHTS of the STATES, without diminution, as guaranteed thereby." "Discarding all sectional feeling, laying aside all party bias," the *Gazette* claimed, "it [the new party] will combine all those true, calm, conservative elements, to be found in the honest, country-loving hearts of the people, without which the government . . . would have long since gone to perdition."⁶⁹ Bell, meanwhile, concluded that only in the ranks of the Americans "are to be found all the truest friends of the Union, and such as have maintained a resolute opposition to the disorganizing doctrines of nullification and secession—all the more temperate and considerate portion of the southern people, who have cultivated a fraternal feeling between the two great sections of the Union, and have always been disposed to bear and forbear, while, at the same time, they have been equally determined, with the most rash and violent, to resist any invasion of their constitutional rights."⁷⁰

The early successes of Americanism inspired conservative Whigs to believe that, behind the new party, they could recapture the governor's office in 1855. To emphasize the popular roots of the new organization, neither Americans nor the remnants of the Whigs held a nominating convention; instead, newspapers began to promote former Representative Meredith P. Gentry as the candidate chosen by the people "to discard the past, and to turn the attention of the people to the questions of the present and the future." In February, Gentry announced his candidacy, and in the summer canvass, Gentry declared himself a member of the American order.[71] Behind their candidate, the new American party launched an aggressive campaign that combined the attack on foreigners and Catholics with an assault upon "the reign of Johnsonism and Socialism in Tennessee." The incumbent's radical ideas made him "the most mischievous man in Tennessee," Gentry charged, since "his radical, transcendental, sublimated, double-distilled Johnsonian Democracy, placed him beyond his own party, and out of reach of the sympathy of the true old-fashioned Democracy, upon whose platform he did not stand, and making him stand upon a platform of his own." Gentry also reminded voters that Johnson's "White Basis" plan of representation "endangered the safety of the weakest part of the citadel of the Constitution—the institution of slavery." The challenger attempted to broaden his appeal by declaring himself in favor of a law requiring a license for the sale of "intoxicating liquors, in small quantities," a position that he hoped would win the support of the state's recently politicized temperance movement.[72] A committee of the State Temperance Convention concluded that Gentry's position "does not go far enough" and refused to endorse a gubernatorial candidate, but in a contest pitting Americanism against "Progressive Democracy," leaders of the newest party nevertheless expected Gentry to carry the temperance forces and gain control of the state government.[73]

Democrats responded quickly and angrily to the conservative Whigs' migration to Americanism. From its earliest appearance, Democratic spokesmen denounced Know-Nothingism itself as an ally of Abolitionism. When Democrats were lured to join American orders, party leaders released their sharpest attacks against the intolerant features of Know-Nothingism as threats to republican liberty. The secrecy of the Know-Nothings' organization prevented open political discussion and would allow an "unholy combination" to gain, "by secret means, the management of the government," while "the rights of the humble citizen, natural and acquired, civil and religious," would be "degraded." Assaults on Catholics represented an attack on "the right of every man to worship God according to the dictates of his conscience" and threatened the power of the state with a "Protestant Jesuitism, which would steal the implements of the Inquisition to torture Catholics with."[74] In fact, Democrats maintained, Know-Nothingism was really nothing more than a new disguise for their old

Whig enemies, for those ambitious politicians had taken up secret organization and the false issue of immigration restriction as a means to return to power.⁷⁵ No Democrat could accept the Know-Nothing platform and remain loyal to Democratic principles, party leaders warned, while those who deserted the party would find themselves locked into an organization led by abolitionists and "bound by an oath to vote for President for the man whom these abolitionists dictate."⁷⁶

Though Americans claimed that the issues separating the old parties had passed away, Democrats maintained that their own party stood intact and still pledged to fight the enemies of freedom. "If Know-Nothingism is sustained, farewell to the liberties of America," Democrats asserted. "The two things are absolutely, and essentially incompatible. . . . If Know-Nothingism is perpetuated[,] Republicanism is at an end!"⁷⁷ The Democrats' mission thus became, as the *Union and American* declared,

> to begin back again in politics at the Declaration of Independence and the adoption of the Constitution, and fight over again, with the enemies of free government and liberty of conscience the great battle of equal government and religious freedom. Our opponents have gone into secret lanes and dark holes and sworn a horrible oath to require a religious test as a qualification for office. They are making an effort to revive a still more odious policy than that which consigned to lasting disgrace the administration of JOHN ADAMS. It is again the mission of the great democratic party to protect and defend the inalienable right of every man to worship God according to the dictates of his own conscience.⁷⁸

Andrew Johnson personally led the Democrats' counteroffensive against Americanism. After the state party convention nominated him for another term, the governor—recognizing a serious challenge to his career—met Gentry in the canvass head-on with his own aggressive campaign. Johnson particularly assailed his opponent's record in Congress, especially Gentry's support for a protective tariff; his 1850 vote for the bill to abolish the slave trade in Washington, D. C.; his preference in 1852 for the presidential candidacy of former Federalist Daniel Webster; and, since his retirement, his failure to take a position on the Kansas-Nebraska Act.⁷⁹

The governor unleashed his most savage attacks on Know-Nothingism's threats to republican government. He ridiculed the order's work in Tennessee, because of the small number of foreigners and Catholics in the state. "There were in Tennessee, one hundred and thirty-four native born Americans, to one foreigner," Johnson noted, "and was it necessary for one hundred and thirty-four to band together to control one man? Must you come together in secret conclave, with solemn oaths, to protect yourselves?" If the Know-Nothings succeeded in expelling Catholics from the country simply because of their "objectionable tenets," they "would be strong enough to put up another on account of their acceptable and approved religious principles. This being so, is a practical union of church and State, and would in short time be followed by legislative enactments making it the established church or religion of the land."[80] The heart of Johnson's campaign remained what it had been in 1853: that the Democratic party still stood ready to defend the people against their perpetual enemies. "This *secret political* organization," Johnson declared, "though recent and new, among the people of this country, was nothing more nor less than ancient *Federalism*, making its appearance under a new name, as it had done at various periods since the formation of the Constitution of the United States."[81]

Against Americanism, Johnson faced a more difficult opponent than he had two years earlier. Ultimately, the governor and his party benefited less from their own efforts than from developments that weakened the American cause. Most ominous for Americans was the split in the national party meeting in Philadelphia in June. Delegates from several northern states—including those where the party had run strongest in state elections—walked out of the meeting after the convention accepted a resolution committing the party to regard all existing legislation on the slavery issue, including the Kansas-Nebraska Act, as final. The document approved by the remaining members coincided with the Tennessee Americans' determination to ignore future sectional issues, but its passage by a rump national meeting diluted the new party's claim to nationality—a fact that Democrats made clear to voters. Although some Americans, like the editor of the *True Whig*, welcomed the withdrawal and maintained that their party had been "thoroughly purged of Abolition agitation," Democrats countered that the American platform "was passed by the representatives of the States where know-nothingism has no hope of success."[82]

Most devastating to the American cause was the rejection of the movement by a significant portion of Tennessee's Whigs. Once again, Senator James C. Jones led the resistance to a movement that ultimately would enhance John Bell's standing in state and national politics. Newspapers allied with the junior senator at first urged a state convention and hesitated to support Gentry because of his refusal to accept Scott in 1852, although most of them eventually gave at least token endorsement to the candidate.[83] Jones himself, meanwhile,

James C. Jones, by Washington B.Cooper, c. 1842. Library Collection, Tennessee State Library and Archives, Nashville. Reproduction courtesy of Tennessee State Library and Archives, Nashville.

publicly kept his distance from the American movement until May, when he issued a public letter declaring his refusal to join the order because of its secret organization and its political proscription of Catholics. Moreover, Jones proclaimed that he looked upon the conflict in Tennessee "with but little interest," because the battle over foreign influence only distracted southerners from the war being waged against them by antislavery advocates in the North. While southerners engaged in a "war of self-immolation" in an insignificant party contest over foreign influence, Jones asserted, "the enemies of our rights and institutions are banded together. Strengthened by our dissensions, arrogant and self-possessed, they send out their notes of defiance, proclaiming a war of extermination to our institutions of the South." The senator then called upon Tennessee's voters to accept "an abandonment of petty hostilities, a burying of ancient feuds and prejudices," and to join together in "a union of all for the sake of the Union—a union of the South for the safety of the South."[84]

With this declaration, Jones became the most visible member of a faction of "Old Line Whigs" in Tennessee. These Whigs not only refused to accept the American party and maintained their separate identity, but also they now insisted that the defense of southern rights within the Union presented the most crucial issue facing the country. In the past it had been safe for southerners to divide into parties, Jones explained, but now, "grown in numbers, strengthened by madness, *(and our forbearance)* [and] supported by law," the enemies of the South "present themselves in bold, arrogant defiance, threatening the destruction of our rights, even, at the expense of the Union."[85] The current state canvass thus held little attraction for Old Line Whigs, and they displayed no enthusiasm for supporting either a radical Democrat or a former Whig who had contributed to the disintegration of the national party. All the while, Jones worked behind the scenes to thwart the Americans' efforts. "Jones seems to be against us," Zollicoffer noted in June. Another American reported that Jones backed a Whig challenger to the Americans' congressional candidate in Memphis and that, when the senator returned to the city, he set "at work there in poisoning the minds of Whigs from not voting for Gentry."[86]

The recalcitrance of Old Line Whigs ultimately cost the American party the election that produced the first disruption of traditional voting patterns since 1839. The Henrymander preserved an anti-Democratic majority in the assembly, although Democrats gained a one-seat advantage in the house. Nevertheless, the Henrymander failed to preserve the dominance of the congressional delegation, as each party carried five of the state's ten districts. Johnson again eked out a narrow victory in the gubernatorial contest, winning reelection by about twenty-one hundred votes. Both Democratic and American observers agreed that the Old Line Whigs had determined the result; the *Union and American*'s editors proclaimed that they had "no doubt, and we very cheerfully make the admission, that JOHNSON would this time have been defeated but for whig votes."[87]

The vigorous campaigning by both parties encouraged an eight-thousand-vote increase in turnout over that of 1853, and the returns indicated that the American cause ran strongest in Johnson's East Tennessee. In Middle and West Tennessee, Old Line Whigs had the most impact. Gentry's total increased only 750 votes over Henry's in the central division, while Johnson drew 2,200 more votes than he had in 1853 and carried Middle Tennessee by almost 5,000 votes. In traditionally Whig West Tennessee, the candidates ran a close race, and Gentry prevailed in the division by only 300 votes. Despite the apparent strength of the parties, Democratic and American leaders believed that substantial numbers of voters had switched allegiance. The *Union and American*, for one, estimated that about 5,000 Whigs and 5,000 Democrats each had crossed party lines. Brownlow, meanwhile, attributed Johnson's strength in West Tennessee "to the account of James C. Jones, who has gone over, soul and body, to his old political enemies."[88]

The loss of the governor's election came as a severe blow to American leaders, and they entered the 1856 campaign aware that the future of their party depended on the result of the presidential election.[89] The defection of the Old Line Whigs, combined with the national issues involved in the presidential contest, compelled Americans to shift their emphasis toward the sectional controversy. At its state convention in February, the party abandoned its secret organization. The convention's president, William M. Cocke, set the meeting's tone with a speech linking the Americans' hostility to immigrants and Catholics to the defense of southern rights. At the end of its proceedings, the convention approved a series of resolutions that made no mention of the Americans' nativist principles, beyond endorsing the national party platform, while encouraging the national Americans to repeal "all ceremonial of initiation into the American party, and all obligations of secrecy" and pledging the state party to oppose "any and all further agitation" upon the slavery question.[90]

This convention signaled the Tennessee Americans' intention to stake their party's future—as they had done in 1851, as Whigs—upon their claim to stand as the conservative party of Union. This claim received a boost when the national American convention at Philadelphia nominated Millard Fillmore as the party's presidential candidate. Privately, Americans complained about the choice of Tennessean Andrew J. Donelson as the vice-presidential nominee—"He has so many political sins to answer for to the Whigs, and the democrats look on him as a traitor," one young American observed[91]— but the conjunction on the ticket of the former Whig president and the nephew of "Old Hickory" fit perfectly the Americans' plan to enter the canvass as the national alliance of "Americans, Old Line Whigs, and Union Democrats," who would "fall back upon the Fillmore ticket as the only hope of defeating southern Democratic and Northern Black Republican *Disunionists.*"[92]

Americans met a Democratic party also proclaiming its national character, because the election had taken on portentous implications for the future of the Union. Sectional hostility had intensified since the passage of the Kansas-Nebraska Act had reopened the issue of slavery's expansion. Tensions exacerbated even more after a virtual civil war broke out in Kansas between settlers from northern and southern states.[93] In June, the Republican convention nominated John C. Frémont as its presidential candidate. Despite the Republicans' promises only to restore the Missouri Compromise line in the Louisiana Purchase territory and to respect slavery where it already existed, southern voters feared that the result of a Republican administration would be "to prohibit and exclude slavery from all the Territories of the United States." Such a result would effectively deny southerners "their equality in the Union" and "greatly endanger if not utterly destroy the integrity of the Union." So powerful was their fear that politicians in the Lower South threatened to lead their states in secession, should the abolitionists' candidate prevail.[94] The only hope for the Union appeared to be the success of a party with a national following, committed both to the preservation of the Union and the protection of southern rights. Only such a national party could prevent the Republicans from coming into power, respect southern rights in slave property, respect the region's equality in the Union, and remove from Lower South demagogues any justification for dissolving the Union. In Tennessee, the 1856 election would be fought over which party, Americans or Democrats, actually did stand as the true national party. The support of the Old Line Whigs would determine the outcome.

The close result of the 1855 elections reminded Democrats of the need to wage an aggressive campaign. At the national convention, the state's delegation voted for the incumbent, Franklin Pierce, on the first five ballots; but on the next ballot, the delegates switched their votes to the eventual victor, Pennsylvania's James Buchanan. This switch probably reflected the influence of Aaron V. Brown, who took the lead in the canvass for Buchanan upon returning to Tennessee.[95] Few members of the party were inspired by the nominee. "There is not much feeling with the democrats here for Buchanan," Andrew Johnson concluded. "There is an acquiescence in his nomination; but no decided zeal felt or manifested for him."[96] Nevertheless, Johnson took the stump for the party's candidate, and Democrats entered the canvass with a conviction that they had the best opportunity to carry the state for a presidential candidate since the days of Andrew Jackson.

The Democrats' message directly challenged the Americans' claim to stand as the party of Union. According to Democrats, the only real contest pitted their own party against the Black Republicans of the North, for the Know-Nothings had no substantial following in the country and no chance to win the national election. "The hope of the opponents of the democracy," party spokesmen maintained, "is, by running a third ticket to take away from the democratic candidates three or four southern States, and thus throw the election into the House of Representatives." Even if the Americans did present a national organization, they offered no solution to the sectional crisis. Their platform promised only to avoid all sectional issues, a position that revealed the party's inability to agree upon the most vital issue before the public.[97]

Democrats, on the other hand, promised to apply the principle of popular sovereignty to all territories as the only just solution to the question of slavery's expansion. Since northern and southern Democrats alike agreed to abide by nonintervention, the National Democracy alone stood pledged to protect southern rights. And since the Democratic party alone enjoyed a following in all states, that party alone had the opportunity to prevent the election of a Black Republican and the attack on southern rights that inevitably would follow. "The conviction is becoming more firmly fixed in the minds of the people," the *Memphis Appeal* concluded, "that the Democratic party is the great conservative and constitutional party upon which the country must mainly rely for its prosperity and salvation." Likewise, the *Union and American* proclaimed that "the people of the United States are now satisfied that there is but one *National Party*. In other days of trouble they have looked to the Democracy, and they have never looked in vain."[98]

Fillmore's backers countered by attacking the weaknesses of the Democratic candidate. Buchanan, they noted, had begun his political career as an avowed Federalist; Jackson himself had distrusted the Pennsylvanian, since he had encouraged "Old Hickory" to negotiate a "corrupt bargain" with Henry Clay for the presidency in 1824. The candidate's entire career had epitomized that of the greedy spoilsman—"A Politician But Not A Statesman"—striving to advance his personal ambitions with little concern for the good of the people.[99] Likewise, Americans charged that Buchanan's party could never resolve the crisis facing the country. Democratic leaders, "for the purpose of individual aggrandizement and party ascendancy," themselves had reopened the debate over slavery's expansion. Now the party based its nationality on its popular sovereignty doctrine; but actually it trumpeted the "squatter sovereignty" version of the doctrine in the North, while maintaining in the South that slavery's status could only be decided by a state government.[100] In fact, southern voters could trust only the American party to defend their rights. The party stood pledged to uphold the country's laws, and currently the laws allowed settlers to take slave property into territories before the organization of a state government. Moreover, the Americans' determination to prevent "newly landed" immigrants from voting would neutralize the influence of slavery's most "earnest, resolute, [and] uncompromising foe," the nation's foreign population.[101]

Still, the heart of the American appeal remained its claim to be the only party that could prevent dissolution of the Union. Both the Republicans and the Democrats "are *sectional*, and the open and avowed advocates of disunion," the *Knoxville Whig* explained, while the Democrats' extreme defense of southern rights showed that it "has been Calhounized into a Southern Sectional Division party." The sectional support for the Democrats showed that they had no chance to win the election, but they presented Buchanan as a candidate only for the purpose of drawing support from Fillmore and contributing to Frémont's election. That event would justify secession and the formation of the southern confederacy the nullifiers had long desired.[102] Since the Democrats had dwindled to a minority faction with only southern support, the only hope to prevent disunion lay in the triumph of "the only true and reliable Union party in the country" and its candidate, "a distinguished Ex-President of the Republic, whose patriotic and successful efforts in a trying crisis, have given him an endearing [*sic*] hold upon the heart of the nation." "The Union is the only sure protection of slavery," the *Athens Post* explained, "and Mr. Fillmore's election and the triumph of Americanism constitute the only sure guarantee of the protection of the Union."[103]

Still, Americans found winning the support of the Old Line Whigs a difficult task. The party's claim to nationality was severely weakened by the failure of the national American party's convention to unite its northern and southern wings. After nominating Fillmore and Donelson, the convention divided when several northern delegates again walked out of the meeting, this time because the party refused to call for a restoration of the Missouri Compromise.[104] In April, Senator Jones issued a public letter stating his intention "to wait and see who the Democratic party will present to us" and promising to "cast my vote for that man and with that party which I think most likely to protect the Constitution, [and] preserve the Union." In the same month, James Williams, a former Whig legislator, began publishing a series of anonymous letters in the *Union and American* under the pseudonym "An Old Clay Whig." These letters presented a scathing critique of the American movement and denounced the new party as an "abandonment and repudiation of old whig principles." Upon Buchanan's nomination, the "Old Clay Whig" urged his compatriots to join him in supporting the Democrats and "the eminently National and Constitutional platform upon which they stand"; that platform, Williams explained, "cannot fail to attract to their support the conservative elements of all political organizations, North and South, which have divided the country." The *Union and American* reported that Williams's articles "produced quite a fluttering in the ranks of the opposition," and editor E. G. Eastman observed that Old Line Whigs took prominent roles at county meetings ratifying the Democratic nomination. Most of these Whigs probably agreed with the reasoning of Memphis's William T. Avery, who made a full conversion to the Democrats, "1st. Because I am with them in the main issues which will be before the Country—and 2dly. Because I think it is the only party in existence which combines any elements of organized strength at the North, favorable to the South—in other words *national*." To no one's surprise, Jones announced in August his determination to vote for Buchanan. Upon returning to Tennessee from Washington, the senator spoke at Democratic rallies in favor of the Democratic ticket, as "affording the only and last hope of security to the South."[105]

While Old Line Whigs remained aloof from the Americans, Democrats who had supported the new movement began to move back to their original party. Many Democratic Americans followed the course of Alfred Robb. Robb had been elected mayor of Clarksville when the American movement made its first stirring in 1854, but during the presidential campaign, he announced that he would vote for Buchanan, because national developments had convinced him that an antislavery coalition among "the Fillmore and Frémont men north, acquiesced and winked at, by the south," had conspired against the Democratic nominee.[106] Gentry's loss in 1855 and the declining prospects of the new party encouraged aspiring Democrats—most likely including Robb—to make amends with their old political allies. In any case, in mid-July James McCallum informed Bell from Pulaski that there were "but very few American democrats in this county, but are now for Buchanan.[107] As the campaign progressed, it became increasingly apparent that the Americans, despite their claim to present an alliance of "Americans, Old Line Whigs, and Union Democrats," enjoyed the support only of the Bell faction of the old Whig party.

Americans nevertheless kept up their offensive and expressed their enthusiasm about Fillmore's prospects. In September, John Bell and sixteen other Fillmore supporters tried to lure Old Liners once and for all by attending a makeshift national Whig convention at Baltimore that promptly endorsed Fillmore's candidacy.[108] The American cause suffered its most severe setback, though, in October, when state elections in Pennsylvania and Indiana resulted in Democratic victories. These results showed the extent of the Democrats' strength in important northern states and indicated that Buchanan would carry them in the November election. In those states, meanwhile, the Americans were believed to have formed fusion tickets with Republicans—a charge that not only revealed the limits of the party's claim to nationality but also suggested that its northern wing indeed had been "abolitionized."[109] In desperation, Fillmore's supporters pleaded with voters to consider their candidate the only defender of the Union against sectional extremists. Nevertheless, by November it had become clear to voters that the Democratic party alone enjoyed a national following. To prevent the election of a Black Republican—and hence prevent disunion—Old Line Whigs would have to cast their votes for the Democratic candidate.

Few were surprised, then, when Buchanan carried Tennessee on his way to victory in the national election. Fillmore, in fact, suffered a more devastating defeat than had Winfield Scott four years earlier, as the American candidate won the electoral votes only of Maryland. The Democratic nominee carried all other slave states and five free states, while Frémont prevailed in all of the remaining northern states. In Tennessee, the shift of the Old Line Whigs gave the Democrats a margin of over six thousand votes. The tallies closely followed traditional party lines in the eastern and middle Grand Divisions, although the victors did increase their majority in Middle Tennessee to almost seven thousand votes. In Jimmy Jones's West Tennessee, Buchanan won over twenty-seven hundred more voters than Johnson had the previous year, and Democrats carried the region for the first time since 1832.

Democrats throughout the state celebrated their triumph—as Whigs had five years earlier, ironically—as a victory for the nation's conservative party of Union. "The democracy have won their victory of peace—over fierce fanaticism, unholy combinations, secret conclaves, malignant and aimless abuse, and unprincipled demagogueism—and the country is safe," William F. Cooper concluded. "The patriot may sleep in peace for at least four years." "The victory has been achieved, and it is a National one, . . ." the *Appeal* echoed. "Sectionalism is trampled under foot, and the whole Union has good cause to feel proud of the triumphs achieved."[110] The Democrats' opponents, meanwhile, could do little but wait for further developments to show them their future path. Many Americans no doubt agreed with the sentiments of one Fillmore supporter. "We have had a terrible thrashing but we all console ourselves with the reflection that our Candidate was the most conservative and union loving in practice of the trio," Lucius J. Polk observed, concluding, "We are delighted however that Frémont has been defeated instead of Buchanan."[111]

In five brief years, Democrats had rebounded from their subordinate position to become the dominant party in Tennessee. The refusal of the Old Line Whigs to follow their former compatriots into the American party gave Democrats a commanding majority among voters. Americans, meanwhile, were left broken, discouraged, and on the defensive; they had little with which to appeal to voters, other than the Whigs' traditional opposition to Democrats.

The new majority party consolidated its control of the state by demolishing its opponents in the 1857 state elections. Southern Rights Democrat Isham G. Harris easily won the governor's office over American Robert S. Hatton, a thirty-one-year-old political novice whose nomination, the *Clarksville Jeffersonian* observed, showed that the Americans' "leading men had no desire to sacrifice themselves for the good of the party." Not even the Henrymander could save the party, for Democrats won seven of ten congressional seats and a commanding twenty-seat majority in the General Assembly. "The American party are completely routed & broken down, and at present have no future prospects," William Campbell concluded. "They must await for future developments and the actions of the two great sectional parties."[112] Such a strong result helped to harmonize the Democrats' factions, since the party now controlled enough offices to satisfy its prominent men. The assembly's majority gladly cast "Lean Jimmy" Jones into political oblivion, replacing him in the Senate with the "mechanic statesman," Andrew Johnson. So assured of popular approval were Democrats that the assembly did not hesitate to elect Johnson's ally, A. O. P. Nicholson, to succeed John Bell for the term that would begin when Bell's expired in 1859. And Tennessee's most prominent advocate of southern rights, Aaron V. Brown, observed these operations from Washington, where he enjoyed his new position as Postmaster General, his reward for his service to the Buchanan ticket in Tennessee.

Democrats prevailed during the political crisis of the 1850s because they succeeded in convincing a majority of voters, and especially Old Line Whigs, that the party of Jackson was the only party in the country with a national following. That party remained committed to defending the right of southerners to take slave property into the territories, but it denied flatly any intention to accept disunion as an option and offered popular sovereignty as the best way to preserve the Union. Democrats profited largely from the dissolution of the national Whig party and from the division within the state Whig party. Old Liners had nowhere to turn in national politics but either to their old enemies or to a new party with clandestine origins. The Americans were unable to convince a number of them that their party had a national following. Moreover, the bitter rivalry between Tennessee's two Whig senators made it difficult for Jones supporters to accept a movement that ultimately would preserve the predominance of Bell's wing. Equally crucial to the Democrats' success was Andrew Johnson's revival of the party earlier in the decade. Before Old Line Whigs could be persuaded to support a new party of Union, the Democrats' own rank and file had to be reassured that their own party sought to defend the liberty of all citizens and not just the interests of slaveholders. The populist campaign of the "mechanic statesman" successfully distanced Democrats from the "disunionist" label they had acquired in 1850, and it restored the faith of Democratic voters that their party still stood, as it had in the days of Jackson and Polk, as the party of equal rights, strict construction, and opposition to the schemes of Federalists and Abolitionists.

Despite the Democrats' success, the basis of Tennessee's two-party system survived. Only a few Old Line Whigs converted to the Democratic party. Most still clung to the Whig name and promised to work with whichever party appeared able to form a national coalition to preserve the Union. Should the Whig-Americans ever construct a national coalition, Old Liners indicated, they would gladly rejoin their former comrades. As a result, the survival of the party system profoundly shaped voters' outlook on the growing sectional rift in the nation. In the Lower South, the collapse of the Whig party encouraged Whigs, in desperation, to make more extreme demands on Democrats to prove their loyalty to slavery. In Tennessee, however, the continued possibility of victory—along with the legacies of the Democrats' stumbling over the politics of slavery during the Crisis of 1850 and of Jackson's condemnation of Nullification—led both Whigs and Democrats to couple the defense of slavery with conservative claims that their respective organizations offered the best defense of the Union. A national party resisting the sectional demagoguery of both the "Black Republicans" and the southern Fire-Eaters, both parties argued, provided the only hope for preserving the Union and, hence, for protecting slavery. With this argument apparently confirmed in the 1856 presidential election, both Whig and Democratic voters continued to believe that the efforts of a national party, committed to the defense of both slavery and Union, somehow could avert sectional conflict.

As the national party system devolved into two sectional organizations, a majority of Tennessee's voters could take some comfort in their belief that the success of their dominant party could perpetuate the constitutional Union that guaranteed their freedom. Yet the strength of the Republican party in the North must have disturbed them. Almost immediately after learning the results of the 1856 contest, the remnants of the American party began to warn voters that

Buchanan's election would not remove the specter of disunion."What will be the consequence[,] time alone can develop," Campbell observed."I have no doubt that in the next congress parties will assume an absolute sectional condition & our next presidential canvass will be entirely sectional." Brownlow's *Knoxville Whig* bluntly stated the issue for its readers:"It is now apparent to every candid mind, and to every reading man, who is not biased by prejudice, that the Democratic party in this country, is the *Disunion* party—seeking to destroy the Constitution, and form a *Southern Confederacy*, to be composed of the Slave States alone.The Democratic party at the North is *abolitionized*, and will favor a dissolution, intending to have a *Northern Confederacy*, composed alone of the Free States. Hence, the next Presidential contest will be fought directly upon this issue."[113]

The failure of popular sovereignty to resolve the issue of slavery's expansion insured that the sectional conflict would dominate Buchanan's administration, and the division of the Democratic party at the next presidential election would leave voters with no clearly national organization.The response of Tennessee's voters to the result of that election marked the end of their antebellum party system, while the events of the following months led them into a new political era.

EIGHT

The Politics of Revolution: Tennessee in the Crisis of Union
1858–1861

Tennessee's antebellum party system would end with the presidential election of 1860. In that election, most voters still acted out of their traditional party loyalties, but the national victory of Republican candidate Abraham Lincoln and the secession of the Lower South states presented voters with an issue that cut across the long-standing party lines. Democratic and Whig leaders both proclaimed the old parties obsolete, as they called upon voters to unite behind the new cause of either the South or the Union.

Despite the demise of the party system, the voters' understanding of politics persisted through the crisis of Union. Historians have long recognized the unusual course pursued by Tennesseans during the winter of secession. Voters at first overwhelmingly rejected secession and made Tennessee one of the Upper South border states that refused immediately to join the Lower South. After the outbreak of war at Fort Sumter, citizens in West and Middle Tennessee quickly reversed their position, as they rushed their state into the Confederacy; while in East Tennessee a majority remained loyal to the Union throughout the conflict. The voters' experience in the political system that had existed for the past thirty years profoundly influenced their response to the crisis. Indeed, it is difficult, if not impossible, to understand Tennessee's experience in the crisis of Union without viewing it in the context of the state's antebellum political world.

After the American party's losses in 1856 and 1857, the Democrats' opponents appeared to have little ammunition with which to challenge the new majority party. John Bell attempted to provide an issue at the end of February 1857 when he introduced into the Senate a bill providing for distribution to the states of the public lands and the proceeds from their sale. Gubernatorial candidate Robert Hatton staked his candidacy upon the distribution issue, along with a call for the restriction of foreigners' voting in territories. At the same time, Hatton persisted in charging that his Democratic opponent, Isham G. Harris, was "himself as much a nullifier as any hot blooded South Carolinian."[1] Harris's landslide victory revealed the futility of the distribution and anti-foreign appeals, while Millard Fillmore's dismal showing made the American party's attacks on the Democrats' nationality seem groundless. With Hatton's loss, the Know-Nothing movement withered away in Tennessee. The *Republican Banner* noted shortly after the contest that "it would be difficult for any one to predict, with any certainty, into what political association he may—or may not—be thrown, within the next 2 or 3 years."[2]

The suspension of specie payments in consequence of the Panic of 1857 allowed remnants of the Whigs to experience a brief revival. Discarding the name "American party" for the more generic label "Opposition," party spokesmen revived the accusation that hard times were the consequence of the Democrats' long-standing hard-money doctrines. Behind gubernatorial nominee John Netherland, the Opposition based its 1859 campaign on the promise to recharter the Union and Planters' banks in Nashville, as the surest guarantee of a stable currency.[3] The elections' results offered hope for the Democrats' challengers. Although Netherland lost to the incumbent Harris, the statewide anti-Democratic total increased by almost eight thousand votes over that of 1857. In the assembly, the Opposition cut the Democratic majority in half, to only ten seats. Most astonishingly, Opposition candidates won in seven of the ten congressional districts. "In these elections Tennessee administers a rebuke to the leaders of the Democratic party which they cannot but feel,..." the *Athens Post* exclaimed. "It is but an intimation of what is in store for them in 1860."[4]

The Opposition's jubilance actually rested upon a weak foundation. Although the party did increase its tally over the 1857 American vote, it still fell short of the usual Whig turnout; and the successes in the congressional elections depended primarily on the "Henrymander," the favorable apportionment of districts devised by the Whig majority in the 1851 assembly. The currency issue also had run its course even before the opening of the 1859 canvass, because the banks had resumed specie payments in the previous year.[5] Democrats channeled concern over the currency into their own traditional opposition to irresponsible corporations whose power threatened popular control in the state. Promising to rein in the banks with a series of reforms that would secure "a sufficient supply of specie to take the place of the shinplasters which have been circulating in this State," Democrats maintained that the 1859 contest centered upon "the simple question" of: "Shall the banks govern the people, or shall the people govern the banks?"[6] The Opposition's reliance upon economic issues thus failed to weaken severely the Democratic following. Instead, it allowed the majority party to reassert its own position as the enemy of an aristocratic "money power."

The persistent controversy over the expansion of slavery proved most beneficial to the Democrats. Sectional concerns dominated James Buchanan's administration from its outset. Two days after the new president's inauguration in 1857, the Supreme Court, in the case of *Dred Scott v. Sandford,* declared that Congress had no authority to prohibit slavery in the territories. During the winter and spring of 1858, Congress engaged in a rancorous debate over Kansas's application for admission to the Union as a slave state. These developments strengthened the Republican party in the North and raised the serious possibility of a "Black Republican" triumph in the presidential election of 1860.[7] While Netherland and the Opposition asserted that the currency issue presented the central question of the 1859 election, Democrats responded that the defense of southern rights and the Union remained the state's and the nation's preeminent concern.[8] As long as the Republican threat remained at the forefront of politics—and as long as the national Democratic party appeared to be the only party that could preserve the Union while protecting southern rights—the Opposition had little chance to regain the majority in Tennessee.

The debate over Kansas's admission, however, severely strained national and state Democratic unity. Kansas had been organized as a territory by the Kansas-Nebraska Act, but its slave status was to be decided by the principle of popular sovereignty. Its admission was at first expected to provide Democrats with proof of the validity of their solution to the problem of slavery's expansion, but the election of delegates to the constitutional convention to be held in the town of Lecompton produced clearly fraudulent returns favoring proslavery advocates. Moreover, the convention refused to submit its work to a popular referendum; settlers would be allowed to vote against the importation of new slaves into the state, but, under the Lecompton constitution, those slaves already in Kansas and their descendants would remain in bondage. President Buchanan announced that the constitution met the requirements of the law and that he would support its acceptance by Congress. To Buchanan's surprise, the Lecompton constitution's strongest opponent proved to be the father of the Kansas-Nebraska Act and the champion of popular sovereignty, Senator Stephen A. Douglas of Illinois. Douglas charged that the fraudulent election and the failure to submit the constitution for popular approval made a mockery of Democratic principles. Popular sovereignty, if properly applied, could indeed resolve the slavery controversy, he maintained, but Kansas's admission under Lecompton would only exacerbate already strained sectional tensions. With the senator as the most prominent opponent of the Lecompton constitution, enough northern Democrats joined Republicans to prevent Kansas's admission.[9]

The mass of Tennessee Democrats supported Buchanan's argument that Kansas and Lecompton represented a vindication of Democratic principles.[10] Douglas's challenge to Buchanan, though, placed the party in a serious predicament. Since his sponsorship of the Kansas-Nebraska Act, the senator had been one of the northern Democrats most popular in the South. He had been looked upon as the most likely successor to Buchanan as the 1860 presidential candidate, but his challenge to Kansas's admission now marked him as an opponent of what many viewed as a vital southern measure. More shocking, Douglas—during his campaign for reelection to the Senate, running against Republican candidate Abraham Lincoln; and in an 1859 article in *Harper's* magazine—also revealed his belief that slavery could be kept out of a territory, notwithstanding the *Dred Scott* decision, if the territory's residents refused to adopt legal protection for slave property.[11] To most southern Democrats, this statement now revealed Douglas as a proponent, not of the South's version of popular sovereignty, but of "squatter sovereignty," the right of settlers to prohibit slavery in a territory before it became a state. What Whig candidates long had charged now appeared to be the true interpretation of Democratic doctrine.

Most Democrats immediately condemned Douglas's views as unacceptable. Even Unionist Democrats who had been favorable to Douglas now recognized him as a damaged candidate. Nevertheless, Douglas had strengthened his support among the party's northern wing, and, since northern delegates would constitute a majority at the national convention in Charleston, there was a strong possibility that he would be nominated, regardless of southern opposition. While the Southern Rights wing remained firm in its rejection of the Illinois senator, moderate party leaders began to reconcile themselves to the prospect of Douglas's candidacy.[12] These Democrats knew that Douglas would be a difficult candidate to present in the state. "While the Democratic masses would probably, *tolerate* Douglass, and vote for him, if the Democratic nominee, on the low ground of *choice of evils*," David M. Currin wrote from Memphis, "yet scarcely any one here avows Douglas his *first* choice." "Whilst the great body of the party might vote for him, as a choice of evils, . . ." the *Union and American* observed, "he would be 'a bitter pill, a very bitter pill.'"[13]

A fraction of Unionists, while publicly disclaiming any partiality for Douglas, continued to champion the senator's cause. Disagreeing with Douglas's opposition to the Lecompton constitution, this group—including James K. Polk's brother, William H. Polk; their nephew, J. Knox Walker; Memphis postmaster William H. Carroll; former U.S. Representative Harvey M. Watterson; former Mississippi Governor Henry S. Foote; and the editors of the *Memphis Appeal*—nevertheless maintained that Douglas already had proven his fidelity to the South through his support of the Kansas-Nebraska Act and of Buchanan's election. His dispute with the administration on the Kansas issue, they argued, "arose on a question of fact rather than of principle," and, despite the controversy, Douglas still upheld the principle of popular sovereignty that long had been sustained by the Democratic party. Southern Democrats needed "to bury past differences, and to act harmoniously and without recrimination" toward Douglas, for the senator still presented the only reliable candidate who could unite northern and southern Democrats and preserve the Union. "Has not the whole Democratic party until of late maintained the very same doctrine which he yet continues to assert, . . ." Foote asked. "Above all, is it not certain that it is only by carrying into faithful execution this very theory, that the agitation of the question of slavery in Congress will ever be effectually suppressed?"[14]

Douglas's cause found a major asset in the support of the Old Line Whigs, whose votes had sustained the Democratic majority since 1856. The Old Liners' hero, former Senator James C. Jones, had been ostracized by the leadership of both of Tennessee's parties; hence, in 1858 he supported Douglas as a middle course between northern and southern extremists. Jones, in fact, campaigned in Illinois that year for Douglas's reelection to the Senate; and in June 1859 he issued a public letter declaring his support for Douglas, because he believed "that he is the only man north of Mason and Dixon's line that can be elected, that would be true to the South."[15] Jones's death in October removed him as a leader of the Douglas forces in Tennessee, but, as his followers joined with prominent Democrats, the state Democratic party could little afford completely to ignore the Illinois senator's claims, as it sought to retain its hold on the state.

Douglas's challenge to Buchanan shook the Democrats' image as the party of both Union and southern rights. Either the division among national leaders would weaken the party's prospects for a national victory, or their nominee might be a candidate whose respect for southern interests was suspect. This blow came at a time which appeared especially crucial for the survival of the Union. The Republicans' increasing strength in the North since 1856 had encouraged that party to continue standing on its antislavery appeal. Even with a united Democratic opposition, there seemed a good chance that a Republican president could be elected with votes from the nonslaveholding states alone.[16] John Brown's attempt to incite a slave insurrection at Harper's Ferry, Virginia, in October 1859, which leaders of both parties saw as "in strict connection with the whole teachings of the Republican party," indicated the likely consequences of a Republican victory.[17] Yet Republican rule also would mean the end of the Union, for Lower South politicians once again pledged secession of their states in the event of the northern sectional party's triumph.

Still, Democrats entered the 1860 canvass with the hope that the Douglas dilemma somehow could be resolved. This hope encouraged party leaders to seek unity in the state convention, so that Tennessee's delegation might have a strong voice in the national convention. Unity would be difficult to achieve. Douglas's weakened position seemed to leave the presidential nomination open, and various Tennesseeans sought to promote their favorite's or their own prospects. Aaron V. Brown had begun to suggest his own name in the press before his death in March 1859. Isham Harris, Brown's successor as the leader of the party's Southern Rights wing, advocated through his own organ, the *Memphis Avalanche*, the cause of Oregon Senator Joseph Lane, the northern favorite of Lower South Democrats. Also, the Southern Rights faction hoped to secure in the state platform a resolution supporting the chief demand of the Fire-Eaters, a declaration that the federal government should provide protection for slave property in all of the territories. Douglas's supporters strongly resisted the resolution, as a repudiation of their candidate. They hoped the state party would express no preference for the nomination, so that they could try to bring Tennessee to Douglas's side at the Charleston convention.[18]

Although the editor of the Opposition's *Banner* called the Democratic state convention "the most stormy and discordant we have ever attended," the meeting did manage to present a unified front. Southern Rights delegates pushed for a change in the convention's rules to allow voting on the platform by county, weighted according to the strength of the Democratic vote in the last gubernatorial election. By using this method, rather than the usual one of voting by congressional district, they hoped to dilute the influence of East Tennessee and increase the chance of including in the platform a resolution asserting the duty of Congress to protect slavery in the territories. The majority of delegates rejected this change, but when the platform committee's report merely endorsed the *Dred Scott* decision and affirmed the popular sovereignty resolutions passed by the national convention at Cincinnati in 1856, Southern Righters again objected that the report "did not go far enough." After bitter debate, the convention recommitted the platform and accepted a compromise that declared the Cincinnati platform "a true exposition of our doctrine on the subjects embraced" but also included a resolution stating that the federal government had no duty to perform regarding slavery in the territories other than "to protect the rights of the owner from wrong and to restore fugitives from labor." While this wording fell short of a declaration in favor of congressional protection, it proved sufficiently acceptable to both Douglas and anti-Douglas Democrats.[19]

Democrats likewise presented the appearance of unity when the convention agreed unanimously to nominate Andrew Johnson for the presidency. A large contingent of both Southern Righters and Unionists had favored making no declaration for a candidate, and most Southern Rights Democrats found the senator's nomination particularly distasteful. Douglas supporters, though, while failing to secure a seat for Knox Walker in the national delegation, endorsed Johnson as a means to try to win his assistance for their own candidate. Governor Harris meanwhile encouraged his associates to accept Johnson's nomination and the moderate platform, apparently in exchange for a promise that the governor himself would be nominated for vice-president, should a northern Democrat receive the presidential bid.[20] Johnson recognized that his candidacy was a long shot; the day before the Charleston convention opened, in fact, he indicated his willingness to support Douglas, in exchange for his own vice-presidential claims.[21] Nevertheless, given the uncertainty that plagued the party in the spring of 1860, a dark-horse candidacy was worth pursuing. For Democrats of all factions, the senator's nomination provided the unity from which the state's delegation perhaps could influence the final outcome at Charleston.

After the national convention opened on April 23, Tennessee's delegation voted unanimously for Johnson on the first twenty-nine ballots for a presidential nominee. Two members then switched to Kentucky Senator James L. Guthrie until, on the thirty-seventh vote, the delegation withdrew from Johnson and, for the final twenty votes, cast a majority for Guthrie, with one vote for Douglas. Even before the balloting began, disruption at the convention had made it doubtful that the meeting could select any candidate. Lower South delegates, led by Alabama's William L. Yancey, demanded that the platform include a resolution calling for federal protection of slave property; when the convention adopted a platform without Yancey's resolution, the delegates from eight southern states walked off the floor.[22]

Tennessee's delegates voted eleven to one against the party platform without the slave protection resolution. Rather than join the seceding delegates, however, they consulted with Virginia's and Kentucky's representatives and decided to remain in the convention; their withdrawal, they concluded, would allow Douglas's supporters to claim the nomination with a vote of two-thirds of the delegates present. As a condition of their remaining, Tennessee's delegation demanded that the two-thirds rule be applied to the entire convention, including those members not present. Douglas thus led the balloting on every vote but failed to garner the necessary two-thirds majority. Cooperating with New York's delegation, Wilson County's John K. Howard proposed a compromise resolution that would withhold the call for federal protection of slavery but declare that "neither the right of persons nor property can be destroyed or impaired by Congressional or Territorial legislation." Before the convention could act on this "Tennessee Platform," though, the majority of delegates voted on May 3 to adjourn and to reconvene six weeks later in Baltimore.[23]

The disruption of the Charleston convention severely damaged the Democratic party's image as a national organization. In its wake, the Tennessee party now divided over what course to pursue. Robert Johnson reported to his father that "some of the Tennessee delegates were stricken with the fire-eating movement and were ready to go off with the Others." These members joined with Southern Righters to call for the selection of new delegates to attend a convention at Richmond, Virginia, which the Charleston seceders had called for the purpose of nominating a candidate, should the Baltimore meeting fail to unite the party.[24] The mass of Democrats rejected this plan and preferred to send the original delegates to Baltimore. While Douglas Democrats retained hope of their favorite's nomination, most party leaders believed that pushing the Tennessee Platform on the convention would force Douglas to withdraw; or, if Douglas persisted in his stand for the nomination, he at least might be compelled to accept a platform more acceptable to the South. Some clung to the belief that the Illinois senator's nomination still could be made palatable to Tennessee voters by placing Andrew Johnson on the ticket as the vice-presidential candidate. Others recognized a greater antipathy to Douglas among Democrats and saw the senator's withdrawal as the party's only salvation. "The masses of the people are against Douglass in this section of the State," delegate W. C. Whitthorne wrote upon his return to Columbia. "They are not only against him, but warmly so, and whilst a majority of the party would support him, if nominated, yet we would hopelessly loose [sic] the State."[25]

The reassembled Democratic national convention at Baltimore never had the opportunity to find a solution. When several of the seceding delegates arrived to rejoin the convention, that body refused to seat most of them and instead recognized new sets of delegates who had been selected by pro-Douglas meetings in the Lower South states. The majority of Tennessee's delegates saw the committee's action as a clear attempt to pack the meeting with Douglas supporters; it now appeared that "the single and isolated purpose of the adherents of Mr. DOUGLAS was, regardless of all other considerations, to *force* the nomination of their leader, whether such a nomination would keep together the party or not, and whether the means necessary to accomplish their end should be foul or fair."[26] Twenty-one of the twenty-four Tennessee delegates, encouraged by Governor Harris, now joined the seceders in a convention newly organized at another location in Baltimore. The three remaining delegates stayed with the rump convention as it nominated Douglas unanimously, upon a platform that would leave to the Supreme Court the dilemma over popular and "squatter" sovereignty. The majority, meanwhile, endorsed the "Conservative" Democrats' ticket of John C. Breckinridge and Joseph Lane, upon a platform that declared "the duty of the Federal Government to protect, when necessary, the rights of persons and property . . . in the Territories, or wherever else its constitutional authority extends."[27]

Thus was shattered the image of a national Democratic party, upon which Tennessee's Democrats had relied since 1856. Nevertheless, the majority of the state party proceeded with a campaign based upon asserting the national character of the southern Democratic faction, as they accepted the delegates' bolt at Baltimore and endorsed the Breckinridge-Lane ticket. According to these Democrats, the disruption of the party occurred because the Douglas forces had gained control of the convention through a manipulation of party machinery. With the removal of Douglas and his allies, the party had been "purified and nationalized" and strengthened in its struggle against the "Black Republicans," for the platform upon which Breckinridge stood—with its clear declaration of the federal government's duty to protect slave property in the territories—offered the only platform that would guarantee southern rights and state equality. Only the bold assertion of those rights and their acceptance by the North could calm the agitation over slavery's expansion. "Those who deny the doctrine of State rights and State equality are *the real disunionists* as they are contributing to advance a policy which must inevitably lead to a dissolution of the Union or cause the people of the South to occupy in our Federal relations the position of *uncivilized, immoral inferiors,*" Democrats argued. Behind Breckinridge and Lane, Democrats insisted that they presented "the best Constitutional ticket, the best State Rights ticket, and the best Union ticket now before the country."[28]

The national party's division only drove a wedge into the state party. William H. Carroll and Harvey M. Watterson, two of the delegates who had refused to withdraw at Baltimore, returned home to announce that they intended "to stand by the nominees of the only Democratic national convention which has assembled since 1856." Douglas supporters then organized a state "National Democratic" convention in Nashville in July; this body condemned the secession of the Tennessee delegation, approved the nomination of Douglas and the Baltimore convention's platform, and selected a ticket of Douglas electors—with Watterson and William H. Polk at its head, as the at-large candidates. These spokesmen charged into the canvass with the claim that the Illinois senator alone "has been put before the country by a *regular* national Democratic convention, and in accordance with the *regular* usages of the party." The platform approved by that convention, Douglas supporters argued, revealed that Douglas stood "fairly and squarely upon the great Democratic principle of non-interference by Congress with the question of slavery, and the right of the people in Territories and States to form and regulate their domestic institutions in their own way."[29]

With a full ticket of electors, Douglas supporters centered their campaign on the claim that they represented the true national Democratic party. The Breckinridge candidacy, they charged, was sponsored by the southern disunionists. The disruption of the national convention had been brought on by "the deep-laid and well-concocted plan of disunion and treason . . . " devised "by some of the ablest men in the South, Mr. Yancey being the chief instigator and prime mover of the damnable conspiracy." Tennessee's party had, "in a moment of excitement, allowed the Disunionists to overreach them" and to commit the state party to "that faction, which is determined to dissolve the Union." Douglas loyalists, on the other hand, promised to stand by the legitimate party nominee as part of the battle to preserve the

Union. Their candidate alone could defeat Lincoln in the free states, and "by making an *effort*," they would "hold up the hands of our Democratic friends North, as well as all other conservative men there, in their great struggle with the cohorts of abolitionism."[30]

This condemnation of Breckinridge coincided with the appeal of the Opposition, which long since had indicated its intention to revive its position as the conservative party of Union. Despite the failure of the American party, John Bell and his adherents retained their faith that a party opposed to the extremists in both sections could replace the Democrats as a national organization. At the conclusion of the 1856 contest, Bell began to work to insure that he would be the presidential nominee of such an organization. The senator at first hoped to unite the southern Opposition with the moderate wing of the Republicans; should sectional issues fail to dominate Buchanan's administration, Bell wrote in early 1857, "the Republicans will look to some modification of their policy and a union with the Americans and old Whigs of the South."[31] Bell abandoned this strategy after the Lecompton debate strengthened the Republicans' sectional appeal in the North—and after his supporters in Tennessee warned him that an alliance with the northern party would destroy the Opposition in the state. Instead, Bell and his Whig allies again sought to form a new national party that would stand against both the Abolitionized Republicans and the fire-eating Democrats. "The country has had enough of Northern and Southern agitation," the *Athens Post* concluded. "What is needed, is, the formation of a great National party—a party, *national* in spirit and in deed, in its teachings and its practice."[32]

As a result of this effort, Bell became one of only two southern senators to vote against Kansas's admission under the Lecompton constitution; he justified his course on the grounds that the issue was another tool of the demagogic politicians who, to attain their selfish ends, were threatening the Union.[33] In Tennessee, Bell's adherents again endorsed the senator's course and reminded voters that "the South has no sectional interests in the great question of admitting Kansas under the Lecompton Constitution." Although several prominent Opposition leaders, including Tennessee's three Opposition members of Congress, favored Kansas's admission, Bell managed to keep the party united behind his presidential prospects.[34] Opposition newspapers kept Bell's name before the public as a presidential contender, before coming out openly for Bell in early 1860. That January, Opposition legislators recommended Bell for president and called for a state convention to be held on George Washington's birthday, February 22. This convention charged the state's delegates to the National Opposition convention in May to "use all honorable means" to procure Bell's nomination, and it resolved that "the continued agitation of the slavery question, while it promises no profitable result to any section, is fraught with infinite mischiefs to the whole country . . . and that it ought therefore to cease." The national convention adopted the name "Constitutional Union" party, nominated Bell on the second ballot, and resolved to present no platform beyond a declaration in favor of "The Constitution, The Union, and The Enforcement of its Laws."[35]

Under yet another new name, Whigs once again presented their own party as the only hope to preserve the Union. The division of the Democrats had resulted in the nomination of two additional sectional tickets, they maintained, "the one of the Southern Disunionists, the other of the Northern Free Soil wing of the Democratic party."[36] Like Douglas's supporters, Constitutional Unionists presented Breckinridge's candidacy as the most dangerous, for Tennessee's Democrats, they maintained, had joined in the plot to dissolve the Union.[37] Unionists denounced the slavery issue as "a mere abstraction involving no practical result," for "climate, soil and the laws of nature are the first tribunal, before which the question of slavery in the Territories must come for settlement." Thus Bell's supporters promised to ignore slavery as a political issue and "to leave the question of protection to slavery where it belongs, to the arbitrament of the judicial tribunals, according to the Constitution and the Laws." Meanwhile, Constitutional Unionists invited "the co-operation of the Union-loving and conservative men of all parties to aid us in our efforts to remove the government from the hands of extremists North and South, and place it where our fathers placed it, a guarantee of the rights of all." "It is to the National Union party of the country, composed of the conservatives of all parties, that our people are prepared to look for safety," a Bell meeting in Memphis declared; "while the republican party of the North is purely sectional and fanatical, the great national democratic party lives only in history, powerless from its own dissentions, and rent by civil feuds."[38]

As in 1856, in 1860 Tennessee's presidential campaign devolved into a struggle to win the support of a minority faction. This time Democrats rather than Whigs faced the more difficult task. Breckinridge supporters warned Douglas loyalists that a divided Democratic vote would give the state to Bell, but the "bitter and deep rooted" split in the national party, along with any candidates' bleak prospects in the national election, made victory in Tennessee seem less urgent than it had four years earlier.[39] A proposal from Douglas elector James Britton in October for fusion of the Breckinridge and Douglas tickets met little enthusiasm from either faction. Most Douglas supporters denounced the proposal as a trick sponsored by the Breckinridge faction. Bell's proponents, meanwhile, recognized that there was no need to convert Douglas Democrats; they merely needed to legitimize Douglas's candidacy as a means to draw votes from Breckinridge. Constitutional Union newspapers reported favorably on the effort for Douglas. Bell and Douglas spokesmen limited criticism of each other's candidates throughout the canvass and instead joined together in attacks on Breckinridge. Breckinridge Democrats complained, too, that Whigs attended Douglas meetings to make his cause appear stronger than it was, and they charged that the Bell organization secretly funded the Douglas effort in the state.[40]

Voters must have recognized that the contest in Tennessee was merely a sideshow in the national election. The Democrats' division, the strengthened position of the Republicans in the North, and the fact that Republican nominee, Abraham Lincoln, needed only to carry free states in order to win a majority in the electoral college would make it difficult for any of the parties running in Tennessee to secure a national victory. Adherents continued to promote their candidates in the hope that Lincoln's election somehow could be avoided, but throughout the campaign, voters reflected the sense that they were going through the motions of a canvass, until the dreaded result could be ratified. Electoral candidates pressed their opponents to state whether they would favor disunion in the event of Lincoln's election; as summer passed into autumn, newspapers already were considering what course to pursue in the case of that result. The results of northern state elections in October dashed any remaining hopes of averting disaster, as Republican victories revealed the party's strength. On the eve of the election, spokesmen for both parties admitted that the Union was in peril, as they appealed for votes on the basis of the need for a united South. Behind Breckinridge, Democrats argued, southern unity would present a strong warning to the abolition president not to act against southern rights; behind Bell, Constitutional Unionists countered, southern unity would weaken the schemes of the disunionists by declaring the region's support for Union, no matter what the outcome.[41]

When the results were tallied, Douglas's candidacy indeed had divided the Democratic vote sufficiently to allow Bell to carry Tennessee. The Constitutional Union candidate won the same proportion of the state vote that Millard Fillmore had won in 1856, but Douglas carried almost 8 percent of the total, to give Bell a forty-six-hundred-vote margin over Breckinridge. Douglas's support came mostly from West Tennessee; the Illinois Democrat received over 20 percent of the votes cast in this division. Old Line Whigs—still following the lead of James C. Jones even after his death—possibly accounted for the bulk of the turnout in favor of Douglas.

Regardless of the returns in Tennessee, the national contest resulted in the outcome that southern voters had feared. Lincoln carried every free state and won a commanding majority in the electoral college, despite receiving less than 40 percent of the popular vote and no votes in the southern states. As promised, South Carolina seceded from the Union on December 20. By February 1, 1861, six other Lower South states had joined South Carolina, and organization of the Confederate States of America had begun.

Tennessee voters now faced an unprecedented choice. For the past decade, they had worked to preserve the Union through support for a national party. Now that separation had occurred, citizens confronted the prospect of war. The Lower South states already had pledged their determination to defend on the battlefield their right to secede, while the Republicans refused to acknowledge that right. Voters had to decide whether their liberty would be better protected in a Union dominated by the abolitionist "Black Republicans," or in a southern republic inaugurated by the disunionist Fire-Eaters. They also knew that whatever course they took might determine whether the Union would be saved or permanently divided.

Yet, for voters, the choice was unclear, for the crisis put into direct conflict two cardinal values in the state's political culture. On the one hand, the election of a president from the Republican party seemed to present a clear threat to the constitutional rights and domestic peace of southern citizens. The right of a state to permit the holding of property in slaves had been guaranteed by the federal Constitution; although the great majority of white Tennesseans owned no slaves, they upheld this right and believed slavery to be the only appropriate relationship between the white and black races. Abolition of the institution would only bring chaos and race war to southern society.[42] Northern abolitionists had waged war against southern rights in slave property for thirty years, and, despite moderate declarations, the Republican party had proven itself to Tennesseans to be the political expression of Abolitionism. Not only did that party attempt to obstruct the execution of the fugitive slave law and prevent southern citizens from taking slave property into the territories, but its members had encouraged slave rebellion and left no doubt that their ultimate goal was the extinction of the institution. The election thus had brought into power the "eternal enemies to slavery and Southern rights," and it seemed entirely plausible that the new administration would move quickly to limit those rights.[43]

On the other hand, voters had also been conditioned to believe that their own liberty depended upon the perpetuation of the Union of states. The American Revolution, it was understood, had created the federal Constitution as an experiment in the human capacity for self-government, and Andrew Jackson's firm denunciation of Nullification in 1833 had sealed for Tennesseans the conviction that liberty and Union were inextricably linked. "For we are the last hope of liberty— the last resource for the restoration of the lost rights of man," the *Republican Banner* had declared in 1857. "Blot out this Republic, and the last ray of hope is extinguished.... There is no longer any check upon the cruelty of tyrants, and the night of despotism will again settle upon the world." Despite the threat to southern rights posed by the "Black Republicans," dissolution of the Union would result in the destruction of "the wisest [government] ever yet devised by man." There was no guarantee that a newly constructed government in a southern nation would preserve the same freedoms enjoyed under the Constitution. "I wish we could form a southern confederacy, if such a thing could be affected," John F. Henry told his mother, "but when we cut the cord that now binds the Union together, no man can tell when the scattered Fragments can ever be gathered together again[;] each state will fly off with its own notions of Gov. which it will not be willing to surrender to any others."[44]

While Tennesseans sympathized with the Lower South's fears concerning the prospects of Lincoln's administration, the majority hesitated to endorse secession. Despite the possibility of an assault on southern rights, the Republicans had not performed any overt or hostile action through the federal government. Lincoln's administration, in fact, had not taken office at the time of the organization of the Confederate States. Moreover, after trying to maintain a middle ground for the past decade, most Tennesseans believed that the country had been thrown into the crisis because of the actions of the sectional extremists. Former Whigs now leading the Constitutional Union party thus immediately declared their fidelity to the Union. A moderate course by Tennessee and the other border slave states, they claimed, perhaps could provide the basis for a settlement that would preserve the integrity of the Constitution and the Union from the assaults of sectional extremists. Unionist Democrats, including Cave Johnson, William H.

Polk, Harvey M. Watterson, William H. Carroll, George W. Jones, and, most visibly, Andrew Johnson, endorsed the Unionist sentiment of their erstwhile opponents.[45] These Democratic and Opposition spokesmen now proclaimed the old party system obsolete, as they called upon voters to unite in defense of the Union. The argument presented by this new alliance laid the foundation for a new Union party. This party, Unionists hoped, would represent the true sentiments of the Union-loving people in the state and throughout the country, and frustrate the schemes of disunionist demagogues.

According to the Unionists, the present crisis had yet to produce a need for separation. Disunion, in fact, presented a greater threat to slavery than did a Republican president. The Republican platform appeared threatening, to be sure, but Lincoln was known to be a moderate member of the party, and as chief executive he would be compelled to act according to the Constitution. Likewise, the new president, whatever his personal views, "will be utterly powerless against slavery," because Democrats and Opposition men still controlled Congress, and because the Supreme Court was dominated by men sympathetic to southern rights.[46] As part of a southern republic, Tennessee no longer would enjoy the protection of the fugitive slave law, and northerners would have no obligation to return slaves escaped from the state. As citizens of a foreign country, Tennesseans would forfeit the right to hold slave property in United States territories, the right for which southern politicians had battled for more than a decade. In a separate country, voters would find themselves isolated and lacking the protection of an established central government, in a world growing increasingly hostile to slavery. Disunion "will bring about the overthrow of slavery, one hundred years sooner than the Republican party could have done it," the *Knoxville Whig* concluded, while the *Republican Banner* assured voters that "the Union offers them a surer and more speedy defence of their Constitutional rights, even with Abraham Lincoln at the head of the Executive Department, than they could hope to attain in a Southern Confederacy, surrounded by a hostile Northern Confederacy."[47]

Inadequate protection for slavery presented only a minor disadvantage of a separate southern confederacy. For the past decade, both Opposition and Democratic spokesmen had warned that disunion was the goal of demagogic politicians; the secession of the Lower South states merely fulfilled the Fire-Eaters' alleged long-standing design to create a government of their own. The disunionists long had made clear their dissatisfaction with popular government, Unionists charged; and now they intended to establish a landed oligarchy—perhaps even a monarchy—that would make Tennessee's citizens "hewers of wood and drawers of water for a set of aristocrats and over-bearing tyrants." "With all power concentrated in the hands of a few," the *Republican Banner* announced, the southern republic "would, from the beginning, be a centralised despotism, and within a very short period it would become a military one; and in no long period, a great Southern Kingdom." Secessionist leaders already had indicated that the southern constitution would contain a property requirement for voting, and the cotton states' obsession with the doctrine of free trade would force the new country to maintain a low tariff that would necessitate a system of oppressive taxation. "The vile and wicked leaders who will *precipitate revolution*, . . ." Brownlow warned, "will manage to hold civil and military offices, with large salaries, to pay for which, money will be coming from the common people, by a system of *direct taxes*."[48]

According to Unionists, the best security for the citizens' liberty was to remain in the Union. Since demagogic politicians, north and south, had brought on the crisis, the real people of the country would rebuke the Republicans and the Fire-Eaters and assert their devotion to the Constitution. "The people are sound to the core," the *Banner* explained. "It is only the leaders who are at fault, and who have raised a storm which they have not power to still." By remaining loyal, Tennessee's voters would encourage northern voters that the Union could be preserved. At the same time, they could join with citizens in the other border slave states to demand a compromise that would force northerners forever to abandon attacks on slavery and to respect southern rights. Such a compromise, in turn, would allow the people of the Lower South to repudiate secession with dignity. Even if politicians obstructed efforts at compromise, Tennesseans would become crucial constituents in a new national Union party that would keep the Republican administration in check until Lincoln and his party could be defeated at the next election. "We have a million and a half good friends in the northern States, and it is not only suicide but ingratitude combined, to desert them when they would do us all the service in their power," one correspondent told Senator Johnson.[49] As George W. Jones saw it,

> in 1864 he [Lincoln] and his party will be swept from the high places of trust in the government and from official existence, in the up rising of the people, in vindication of their rights, by a political revolution more marked and decided, than has ever before characterized a Presidential election. Better, it seems to me, for us to hold on to our rights under the Constitution, and in the Union, with both branches of Con-

gress and the Supreme Court of the United States, to guard, protect and shield us from wrong; with the certainty that at the end of four years the people themselves will vindicate our every right.[50]

Unionists acknowledged their loyalty to be conditional. Should Lincoln, with the approval of the people of the North, attempt to carry out the Republican party's mission to assail southern rights, the spirit as well as the letter of the Constitution would be abrogated. Although most Unionists rejected the principle of secession, they warned Republicans not to attempt to coerce the withdrawn states back under the authority of the Union. While secession would make any government unworkable, "when any form of government becomes oppressive the people have a right to throw it off—a natural, not a constitutional right." Even though Unionists disagreed over the extent of the Republican threat and even though demagogues had misled them, the people of the South had opted to exercise their right of revolution. "However much the doctrine of secession may be denied, it would be absurd to declare that those States are not, as far as they have gone, in a state of successful revolution," the *Nashville Patriot* observed. "No power on earth can compel them to resume their allegiance to the Union." Should the administration embark upon a policy of coercion, Tennessee's citizens would have no alternative but to defend their southern brothers. "We would cease to value a Union maintained by force," one correspondent wrote from Memphis, "and our sympathies with the Cotton States would readily induce us to espouse their quarrel."[51]

Nevertheless, throughout the winter, Unionists remained firm in their belief that there would be no need for their state to resort to its own right of revolution. Northern newspapers, they maintained, daily brought further evidence of Lincoln's moderation and of the northern electorate's desire for compromise. Meanwhile, they pointed to compromise proposals before Congress, principally that of Kentucky's Senator John J. Crittenden, as bases for an impending settlement. "The true position of Tennessee is to occupy neutral ground—to stand as a rock between the waves of Northern and Southern fanaticism," Unionists argued.[52]

Throughout the winter of secession, with the hope of a peaceful adjustment apparently promising, Unionists believed that their position reflected the sentiment of the majority of Tennessee's voters. "Nearly every body hopes & wishes that the controversy may be settled, in the Union, honorably & safely," Henry G. Smith observed in Memphis. And Robert Johnson wrote to his father, the senator, "If the Crittenden proposition will only pass, Tennessee will accept it by an overwhelming majority. Disunion will be burried [sic] so deep that it can never be resurrected."[53]

Southern Rights Democrats, meanwhile, led by Governor Harris, East Tennessee's Landon C. Haynes, and the West Tennessee congressman William T. Avery, were joined by a few wavering Unionists, including leading Douglas advocates Henry S. Foote and the editors of the *Memphis Appeal*, in rejecting the Unionists' plea. These Democrats at first called upon Tennessee to meet in convention with all of the slave states, to present an unyielding demand for constitutional guarantees for southern rights in slavery. Republican successes presented a dire threat to those rights, they maintained: "There is no better time than the present to determine and ascertain whether the Union is to be used as a Black Republican engine to depreciate and degrade the South, or whether we are to have peace, equality, and respect in it." As the Lower South states seceded, Southern Righters concluded that the Union now was irreparably destroyed, and they openly advocated secession. While remaining in the Union, Tennesseans could expect a Republican attack on slavery; it might come in the form of a direct military assault or through more subtle political maneuvers, whether through building an Abolition party in the state or through admitting the remaining territories as free states and using them to ratify a constitutional amendment eliminating the institution. In either case, without explicit renunciation of the abolitionists' antislavery program, there would be no need to remain in the Union to await the inevitable assault. "We may demand our rights, demand redress for past wrongs and security for the future as some contend for," James L. Thompson proclaimed in the state senate, "but it will be in dishonor and will avail us nothing, and will only amount to delay."[54]

Advocates of separation accepted secession as a constitutional principle and insisted that a state government had the right to withdraw from the federal compact if its citizens' liberties no longer were protected. Recognizing the doctrine's close association among voters with Nullification, though, these secessionists focused their appeal on the dangers of "coercion" and maintained that Lincoln intended to force the Lower South back into the Union at the first opportunity. Force likewise would transform free states into "conquered provinces" and negate the principle of self-government established by the Constitution. "The day, therefore, that Lincoln would attempt by military force to coerce a State would mark his administration with the usurpations of a tyrant," Haynes concluded. "It would be a subversion of all written limitations of power and a conversion of the Federal Government into a military despotism." No citizen could submit to the authority of such a dictatorship, secessionists claimed, and should Tennessee fail to act, it would soon find itself "the southern tail to a northern abolition Confederacy." Conflict could be avoided only if all of the slave states united to show the Republicans the futility of force, and Tennesseans could contribute to preserving the peace by arming their state and providing for a quick alliance with the southern republic. "The South must consolidate for safety," the *Appeal* admonished. "The prompt secession of some, if not all of the border slave States, alone can save us from the horrors of civil war."[55]

While warning of the threat of coercion, secessionist spokesmen assured voters of the advantages of membership in a southern republic. Obviously, slavery would be sustained by the central government, and there would be no abolitionist element in the confederacy to endanger the institution. Nonslaveholders as well as slaveholders would benefit. Tennessee's railroad connections linked the state to the Cotton South, while her trade in produce predominantly headed for those same states. In the southern confederacy, Tennessee farmers would find these markets guaranteed, without competition from the Northwest, and they would prosper with other border-state yeomen as the republic's chief supplier of food and livestock. Moreover, the South's need for finished products would stimulate expansion of the state's mining operations and establishment of profitable manufacturing ventures. "Place Tennessee in a Southern Confederacy with her manufacturing, mineral and agricultural resources," the *Union and American* exhorted, "and what limit can there be to her material prosperity!"[56]

Economic considerations aside, secessionists maintained that the southern republic would provide the surest guarantee of republican liberty. Repudiating charges that Lower South planters favored an aristocracy, they insisted that the new confederacy would be built upon the same constitutional principles that had provided the foundation for the Union before it had been subverted by the northern abolitionists. "We will not secede from the principles, the spirit of the Union," secessionists promised; "we will carry with us the form of government, the Constitution, the laws, the judiciary that we now have. In a word we will take the Union and the Constitution of our fathers and leave the enemies of both to enjoy alone their mad revel of Black Republican fanaticism."[57]

Although presenting contrasting courses to voters, Unionist and secessionist leaders agreed that Tennessee needed to take at least some sort of action in the crisis. When Governor Harris on December 7 issued a proclamation calling the General Assembly into a special session in January, most assumed, as the *Banner* explained, that the

Isham G. Harris, c. 1858. Tennessee Historical Society Picture Collection. Reproduction courtesy of Tennessee State Library and Archives, Nashville.

legislature would "provide for a Convention of the people, upon which body will devolve the responsibility of defining the position of the State with reference to the pending movements in the South." Several Unionists saw a convention as a means to promote a national compromise and approved the propriety of Harris's proclamation.[58] As secessionist spokesmen became increasingly aggressive, however, Unionists expressed fear that the governor and his allies intended to use a convention to achieve a separation, regardless of the popular will. These demagogues, Unionists maintained, first would try to excite public opinion into an anti-northern frenzy, so that voters would approve their devious course; yet whatever the effect of their campaign might be, they would provide a convention with the authority to secede and to carry the state into the southern republic, even if the majority disapproved that course.[59]

The opening of the legislative session confirmed these fears. Harris and pro-secession legislators launched an offensive that seemed designed to align Tennessee with the seceded states. In his message to the assembly, the governor retraced the history of "the systematic, wanton, and long continued agitation of the slavery question, with the actual and threatened aggressions of the Northern States and a portion of their people, upon the well-defined Constitutional rights of the Southern citizen." After recommending submitting the question of a convention to the voters, Harris encouraged the legislature to adopt resolutions demanding from the North five constitutional amendments that would "secure" southern rights, but whose extreme stipulations clearly would be unacceptable to Republicans.[60] Harris also stated his belief that, given the current division of the country, "Tennessee will be powerless in any efforts she may make to quell the storm that pervades the country." Hence, he asserted, "the work of alienation and disruption has gone so far, that it will be extremely difficult, if not impossible, to arrest it; and before your adjournment, in all human probability, the only practical question for the State to determine, will be whether she will unite her fortunes with a Northern or Southern Confederacy; upon which question, when presented, I am certain there can be little division in sentiment, identified as we are in every respect with the South."[61]

Leroy Pope Walker and Thomas Wharton, agents from Alabama and Mississippi, respectively, received permission to address a joint session of the legislature, and they echoed Harris's warnings of the impending danger facing the South.[62] With these prefaces, secessionist legislators proposed even more drastic measures than the governor's constitutional amendments. Among the barrage of resolutions they introduced were declarations denouncing the North's aggression, providing for negotiations for Tennessee's participation in the creation of the southern republic, and establishing an effectual separation from the northern economy. Included were proposals to establish commercial nonintercourse with the North and to encourage foreign importations through Lower South ports. To insure the state's military readiness, secessionists supported a bill "to enable the State of Tennessee to repel invasion and suppress insurrection," which would create a state army under the direction of Governor Harris. For good measure, secessionist legislators sought vengeance against Andrew Johnson—the senator they had elected but who now proved to be the South's most vocal Unionist—with resolutions instructing him to resign his seat in the Senate.[63]

Unionists in the legislature frustrated the secessionists' offensive. Roll-call votes in the assembly revealed the importance of both the Whig and Democratic party traditions as bases for the Unionist and secessionist forces and the role of the Unionist Democrats in the coalescing Unionist party. The assembly agreed unanimously to pass the bill establishing a referendum on a convention and providing for the election of delegates on the same day. Secessionists, though, appeared willing to leave the final decision on the state's course in the convention's hands; when Opposition members moved to amend the bill with a provision requiring that any convention action "having for its object a change of the position or relation of this State" be submitted to a popular vote, a substantial number of Democrats abandoned their traditional reliance on popular sovereignty and voted against the proposal. The remaining Democrats joined Opposition members to carry the amendment and to withstand the secessionists' attempts to lower its standard to require a simple majority—rather than a majority of the number of votes cast at the last gubernatorial election—to approve the convention's decisions. The Unionist coalition also required that a referendum could be delayed until at least twenty days after the convention's action. Without these provisions, it seemed to Unionists, the convention could approve secession and then force its decision through delaying the electorate's opportunity to resist and through intimidation at the polls. Despite the apparent unity behind the convention bill, the assembly's deliberations made it appear that secessionists hoped to bring about separation and affiliation with the Lower South, regardless of the opinion of the voters.[64]

The rest of the secessionists' program likewise went down to defeat. Most of the pro-separation resolutions, including the instructing resolutions to Senator Johnson, died in committee. Democratic strength in the senate passed the resolution supporting commercial nonintercourse with northern citizens and the bill encouraging foreign importations, but the Unionist coalition in the house killed both measures. Likewise, the army bill received approval in the senate but met defeat in the house, when a one-vote majority tabled it.[65] The army bill particularly had frightened Unionists, for it implied that Governor Harris and his followers might take drastic measures, perhaps even martial law, if necessary, to achieve Tennessee's secession. Its defeat, however, marked the assembly's rejection of precipitous measures and left the secessionists branded as the proponents of dangerous, anti-republican policies. "The disunionists here, who hoped for great results from the legislature," Return J. Meigs reported to Senator Johnson after the proposal's failure in the house, "have sustained a disastrous rout; and the result of Saturday's vote [on the army bill] will finish them, I trust, for good."[66]

While rejecting separation, the assembly's Unionists made it clear that their position did not imply accepting submission to the North; instead, they continued to try to place Tennessee upon the middle ground between the sectional extremes. The house and senate both easily passed a resolution asking the president of the United States and the leaders of the southern states to maintain "the *status quo* of all movements tending to coercion, collision, and concerning the forts and arsenals of the nation." When members learned that the New York legislature had offered men and money "to be used in coercing certain sovereign States of the South into obedience to the Federal Government," Unionists joined with secessionists to pass their own declaration that "the people of Tennessee . . . will, as one man, resist such invasion of the soil of the South at any hazard, and to the last extremity." Even though Unionists rejected the army bill, the assembly did pass an act repealing an 1857 act abolishing the militia, and this repeal allowed companies to organize for the state's defense.[67]

The assembly's official statement on the crisis came in the form of a series of resolutions—passed after a lengthy and often heated debate—that proposed to amend the federal Constitution with the propositions recommended by Governor Harris. The legislature's version, though, reflected the desire for compromise. Unionists toned down the governor's more extreme demands, and the series included an invitation to delegates from all of the slaveholding states to convene in Nashville to "define a basis upon which, if possible, the Federal Union and the Constitutional rights of the slave States may be perpetuated and preserved." Moreover, the assembly further recommended a national convention at Richmond, to meet after the Nashville convention had completed its work, "to revise and perfect such plan of adjustment." Should the Richmond convention fail, the assembly sanctioned, not separation into a separate southern republic, but a reconstruction of the Union based upon the Constitution, "with such amendments as may be satisfactory to the slaveholding states" and including those northern states willing to respect southern rights, "severing at once all connections with States refusing such reasonable guarantees to our future safety."[68]

Secessionist legislators resisted the calls for conventions at Nashville and Richmond, but they lined up behind the resolutions calling for Harris's constitutional amendments. Unionists, meanwhile, accepted the resolution providing for a reconstruction, probably believing that the proposed conventions could work out some arrangement without resorting to this extreme. Unionists, too, could accept the resolutions in their final form, because they made clear Tennessee's determination to occupy middle ground between North and South, notwithstanding the secessionists' efforts to ally the state with the embryonic southern republic. When the resolutions first emerged from a committee, they included a provision to send delegates to the upcoming convention of the seceded states in Montgomery, Alabama, but Unionists quickly replaced this provision with the call for a convention at Nashville. Although Democrats united to elect three members of Tennessee's twelve-member delegation to the proposed convention, the Unionist coalition selected eight delegates with clearly pro-Union sympathies. Democratic members of the senate tried to get at least token representation at Montgomery by proposing to allow the governor to appoint a three-man commission to attend that convention, but one Democrat broke ranks and united with the Opposition to defeat the proposal. And when other southern states ignored Tennessee's invitation to Nashville, the assembly again exhibited its desire for an adjustment by directing the delegation it had elected to attend the peace conference gathering in Washington.[69]

The outcome of the legislative session dealt the Southern Rights movement in Tennessee a severe blow, for the extreme stand taken by Governor Harris and his allies created the impression among voters that the governor's faction desired "to rush the people of the State into the vortex of secession," regardless of the popular will. Unionists condemned Harris's message to the legislature as "incendiary," while they accused "the Disunion leaders in Tennessee" of attempting "to force a false issue upon the people, by falsely presenting, that we must either go with the *Northern Fanatic* or with the *Southern Distructive* [sic]." Some charged that Harris had ordered his friends to instruct Johnson out of the Senate so that the governor himself could be chosen as his successor. Most damaging were the Southern Righters' willingness to let a state convention provide for Tennessee's secession without popular approval, and their attempt to create a standing army in the state, for these measures evoked the specter of the establishment of an unrepresentative, authoritarian government. While condemning the "Black Republicans" for attempting to create a military despotism in the United States, Southern Rights advocates in Tennessee now found themselves attacked by Unionists for trying to create the same danger within the state itself.[70]

This stigma burdened Secession advocates in the referendum on a convention and the election for delegates. The legislature's designation of February 9 as the election date left only three weeks to organize a campaign, but secessionists moved quickly to nominate as candidates "men who are opposed to all compromises that do not *promptly* and *forever* settle the differences existing between the Black Republicans and the South." Nominated as "States Rights Anti-Coercion" candidates, secessionists denied that they advocated immediate separation. Instead, in the convention they would present a final ultimatum to the North; if it were not accepted before March 4, the date of Lincoln's inauguration, they would move to unite Tennessee's destiny with the seceded states. Their opponents, these anticoercionists charged, favored "submission" to the Republicans, and they warned that the election of "submissionists" would be interpreted in the North as Tennessee's willingness to sacrifice its rights for the sake of the Union. Republicans then would proceed with their plan to coerce the seceded states, confident that Tennessee would offer no resistance. Indeed, secessionists charged, Tennesseans would find themselves compelled to assist in the new administration's tyranny. Unionists were deluding voters with their insistence that the Union could still be preserved. The withdrawal of the Lower South states had permanently dissolved the Union, and the true issue in the election was whether Tennessee would side with the abolitionists or with their fellow southerners. "The question for the people of Tennessee, is not one of Union or Disunion," the *Union and American* explained. "The Union is already dissolved. The question is: Shall we take the Union without the Constitution, or the Constitution without the Union?"[71]

Unionists met the anticoercionists with "States Rights Union" tickets of candidates who charged their opponents with attempting to force the voters into accepting secession. Denying charges of "submission," these spokesmen promised to stand behind the Crittenden proposals as an ultimatum but refused to place any deadline upon the North. As the *Banner* explained, "We should give the people of the North ample time to retrace their steps, and repeal their hostile measures. We should not endeavor to drive them into hasty concessions and ill-considered compromises." Promoting their candidates as "men devoted to the interests of the South, but yet who are not willing ruthlessly to pull down the pillars of the temple of liberty," Unionists argued that their opponents' impatience revealed that they really sought separation at any cost, regardless of the popular will. "Whatever may be their declarations of attachment to the Union," the Union committee in Nashville stated, "you may rely upon it[,] their object is secession now, by separate State action, and the formation, with the Cotton States, of a Southern Confederacy." "If the PEOPLE do not rise in their strength and put back meddling politicians, the latter will *chloroform* them with 'sectional prejudice,' and then ride over them rough-shod before they can recover from the narcotic," the *Banner* warned. "The political tricksters who see their *power* slipping from their grasp, are playing a desperate game and will not 'lose a trick' if they can help it."[72]

The crucial issue in the February election thus became, not whether to hold a convention, but whether to select advocates of Union or secession to attend that convention. Regardless of whether or not the proposed convention would meet, the victory of Unionist or anticoercion delegates would indicate whether public opinion favored a moderate or an extreme position in the crisis. Unionists throughout the canvass perceived that the secessionist cause was alienating arti-

Table 11. Results of Tennessee Election for Convention and Delegates, February 9, 1861, by Grand Division

	Convention	Percent	No Convention	Percent
East	7,867	19.1	33,309	80.9
Middle	26,879	49.1	27,894	50.9
West	23,052	73.1	8,488	26.9
State	57,798	45.3	69,691	54.7

| | Secession | | Union | |
	Delegates	Percent	Delegates	Percent
East	5,577	15.3	30,903	84.7
Middle	9,828	21.1	36,809	78.9
West	9,344	30.7	21,091	69.3
State	24,749	21.8	88,803	78.2

Source: *Nashville Republican Banner*, Mar. 5, 1861.

sans and workers in towns, as well as yeoman farmers—the vast majority of whom were nonslaveholders—in the countryside.[73] The election results confirmed this belief. A convention was voted down by a twelve-thousand-vote majority. West Tennessee voters overwhelmingly approved the meeting, but East Tennesseans returned an even greater majority against it. Likewise, slaveholders—particularly Democratic owners—tended to support the convention, while nonslaveholders strongly opposed it. Several Unionist leaders had expressed their willingness to hold a meeting, but the aggressive tone of the anticoercionists' appeal convinced voters "in the hills and hollows" that a convention might force disunion despite the voters' preference. "They were fearfull that the same outrageous disregard for the spoken will of the people in Georgia would characterise their convention should they Elect one," C. H. Mills reported to Andrew Johnson.[74]

In the choice for Union or for secession, Unionists triumphed even more overwhelmingly. No anticoercion candidate won his race, and in each Grand Division, voters approved Unionist candidates with more than two-thirds of the vote. In East Tennessee, the pro-Union total approached 85 percent. As Unionists expected, the votes of nonslaveholding Democrats accounted for the lopsided margin, as most refused to follow the lead of Governor Harris and chose instead either to endorse Union candidates or abstain (see table 11).[75] The result of the delegate elections was a moot point, for the outcome of the voting meant that no convention would be held. The referendum showed primarily that Tennessee's voters overwhelmingly favored remaining in the Union to fight the Republicans and their abolitionist allies. While slavery was an accepted institution and southern rights did appear endangered, most voters as yet saw no reason to destroy the Union. The state's loyalty appeared to provide the surest way to promote a sectional agreement that could reunite the country. Peace could be preserved best by compelling the new administration to avoid an attack upon the seceded states.

The February results revealed that the alignment that had formed in the legislature in January now extended into the electorate. Whigs and Unionist Democrats, whose followers were principally nonslaveholding Democrats, predominantly voted for pro-Union candidates; while anticoercion candidates drew support chiefly from the Democratic party's Southern Rights wing. The Unionist coalition thus provided the foundation for a new party that stood ready to challenge Governor Harris and his allies for control of the state government. Advocates of southern unity, meanwhile, recognized that the referendum had damaged their cause tremendously. Not only had their program for resolving the crisis been repudiated, but now they stood condemned by voters for their apparent disregard of popular sovereignty. "I do hope and trust that the fate (politically) of Harris Haynes and others are [sic] forever sealed," John McGaughey wrote, while another East Tennessean agreed that "Gov Harris is buried so deep that no political resurrection horn can ever toot him up."[76]

Despite their loss, secession advocates continued their offensive. Republican hostility and the absence of any sectional agreement, they believed, would weaken the voters' confidence in the Union and would allow secessionists to persuade them in the coming state elections in August to reverse their February decision. "So brief and fleeting has been the campaign just past—so rapid the late political transactions around us—that the advocates of southern independence have had but little opportunity to place the true issue before the masses, . . . " the *Appeal* encouraged its allies the day after the election; "with us, *the canvass has but just begun.* We shall be daunted naught by the first and *only* defeat. The election of yesterday is but the first act in the great drama which is yet to be played." As they planned to hold a state convention on May 11 to nominate a gubernatorial candidate, secessionist newspapers continued to warn voters of the Republicans' impending attempt to establish a military dictatorship and insisted that Tennessee's only safe course lay in going with a united South. "The people are beginning to learn that their hopes are to be sadly disappointed," the *Union and American* stated, "that satisfactory guarantees will not be granted by the Black Republicans, that the seceded States will not return and that the Union is as to them finally dissolved, and that coercion is to be the policy of the Lincoln administration, and that war is a necessary consequence of such a policy."[77]

Unionists expressed concern that the secessionists' persistence might succeed.[78] Developments in the two months following the February election exacerbated the Unionists' anxiety. Lincoln's inaugural address secessionists interpreted as *"a declaration of war against the seceded States,"* for the new president affirmed his belief in the perpetuity of the Union and promised to execute the law, including the collection of tariff revenues, in all the States. In its first few weeks, the new administration issued no endorsement of any of the compromise proposals before Congress. Although rumors from Washington indicated that the administration intended to abandon Fort Sumter, South Carolina, and Fort Pickens, Florida, the two remaining federal military installations in the seceded states, its official policy on these institutions remained unclear. Republicans in Congress, meanwhile, introduced bills to raise tariff rates to protect northern industry, as well as a "force" bill that would authorize military action against the Lower South. As the administration appeared to move away from conciliation, the Montgomery convention completed the constitution of the Confederate States. Contrary to Unionist warnings of monarchy, the government created was essentially the same as that of the United States.[79] "The uncertainty of policy by the Administration is weakening Union men, . . ." Jeptha Fowlkes warned Andrew Johnson from Memphis, while the Confederate constitution "is generally recd. well by all Union men! while applauded by seceders—vehemently—& is taking here!" These facts, Fowlkes feared, augured ill for the Union cause: "My opinion, is, soon, a large number of Union-Conservative men in Tene. will become reconciled to separation—and indeed, go over to the Seceders. This seems to me the tendency;—& rendered, so because they find, a something fixed—& definite South: while, all, is doubt, hesitation & uncertainty, with our Northern friends!"[80]

Unionists thus expected a difficult canvass in the summer of 1861. Still, they were confident that their own cause would remain strong. Party spokesmen assured voters that Lincoln's inaugural address in no way threatened coercion, that Republican moderates indicated their support for a sectional compromise, and that the Republicans' opposition in Congress would defeat the tariff and force bills. Likewise, they noted that the Confederate constitution had not been submitted to the people for ratification and that it prohibited protective tariffs; this provision guaranteed that tariff rates would be kept so low that the government would have no alternative but to resort to direct taxation. And they continued to insist that Tennessee's fidelity could still work toward a preservation of the Union. With no assault yet from the administration on the seceded states, with the several compromise proposals still before the country, and with secessionists still stigmatized for their attempt to force the state into disunion, Unionists eagerly awaited the summer canvass. "Our people will not consent to go into a southern Confederacy," Samuel Williams reported to Johnson from Trenton in Gibson County, while Thomas J. Campbell wrote from Cleveland in East Tennessee that, in that section, "the people are more warmly Union than ever."[81]

Between the election of 1860 and the spring of 1861, then, Tennessee's parties became realigned to form a new party system founded upon the question of the state's response to the sectional crisis. As the newborn Unionist and secessionist parties prepared to fight the question over the summer, voters appeared to be settling into a new party system that would last at least for the duration of the Lincoln administration.

Conflict at Fort Sumter quickly destroyed this new political alignment. Confederate batteries opened fire on the fort on April 12, in order to remove this symbol of federal authority from Charleston harbor. President Lincoln two days later responded to the attack with a call for seventy-five thousand militia troops from the loyal states to assist in suppressing the seceded states' rebellion.[82]

Tennesseans followed the battle in Charleston harbor attentively, but Lincoln's call for volunteers—particularly the request for Tennessee to supply two regiments—met widespread condemnation in the middle and western Grand Divisions. This response permanently altered the state's political configuration. To voters in these regions, the "Black Republicans" had demonstrated their intention to coerce the seceded states back into the Union and to create a military dictatorship. With this design now apparently revealed, secession advocates were transformed from anti-republican disunionists into prophetic statesmen. They alone had warned of the true dangers presented by a Republican administration, it now appeared, for their predictions of an inevitable assault on southern rights seemed to have been proved true.

Northern aggression undermined the Unionist party's basis for existence. Unionism had been premised upon certain assumptions: that Lincoln would be compelled to observe the Constitution and the laws, that a sectional compromise could be achieved, and that the border states' loyalty would contribute to the Republicans' defeat at the next national election. Underlying these convictions had been the assumption that, in the North, a conservative sentiment favoring preservation of the Union prevailed. Lincoln's call for volunteers indicated that the new president would neither abide by the Constitution nor respect southern rights, and northern public approval of the call left most Unionists to conclude that the Union no longer presented the surest guarantee of liberty. Citizens now had no alternative but to resort to their right of revolution to throw off an oppressive, despotic government.[83] "I would have given all I have to preserve the union, and the rights and benefits of the South," wrote Felix Zollicoffer. "But our reasonable demands were refused—security and equality of rights were denied us—we could obtain no safety to our institutions. They would sustain the Union by force—a Union in which our institutions are constantly menaced—while they deny us terms of safety in the Union. They are now united in a purpose to overwhelm and humiliate us. They are enraged, and full of vindictive feeling. There is nothing left to us but to fight, or to be crushed and humiliated."[84]

Prominent Unionist leaders, who initially persisted in calling for moderation, quickly gave in to calls for Tennessee's separation from the United States. In Nashville, Unionist spokesmen at first tried to forestall precipitate action and encouraged their state to maintain a neutral stance. In an address signed by eleven of the most prominent Middle Tennesseans—including John Bell, John S. Brien, Neill S. Brown, Andrew and Edwin Ewing, Cave Johnson, and Balie Peyton—Unionists approved Harris's refusal to comply with Lincoln's request for troops but stated their belief that Tennessee "ought, as we think[,] to decline joining either party." Within a week after publication of the address, public pressure compelled these Unionists to accept resistance by a united South. Brien, Brown, and Andrew Ewing joined secessionists at a public meeting to declare themselves "in favor of Tennessee's arming herself without delay, and defending herself and the whole South against the menaced aggressions." Even Bell, Tennessee's longtime champion of a conservative party of Union, acknowledged, a week after the conflict began, that "the reports wafted to us on every breeze that comes from the North" brought news "of the intense and increasing excitement in that section and the united and determined purpose to wage a war for the subjugation of the South." "The events of the last few days have effected a wonderful change in the minds of the people here," one observer told William Campbell; "our most influential and strongest

Union men of yesterday are to day carried by the vortex of circumstances into that powerful stream of public opinion on which they float too weak and powerless to stem the current which will inundate the whole country in a most horrid civil war."[85]

Secessionists wasted no time capitalizing on public indignation. "The *Constitutional* Government of the United States is this day at an end by usurpation of the tyrants who hold their councils in the White House, . . . " the *Union and American* proclaimed. "Tennessee is today by the act of the President and his Cabinet, absolved from all allegiance to the government of the tyrants who have usurped powers which belong neither to them nor to the Congress of the United States."[86] With the outbreak of hostilities, panic gripped the public that the state was unprepared to meet the inevitable northern invasion, so secessionists urged organization for defense, while they insisted that Tennesseans faced no alternative but to unite with the rest of the South in the Confederate States. Only in southern unity could Tennesseans find sufficient military strength to resist the North, they argued, and only in the Confederacy could citizens find the constitutional form of government that would respect and preserve their freedom. Once again Governor Harris took the initiative in urging the state to take action. First, the governor responded to Secretary of War Simon Cameron's request for volunteers with a terse reply asserting that "Tennessee will not furnish a single man for purposes of coercion but 50,000 if necessary for the defence of our rights and those of our Southern brothers." Three days later, on April 18, Harris issued a proclamation calling the General Assembly into another extra session, to meet on April 25.[87]

Within two weeks, the legislature had carried through Tennessee's revolution. Meeting in secret, the assembly followed Governor Harris's recommendation to bypass a convention and to act upon its own position as the people's representatives, a method of action that "will be attended with less expense to the State." The legislature quickly adopted a "Declaration of Independence" that waived "any expression of opinion as to the abstract doctrine of secession," and secessionists—now with no fear of public opinion—agreed to submit the declaration to a popular vote in a referendum requiring voters to choose between "Separation" and "No Separation." Voters also would decide whether to send delegates to the provisional Confederate Congress, in a vote between "Representation" or "No Representation." Even before the day of the election, however, the process of aligning Tennessee with the Confederate states would be well under way. On May 1, the assembly approved a resolution authorizing Governor Harris to appoint three commissioners to negotiate a military alliance with the Confederacy. Five days later, legislators approved an act creating a provisional army in the state. This act authorized Governor Harris to appoint officers and to issue five million dollars in bonds to pay for the military force, and it instituted a property tax and a sales tax to fund the debt. The next day, Harris's commissioners—Gustavus A. Henry, A. O. W. Totten, and Washington Barrow—signed a "Convention" between Tennessee and the Confederacy that placed the state's defense under the direction of Confederate President Jefferson Davis, while anticipating Tennessee's "speedy admission into the Confederacy." Later that day, the assembly ratified the Convention, lifted its veil of secrecy, and announced its actions to the state.[88]

In this extra session, unlike the previous one, Democratic unity prevailed, while Opposition members broke away from their allies to approve Tennessee's revolution. Most Opposition legislators accepted the creation of the army to provide for the state's defense, but seventeen of the thirty-seven members voting opposed the military convention with the Confederacy.[89] The resisting Unionists probably held out hope that Tennessee, in some sort of league with other border slave states, especially neighboring Kentucky, could remain neutral in the conflict. With a large portion of the Unionists' former allies now joining their erstwhile opponents, their hope of keeping Tennessee neutral was dashed. Tennessee's revolution and its entrance into the Confederacy thus were carried out a month before citizens had the opportunity to voice their assent.

Despite these precipitate actions, Harris and the legislators were confident that the revolution would meet the approval of the mass of the voters. Only in East Tennessee did there appear to be any strong sentiment in favor of remaining in the Union; and secessionist leaders there were joined by Middle Tennesseeans Henry S. Foote, John F. House, Gustavus A. Henry, and John Bell in canvassing the region in favor of the two issues at hand, separation and representation. Elsewhere in the state, few spokesmen remained for unconditional Unionism. Opponents of the revolution still condemned Lincoln while advocating neutrality as preferable to "Taxing the people ruinously, & *trading our soldiers* off like sheep to be slaughtered."[90] Calls for neutrality and condemnation of "King Harris" failed to stem the tide of public opinion. Across the state, almost 70 percent of those participating in the election approved both separation and representation, and the referendum carried by a majority of fifty-seven thousand votes (see table 12). Slaveholding Tennesseans presented virtually a united front in favor of the revolution, regardless of party heritage or whether they

Table 12. Results of Tennessee Referendum on Declaration of Independence, Passed by General Assembly, June 8, 1861, by Grand Division

	Separation	Percent	No Separation	Percent
East	14,780	31.0	32,923	69.0
Middle	57,767	89.0	7,147	11.0
West	29,625	80.5	7,168	19.5
State	102,172	68.4	47,238	31.6

Source: White and Ash, *Messages of the Governors,* 5:304-5.

had favored the Unionist or the secessionist side during the past winter. In Middle and West Tennessee, the preponderance of nonslaveowners likewise rushed to approve the connection with the Confederacy. In these two divisions, resistance prevailed only in Carroll, Decatur, Hardin, Henderson, Wayne, and Weakley counties along the western ridge of the Highland Rim, and in Fentress and Macon counties in the hills of eastern Middle Tennessee. Elsewhere, voters overwhelmingly approved the legislature's actions; in thirty of the fifty-four counties in the two westerly Grand Divisions, the vote for separation was over 90 percent.[91]

Only in East Tennessee did a majority reject separation, and voters in this division did so by more than a two-to-one margin. Separation gained its strongest following in the southern portion of the region. Meigs, Monroe, Polk, Rhea, and Sequatchie counties approved revolution, and in Hamilton, Marion, and McMinn counties, separation gathered more than 40 percent of the votes cast. In the upper eastern end of the state, separation also won Sullivan County and gained a modest following in Washington County. Throughout the division, the secessionist cause seemed to run well in towns and county seats; the desire to join the Confederacy triumphed in Chattanooga and made a strong showing in the counties containing Knoxville and Athens. In the central counties of East Tennessee, however, revolution gained little support. Ten counties contributed less than 20 percent of their vote for separation, and across the division, Unionism won more than thirty-two thousand votes, compared to less than sixteen thousand for disunion.

The heritage of the antebellum parties heavily influenced the division over disunion in East Tennessee. Areas that had voted Whig in the prewar years tended to oppose separation in the June 8 referendum, while Democratic regions more often supported revolution.[92] Former

Whigs, moreover, provided the bulk of Unionist leadership, although they were joined at the forefront of Unionism by Democratic Senator Andrew Johnson. Lincoln, in fact, had selected Johnson—rather than the expected beneficiary, John Bell—as one of his chief advisors concerning the distribution of patronage in the state. Johnson had condemned secession and had indicated his approval of the idea of coercion in a speech to the Senate in December 1860; and the "mechanic statesman's" image as the champion of the hardworking yeomanry in opposition to a slaveholding aristocracy apparently coincided with the new president's own understanding of the Republican party's appeal. Before April 14, Johnson irritated Whig-Unionists when he seemed partial to Democrats in his recommendations to Lincoln, but his refusal to resign from the Senate, even after Tennessee's withdrawal from the Union—and after most Democrats came out for separation—reingratiated him with Unionists of Whig descent. Whig-Unionists probably saw a channel of access to the national administration through their former enemy—access that might lead to prominence in the state at the end of the conflict. In any case, the alliance between Johnson and the former Whigs represented a continuation of the Unionist coalition in East Tennessee despite its collapse elsewhere in the state, and the presence of a visible, adamant, united leadership contributed greatly in sustaining the loyalty of the Unionist ranks.[93]

The confrontation of party ideologies could survive in East Tennessee, even after its disintegration in the two western Grand Divisions, primarily because of the different nature of slavery in East Tennessee. While whites throughout the state accepted the institution, west of the Cumberland Mountains, slavery appeared to be a social, political, and economic necessity. Bondage in the Middle and Western districts subjugated a substantial black population whose emancipation, whites there believed, would unleash chaos on society. They also understood slavery to be a guarantee of their own liberty and independence, for the availability of black labor prevented whites from becoming a working class dependent upon wealthy planters. For aspiring, hardworking yeomen, moreover, the status of slaveowner seemed an attainable goal. Slavery was vital for the large-scale, labor-intensive cultivation of the state's cotton and tobacco cash crops, while farmers concentrating on the production of corn and livestock aspired to expand their operations through the acquisition of one slave or more. Since ownership in the Middle and West had already penetrated beyond the ranks of the fabulously wealthy to encompass a considerable portion of successful yeomen, it seemed plausible in these regions that diligence and careful management could elevate the average farmer into the slaveholding ranks. In West and Middle Tennessee, then, voters viewed the Republicans' expected attack upon slavery as a threat to their region's social peace, to their own personal autonomy, and to a vital component of their understanding of economic success. When forced to choose between North and South, most saw no alternative but to side "with those to whom we are indissolubly bound by the ties of sympathy and of interest."[94]

In East Tennessee, the situation was quite different. There, slavery never became so deeply entrenched. Slaves comprised only 9 percent of the population in 1860, and their density varied greatly—from areas where a modest number of slaves labored to civil districts where blacks were rarely, if ever, seen. In Bledsoe County, where the density of slaves was highest, they comprised only 15.5 percent of the population. In thirteen of the division's thirty counties, the rate exceeded 10 percent, but in ten of the remaining counties, the proportion fell below 6 percent, with slaves in Scott County comprising less than 2 percent of the population. Abolition, while undesirable, would bring no major disruption to most of East Tennessee society. In this region, too, slavery served no vital economic function, as most slaves worked either as personal servants or as unskilled laborers. Given few slaves and fewer plantations, to East Tennessee whites, slavery appeared less vital as a buffer against proletarianization. And, with slave ownership limited to the wealthiest inhabitants of the mountains, the institution appeared much more an elitist privilege than it did elsewhere in the state.

With slavery's future less of an overriding concern, East Tennesseans relied upon either interest or party identity to guide them in the decision for Union or disunion. The bulk of slaveholders recognized the Republicans' threat to their property, and separation and representation garnered support among town dwellers and ambitious farmers—especially in the counties nearest the cotton states—who hoped to prosper as miners, manufacturers, and food suppliers for the Confederate nation. Democrats likewise recalled their party's warnings that abolitionist aggression was chiefly responsible for the crisis and presented the greatest threat to republican liberty. For most of East Tennessee's yeomen, slavery was not an institution over which to dissolve the Union. Instead—especially since slavery already was associated with the elite—they found more plausible the charge that demagogues from lordly cotton plantations had brought on the conflict and, in the Confederacy, were creating the aristocracy they had long desired.[95]

The dangers presented by a cotton aristocracy appeared confirmed

"Swearing in the Flag, East Tennessee, 1862." From *Harper's New Monthly Magazine* (1862). Reproduction courtesy of Tennessee State Library and Archives, Nashville.

for East Tennessee Unionists when they recalled the course in the crisis of their own state. Governor Isham G. Harris—a West Tennessean who had built his career on aggressive defense of southern rights—and his cohorts had attempted in January to force Tennessee out of the Union, regardless of the people's will, Unionists believed; and they had taken advantage of the confusion over the Fort Sumter conflict to incite popular hysteria in order to attain their ends. With separation a reality, Harris became widely hated in East Tennessee, as the embodiment of the ambitious, fire-eating demagogue. As the governor led West and Middle Tennesseans through the preparation for war, East Tennessee Unionists charged that "King Harris" now sought to establish his own military despotism—backed by an army commanded by his appointees and supported by oppressive taxes—that would extinguish once and for all the freedom of the citizens in Tennessee. "If we loose [sic] then," Brownlow wrote of the June referendum, "our liberties are gone, and we are swallowed up by a Military Despotism more odious than any now existing in any monarchy in Europe." With such a clear case of treason and political usurpation before them, East Tennesseans made no secret of their support for the right of the federal government to reassert its authority. Even before the outbreak of war, they had endorsed Andrew Johnson's belief that the government had the authority "to put down resistance, and effectually to execute the laws as contemplated by the Constitution of the country," and with Tennessee's revolution understood in the East as the *coup* of King Harris, Unionists looked to the previously despised Lincoln as the only hope of their deliverance.[96]

East Tennessee Unionists tried to maintain their allegiance to the federal government despite the legislature's revolution. In Knox County, several leading Unionists organized an East Tennessee Convention that on May 30 condemned the assembly's actions as unconstitutional. After urging the defeat of separation and representation, the convention empowered its president, Representative Thomas A. R. Nelson, to reconvene the body once he learned of the results of the June referendum. When the June 8 referendum confirmed Tennessee's separation, Nelson called the convention to meet in Greeneville on June 17. For four days—and with Confederate troops passing through the town on their way to the front in Virginia—delegates considered Nelson's proposal to declare the state's counties that voted against separation to be the legal government of the state. Ultimately they pursued a more conciliatory approach to resistance: while accepting Nelson's "Declaration of Grievances" and its contention that the recent election "was free, with but few exceptions, in no part of the State, other than East Tennessee," the convention resolved to send Oliver P. Temple, John Netherland, and James P. McDowell as commissioners to the legislature to ask the assembly for "its consent that the counties composing East Tennessee and such counties in Middle Tennessee as desire to co-operate with them may form and erect a separate state." This new state would maintain its allegiance to the Union, and legislative consent would ensure a peaceful separation. Still, in this request Unionists made known their intention to take more direct action, for the delegates authorized Nelson to call yet another meeting, at Kingston in Roane County, should the legislature reject the commissioners' petition.[97]

Tennessee's leaders had no inclination to permit the eastern division's independence, if for no other reason than the fact that the railroad connection from Chattanooga to Virginia provided a crucial transportation route from the Lower South to the expected battlefront near the new Confederate capital at Richmond. Harris already had ordered volunteer troops into East Tennessee, ostensibly to protect the region from northern invasion. A Joint Select Committee in the assembly received the commissioners' petition but recommended its rejection on the grounds that the East Tennessee Convention failed to represent "the sentiment of the people of East Tennessee."[98]

Unionism's strength in the East, though, provided one last hope for the political opponents of the now seemingly invincible Governor Harris. In Middle and West Tennessee, one-time Unionists accepted the state's revolution as an irreversible fact, but they were disturbed by Harris's uncontested power in directing the government since the conflict at Fort Sumter. They also feared that Harris would send the Army of Tennessee, once its organization was completed, to aid the Confederacy in other states, rather than leaving it at home for Tennessee's own defense—a fear that appeared realized when the legislature on June 29 authorized the governor to transfer the command of the army to President Davis. Unionism's strength in East Tennessee offered the opportunity to unite with the governor's opponents in Middle and West Tennessee on the basis of resistance to "King Harris." Such a trans-state alliance conceivably could replace the demagogic governor with a moderate who had Unionist antecedents. This type of executive could make the defense of Tennessee, rather than the military affairs of the entire Confederacy, the state's chief concern. At the same time, removing the hated Harris could forestall East Tennessee's independence, and as a united state, Tennessee still could pursue a conciliatory course in the conflict that might prevent war from reaching Tennessee's borders and encourage a peaceful reconstruction of the Union.[99]

Notwithstanding the frenzy of late April, the Unionist party still held its convention on May 2. In its resolutions, the delegates admitted that "the once Union party of Tennessee ... is a Union party no longer" because "events had transpired in the country which rendered it necessary for that party to abandon the position which it occupied."

Nevertheless, the convention nominated William B. Campbell, "a military chieftain of large experience," to challenge Governor Harris, despite the convention's approval of Harris's refusal to honor Lincoln's call for volunteers. Campbell, though, proved an opponent of separation and declined the nomination. The former governor's unconditional Unionism made him overwhelmingly popular among Unionists in East Tennessee and had been one of the primary reasons for the convention's nomination; Harris's opponents therefore pressured Campbell to relent and to challenge the incumbent.[100] As Campbell persisted in his refusal, former Unionists increasingly turned their attention to William H. Polk—one of the state's leading Unionist Democrats, the brother of the former president, and a candidate eager to challenge the reign of "King Harris." The *Nashville Republican Banner* on June 30 endorsed Polk as the candidate most likely "to remove the unhappy estrangement now existing between the people of East Tennessee and the remaining divisions of the State." One week later, Polk announced that he would canvass Middle and West Tennessee in an open challenge to the incumbent.[101]

Polk entered his canvass convinced that a widespread repugnance to Harris prevailed in Middle and West Tennessee, and the challenger and his supporters charged in their campaign that the incumbent had "committed five separate and distinct and flagrant violations of the State Constitution" by appointing five members of the assembly to positions in the provisional army. In these and his other appointments, Polk supporters claimed, Harris had "used the immense patronage of his office to reward the men who have been his partizan adherents." Moreover, Harris displayed his ambition through his willingness to accept a third term, in violation of "a safe and learned precedent" according to which Tennessee governors retire after two terms—although all knew that "his aspirations are fixed upon a seat in the Senate of the Confederate States at its first session." Should Harris succeed in breaking the two-term custom, "the field will be open in Tennessee for the erection of a species of despotism—a 'one man power'—from which the generous freemen of the State will recoil with trembling." These factors all revealed Harris to be a selfish demagogue who was using the crisis to create a powerful clique, dependent upon the army and oppressive taxation, that would endanger the welfare and the liberties of Tennessee's citizens. Like the warfare that Whigs and Democrats had fought against despotic aristocrats, Polk and his advocates would continue the battle for freedom, not only against "Black Republicans" but also against the unconstitutional seizure of power occurring within Tennessee itself.[102]

At the same time, Polk assured voters that his own election would signify no retreat from Tennessee's separation from the Union and allegiance to the Confederacy. The challenger himself had voted in favor of separation and representation, he maintained, and in office he would devote his efforts to maintaining southern independence. Unlike Harris, though, Polk "would step into the arena of action as a vigorous champion of the people—a jealous guardian of their rights." Polk's triumph, moreover, would present the best opportunity to reunite the state. Unionists in East Tennessee despised Harris because of his usurpations, and the middle and western divisions' rejection of the incumbent would signal their willingness to placate East Tennesseans. The election of the moderate Polk, too, would present East Tennessee's Unionists with the promise of a just and fair administration of government, which might induce the dissenters to revive their affection for their fellow Tennesseans, despite their differences on the cause of southern rights. "[I]n view of the profound hostility towards Governor Harris cherished by the people of East Tennessee," the *Banner* explained, "the election of some man not so seriously objectionable to them as his Excellency, might do much by way of just and honorable conciliation, drawing them to us by a new tie of friendship."[103]

East Tennessee Unionists did accept Polk's candidacy, though not without hesitation. At first, because of Campbell's known loyalist sympathies, they hoped he would accept nomination; but when he declined, they attempted to run Knoxville's Connally F. Trigg as an unconditional Unionist. At the same time, two incumbent congressmen, Nelson and Horace Maynard, along with two other aspirants, ran for election to the United States Congress in the four East Tennessee districts, against opponents who pledged to serve in the Confederate Congress. Three days after the *Knoxville Whig* announced Trigg's candidacy, the *Republican Banner* reported that Trigg had withdrawn because he had not resided in the state for the constitutionally required seven years, though in fact East Tennesseans probably had realized the futility of promoting their own candidate.[104] Polk, meanwhile, promised to "clean out the stable" of Harris appointees in East Tennessee and replace them with Union men. This pledge offered Unionists hope of gaining control of the region's railroads and banks, and this control, they believed, would "give a death blow to the secessionists in East Tennessee, and cripple them in Middle and West Tennessee." Despite Polk's vote for separation and representation, then, East Tennessee's unconditional Unionists threw their support to him two weeks before the election. "He is kind in his feelings toward East Tennessee, and East Tennessee Union men, and will do us justice, the very thing Harris and his party will never do," Brownlow explained. "As a choice of evils, and as a peace measure, we go for Polk."[105]

While East Tennessee's Unionists pondered their course, Polk's canvass in Middle and West Tennessee went virtually ignored. Among former Unionist newspapers, only the *Nashville Republican Banner,* the *Memphis Bulletin,* and two minor Middle Tennessee weeklies threw their support behind the challenger. Most others, calling for unity in the crisis, denounced Polk's candidacy as "*partyism*" itself and promised to present "no factious opposition to Gov. Harris, or any other gentleman who may be mutually selected." Polk's appearances were poorly attended and went largely unnoticed, while West and Middle Tennesseans' preoccupation with military preparations left voters, as the *Jeffersonian* observed, "in no humor to rally around a candidate, who like him, is receiving the support of the Union shriekers of East Tennessee."[106]

The Secessionist party convention had met as scheduled on May 11 and concluded that it was "inexpedient to suggest a candidate for Governor at the present time"; instead, the convention urged citizens, "in their primary capacity having buried all party prejudices and erased old divisions," to hold local public meetings on June 15 "for purpose of harmonizing sentiment with regard to their choice for Governor." After these public meetings nominated the governor for a third term, Harris's supporters defended him from Polk's charges, while accusing the challenger of covert Unionism. They also argued that Harris's defeat "would be construed as a condemnation of the policy adopted by such an overwhelming majority by the people, on the 8th of June." The governor himself found his official responsibilities too pressing for him to meet Polk on the stump, though he did try to belie charges of partisanship by appointing as many former Whigs and Unionists as he could as officers in the army.[107]

The incumbent had little reason to worry about Polk's challenge. Nelson and Maynard won reelection to the federal Congress, and Polk carried East Tennessee by a margin of nearly two to one; but with the election occurring less than two weeks after the Confederate victory at the first Battle of Manassas, Harris defeated the challenger by more than thirty-one thousand votes. Even without campaigning, and with Polk touring in the middle and western Grand Divisions, the governor still garnered a majority of forty-four thousand votes in these regions. In eighteen counties, the tally for Harris exceeded 90 percent (see table 13).

With Isham Harris's reelection, citizens in Middle and West Tennes-

Table 13. Results of Tennessee Elections for Governor and for Ratification of the Permanent Constitution of the Confederate States of America, August 1, 1861, by Grand Division

	Harris	Percent	Polk	Percent
East	14,887	35.4	27,115	64.6
Middle	39,404	81.8	8,788	18.2
West	20,682	73.5	7,440	26.5
State	74,973	63.4	43,343	36.6

	For		Against	
	Constitution	Percent	Constitution	Percent
East	15,494	36.7	26,738	63.3
Middle	42,931	95.0	2,264	5.0
West	24,172	92.8	1,868	7.2
State	82,597	72.8	30,870	27.2

Source: *Nashville Republican Banner,* Oct. 31, 1861.

see considered their state wholeheartedly committed to the Confederacy. In these divisions, the ratification of the permanent Confederate constitution—which won approval with 73 percent of the votes cast—provided the most important issue in the August election (see table 13). "Tennessee will share with the Confederate States of the South the fortunes and fate of the Revolution, good or ill as they may be," the *Patriot* concluded. "This is now settled beyond cavil or dispute."[108] With overwhelming popular approval of his course, Harris, the day after the election, exercised his power to transfer authority over the Army of Tennessee to President Davis. Meanwhile, Thomas A. R. Nelson issued a call for the East Tennessee Convention to gather at Kingston on August 31. Confederates feared that the convention would attempt to declare East Tennessee's independence and petition for admission to the United States as a separate state. Virginia troops arrested Nelson, though, while he was traveling to Washington to claim his seat in Congress. On August 16, Governor Harris informed Confederate Secretary of War Leroy Pope Walker that "we can temporize with the rebellious spirit of that people no longer," as he requested sufficient troops to enact "a decided and energetic policy" of suppressing Unionism in East Tennessee. When the new General Assembly convened in October, legislators found all of Tennessee united, albeit forcibly, under the authority of the Confederate States.[109]

Tennessee's experience in the Confederacy proved brief. Forts Henry and Donelson, hastily constructed posts on the Kentucky line at the Tennessee and Cumberland rivers, fell to Union forces in February 1862. As the invading army approached Nashville, Governor Harris directed the legislature to move its deliberations to Memphis. The movement of federal troops into West Tennessee prevented the assembly from gaining a quorum for three weeks, and, with a bare minimum of members present, the assembly adjourned on March 20 after meeting in Memphis for only nine days.[110] After the Battle of Shiloh in April, West Tennessee and the northern half of Middle Tennessee lay under the control of an army of occupation. Confederate troops withdrew from the remainder of Middle Tennessee in January 1863, after the Battle of Stones River near Murfreesborough. With the "liberation" of East Tennessee later that year, the home state of Andrew Jackson once more came under the authority of the federal Union. Unlike the republican government that had left the Union two years earlier, however, Tennessee's administration now was directed by President Lincoln's appointed military governor, Andrew Johnson.

Well before the Union army's occupation, the political world that had existed in Tennessee since the days of Jackson already had come to an end. In that world, trans-state political parties confronted each other upon their interpretations of the republican fear that manipulative demagogues sought to consolidate power in the hands of the few, at the expense of the many. The outbreak of war reshaped the voters' understanding of politics. Thus, the fundamental concern in Middle and West Tennessee became vindication of the South, and in East Tennessee it became perpetuation of the Union. These very different sectional responses in Tennessee's Grand Divisions established the basis for the state's postwar political configuration. In the years after Appomattox, East Tennessee provided one of the few Republican strongholds in the South, while the rest of the state became a component of the Democratic "Solid South." In New South Tennessee, moreover, voters would hear few warnings about potential aristocrats; instead, the "Lost Cause," the legacy of defeat and occupation, and the fear of "Negro Rule" became the most influential tenets.

Perhaps nothing better reveals the transformation of state politics than William Polk's 1861 gubernatorial campaign. Polk built his challenge to Isham Harris upon the same republican fear of despotism that had dominated politics for the past thirty years; in previous campaigns, his ammunition against Harris would have gained him a substantial following. During the *rage militaire* of 1861, however, Polk's canvass scarcely made an impression. Fear of northern aggression subsumed hostility toward the governor's power in Middle and West Tennessee; in East Tennessee, Polk received Unionist support merely as a "choice of evils."

Still, the themes that had guided Tennessee's antebellum party system profoundly affected the state's response to the crisis of Union. The Opposition's revival after the Panic of 1857, on the eve of the conflict, reinforced the parties' traditional appeals as defenders of liberty against either "Federalists" or "Spoilsmen." By this time, the parties long ago had absorbed the sectional issue, including as enemies of freedom either abolitionists in the North or disunionist nullifiers in the South; each group was depicted as using the slavery issue to advance its selfish ends, regardless of the consequences. Both of Tennessee's parties stood against the sectional extremists, but Democrats warned that a greater threat was presented by the "Black Republicans," while their opponents emphasized the danger posed by southern Fire-Eaters. After Lincoln's election and the Lower South's secession, Tennessee voters saw themselves caught in a confrontation between two sets of radical demagogues. Party heritage and the socioeconomic opportunities presented by slavery influenced their choices of position in the crisis. Democrats were most likely to select the Southern Rights cause, and former Whigs almost unanimously pledged their loyalty to the Union. When forced to choose between the two positions, nonslaveholding Democrats abandoned their leaders to form the rank and file of a new Union party.

The hopes aroused by this new party likewise grew out of Tennesseans' antebellum political experience. Democratic and Whig/American/Opposition claims that a national party organization could preserve the Union encouraged the mass of Tennessee's voters to think that a new conservative party of Union could defeat the Republicans and resolve the crisis. Faced with the prospect of military action on the part of the Republican administration, though, voters quickly lost faith in the traditional political system. With the Constitution apparently abrogated by a military despotism, West and Middle Tennessee voters saw no alternative but to act upon their right of revolution. At the same time, with the state government itself apparently taken over by a partisan tyrant, East Tennessee Unionists saw no alternative but to cling to the Constitution of their revolutionary fathers.

Tennesseans thus believed that their actions in 1861 constituted a true revolution—not in the sense of a social upheaval, but as a defensive movement patterned after the upheaval of 1776. They perceived their separation from the Union in this way because, for so long, republican ideology had convinced them that politics involved a constant struggle to defend freedom against scheming conspiratorial demagogues. In the antebellum party system, intensified by an economic crisis, that ideology had been modified to fit new circumstances. In areas where black slavery had grown into an important institution, the understanding of republican freedom had developed to include slavery as a component vital for the protection of social order, economic mobility, and personal autonomy. In areas where slavery was a peripheral element of society, it was considered irrelevant to the attainment of republican ideals. When the outbreak of war revealed that the southern conception of the republic could not be sustained within the Union, most Tennesseans believed that revolution was necessary for the preservation of American freedom. East Tennesseans, however, considered a revolution from their state necessary for the same reason. Yet, whether they cast their lot with the South or the North, citizens believed that the fate of the republican liberty bequeathed to them by the revolutionary generation depended upon their choice.

William H. Mott, a resident of Alexandria, DeKalb County, who served as a major in the Army of Tennessee, spoke for most Tennesseans when, in his journal for 1862, he reflected on the future of republicanism and reaffirmed his commitment to its cause:

> It is a gloomy picture which the future presents even at best, and a still more gloomy one to look back upon the brilliant past, laden with so much of promise & hope to the new world. We have now to build up a new fabric from the ruins of the old, which fanaticism has riddled & torn till the stately old mansion, the temple of our blood purchased liberties[,] has crumbled to atoms[,] and upon its trampled remains are based the elements of a despotism[,] & a Military ruler sits upon the same chair that Washington Jefferson & Adams graced in the earlier and palmier days of the Republic. Is it thus that our great government is to emulate the example of previous experiments of Republicanism, [and] crumble & recede to monarchies, or is there a germ that is to put forth like magic upon the stern old rock of Liberty & grow until its spreading branches shade the fair continent of America[?] I cannot bear even the thought that a tyrant's rule should ever be felt upon the good soil of America that has been fanned so long by the fresh breezes of liberty. I want it all North, South, East, and West to be Republican. If the same government cannot canopy us all[,] let us [(]if separated we *must*[)] at least revere the recollections of the past, nor prove faithless to that trust, transmitted to us by our Fathers of the Revolution. Then let us swear by our lives our fortunes & our sacred honor that America must

& shall be free, and should we fail the goal let us plant it upon the minds of posterity that they may restore what we have lost.[111]

The republic for which Mott fought—and died, at Murfreesborough—perished with the conflict. No longer would citizens in Tennessee, or elsewhere in America, understand their politics in the same terms as they had during the antebellum party system: as a battle for liberty against oppression.

APPENDIX A

Roll-Call Votes Indicating Party Divisions in the Tennessee General Assembly
1839–1845

Session	Democrat Yes-No	% Yes	Whig Yes-No	% Yes
House, 1839-40				
To postpone indefinitely a bill to regulate banks	6-31	16.2	29-1	96.7
To create additional branches of the Planters' Bank	9-30	23.1	27-5	84.4
To pass a bill to encourage manufacturing in the Ocoee District	20-18	52.6	22-8	73.3
To postpone indefinitely a bill to limit the power of corporations	7-28	20.0	29-0	100.0
To pass a bill to repeal laws authorizing the governor to subscribe for stock in internal improvement companies	33-6	84.6	18-13	58.1
To pass a bill to increase the tax on brokers	29-6	82.9	4-4	50.0

To pass a bill to encourage the culture of silk	18-20	47.4	21-10	67.7
Senate, 1839-40				
To pass a bill to regulate banking	12-2	85.7	0-10	0.0
To pass a bill to regulate the power of corporations	12-1	92.3	0-9	0.0
To table an amendment to an insurance company charter restricting the investment of its capital	6-8	42.9	11-1	91.7
To table an amendment to an insurance company charter preventing investment in a public debt or a chartered bank	3-11	21.4	11-0	100.0
To pass a bill to increase the tax on brokers	10-0	100.0	1-8	11.1
To table a bill to encourage the culture of silk	9-3	75.0	2-6	25.0
To pass a bill to establish a lunatic asylum	5-7	41.7	7-3	70.0
To pass a bill to make penal the misuse or misrepresentation of public funds	12-2	85.7	0-8	0.0
To pass resolutions to amend the state constitution to prohibit the state, in the future, from becoming the sole proprietor of a bank	8-6	57.1	8-1	88.9
House, 1841-42				
To pass a bill to dispose of that portion of the money due the state from the sale of public lands	10-20	33.3	34-0	100.0
To pass a bill to encourage domestic manufacturing	13-17	43.3	28-4	87.5

Appendix A

To pass a resolution declaring the state's intention to honor its public debt	20-9	69.0	33-0	100.0
To pass a bill to suppress illegal voting	22-12	64.7	29-6	82.9
To table a resolution condemning the "fallacy" of a gold and silver currency	29-1	96.7	3-35	7.9
To pass a bill to suppress fraud in corporations	33-1	97.1	18-16	52.9
To pass a bill to compel banks to act in accordance with their charters	33-2	94.3	4-33	10.8
To postpone indefinitely a bill to limit the power of corporations	6-30	16.7	32-2	94.1

Senate, 1841-42

To pass a bill to dispose of that portion of the money due the state from the sale of public lands	8-5	61.5	11-1	91.7
To pass a bill to encourage domestic manufacturing	5-8	38.5	9-2	81.8
To pass a bill to encourage the culture of silk	6-7	46.2	9-3	75.0
To pass a resolution declaring the state's intention to honor its public debt	4-9	30.8	12-0	100.0
To pass a bill to suppress illegal voting	5-7	41.7	9-0	100.0
To pass a resolution to amend the state constitution to prohibit the legislature from creating a public debt	9-4	69.2	3-9	25.0

266   Appendix A

To strike from resolutions a preamble renouncing the principle of repudiation	13-0	100.0	0-12	0.0
To table a preamble declaring the state debt too large and pledging the legislature's intention not to increase the debt	5-8	38.5	12-0	100.0
To table a bill to regulate banking	3-10	23.1	11-1	91.7
To postpone indefinitely a bill to compel the banks to act in accordance with their charters	3-10	23.1	10-1	90.9
To adopt an amendment compensating in railroad stock damages to property caused by railroad companies	0-12	0.0	7-2	77.8

House, 1843-44

To pass a bill to increase the rate of the property tax	2-32	5.9	36-2	94.7
To pass a bill imposing a tax on certain civil offices and professions	8-24	25.0	17-16	51.5
To pass a bill chartering the Bank of East Tennessee	5-27	15.6	29-8	78.4
To pass a bill to encourage domestic manufacturing	7-25	21.9	26-6	81.3
To pass a bill to continue encouraging the culture of silk	13-19	40.6	26-12	68.4
To pass a bill to establish an institution for the blind and an asylum for the deaf and dumb	15-15	50.0	25-10	71.4

Appendix A

To pass a bill to appoint commissioners to regulate the affairs of internal improvement companies	12-16	42.9	18-11	62.1
To pass a bill extending the time granted to the Western and Atlantic Railroad to complete the line to East Tennessee	15-12	55.6	32-9	78.1
To pass a bill prohibiting removal of directors of the branches of state bank for "mere noncompliance with instructions," and prohibiting branch banks from operating under more restrictions than the principal bank	1-26	3.7	29-2	93.6
To pass resolutions asking the federal government for an appropriation to remove obstacles from rivers	2-23	8.0	24-10	70.6
To pass a resolution instructing the state's U.S. senators and requesting its U.S. representatives to support a reduction in the price of public land	30-4	88.2	18-19	48.7
To pass a bill to amend the redemption laws	8-25	24.2	26-10	72.2
To pass a bill authorizing the sale of common school lands, at the wish of the people of the township where the lands are situated	19-7	73.1	14-21	40.0

Senate, 1843-44

To pass a bill to increase the rate of the property tax	2-9	18.2	14-0	100.0
To pass a bill chartering the Bank of East Tennessee	1-7	12.5	12-1	92.3

To pass a bill to continue encouraging the culture of silk	5-6	45.5	8-4	66.7
To pass a bill authorizing the sale of common school lands, at the wish of the people of the township where the lands are situated	10-0	100.0	6-7	46.2
To pass a bill prohibiting the removal of directors of the branches of the state bank for "mere noncompliance with instructions," and prohibiting branch banks from operating under more restrictions than the principal bank	0-9	0.0	13-1	92.9
To pass a resolution to amend the state constitution to prohibit the legislature from creating corporations with banking privileges unless the stockholders were made individually liable for the debts of the corporation	11-0	100.0	1-12	7.7
To pass a resolution to amend the state constitution to prohibit a public debt	6-4	60.0	2-12	14.3
To pass a bill to authorize the governor to subscribe for stock in the Bank of East Tennessee	1-8	11.1	7-7	50.0
To pass a bill to provide for the gradual extinguishing of the public debt	2-8	25.0	9-4	69.2
To pass a resolution requesting U.S. senators and representatives to support the distribution to the states of the proceeds from the sale of public lands	0-10	0.0	14-0	100.0

Appendix A

To pass a bill to establish an institution for the blind and an asylum for the deaf and dumb	3-8	27.3	10-4	71.4
To pass a bill to appoint commissioners to regulate the affairs of internal improvement companies	3-7	30.0	9-4	69.2

APPENDIX B

Roll-Call Votes in the First Extra Session of the Tennessee General Assembly
January 7–February 4, 1861, by Party Affiliation

	Opposition		Democrat	
	Yes-No	% Yes	Yes-No	% Yes
House				
To adopt amendment to bill providing for referendum on state convention: "That no ordinance or resolution which may be adopted by said convention, having for its object a change of the position or relation of this State, shall be of any binding force or effect until it is submitted to, and ratified and adopted by a majority of the qualified voters of the State, taking as a basis the vote cast in the last election for Governor and members of the General Assembly"	32-0	100.0	12-23	34.3
To pass bill providing for a referendum on a state convention	32-0	100.0	39-0	100.0
To pass resolution in response to those passed by the legislature of New York	23-6	79.3	37-1	97.4

Appendix B

Measure				
To table resolution to discourage commercial intercourse with citizens of the northern states	22-3	88.0	10-21	32.3
To postpone indefinitely a bill to encourage foreign importations	25-3	89.3	7-25	21.9
To amend resolution sending delegates to a Southern Convention by striking out "Montgomery" and replacing with "Nashville"	28-1	96.6	22-15	59.5
To pass resolution proposing amendments to the Constitution of the United States and authorizing the appointment of delegates to a Southern Convention	29-1	96.7	28-5	84.5
To proceed with the election of delegates to a Southern Convention	33-0	100.0	6-23	20.7
To pass bill repealing the act abolishing military duty	18-13	58.1	31-7	81.6
To postpone indefinitely a bill "to enable the State of Tennessee to repel invasion and suppress insurrection"	26-5	83.9	6-26	18.8
To pass resolution directing delegates to a Southern Convention to attend the Peace Conference at Washington	30-1	96.8	20-15	57.1

Senate

Measure				
To amend bill providing for the calling of a convention of the people of Tennessee with: "no ordinance or resolution adopted by said Convention, having for its object to change the position or relation of this State to the Federal Union, or her sister Southern States, shall be of binding force until it is submitted to a vote of the people, and ratified by a majority of all the voters in the State, taking the vote in the last Gubernatorial election as the number of qualified voters in the State"	9-0	100.0	5-8	38.5

To amend bill providing for the calling of a convention by striking out reference to voters in last gubernatorial election and replacing with: "by a majority of voters polled, and that before any act or ordinance touching our relations to the Federal Government shall be binding, the same shall be submitted back to the people for their rejection or approval, not sooner than twenty days after the passage of such act or ordinance"	0-11	0.0	13-1	92.9
To adopt resolution to discourage commercial intercourse with the citizens of the northern states	3-5	37.5	10-0	100.0
To proceed to the election of delegates to a convention of slaveholding states	11-0	100.0	2-11	15.4
To pass bill "to enable the State of Tennessee to repel invasion and suppress insurrection"	1-8	11.1	10-0	100.0
To pass bill repealing the act abolishing military duty	2-7	22.2	11-1	91.7
To pass resolution authorizing the governor to appoint three commissioners to the Southern Convention at Montgomery, Alabama	0-10	0.0	9-1	90.0
To pass bill to encourage foreign importations	4-6	40.0	12-1	92.3
To pass bill providing for a referendum on a state convention	11-0	100.0	14-0	100.0
To pass resolution "in regard to the action of the Legislature of New York, tendering men and money to the President of the United States"	5-5	50.0	12-0	100.0
To pass first three resolutions in series proposing amendments to the Constitution of the United States	6-5	54.6	13-0	100.0

Appendix B 273

To pass remaining three resolutions   8-3   72.7   12-0   100.0
in series proposing amendments
to the Constitution of the
United States

APPENDIX C

Roll-Call Votes in the Second Extra Session of the Tennessee General Assembly

April 25–July 1, 1861,
by Party Affiliation

	Opposition		Democrat	
	Yes-No	% Yes	Yes-No	% Yes
House				
To pass resolution to meet in secret	11-11	50.0	22-5	81.5
To pass bill creating a provisional army	20-11	64.5	34-4	89.5
To pass resolution authorizing governor to appoint commissioners to negotiate a military league with the Confederacy	11-21	34.4	29-3	90.6
To pass bill submitting a Declaration of Independence to a popular vote	13-18	41.9	33-3	91.7
To pass bill confirming governor's military appointments	10-21	32.3	28-3	90.3
To pass resolution removing injunction of secrecy on legislature	24-7	77.4	19-11	63.3
To pass resolution ratifying Military League with Confederacy	14-15	48.3	30-1	96.8

Appendix C

To pass bill submitting to a popular vote the adoption or rejection of the permanent Constitution of the Confederate States	12-11	52.2	32-1	97.0

Senate

To pass bill creating a provisional army	7-4	63.6	11-1	91.7
To pass bill submitting a Declaration of Independence to a popular vote	7-4	63.6	14-0	100.0
To pass resolution ratifying Military League with Confederacy	3-5	37.5	11-1	91.7
To pass bill submitting to a popular vote the adoption or rejection of the permanent Constitution of the Confederate States	8-2	80.0	10-0	100.0
To pass resolution requesting U.S. senators to resign their seats	3-7	30.0	10-2	83.3

Notes

Abbreviations

DU	William R. Perkins Library, Duke Univ.
House Journal	Tennessee General Assembly, *Journal of the House of Representatives of the State of Tennessee* (year of session indicated in parentheses)
HSP	Historical Society of Pennsylvania, Philadelphia
LC	Library of Congress, Washington, D.C.
McClung	McClung Collection, East Tennessee Historical Center, Knoxville
NCDAH	North Carolina Dept. of Archives and History, Raleigh
NYHS	New York Historical Society, New York City
Public Acts	Tennessee General Assembly, *Public Acts of the State of Tennessee* (year of session in which act passed indicated in parentheses)
Senate Journal	Tennessee General Assembly, *Journal of the Senate of the State of Tennessee* (year of session indicated in parentheses)
SHC	Southern Historical Collection, Univ. of North Carolina, Chapel Hill
THQ	*Tennessee Historical Quarterly*
THS	Tennessee Historical Society, Nashville
TSLA	Tennessee State Library and Archives, Nashville
UT	James D. Hoskins Library, Univ. of Tennessee, Knoxville

Preface

1. *Nashville Republican Banner,* Apr. 9 and 13, 1861.
2. Previous studies of Tennessee during the secession crisis include Mary E. R. Campbell, *The Attitude of Tennesseans Toward the Union, 1847-1861* (New York: Vantage Press, 1961); James W. Patton, *Unionism and Reconstruction in Tennessee, 1860-1869* (Chapel Hill: Univ. of North Carolina Press, 1934); John Edgar Tricamo, "Tennessee Politics, 1845-1861" (Ph.D. diss., Co-

lumbia Univ., 1965); and Charles L. Lufkin, "Secession and Coercion in Tennessee: The Spring of 1861," *THQ* 50 (Summer 1991): 98-109. The exception to the generalizations of this paragraph is Daniel W. Crofts, *Reluctant Confederates: Upper South Unionists in the Secession Crisis* (Chapel Hill: Univ. of North Carolina Press, 1989). Crofts provides the best recent account of Tennessee from the election of 1860 through April 1861 in an excellent comparative study of Upper South Unionism in Tennessee, North Carolina, and Virginia. His focus on Unionists, however, leads his attention away from state politics to national Unionist negotiations; also, Crofts devotes little attention to local politics after the conflict at Fort Sumter.

3. This expression comes from John William Ward, *Andrew Jackson: Symbol for an Age* (New York: Oxford Univ. Press, 1955).

4. Standard works on Tennessee politics during the era of the second American party system include Thomas Perkins Abernethy, *From Frontier to Plantation in Tennessee: A Study in Frontier Democracy* (Chapel Hill: Univ. of North Carolina Press, 1932); Paul H. Bergeron, *Antebellum Politics in Tennessee* (Lexington: Univ. Press of Kentucky, 1982); Charles G. Sellers, *James K. Polk: Jacksonian, 1795-1843* (Princeton, N.J.: Princeton Univ. Press, 1957); Charles G. Sellers, *James K. Polk: Continentalist, 1843-1846* (Princeton, N.J.: Princeton Univ. Press, 1966); and Frank Mitchell Lowrey, III, "Tennessee Voters During the Second Two-Party System, 1836-1860: A Study in Voter Constancy and in Socio-Economic and Demographic Distinctions" (Ph.D. diss., Univ. of Alabama, 1973).

5. J. Mills Thornton, III, *Politics and Power in a Slave Society: Alabama, 1800-1860* (Baton Rouge: Louisiana State Univ. Press, 1978); Michael F. Holt, *The Political Crisis of the 1850s* (New York: Norton, 1978); Marc W. Kruman, *Parties and Politics in North Carolina, 1836-1865* (Baton Rouge: Louisiana State Univ. Press, 1983); Lacy K. Ford, *Origins of Southern Radicalism: The South Carolina Upcountry, 1800-1860* (New York: Oxford Univ. Press, 1988). See also James M. McPherson, *What They Fought For, 1861-1865* (Baton Rouge: Louisiana State Univ. Press, 1994); and George C. Rable, *The Confederate Republic: A Revolution Against Politics* (Chapel Hill: Univ. of North Carolina Press, 1994).

6. See esp. Stanley John Folmsbee, *Sectionalism and Internal Improvements in Tennessee, 1796-1845* (Knoxville: East Tennessee Historical Society, 1939); William J. Cooper, Jr., *The South and the Politics of Slavery, 1828-1856* (Baton Rouge: Louisiana State Univ. Press, 1978); and Bergeron, *Antebellum Politics in Tennessee*.

7. Bergeron, *Antebellum Politics in Tennessee*, ix.

8. Republicanism, as understood in this work, will be discussed in ch. 1. It is an understatement to say that the literature on republicanism in early America, along with criticism of its historical utility, is voluminous. Good introductions to this literature can be found in Robert E. Shalhope, "Toward a Republican Synthesis: The Emergence of an Understanding of Republicanism in American Historiography," *William and Mary Quarterly* 29 (Jan. 1972): 49-80; Robert E. Shalhope, "Republicanism and Early American Historiogra-

phy," *William and Mary Quarterly* 39 (Apr. 1982): 334-56; Daniel T. Rodgers, "Republicanism: The Career of a Concept," *Journal of American History* 79 (June 1992): 11-38; and Milton M. Klein, Richard D. Brown, and John B. Hench, eds., *The Republican Synthesis Revisited: Essays in Honor of George Athan Billias* (Worcester, Mass.: American Antiquarian Society, 1992). The standard works, which have heavily influenced this study, remain Bernard Bailyn, *The Ideological Origins of the American Revolution* (Cambridge, Mass.: Belknap Press of Harvard Univ. Press, 1967); Gordon S. Wood, *The Creation of the American Republic, 1776-1787* (Chapel Hill: Univ. of North Carolina Press, 1969); and Lance Banning, *The Jeffersonian Persuasion: Evolution of a Party Ideology* (Ithaca, N.Y.: Cornell Univ. Press, 1978). On the power of republicanism in antebellum politics, see the works cited in n. 4 above, along with Harry L. Watson, *Liberty and Power: The Politics of Jacksonian America* (New York: Noonday Press, 1990); Marc W. Kruman, "The Second American Party System and the Transformation of Revolutionary Republicanism," *Journal of the Early Republic* 12 (Winter 1992): 509-37; Major L. Wilson, "The 'Country' versus the 'Court': A Republican Consensus and Party Debate in the Bank War," *Journal of the Early Republic* 15 (Winter 1995): 619-47; and Thomas Brown, *Politics and Statesmanship: Essays on the American Whig Party* (New York: Columbia Univ. Press, 1985), esp. 1-12.

Chapter 1. Politics and Republicanism in Jackson's Tennessee

1. William Carroll to Andrew Jackson, Dec. 26, 1831, Andrew Jackson Papers, LC; George Washington Campbell to Andrew Jackson, Jan. 14, 1831, Andrew Jackson Papers, LC.

2. Alfred Balch to James K. Polk, Jan. 6, 1831, in Herbert Weaver et al., eds., *Correspondence of James K. Polk* (Knoxville: Univ. of Tennessee Press, 1969), 1:375.

3. William Carroll to Robert C. Thompson, qtd. in Robert H. White and Stephen V. Ash, eds., *Messages of the Governors of Tennessee* (Nashville: Tennessee Historical Commission, 1952), 2:200.

4. Andrew Buchanan, speech in Tennessee House of Representatives, qtd. in White and Ash, *Messages of the Governors* 2:191. On the conception of power and liberty in republicanism, see Bailyn, *Ideological Origins*, 55-93.

5. Joseph Kincaid, speech in Tennessee House of Representatives, qtd. in White and Ash, *Messages of the Governors* 2:184; *Nashville Republican*, Feb. 10, 1831.

6. Free blacks made up a small proportion of Tennessee's population and had been permitted to vote under the original state constitution, but because of growing racism and increased abolitionist activity in the 1830s, the 1834 revision specifically limited suffrage to white males over 21. On the ostracism of free blacks, see Anita Shafer Goodstein, *Nashville, 1780-1860: From Frontier to City* (Gainesville: Univ. of Florida Press, 1989), 136-56; see also Arthur F. Howington, "'Not in the Condition of a Horse or an Ox': *Ford v. Ford*, the

Law of Testamentary Manumission, and the Tennessee Court's Recognition of Slave Humanity," *THQ* 34 (Fall 1975): 249-63; and Steve Baker, "Agriculture, Race, and Free Blacks in West Tennessee," *West Tennessee Historical Society Papers* 48 (Dec. 1994): 107-17.

7. On the legal standing of women in antebellum Tennessee, see Lawrence B. Goodheart, Neil Hanks, and Elizabeth Johnson, "'An Act for the Relief of Females . . .': Divorce and the Changing Legal Status of Women in Tennessee, 1796-1860," 2 pts., *THQ* 44 (Fall 1985): 318-39 and 44 (Winter 1985): 402-16. On women's participation in the politics of the second-party system, see Jayne Crumpler De Fiore, "Come, and Bring the Ladies: Tennessee Women and the Politics of Opportunity during the Presidential Campaigns of 1840 and 1844," *THQ* 51 (Winter 1992): 197-212; and Elizabeth R. Varon, "Tippecanoe and the Ladies, Too: White Women and Party Politics in Antebellum Virginia," *Journal of American History* 82 (Sept. 1995): 494-521.

8. *Journal of the Proceedings of a Convention Began and Held at Knoxville, January 11, 1796* (Knoxville, Tenn., 1796; rpt. Nashville: n.p., 1852).

9. There is, unfortunately, no good study of the move for constitutional revision in Tennessee. The calling of the Convention of 1834 is usually attributed to a democratic spirit that prevailed throughout Jacksonian America; see Wallace M. McClure, *State Constitution-Making, With Especial Reference to Tennessee* (Nashville: Marshall and Bruce Co., 1915), 51-57; Abernethy, *From Frontier to Plantation*, 235-37; and Bergeron, *Antebellum Politics in Tennessee*, 38-40. The conclusion here that public dissatisfaction with the state's judicial system was the primary factor behind the calling of the 1834 convention is based on White and Ash, *Messages of the Governors* 2:448-661; *Knoxville Register*, June 19 and Nov. 27, 1833; *Knoxville Register*, Jan. 1, 8, 15, 29, 1834; *Nashville Republican*, May 22-Sept. 9, 1834; J. S. Yerger to Robert L. Caruthers, June 7, 1831, in Robert Looney Caruthers Papers, SHC; William B. Campbell to David Campbell, July 11, 1831, and David Campbell to William B. Campbell, Aug. 17, 1833, both in David Campbell Papers, DU.

10. *Journal of the Convention of the State of Tennessee; Convened for the Purpose of Revising and Amending the Constitution Thereof* (Nashville: n.p., 1834), 187, 193-200, 207, 229-40, 267-73, 280-89, 351-52.

11. Tennessee Constitution, 1834, Art. 3. On republicanism and executive power, see Wood, *Creation of the American Republic*, 148-50.

12. Tennessee Constitution, 1834, Art. 2. The convention increased the maximum number of members permitted in the house of representatives from 40 to 99 and limited the number of senators to one-third of the number of members in the house; throughout the antebellum era, the house would contain 75 seats and the senate 25. The convention also raised the minimum age qualification of senators from 21 to 30 while leaving the qualification of representatives at 21. This distinction proved to have little effect on the membership of either body, as the ages of members of both chambers averaged in the mid-thirties.

13. Wood, *Creation of the American Republic*, 162-63; Kruman, *Parties and Politics in North Carolina*, 45-54; Thornton, *Politics and Power in a Slave Society*, 59-60, 80-87.

14. On Federalist opposition to Tennessee's admission, see Abernethy, *From Frontier to Plantation,* 138-43; and William H. Masterson, *William Blount* (Baton Rouge: Louisiana State Univ. Press, 1954), 294-98.

15. U.S. Census Office, *Sixth Census of Enumeration of the Inhabitants of the United States* (Washington, D.C.: Blair and Rives, 1841), 264-74; U.S. Census Office, *Seventh Census of the United States: 1850* (Washington, D.C.: R. Armstrong, 1853), 584; Donald L. Winters, *Tennessee Farming, Tennessee Farmers: Antebellum Agriculture in the Upper South* (Knoxville: Univ. of Tennessee Press, 1994), 30-75; Robert Tracy McKenzie, *One South or Many? Plantation Belt and Upcountry in Civil War Era Tennessee* (Cambridge, England: Cambridge Univ. Press, 1994), 11-55; Stephen V. Ash, *Middle Tennessee Society Transformed, 1860-1870: War and Peace in the Upper South* (Baton Rouge: Louisiana State Univ. Press, 1988), 13-32; Donald L. Winters, "The Agricultural Ladder in Southern Agriculture: Tennessee, 1850-1870," *Agricultural History* 61 (Summer 1987): 36-52. On safety-first agriculture, see Gavin Wright, *The Political Economy of the Cotton South: Households, Markets, and Wealth in the Nineteenth Century* (New York: Norton, 1978), 62-74. See also J. Mills Thornton, III, "The Ethic of Subsistence and the Origins of Southern Secession," *THQ* 48 (Summer 1989): 67-85.

16. Kruman, *Parties and Politics in North Carolina,* 50. The standard definition of "planter" as a person owning 20 or more slaves was first proposed by U. B. Phillips, *Life and Labor in the Old South* (1929; reprint, Boston: Little, Brown, 1963).

17. McKenzie, *One South or Many?,* 56-84; Ash, *Middle Tennessee Society Transformed,* 42-48; Donald L. Winters, "'Plain Folk' of the Old South Reexamined: Economic Democracy in Tennessee," *Journal of Southern History* 53 (Nov. 1987): 571; see also Lee Soltow, "Land Inequality on the Frontier: The Distribution of Land in East Tennessee at the Beginning of the Nineteenth Century," *Social Science History* 5 (Summer 1981): 275-91.

18. *Nashville Whig,* July 11 and 18, 1821; Robertson Topp to Elizabeth L. Topp, July 1, 1837, Robertson Topp Papers, Burrow Library, Rhodes College, Memphis, Tenn.; William B. Campbell to Mary H. Campbell, Aug. 1, 1831, and B. R. Owen to William B. Campbell, Jan. 10, 1839, both in Campbell Papers, DU; *Nashville National Banner,* Feb. 18, 1834; *Athens Post,* Oct. 7, 1853. See also Harry L. Watson, "Conflict and Collaboration: Yeomen, Slaveholders, and Politics in the Antebellum South," *Social History* 10 (Oct. 1985): 273-98.

19. U.S. Census Office, *Sixth Census,* 264-74; U.S. Census Office, *Seventh Census,* 584; U.S. Census Office, *Population of the United States in 1860; Compiled from the Original Returns of the 8th Census, Under the Direction of the Secretary of the Interior, by Joseph C. G. Kennedy* (Washington, D.C.: Government Printing Office, 1864), 471; Robert M. McBride and Dan M. Robison, *Biographical Directory of the Tennessee General Assembly,* 3 vols. (Nashville: Tennessee State Library and Archives and the Tennessee Historical Commission, 1975). Some of the data for the 1850 and 1860 legislators were provided by Ralph A. Wooster, who shared the notes used for his study of legislative membership in *Politicians, Planters, and Plain Folk:*

Courthouse and Statehouse in the Upper South, 1850-1860 (Knoxville: Univ. of Tennessee Press, 1975). Rather than assuming, as Wooster does, that a legislator not found on the 1850 and 1860 census schedules of slaves and slave owners was a nonslaveholder, I assumed that, since the same census taker compiled both schedule 1 (population) and schedule 2 (slave owners and slaves), legislators found on schedule 1 but not schedule 2 owned no slaves. Those found on neither schedule 1 nor schedule 2 are not included in the analysis of slaveholding. See also Kruman, *Parties and Politics in North Carolina*, 45-51; and Thornton, *Politics and Power in a Slave Society*, 60-68.

20. See, e.g., Abernethy, *From Frontier to Plantation*, 358-64; Richard P. McCormick, *The Second American Party System: Party Formation in the Jackson Era* (New York: Norton, 1966), 222-25; and John Foreman to Abia Hodgson, Mar. 8, 1817, William Brown Hodgson Papers, DU.

21. Alfred Balch to James K. Polk, Jan. 6, 1831, in Weaver et al., *Correspondence of James K. Polk*, 1:376; *Nashville Republican*, July 28, 1831; McBride and Robison, *Biographical Directory*, 1:145-46.

22. *Nashville Republican*, June 4, July 9 and 28, 1835; *Nashville National Banner*, July 10 and 29, 1835; *Nashville Union*, July 1, 3, and 31, Aug. 26, 1835.

23. *House Journal* (1831-32), 134; *Senate Journal* (1833-34), 191-92; McBride and Robison, *Biographical Directory*, 1:170.

24. The rate on the poll tax eventually increased to 50 cents, and the property tax rate to 13 1/16 cents by 1860. These rates were still low compared to those of postbellum Tennessee, though in 1859 the state comptroller recommended a reduction in tax rates. See "Report of James T. Dunlap, Comptroller of the Treasury, to the General Assembly of Tennessee, October, 1859," *Appendix to House and Senate Journals* (1859), vi, vii, 17.

25. *Public Acts* (1835), 58-66; (1844), 141, 173. *Senate Journal* (1845-46), app., p. 115. *House Journal* (1847-48), app., p. 96.

26. William Carroll to Andrew Jackson, Dec. 2, 1832, in Andrew Jackson Papers, LC.

27. U.S. Census Office, *Sixth Census*, 264-74; U.S. Census Office, *Seventh Census*, 584-90; U.S. Census Office, *Population of the U.S. in 1860*, 132-39; Folmsbee, *Sectionalism and Internal Improvements*, 1-2.

28. Nathaniel Kelsey, circular, July 25, 1833, in Thomas Amis Rogers Nelson Papers, McClung; Folmsbee, *Sectionalism and Internal Improvements*, 10-14; William G. Brownlow, *A Political Register, Setting Forth the Principles of the Whig and Locofoco Parties in the United States, with the Life and Public Services of Henry Clay. Also an Appendix Personal to the Author; and a General Index* (Jonesborough, Tenn.: n.p., 1844), 24.

29. Folmsbee, *Sectionalism and Internal Improvements*, 2-3; Goodstein, *Nashville, 1780-1860*, 1-70; Ash, *Middle Tennessee Society Transformed*, 1-22; Abernethy, *From Frontier to Plantation*, 188; Thomas Perkins Abernethy, "The Early Development of Commerce and Banking in Tennessee," *Mississippi Valley Historical Review* 14 (Dec. 1927): 311-19.

Notes to pages 16-19 283

30. U.S. Census Office, *Sixth Census,* 264-74; U.S. Census Office, *Agriculture of the United States in 1860; Compiled from the Original Returns of the Eighth Census, Under the Direction of the Secretary of the Interior, by Joseph C. G. Kennedy, Superintendent of Census* (Washington, D.C.: Government Printing Office, 1864), 132-39; Ash, *Middle Tennessee Society Transformed,* 16-18.

31. U.S. Census Office, *Sixth Census,* 264-74; U.S. Census Office, *Seventh Census,* 584-90; U.S. Census Office, Seventh Census, MSS, Agriculture, Maury County, Tenn.; Ash, *Middle Tennessee Society Transformed,* 15-16.

32. Winters, *Tennessee Farming, Tennessee Farmers,* 76-95; Ash, *Middle Tennessee Society Transformed,* 9-11; Folmsbee, *Sectionalism and Internal Improvements,* 14-17; Goodstein, *Nashville, 1780-1860,* 19-24; Allen Brown to James K. Polk, Mar. 14, 1834, in Weaver et al., *Correspondence of James K. Polk,* 2:358; H. Phillip Bacon, "Nashville's Trade at the Beginning of the Nineteenth Century," *THQ* 15 (Mar. 1956): 30-36.

33. Folmsbee, *Sectionalism and Internal Improvements,* 3-4; Bette Baird Tilly, "Aspects of Social and Economic Life in West Tennessee Before the Civil War" (Ph.D. diss., Memphis State Univ., 1974), 42-177; Samuel C. Williams, ed., "Journal of Events (1825-1873) of David Anderson Deaderick," East Tennessee Historical Society *Publications* 8 (1936): 130.

34. U.S. Census Office, *Sixth Census,* 264-74; U.S. Census Office, *Seventh Census,* 584-90; U.S. Census Office, *Agriculture of the U.S. in 1860,* 132-39; Tilly, "Aspects of Social and Economic Life in West Tennessee," 88-103.

35. Tricamo, "Tennessee Politics," 10, 72-110; Folmsbee, *Sectionalism and Internal Improvements,* 70-147; William B. Campbell to David Campbell, Nov. 20, 1851, in Campbell Papers, DU.

36. *Journal of the Convention of Tennessee, 1834,* 87-93, 125-30; Abernethy, *From Frontier to Plantation,* 104, 112-13; Chase C. Mooney, *Slavery in Tennessee* (Bloomington: Indiana Univ. Press, 1957); Arthur F. Howington, *What Sayeth the Law: The Treatment of Slaves and Free Blacks in the State and Local Courts of Tennessee* (New York: Garland, 1986); and John Cimprich, *Slavery's End in Tennessee, 1861-1865* (University: Univ. of Alabama Press, 1985), 6-18.

37. On white southern and American assumptions about slavery and race, see George M. Fredrickson, *The Black Image in the White Mind: The Debate on Afro-American Character and Destiny, 1817-1914* (Middleton, Conn.: Wesleyan Univ. Press, 1971), 43-96; James Oakes, *The Ruling Race: A History of American Slaveholders* (New York: Vintage, 1982), 123-50; and Winthrop D. Jordan, *White Over Black: American Attitudes Toward the Negro, 1550-1812* (Chapel Hill: Univ. of North Carolina Press, 1968).

38. *Public Acts* (1831-32), 121-22; (1835-36), 145-46; (1839-40), 82-83; (1853-54), 121-22. White and Ash, *Messages of the Governors* 5:174-208. A good survey of Tennessee's slave laws can be found in Mooney, *Slavery in Tennessee,* 7-28.

39. See, e.g., *House Journal* (1835-36), 564; (1839-40), 350; (1853-54), 708-9; and *Senate Journal* (1835-36), 463; (1839-40), 182; (1853-54), 629.

40. William B. Campbell to David Campbell, Dec. 17 and 24, 1856, both in Campbell Papers, DU; William F. Cooper to Matthew D. Cooper, Dec. 29, 1856, in Cooper Family Papers, TSLA; Benjamin F. Allen to William Trousdale, Jan. 8, 1857, in William Trousdale Papers, THS. *Clarksville Jeffersonian*, Nov. 26 and Dec. 3, 1856; *Nashville Union*, Dec. 11, 1856.

41. U.S. Census Office, *Preliminary Report on the Eighth Census: 1860* (Washington, D.C.: Government Printing Office, 1862), 130-31; Kruman, *Parties and Politics in North Carolina*, 49.

42. Winters, *Tennessee Farming, Tennessee Farmers*, 138-41; McKenzie, *One South or Many?*, 14-16; Blanche Henry Clark, *The Tennessee Yeoman, 1840-1860* (Nashville: Vanderbilt Univ. Press, 1942), 28; Mooney, *Slavery in Tennessee*, 104-5.

43. *Journal of the Convention of Tennessee, 1834*, 125-26, 201.

44. *Knoxville Register*, Jan. 29, 1834; *Jonesborough Whig*, Mar. 16, 1842; Lawrence B. Goodheart, "Tennessee's Antislavery Movement Reconsidered: The Example of Elihu Embree," *THQ* 41 (Fall 1982): 224-38.

45. Lawson Gifford to James K. Polk, Feb. 4, 1839, in Weaver et al., *Correspondence of James K. Polk*, 5:45; Bryson B. Trousdale to William Trousdale, Nov. 23, 1848, in William Trousdale Papers, TSLA; *Knoxville Register*, Apr. 27, 1831; *Jackson (Tenn.) Southern Statesman*, July 23, 1831.

46. *Nashville Union*, July 29, 1835; *Nashville Whig*, Feb. 23, 1843. On the importance of black slavery to the southern understanding of white freedom, see Fredrickson, *Black Image in the White Mind*, 43-96, 130-64; and Edmund S. Morgan, *American Slavery, American Freedom: The Ordeal of Colonial Virginia* (New York: Norton, 1975), esp. 295-387.

47. Charles G. Sellers, "Jackson Men with Feet of Clay," *American Historical Review* 62 (Apr. 1957): 537-51; Charles G. Sellers, "Banking and Politics in Jackson's Tennessee, 1817-1827," *Mississippi Valley Historical Review* 41 (June 1954): 61-84; Sellers, *James K. Polk: Jacksonian*, 66-99; and Abernethy, *From Frontier to Plantation*, 227-49.

48. *Knoxville Register*, Nov. 19, 1828, and July 25, 1832; *Nashville Republican*, Jan. 1, 1832. On Jackson's popularity, see Ward, *Andrew Jackson: Symbol for an Age*.

49. *Nashville Republican*, Apr. 15, 1825; *Knoxville Register*, Feb. 4, 1825, and Mar. 12, 1828.

50. *Knoxville Register*, Apr. 9, July 2, and Oct. 1, 15, and 22, 1828; *Nashville Republican*, Apr. 16 and 23, 1825, and Apr. 7, 1827; White and Ash, *Messages of the Governors* 2:233.

51. *Knoxville Register*, Jan. 19, 1831; William B. Campbell to David Campbell, July 11, 1831, in Campbell Papers, DU.

52. During Jackson's presidency, two of his critics managed to get elected to Congress, but their success represented temporary triumphs made possible by special circumstances, rather than a groundswell of opposition to the president. Thomas D. Arnold in 1831 defeated the "Jackson man" Pryor Lea for the seat from the Knoxville district by relying, first, upon the support of John Williams, whom Jackson's supporters had defeated for the Senate in 1823, and, second, upon the charge that Lea favored reopening the African

slave trade. Arnold declined to run for reelection, probably recognizing the tenuous nature of his majority, and Lea's brother Luke replaced Arnold in the Congress of 1833. David Crockett had represented Tennessee's Western District since 1827 and had supported Jackson's election in 1828, but he broke with the Administration when he opposed a bill that would have ceded to Tennessee title to unappropriated lands in Crockett's district, a move that Crockett feared would leave squatters in his district at the mercy of speculators. Crockett's opposition led to his defeat in 1831 by William Fitzgerald; he returned to Congress in 1833, after a close election, by supporting Jackson's stand against Nullification and by attacking Fitzgerald for overcharging Congress for transportation expenses. Once back in Congress, he again opposed the Administration and suffered his final defeat against Adam Huntsman in 1835. *Knoxville Register,* July 27, Aug. 3, Sept. 14, 1831. *Nashville Republican,* Mar. 15, 1831. *Jackson Southern Statesman,* Aug. 20, 1831; June 29, July 6 and 20, Aug. 10, 1833. *Nashville National Banner,* July 26, 1834. David Crockett to William T. Yeatman, June 15, 1834, Yeatman-Polk Collection, TSLA. James K. Polk to Davidson McMillan, Jan. 16, 1829, in Weaver et al., *Correspondence of James K. Polk,* 1:229-31. Abernethy, *From Frontier to Plantation,* 259-60. Sellers, *James K. Polk: Jacksonian,* 122-28.

53. *Knoxville Register,* Dec. 29, 1830; Jan. 12, Mar. 2, 1831; July 25, Aug. 15, Dec. 12, 1832; Jan. 2, 1833. *Nashville Republican,* Dec. 22, 1830; June 27, July 23, Nov. 30, 1832. *Nashville National Banner,* Jan. 2, 1833. *Jackson Southern Statesman,* Sept. 3, 1831; July 28, 1832.

54. *Nashville Republican,* May 3, June 1, 1832. On the formation of the Jackson coalition that provided the basis for the Democratic-Republican party, see Richard B. Latner, *The Presidency of Andrew Jackson: White House Politics, 1829-1837* (Athens: Univ. of Georgia Press, 1979), 7-30; Richard H. Brown, "The Missouri Crisis, Slavery, and the Politics of Jacksonianism," *South Atlantic Quarterly* 65 (Winter 1966): 55-72; and Donald B. Cole, *The Presidency of Andrew Jackson* (Lawrence: Univ. Press of Kansas, 1993).

55. The phrase "revolt against Jackson" is that of Powell Moore, "The Revolt Against Jackson in Tennessee, 1835-1836," *Journal of Southern History* 2 (Aug. 1936): 335-59.

Chapter 2. The Presidential Candidacy of Hugh Lawson White, 1832-1836

1. James K. Polk to William B. Lewis, Aug. 13, 1833, in Weaver et al., *Correspondence of James K. Polk,* 2:100; *Nashville Republican,* Sept. 14, 1833; *Nashville National Banner,* Nov. 18, 1833.

2. The best accounts of the Nullification Crisis are William W. Freehling, *Prelude to Civil War: The Nullification Controversy in South Carolina, 1816-1836* (New York: Harper and Row, 1965), 89-218; Richard E. Ellis, *The Union at Risk: Jacksonian Democracy, States' Rights and the Nullification Crisis* (New York: Oxford Univ. Press, 1987), 41-101; and Ford, *Origins of Southern Radicalism,* 99-153.

3. Andrew Jackson to Joel R. Poinsett, Nov. 7, 1832, in *Correspondence of*

Andrew Jackson, ed. John Spencer Bassett (Washington, D.C.: Carnegie Institute, 1929), 4:486; James D. Richardson, *A Compilation of the Messages and Papers of the Presidents,* 20 vols. (New York: Bureau of National Literature, 1898), 3:1206; Richard B. Latner, "The Nullification Crisis and Republican Subversion," *Journal of Southern History* 43 (Feb. 1977): 19-38; Ellis, *Union at Risk,* 74-101.

4. Richardson, *Compilation of Messages and Papers,* 3:1217.

5. Freehling, *Prelude to Civil War,* 260-97; Ellis, *Union at Risk,* 158-77.

6. "Preamble and Resolutions by the Citizens of Elizabethton, in Response to Hearing Jackson's Proclamation of Nullification, Dec. 20, 1832," in Nelson Papers, McClung. William Carroll to Andrew Jackson, Dec. 18, 1832, in Jackson Papers, LC. Edmund Dillahunty to Robert L. Caruthers, Dec. 28, 1832, in Caruthers Papers, SHC. *Nashville Republican,* Apr. 10, Oct. 10, Aug. 6, Dec. 28 and 31, 1832. *Nashville National Banner,* July 2, 3; Dec. 10, 12, 19, 20-22, 1832; Jan. 3 and 16, Feb. 7 and 13, Mar. 14 and 18, 1833. Letters in Weaver et al., *Correspondence of James K. Polk*: John W. Childress to James K. Polk, Dec. 20, 1832, on p. 1:594; Isaac J. Thomas to Polk, Dec. 24, 1832, on p. 1:588; Archibald Yell to Polk, Dec. 27, 1832, on p. 1:591; Samuel H. Laughlin to Polk, Jan. 8, 1833, on p. 2:11-12; Aaron V. Brown to Polk, Jan. 20, 1833, on p. 2:34. See also Paul H. Bergeron, "Tennessee's Response to the Nullification Crisis," *Journal of Southern History* 39 (Feb. 1973): 23-44.

7. "Preamble and Resolutions by the Citizens of Elizabethton, in Response to Hearing Jackson's Proclamation of Nullification, Dec. 20, 1832," in Nelson Papers, McClung; *Nashville Republican,* Nov. 30, 1832; *Nashville National Banner,* May 16, 1833.

8. Joseph Howard Parks, *Felix Grundy: Champion of Democracy* (Baton Rouge: Louisiana State Univ. Press, 1940), 182-215; James Campbell to [David Campbell], Oct. 23, 1831, in Campbell Papers, DU; *Nashville Republican,* July 16, Oct. 13, 20, 27, Nov. 1, 1831; May 14, June 6, 1832.

9. On the "Eaton Affair," see Richard B. Latner, "The Eaton Affair Reconsidered," *THQ* 36 (Fall 1977): 330-51; Latner, *Presidency of Andrew Jackson,* 59-68, 81-85; and Cole, *Presidency of Andrew Jackson,* 81-88.

10. William Carroll to Andrew Jackson, Sept. 27, 1831; Robert M. Burton to Jackson, Oct. 5, 1831; Carroll to Jackson, Nov. 13, 1831; and Carroll to Jackson, Dec. 3, 1833, all in Jackson Papers, LC. W. A. Wade to William B. Campbell, Sept. 7, 1831; James Campbell to [John] Campbell, Oct. 2, 1831; and Wade to Campbell, July 1, 1832, all in Campbell Papers, DU. Daniel S. Donelson to Andrew J. Donelson, Oct. 31, 1831, in Dyas Collection, John Coffee Papers, THS. William Brady to Robert L. Caruthers, Nov. 4, 1831, in Caruthers Papers, SHC. *Nashville Republican,* Sept. 27 and 29, 1831.

11. Andrew Jackson to Ephraim H. Foster, June 22, 1832, and Jackson to [Members of the Tennessee Legislature], Sept., 1832, both in Jackson Papers, LC. Foster to Dixon Allen, July 2, 1832, Campbell Papers, DU. John H. Dew to Robert L. Caruthers, Sept. 10, 1832, Caruthers Papers, SHC. *Nashville Republican,* Oct. 8, 1832. The 1832 extra session had been called by Governor

Carroll to redraw the state's legislative and congressional districts and to pass a law providing for the election of presidential electors.

12. Felix Grundy to Andrew Jackson, May 6, 1833; Grundy to Jackson, Aug. 7, 1833; and William Carroll to Jackson, Dec. 3, 1833, all in Jackson Papers, LC. Grundy to Cave Johnson, Aug. 29, 1833, Felix Grundy Papers, TSLA. William B. Campbell to David Campbell, Oct. 23, 1833, Campbell Papers, DU. Balie Peyton to John C. McLemore, Oct. 5, 1832, Murdock Collection-Overton Papers, THS. *Nashville Republican,* July 10, Oct. 8, 1833; *House Journal* (1832, extra sess.), 89; *House Journal* (1833-34), 94.

13. William B. Campbell to David Campbell, Oct. 22, 1832, Campbell Papers, DU.

14. On the Second Bank of the United States, see Peter Temin, *The Jacksonian Economy* (New York: Norton, 1969), 44-58; and Bray Hammond, *Banks and Politics in America from the Revolution to the Civil War* (Princeton, N.J.: Princeton Univ. Press, 1957), 286-450.

15. Sellers, "Banking and Politics in Jackson's Tennessee," 75-84; Watson, *Liberty and Power,* 132-71.

16. Charles G. Sellers, *The Market Revolution: Jacksonian America, 1815-1846* (New York: Oxford Univ. Press, 1991), 321-31; Hammond, *Banks and Politics,* 405-450; Frank Otto Gatell, "Spoils of the Bank War: Political Bias in the Selection of Pet Banks," *American Historical Review* 70 (Oct. 1964): 35-58.

17. *Knoxville Register,* Aug. 15, 1832; George C. Childress to Dixon Allen, Aug. 4, 1832, Campbell Papers, DU; Willie Blount to Andrew Jackson, Sept., 1831, Jackson Papers, LC; Claude A. Campbell, *The Development of Banking in Tennessee* (Nashville: n.p., 1932), 43-50; Sellers, "Banking and Politics in Jackson's Tennessee," 64-75.

18. *Knoxville Register,* May 4, 1831; Sellers, "Banking and Politics in Jackson's Tennessee," 77-78; Claude Campbell, *Development of Banking in Tennessee,* 50-62; Larry Schweikart, "Tennessee Banks in the Antebellum Period," *THQ* 45 (Summer 1986): 119-21, 126-27.

19. Samuel G. Smith to James K. Polk, Feb. 8, 1834, in Weaver et al., *Correspondence of James K. Polk,* 2:299. *Nashville Republican,* Nov. 14 and 19, 1833. *Nashville National Banner,* July 31, Nov. 27, 1832; Apr. 5, Nov. 15, 1833. *Public Acts* (1832), 2-13; (1833), 30-42, 60-66.

20. Stephen Adams to James K. Polk, Mar. 24, 1834, on p. 2:374, and James Walker to Polk, May 29, 1834, on p. 2:421, both in Weaver et al., *Correspondence of James K. Polk. Nashville National Banner,* May 4, Oct. 3, 1833; Aug. 15, 19, 1834.

21. *Nashville National Banner,* Jan. 6, 1832. Terry H. Cahal to James K. Polk, May 4, 1832, in Weaver et al., *Correspondence of James K. Polk,* 1:470. William B. Campbell to David Campbell, Mar. 4, 1832, and James Campbell to John Campbell, July 24, 1833, both in Campbell Papers, DU.

22. *Nashville Republican,* June 13, 1832, and Dec. 24, 1833; *Nashville National Banner,* July 20, Dec. 17, 1832.

23. *Nashville National Banner,* Mar. 25, Apr. 3, 1833.

24. James Campbell to David Campbell, Nov. 7, 1833, Campbell Papers, DU; *Nashville Republican,* Oct. 3, 1833, and Nov. 18, 1834; *Nashville National Banner,* Aug. 15, 1834; Samuel H. Laughlin to James K. Polk, Oct. 20, 1834, in Weaver et al., *Correspondence of James K. Polk,* 2:534-35.

25. Robert M. Burton to James K. Polk, Aug. 27, 1834, in Weaver et al., *Correspondence of James K. Polk,* 2:461; Burton to Robert L. Caruthers, Aug. 17, 1834, Caruthers Papers, SHC; *Nashville Republican,* May 14, 1832, and Sept. 4, 1834; *Nashville National Banner,* June 13, 1832, and Aug. 15, 1834; *Columbia (Tenn.) Observer,* Sept. 19, 1834; Parks, *Felix Grundy,* 166-81, 216-42; Sellers, *James K. Polk: Jacksonian,* 76-98, 142-240.

26. McBride and Robison, *Biographical Directory,* 1:257-58; Archibald Yell to James K. Polk, Mar. 2, 1828, in Weaver et al., *Correspondence of James K. Polk,* 1:159; David Campbell to James Campbell, Sept. 15, 1833, Campbell Papers, DU; *Nashville Republican,* Mar. 10, 1832, and Sept. 4, 1834; Joseph Howard Parks, *John Bell of Tennessee* (Baton Rouge: Louisiana State Univ. Press, 1950), 37-83.

27. Andrew Jackson to Andrew J. Hutchings, June 26, 1835, in Dyas Collection, Coffee Papers, THS; James K. Polk to James Walker, Jan. 18, 1835, in Weaver et al., *Correspondence of James K. Polk,* 3:40; *Nashville National Banner,* Sept. 7, 1833; *Nashville Republican,* May 9, 1835; Parks, *John Bell of Tennessee,* 97-99.

28. *Nashville Republican,* Nov. 22, 1831; Apr. 14, 1832; Sept. 4, 1834. Parks, *John Bell of Tennessee,* 58-83.

29. *Nashville National Banner,* June 14, Sept. 17, 1834; *Nashville Republican,* Sept. 4, 1834; Parks, *John Bell of Tennessee,* 70-75; Sellers, *James K. Polk: Jacksonian,* 234-42, 256-57.

30. Alfred Balch to Andrew Jackson, Oct. 30, 1834; Jackson to Balch, Nov. 5, 1835; and "Note," n.d., all in Jackson Papers, LC. Samuel H. Laughlin to James K. Polk, May 30, 1835, in Weaver et al., *Correspondence of James K. Polk,* 3:207. Jackson to Andrew J. Hutchings, June 26, 1835, in Dyas Collection, Coffee Papers, THS. *Nashville Union,* Sept. 18, 1835.

31. *Nashville Republican,* Feb. 24, 1835. James K. Polk to James Walker, Dec. 24, 1834, on pp. 2:598-601, and Polk to Walker, Dec. 25, 1834, on pp. 2:603-5, both in Weaver et al., *Correspondence of James K. Polk.* Sellers, *James K. Polk: Jacksonian,* 259-62. Parks, *John Bell of Tennessee,* 84-87. Nancy N. Scott, ed., *A Memoir of Hugh Lawson White* (Philadelphia: J. B. Lippincott, 1856), 253-64. One congressman, Cave Johnson, attended the meeting but refused to sign the letter; see *Nashville Union,* June 29, 1835.

32. *Nashville National Banner,* July 30, 1832; *Knoxville Register,* July 18, Aug. 1, 1832; Scott, *Memoir of Hugh Lawson White,* 81-112.

33. Alfred Balch to Andrew Jackson, Nov. 29, 1833, Jackson Papers, LC; A. O. P. Nicholson to James K. Polk, Dec. 5, 1833, in Weaver et al., *Correspondence of James K. Polk,* 2:157-58; Jackson to Felix Grundy, Sept. 24, 1835, Felix Grundy Papers, SHC; *Nashville Republican,* May 10, 1834, and Feb. 24, 1835; *Nashville National Banner,* Oct. 1, 1834.

34. Thomas P. Abernethy, "The Origin of the Whig Party in Tennessee," *Mis-

sissippi Valley Historical Review 12 (Mar. 1926): 507-8; Moore, "Revolt Against Jackson in Tennessee," 335-37; Scott, *Memoir of Hugh Lawson White*, 245-70. White's opinion on the unconstitutionality of a United States Bank, it should be noted, did permit the possibility of a bank, chartered in the District of Columbia, that could regulate the currency through arrangements with state banks; see Hugh L. White to Andrew Jackson, Apr. 11, 1833, Jackson Papers, LC.

35. *Nashville Republican*, Jan. 22, Feb. 24, 1835, and Oct. 1, 1836; *Nashville National Banner*, Mar. 25, 1835; Thornton, *Politics and Power in a Slave Society*, 31-33.

36. Samuel G. Smith to Polk, Feb. 13, 1835, on pp. 3:99-100, and James Walker to James K. Polk, Feb. 28, 1835, on p. 3:119, in Weaver et al., *Correspondence of James K. Polk; Nashville National Banner*, Oct. 1, 1834.

37. Samuel G. Smith to James K. Polk, Feb. 3, 1835, in Weaver et al., *Correspondence of James K. Polk*, 3:82; *Nashville Republican*, Jan. 22, 1835.

38. *Nashville Republican*, Feb. 10, 1835.

39. *Nashville Republican*, Jan. 22, May 30, 1835; *Nashville National Banner*, Jan. 5, Apr. 1, 1835. James Walker to James K. Polk, Jan. 7, 1835, on p. 3:25, and William G. Childress to Polk, Feb. 14, 1835, on pp. 3:100-101, in Weaver et al., *Correspondence of James K. Polk*.

40. *Nashville Republican*, Oct. 3, 1835.

41. *Nashville Republican*, May 21, 1835, and July 16, 1836; *Nashville National Banner*, July 15, 1836. John Bell, *Speech of the Hon. John Bell, Delivered at Vauxhall Garden, Nashville, on the 23rd of May, 1835* (Nashville: W. Hasell Hunt, 1835), 32-33.

42. *Nashville Republican*, Feb. 14 and May 3, 1832; *Knoxville Register*, Feb. 8, 1832. John H. Eaton to Andrew Jackson, Mar. 13, 1832, and William Carroll to Jackson, Feb. 20, 1834, both in Jackson Papers, LC. James Campbell to David Campbell, Feb. 15, 1832, and W. A. Wade to William B. Campbell, Mar. 1, 1832, both in Campbell Papers, DU.

43. *Nashville Republican*, Jan. 22, Mar. 3, Apr. 4, 1835; *Nashville National Banner*, Feb. 23, Mar. 4, 1835.

44. *Nashville Republican*, June 2, 1835, and Aug. 9, 1836.

45. *House Journal* (1835), 121; *Nashville Republican*, Nov. 18, 1834, and May 17, 1836; *Nashville Union*, June 1, 1835. On the idea of party in the early 19th century, see Major L. Wilson, "Republicanism and the Idea of Party in the Jacksonian Period," *Journal of the Early Republic* 8 (Winter 1988): 419-42; Richard Hofstadter, *The Idea of a Party System: The Rise of Legitimate Opposition in the United States, 1780-1840* (Berkeley: Univ. of California Press, 1969); and Donald B. Cole, *Martin Van Buren and the American Political System* (Princeton, N.J.: Princeton Univ. Press, 1984), 101-41, 256-81. See also Ralph Ketcham, *Presidents Above Party: The First American Presidency, 1789-1829* (Chapel Hill: Univ. of North Carolina Press, 1984).

46. *House Journal* (1835), 121; *Nashville Republican*, Aug. 9, 1836; Bell, *Speech of Bell at Vauxhall Garden*, 4-19.

47. *Nashville Republican*, June 2, 1835.
48. *Nashville National Banner*, Apr. 22, May 8, 1835; *Nashville Republican*, June 2, Aug. 25, Oct. 24, 1835; *Memphis Enquirer*, Oct. 7, 1836.
49. *Nashville Republican*, Dec. 24, 1835; Sellers, *James K. Polk: Jacksonian*, 292-97.
50. *Nashville National Banner*, Feb. 13, Apr. 22, 1835; *Nashville Republican*, Mar. 14, June 23, July 2, Nov. 5, 1835; *Memphis Enquirer*, Apr. 5, 1836.
51. Bell, *Speech of Bell at Vauxhall Garden*, 36-37; *Nashville Republican*, Mar. 10, 1835; *Nashville National Banner*, Apr. 29, 1835; *Nashville Republican*, Mar. 14, May 5, 1835.
52. *Nashville National Banner*, May 8 and 25, 1835; Samuel H. Laughlin to James K. Polk, Oct. 20, 1834, on pp. 2:534-37, and Polk to Francis Preston Blair, Oct. 3, 1835, on p. 3:317, in Weaver et al., *Correspondence of James K. Polk*.
53. James Walker to James K. Polk, Feb. 24, 1835, in Weaver et al., *Correspondence of James K. Polk*, 3:109-10. A Tennessean who happened to be in Baltimore at the time of the convention, Edmund Rucker, was persuaded to attend and cast Tennessee's electoral votes for Van Buren and Johnson. Rucker's participation lent credence to the White supporters' charge that the "Ruckerized" convention was not a representative body but a "packed jury"; see *Nashville Republican*, June 4, 6, 9, 1835; Samuel Powel to Robert L. Caruthers, July 25, 1835, Caruthers Papers, SHC.
54. John Catron to Andrew Jackson, Mar. 21, 1835, and Felix Grundy to Jackson, Mar. 28, 1835, both in Jackson Papers, LC. Edmund Dillahunty to Robert L. Caruthers, Oct. 24, 1835, Caruthers Papers, SHC. *Nashville Union*, June 3, 1835.
55. James K. Polk to James Walker, Feb. 7, 1835, on p. 3:85; Andrew Jackson to Polk, May 12, 1835, on p. 3:191; and Jackson to Polk, Aug. 3, 1835, on pp. 3:251-54, all in Weaver et al., *Correspondence of James K. Polk*. Jackson to John Donelson Coffee, June 1, 1835, Dyas Collection, John Coffee Papers, THS.
56. Andrew Jackson to James K. Polk, May 12, 1835, in Weaver et al., *Correspondence of James K. Polk*, 3:191.
57. James Campbell to David Campbell, Apr. 5, 1835, Campbell Papers, DU; Sellers, *James K. Polk: Jacksonian*, 270-79; *Nashville Republican*, Mar. 17, Sept. 1, 1835; *Nashville Union*, Mar. 30, 1835; Paul H. Bergeron, "James K. Polk and the Jacksonian Press in Tennessee," *THQ* 41 (Fall 1982): 257-77.
58. Jackson to Polk, May 3, 1835, in Weaver et al., *Correspondence of James K. Polk*, 3:182; *Nashville Union*, Sept. 4, 1835; James K. Polk, *Speech of the Hon. James K. Polk, Delivered at a Public Dinner at Mooresville, Maury County, Tennessee, on the 22d Day of October, 1835* (Nashville: n.p., 1835), 2-4.
59. *Nashville Union*, Apr. 20, 1835; Andrew J. Donelson to Robert L. Caruthers, Jan. 25, 1835, and Samuel Powel to Caruthers, July 25, 1835, both in Caruthers Papers, SHC.
60. *Nashville Union*, Apr. 15 and 20, May 22, Aug. 28, 1835; Andrew J.

Donelson to Stockley Donelson, June 1, 1835, Andrew Jackson Donelson Letters, UT; Greenville Cook to James K. Polk, Jan. 1, 1836, in Weaver et al., *Correspondence of James K. Polk*, 3:420; Andrew Jackson to Andrew J. Hutchings, June 26, 1835, Dyas Collection, John Coffee Papers.

61. *Nashville Republican*, Feb. 10, Mar. 17, July 18 and 23, Sept. 1, 1835; *Nashville National Banner*, Mar. 20, 1835; *Nashville Union*, Mar. 30, Apr. 21, 1835.

62. *Nashville Republican*, Oct. 24, 1835.

63. *Knoxville Register*, Sept. 21, 1836; *Nashville Republican*, Jan. 16, Mar. 15, 1836.

64. *Knoxville Register*, Apr. 14, Aug. 25, 1836. David Campbell to William B. Campbell, Apr. 8, 1835, and William B. Campbell to David Campbell, Oct. 6, 1835, both in Campbell Papers, DU.

65. *Nashville Republican*, Oct. 24, 1834; Jan. 14, June 4, Sept. 13, 1836.

66. Alfred Balch to Andrew Jackson, Aug. 12, 1835, Jackson Papers, LC.

67. Ibid.; Andrew Jackson to James K. Polk, Aug. 3, 1835, in Weaver et al., *Correspondence of James K. Polk*, 3:251-54; Polk, *Speech of Polk at Mooresville*; *Nashville Union*, Nov. 3, 7, 9, 17, Dec. 26, 1835.

68. Samuel H. Laughlin to Andrew J. Donelson, Oct. 21, 1835, Andrew Jackson Donelson Papers, THS; Sellers, *James K. Polk: Jacksonian*, 263-66.

69. Joel H. Silbey, "Election of 1836," in *History of American Presidential Elections, 1789-1968*, ed. Arthur M. Schlesinger, Jr., 4 vols. (New York: McGraw-Hill, 1971), 1:577-640; John Bell to Hugh L. White, May 2, 1835, Murdock Collection-Overton Papers, THS; *Nashville Union*, May 13, Dec. 5, 1835; Richard P. McCormick, "Was There a 'Whig Strategy' in 1836?" *Journal of the Early Republic* 4 (Spring 1984): 47-70; Thomas Brown, "From Old Hickory to Sly Fox: The Routinization of Charisma in the Early Democratic Party," *Journal of the Early Republic* 11 (Fall 1991): 339-69.

70. *House Journal* (1835), 14, 34-35, 67-71; *Senate Journal* (1835), 21-23, 43-47.

71. *Nashville Union*, Nov. 24, 1835; Samuel H. Laughlin to James K. Polk, Oct. 21, 1835, in Weaver et al., *Correspondence of James K. Polk*, 3:344-45; Josephus C. Guild, *Old Times in Tennessee* (Nashville: Tavel, Eastman & Howell, 1878), 143-56.

72. *Nashville Republican*, Oct. 6, 1835; see also Scott, *Memoir of Hugh Lawson White*, 180-96.

73. Andrew Jackson to James K. Polk, Aug. 3, 1835, on p. 3:252; Jackson to Polk, Oct. 20, 1835, on pp. 3:342-43; and Polk to Samuel H. Laughlin, Jan. 8, 1836, on p. 3:431, all in Weaver et al., *Correspondence of James K. Polk*.

74. *House Journal* (1835), 469-70, 619, 682-85; *Nashville Union*, Jan. 26, Feb. 18, 1836; Aaron V. Brown to James K. Polk, Aug. 27, 1835, in Weaver et al., *Correspondence of James K. Polk*, 3:277; A. O. P. Nicholson to Andrew Jackson, Jan. 26, 1836, Jackson Papers, LC.

75. Balie Peyton to Robert L. Caruthers, Apr. 16, 1836, Caruthers Papers, SHC; *Memphis Enquirer*, May 18, 1836; *Nashville Republican*, Apr. 14, June 4, Oct. 1, 1836.

76. *Nashville National Banner,* Jan. 8, Mar. 28, Aug. 17, 1836.
77. *Nashville Union,* Feb. 6, 25, Mar. 3, 1836; A. O. P. Nicholson to James K. Polk, Jan. 31, 1836, on pp. 3:479-80, and Nicholson to Polk, Feb. 7, 1836, on p. 3:486, in Weaver et al., *Correspondence of James K. Polk; Nashville Republican,* Sept. 27, 1836.
78. James Walker to James K. Polk, June 6, 1836, in Weaver et al., *Correspondence of James K. Polk,* 3:656; Bergeron, "James K. Polk and the Jacksonian Press in Tennessee," 263-64.
79. *Nashville Republican,* July 28, Sept. 15, 1836; Jackson to Amos Kendall, Aug. 12, 1836, Jackson Papers, LC.
80. John S. Brien to William B. Campbell, Sept. 14, 1836, and William Martin to William B. Campbell, Sept. 10, 1836, both in Campbell Papers, DU. John S. Young to James K. Polk, Aug. 11, 1836, in Weaver et al., *Correspondence of James K. Polk,* 3:700-701; Thomas A. R. Nelson to Hugh L. White, Sept. 21, 1836, Nelson Papers, McClung; *Nashville Republican,* Aug. 20, 1836.
81. *Nashville Republican,* Sept. 10, 15, 1836; *Nashville National Banner,* Aug. 3, 1836.
82. *Knoxville Register,* Sept. 21, 1836; *Nashville Republican,* Sept. 3, 15, 1836; *Memphis Enquirer,* Aug. 25, Sept. 22, 1836; James D. Smith to William B. Campbell, Sept. 7, 1836, Campbell Papers, DU.
83. William B. Campbell to David Campbell, Oct. 6, 1835, Campbell Papers, DU.
84. *Nashville National Banner,* Aug. 29, 1836.

Chapter 3. The Creation of Tennessee's Party System, 1837-1839

1. James Campbell to David Campbell, Feb. 8, 1837, Campbell Papers, DU; *Nashville National Banner,* Nov. 30, 1836; *Memphis Enquirer,* Dec. 10, 1836.
2. Samuel Powel to Samuel Bunch, Jan. 9, 1837, Samuel Powel III Papers, DU. George Gammon to Polk, Dec. 28, 1836, on p. 3:806; Hopkins L. Turney to Polk, Jan. 4, 1837, on p. 4:10; A. O. P. Nicholson to Polk, Jan. 22, 1837, on pp. 4:42-43, all in Weaver et al., *Correspondence of James K. Polk.*
3. *Memphis Enquirer,* Feb. 25, 1837; Balie Peyton to William B. Campbell, Dec. 30, 1836, Campbell Papers, DU; Felix Grundy to William Trousdale, Apr. 14, 1837, Trousdale Papers, TSLA; John H. Dew to James K. Polk, Dec. 25, 1836, on p. 3:802, and John F. Gillespy to Polk, May 5, 1837, on p. 4:113, both in Weaver et al., *Correspondence of James K. Polk.* The U.S. senators' terms expired in March of odd-numbered years, when the legislature was not in session; the biennial meeting schedule of the General Assembly thus forced legislators to elect a new senator either two years prior to a term's expiration or more than six months after a vacancy had occurred. Traditionally, Tennessee's legislature elected senators in the session after the expiration of an incumbent's term. See Brian G. Walton, "A Matter of Timing: Elections to the United States Senate in Tennessee Before the Civil War," *THQ* 31 (Summer 1972): 129-48.

4. George Gammon to James K. Polk, Dec. 28, 1836, on p. 3:806; John W. Childress to Polk, Feb. 17, 1837, on p. 4:65; and William Bobbitt to Polk, Nov. 30, 1836, on p. 3:789, all in Weaver et al., *Correspondence of James K. Polk*. [Andrew J. Donelson] to [Martin Van Buren], Apr. 3, 1837, Andrew Jackson Donelson Papers, LC.

5. *Nashville Republican*, May 6, 1837; *Memphis Enquirer*, Feb. 25, 1837; Balie Peyton to William B. Campbell, Dec. 30, 1836, Campbell Papers, DU. In the first session of Congress to meet after the presidential election, John Bell introduced a bill that apparently was intended to provide a hobby both for the congressman and for the opposition cause in Tennessee. This "bill to secure the freedom of elections" proposed to punish by fine and removal from office any federal official who, "by the contribution of money or any other valuable thing, or by the use of the franking privilege, or by the abuse of any other official prerogative or function," "intermeddled" in an election. Congress never passed this bill, and it soon became lost in the debate over the federal government's fiscal policy, though Tennessee and Kentucky Whigs occasionally returned to the bill and promoted it as an original Whig measure. See *Congressional Globe*, 24th Cong., 2d sess., 124; *Nashville Union*, Feb. 23, 1837; John Bell, *Speech of Mr. Bell, of Tennessee, on the Bill to Secure the Freedom of Elections: Delivered in the House of Representatives, January, 1837* (Washington, D.C.: William W. Moore, 1837); *Nashville Whig*, Jan. 9, 1839; *Nashville Republican Banner*, Apr. 25, 1839.

6. Balie Peyton to William B. Campbell, Dec. 30, 1836, Campbell Papers, DU.

7. *Memphis Enquirer*, Nov. 1, 1836; *Nashville Union*, Apr. 29, 1837; *Nashville Republican*, Apr. 27, 1837.

8. *Nashville Republican*, Apr. 25, May 23, 1837; *Nashville National Banner*, May 17, 22, 24, 26, 1837; *Memphis Enquirer*, May 27, 1837; Andrew Jackson to Francis Preston Blair, Apr. 18 and 24, 1837, Jackson Papers, LC. Most historians now attribute the panic to developments in the international economy rather than to the effects of Jackson's fiscal policies; see Temin, *Jacksonian Economy*, 113-47; Larry Schweikart, *Banking in the American South from the Age of Jackson to Reconstruction* (Baton Rouge: Louisiana State Univ. Press, 1987), 48-82.

9. Jacob S. Yerger to William B. Campbell, May 5, 1837, Campbell Papers, DU; Robert Armstrong to James K. Polk, July 16, 1837, in Weaver et al., *Correspondence of James K. Polk*, 4:182. See also Michael F. Holt, *Political Parties and American Political Development from the Age of Jackson to the Age of Lincoln* (Baton Rouge: Louisiana State Univ. Press, 1992), 151-91.

10. John Catron to James K. Polk, Sept. 27, 1837, in Weaver et al., *Correspondence of James K. Polk*, 4:253; *Nashville Union*, Apr. 26, 1838. The legislative investigating committee cleared both banks of the charge of favoritism in their lending policies; see Claude A. Campbell, *Development of Banking in Tennessee*, 77-78, 80-93.

11. *Nashville Union*, May 9, 1837.

12. *Nashville Republican*, June 1, 1837; *Nashville Union*, May 25, Nov.

25, 1837. On the state's prohibition of the issuance of small notes, see *Public Acts* (1832) 9; (1833) 38, 63.

13. *Memphis Enquirer,* June 10, 1837; James Campbell to David Campbell, June 1, 1837, Campbell Papers, DU; W. B. Robinson to Robert H. McEwen, May 21, 1838, Robert Houston McEwen Papers, TSLA; *Nashville Union,* May 25, 27, Nov. 14, 1837; *Nashville Republican,* June 27, 1837.

14. *Nashville Republican Banner,* Sept. 15, 1837; *Nashville National Banner,* Aug. 11, 1837; *Nashville Republican,* Apr. 29, 1837; Williamson Smith to James K. Polk, Oct. 21, 1836, in Weaver et al., *Correspondence of James K. Polk,* 3:768. On Jackson's fiscal policies, see Temin, *Jacksonian Economy,* 59-112; Hammond, *Banks and Politics,* 454-60; John M. McFaul, *The Politics of Jacksonian Finance* (Ithaca, N.Y.: Cornell Univ. Press, 1972), 58-177; Latner, *Presidency of Andrew Jackson,* 185-92.

15. *Memphis Enquirer,* Apr. 15 and May 6, 1837; *Nashville Republican,* Oct. 13, 1836, and Apr. 6, 1837; *Knoxville Register,* Sept. 21, 1836; Richard H. Timberlake, "The Specie Circular and Distribution of the Surplus," *Journal of Political Economy* 68 (Apr. 1960): 109-17.

16. *Nashville Republican,* Dec. 20, 1836, and Apr. 22, 1837; *Memphis Enquirer,* July 22, 1837.

17. *Memphis Enquirer,* June 8, 1836, and Apr. 22, 1837; *Nashville National Banner,* Sept. 21, 1836, and June 12, 1837; *Nashville Republican,* Apr. 22, June 3, 1837.

18. *Memphis Enquirer,* July 22, Aug. 12, Sept. 2, 1837; *Nashville Republican,* June 22, July 25, Aug. 15, 1837.

19. *Nashville Republican,* June 13, July 22, 1837. Josephus C. Guild to James K. Polk, July 11, 1837, on p. 4:174, and Polk to Andrew Jackson, May 19, 1837, on p. 4:121, both in Weaver et al., *Correspondence of James K. Polk. Memphis Enquirer,* Apr. 22, July 1, 1837. David Campbell of Lebanon to William B. Campbell, June 3, 1837, and Balie Peyton to William B. Campbell, July 19, 1837, both in Campbell Papers, DU.

20. *Nashville National Banner,* May 31, 1837; John S. Brien to William B. Campbell, Jan. 8, 1838, Campbell Papers, DU.

21. *Nashville Union,* Apr. 13, 29, 1837; James K. Polk to Martin Van Buren, May 29, 1837, on pp. 4:153-54, and Polk to William Warner, June 19, 1837, on pp. 4:131-32, both in Weaver et al., *Correspondence of James K. Polk;* Andrew Jackson to Francis Preston Blair, Jan. 16, 1838, Jackson Papers, LC; Felix Grundy to Randall McGavock, May 29, 1838, McGavock Family Papers, SHC.

22. Andrew Jackson to Moses Dawson, May 26, 1837, Jackson Papers, LC; William R. Rucker to James K. Polk, June 30, 1837, in Weaver et al., *Correspondence of James K. Polk,* 4:165.

23. Andrew Jackson to Francis Preston Blair, Apr. 18, 1837, Jackson Papers, LC. Andrew J. Donelson to James K. Polk, Jan. 4, 1838, on p. 4:314, and James Walker to Polk, Feb. 7, 1838, on p. 4:362, both in Weaver et al., *Correspondence of James K. Polk. Nashville Union,* Apr. 29, 1837.

24. James Walker to James K. Polk, Aug. 19, 1837, on p. 4:214; and Levin H. Coe to Polk, June 11, 1837, on p. 4:141, both in Weaver et al., *Correspon-*

Notes to pages 62-65

dence of James K. Polk.
25. James Walker to James K. Polk, Aug. 19, 1837, on p. 4:214, and Levin H. Coe to Polk, Aug. 8, 1837, on pp. 4:203-4, both in Weaver et al., *Correspondence of James K. Polk. Memphis Enquirer,* July 1, 1837; *Nashville Union,* June 28, July 8, 1837.
26. William R. Rucker to James K. Polk, June 30, 1837, on p. 4:165, and John H. Bills to Polk, July 23, 1837, on p. 4:190, both in Weaver et al., *Correspondence of James K. Polk.*
27. *Nashville Republican,* Mar. 16 and 21, 1837; *Nashville Union,* May 15, June 13, July 11, 1837; *Nashville National Banner,* May 22 and 31, 1837. Catron to James K. Polk, Apr. 22, 1837, on pp. 4:96-97; Polk to Andrew Jackson, May 19, 1837, on p. 4:121; and Daniel Graham to Polk, July 19, 1837, on p. 4:186, all in Weaver et al., *Correspondence of James K. Polk.* Jackson to Amos Kendall, May 22, 1837, Jackson Papers, LC. David Campbell to William B. Campbell, Apr. 3, 1837, Campbell Papers, DU. John Catron to Andrew Jackson, June 21, 1837, Stanley Horn Collection, Andrew Jackson Papers, TSLA. *Memphis Enquirer,* June 10, 1837.
28. Balie Peyton to William B. Campbell, Dec. 30, 1836, Campbell Papers, DU; James Walker to James K. Polk, Feb. 17, 1837, in Weaver et al., *Correspondence of James K. Polk,* 4:68; *Nashville Union,* June 13, 1837; *Nashville Republican,* June 1, 1837; *Memphis Enquirer,* June 3, 10, 1837.
29. George R. Powel to James K. Polk, July 18, 1837, in Weaver et al., *Correspondence of James K. Polk,* 4:184; *Nashville Republican,* Apr. 1 and 28, June 2 and 7, Aug. 16, Nov. 22 and 26, 1836; *Nashville Union,* Aug. 23, 1836; Feb. 14, July 20, 1837; *Memphis Enquirer,* Jan. 28, 1837; Folmsbee, *Sectionalism and Internal Improvements,* 148-53.
30. Joseph H. Talbot to James K. Polk, Apr. 21, 1837, on p. 4:93; John F. Gillespy to Polk, May 5, 1837, on p. 4:113; Gillespy to Polk, July 7, 1837, on p. 4:170; John Catron to Polk, July 7, 1837, on p. 4:169; and Daniel Graham to Polk, July 19, 1837, on p. 4:186, all in Weaver et al., *Correspondence of James K. Polk.* Balie Peyton to William B. Campbell, Dec. 30, 1836; and Jacob S. Yerger to Campbell, May 31, 1837, both in Campbell Papers, DU. *Nashville Union,* July 15, 1837; *Nashville Whig,* July 26, 1839.
31. *Nashville National Banner,* May 22, June 30, July 12 and 14, 1837; *Nashville Republican,* July 6, 1837; *Nashville Union,* June 3, July 6, 1837; William B. Campbell to David Campbell, June 4, 1837, and David Campbell to William B. Campbell, June 19, 1837, both in Campbell Papers, DU.
32. John W. Childress to James K. Polk, July 11, 1837, on p. 4:173; John H. Bills to Polk, July 23, 1837, on p. 4:190; and Aaron V. Brown to Polk, July 18, 1837, on p. 4:183, all in Weaver et al., *Correspondence of James K. Polk;* William Park to James Park, June 28, 1837, Park Family Papers, UT.
33. *Nashville Union,* May 9, Aug. 12, 1837.
34. Joseph H. Talbot to James K. Polk, Apr. 21, 1837, on p. 4:93, and Josephus C. Guild to Polk, Nov. 23, 1837, on p. 4:271, both in Weaver et al., *Correspondence of James K. Polk;* Andrew Jackson to Felix Grundy, Dec. 16, 1837, Jackson Papers, LC.
35. *House Journal* (1837), 85, 402-6, 549-56; *Senate Journal* (1837), 63,

432; *Public Acts* (1837), 454-56; *Nashville Union,* Oct. 7 and 24, 1837; Jan. 25, 1838; *Nashville Republican Banner,* Sept. 27, Oct. 13, Nov. 8, 1837; Daniel S. Donelson to Andrew J. Donelson, Oct. 15, 1837, Bettie M. Donelson Papers, THS; John O. Bradford to James K. Polk, Sept. 2, 1837, on p. 4:220, and Adam Huntsman to Polk, Dec. 16, 1838, on p. 4:652, both in Weaver et al., *Correspondence of James K. Polk.*

36. *House Journal* (1837), 217, 558; Andrew Jackson to Francis Preston Blair, Oct. 31, 1837, Jackson Papers, LC; *Nashville Union,* Oct. 12 and 14, Nov. 30, 1837; *Nashville Republican Banner,* Oct. 13, Nov. 29, Dec. 23, 1837.

37. *House Journal* (1837), 324, 585; *Senate Journal* (1837), 332-33, 358; *Public Acts* (1837), 153-69, 219-20; James Walker to James K. Polk, Dec. 7, 1837, in Weaver et al., *Correspondence of James K. Polk,* 4:263; Felix Grundy to Andrew Jackson, Jan. 18, 1838, Grundy Papers, SHC; *Nashville National Banner,* July 26, 1837; *Nashville Union,* Dec. 23, 1837; *Nashville Republican Banner,* Oct. 12, Nov. 9, 11, 28, Dec. 9, 1837; *Nashville Whig,* Feb. 9, 1838; Folmsbee, *Sectionalism and Internal Improvements,* 162-76; White and Ash, *Messages of the Governors* 3:181-85, 3:288.

38. Andrew Jackson to Francis Preston Blair, July 23, 1837, Jackson Papers, LC; *Nashville Union,* Dec. 5, 1837. On the subtreasury, see Temin, *Jacksonian Economy,* 165-69; and McFaul, *Politics of Jacksonian Finance,* 178-209.

39. John Catron to Polk, Sept. 10, 1837, on pp. 4:229-33; James Walker to Polk, Sept. 7, 1837, on pp. 4:228-29; and Adam Huntsman to Polk, July 30, [1838], on p. 4:515, all in Weaver et al., *Correspondence of James K. Polk;* Catron to Andrew Jackson, Nov. 22, 1837, Jackson Papers, LC.

40. James K. Polk to A. O. P. Nicholson, May 20, 1838, on p. 4:454, and James Walker to Polk, Aug. 27, 1837, on p. 4:217, both in Weaver et al., *Correspondence of James K. Polk.* Andrew Jackson to Francis Preston Blair, Jan. 16, 1838, and Jackson to Amos Kendall, Mar. 27, 1838, both in Jackson Papers, LC. *Nashville Union,* Dec. 5, 1837.

41. Aaron V. Brown to Felix Grundy, Feb. 8, 1838, Grundy Papers, SHC; James Campbell to David Campbell, Jan. 19, 1838, Campbell Papers, DU.

42. *Nashville Republican Banner,* Nov. 25, 1837; *Nashville Union,* Nov. 23, 1837.

43. *Nashville Republican Banner,* Dec. 16, 1837; Mar. 9, Apr. 27, June 16 and 21, Sept. 3 and 7, 1838. *Nashville Whig,* Jan. 9, June 13 and 18, July 9, Aug. 24, Sept. 5, 1838. *Memphis Enquirer,* Dec. 16, 1837. *Nashville Union,* Sept. 5, 1838. A. O. P. Nicholson to James K. Polk, May 25, 1838, in Weaver et al., *Correspondence of James K. Polk,* 4:461. William R. Brown to Jesse Abernathy, Dec. 11, 1837, UT.

44. Scott, *Memoir of Hugh Lawson White,* 356-68; *Nashville Whig,* Aug. 13, 1838; *Nashville Union,* Aug. 27, 1838.

45. *Nashville Whig,* Mar. 21 and May 7, 1838; *Nashville Republican Banner,* Oct. 8 and 20, 1838; William B. Carter to Thomas A. R. Nelson, Mar. 13, 1838, Nelson Papers, McClung.

46. *Nashville Republican Banner,* Mar. 3 and 9, Aug. 17 and 30, Nov. 8, 1838; William B. Campbell to David Campbell, Sept. 7, 1837, and John S. Brien to Campbell, Jan. 8, 1838, both in Campbell Papers, DU; William B. Campbell to Robert L. Caruthers, Sept. 19, 1837, Caruthers Papers, SHC; Campbell to Adam Ferguson, Jan. 30, 1838, Ferguson Family Papers, TSLA.

47. *Nashville Whig,* Feb. 28, 1838; *Nashville Republican Banner,* Mar. 9, Oct. 20, Dec. 4, 1838.

48. *Nashville Republican Banner,* Oct. 13, 1838.

49. *Nashville Whig,* Feb. 28, May 7, 1838; *Nashville Republican Banner,* May 4, 1838; John Bell to Robert L. Caruthers, Mar. 17, 1838, Caruthers Papers, SHC.

50. *Nashville Republican Banner,* Aug. 29, 1838; *Nashville Whig,* Mar. 21, 1838.

51. *Nashville Republican Banner,* July 13, Aug. 15, Sept. 20, Oct. 20, 1838; *Nashville Whig,* Jan. 18, Apr. 2, 1838.

52. *Nashville Whig,* May 7, Oct. 3, 1838; *Nashville Republican Banner,* Oct. 12, 1838.

53. J. B. McCormick to William B. Campbell, May 22, 1838, and Thomas S. Bransford to Campbell, May 21, 1838, both in Campbell Papers, DU; Zachariah G. Goodall to William Trousdale, Aug. 26, 1838, Trousdale Papers, TSLA.

54. Daniel Kenney to James K. Polk, Apr. 13, 1838, on p. 4:423, and Elihu Crisp to Polk, Dec. 20, 1837, on p. 4:301, in Weaver et al., *Correspondence of James K. Polk*; A. O. P. Nicholson to Felix Grundy, Oct. 8, 1838, Grundy Papers, SHC; *Nashville Union,* Feb. 27, July 23, Sept. 26, 1838; *Nashville Whig,* Oct. 3, 1838.

55. James K. Polk to Andrew Jackson, Jan. 7, 1838, on p. 4:319; Polk to Andrew J. Donelson, May 29, 1838, on p. 4:465; John C. McLemore to Polk, June 25, 1837, on p. 4:159; and Polk to Donelson, Aug. 6, 1837, on p. 4:198, all in Weaver et al., *Correspondence of James K. Polk*. Andrew Jackson to Francis Preston Blair, Aug. 16, 1837, Jackson Papers, LC.

56. James Walker to James K. Polk, Jan. 25, 1838, on p. 4:340; Joseph H. Talbot to Polk, Feb. 16, 1838, on p. 4:447; Alfred Balch to Polk, June 15, 1838, on p. 4:477; and William E. Butler to Polk, June 12, 1838, on p. 4:476, all in Weaver et al., *Correspondence of James K. Polk*. John H. Dew to Robert L. Caruthers, Apr. 23, 1838, Caruthers Papers, SHC. *Nashville Whig,* Apr. 4, 1838.

57. *Nashville Union,* Sept. 3, 1838; *Nashville Republican Banner,* Sept. 5, 1838.

58. John Catron to Andrew Jackson, Jan. 4, 1838, and Cave Johnson to Jackson, Aug. 28, 1838, both in Jackson Papers, LC; Sellers, *James K. Polk: Jacksonian,* 350-52.

59. *Nashville Union,* Sept. 3, 1838; Apr. 10, 1839; Joseph H. Talbot to James K. Polk, Sept. 20, 1838, in Weaver et al., *Correspondence of James K. Polk,* 4:558; Sellers, *James K. Polk: Jacksonian,* 356-66.

60. *Nashville Union,* Apr. 10, 1839.

61. *Nashville Union,* Apr. 10, 12, 1839.

62. *Nashville Union,* Apr. 12, 1839.
63. A. O. P. Nicholson to Felix Grundy, Oct. 8, 1838, Grundy Papers, SHC. James K. Polk to Andrew Jackson, Sept. 23, 1838, on p. 4:561; Alfred Balch to Polk, Jan. 3, 1839, on pp. 5:6-7; and William R. Rucker to Polk, Sept. 16, 1838, on pp. 4:550-51, all in Weaver et al., *Correspondence of James K. Polk.* Jackson to Francis Preston Blair, Jan. 29, 1838, Jackson Papers, LC. William B. Campbell to David Campbell, Apr. 28, 1839, Campbell Papers, DU. Adam Ferguson to Felix Grundy, Apr. 14, 1839, Ferguson Papers, TSLA. *Nashville Union,* Jan. 27, Sept. 26, 1838; Feb. 13, Mar. 29, June 12, 1839.
64. *Nashville Whig,* Sept. 7, Oct. 3, 1838; *Nashville Union,* Oct. 12, 1838.
65. John Catron to James K. Polk, Oct. 27, [1838], on p. 4:589, and John W. Childress to James K. Polk, Dec. 12, 1838, on p. 4:644, both in Weaver et al., *Correspondence of James K. Polk*; Jackson to Andrew J. Donelson, Dec. 7, 1838, Andrew Jackson Donelson Papers, LC; *Nashville Republican Banner,* Oct. 12, Nov. 9, Dec. 6, 1838; Apr. 12, 1839; *Nashville Union,* Dec. 14, 1838.
66. *Nashville Republican Banner,* Apr. 16, 22, May 21, 1839; *Nashville Union,* Apr. 22, 24, June 7, July 5, 1839; *Elizabethton Tennessee Whig,* July 30, 1839.
67. *Nashville Whig,* Apr. 12, 1839. *Nashville Republican Banner,* Oct. 25, 29, Nov. 14, 19, 1838; Mar. 20, July 12, 24, 27, Aug. 10, 1839. *Elizabethton Tennessee Whig,* May 23, 30, July 25, 1839. See also [Allen A. Hall], *The Counterfeit Detector, or The Leaders of 'The Party' Exposed* (Nashville: n.p., 1839).
68. *Nashville Republican Banner,* Oct. 12, Nov. 6, Apr. 19, 1839; *Elizabethton Tennessee Whig,* June 27, 1839.
69. Sellers, *James K. Polk: Jacksonian,* 366-73.
70. *Nashville Whig,* Apr. 15, 1839; *Elizabethton Tennessee Whig,* May 16, 1839.
71. *Nashville Republican Banner,* June 29, July 1 and 3, and Aug. 3, 1839; *Elizabethton Tennessee Whig,* May 23, 1839; John Bell to Henry Clay, May 21, 1839, in *The Papers of Henry Clay,* ed. James F. Hopkins et al. (Lexington: Univ. Press of Kentucky, 1988), 9:316.
72. James Campbell to David Campbell, June 16, 1839, Campbell Papers, DU.
73. *Nashville Whig,* Mar. 27, 1839; *Knoxville Argus,* July 18, 1839. E. S. Davis to James K. Polk, Dec. 28, 1838, on p. 4:664; Jesse B. Clements to Polk, Feb. 11, 1839, on p. 5:57; and James Walker to Polk, May 25, 1839, on p. 5:134, all in Weaver et al., *Correspondence of James K. Polk.* J. L. Williams to William B. Campbell, June 30, 1839, Campbell Papers, DU. *Nashville Union,* Dec. 14, 1839.
74. James K. Polk to Andrew Jackson, June 11, 1838, on p. 4:475; James Walker to Polk, June 22, 1838, on p. 4:488-89; and Walker to Polk, June 29, 1838, on pp. 4:495-96, all in Weaver et al., *Correspondence of James K. Polk.* J. B. McCormick to William B. Campbell, May 22, 1838, and B. R. Owen to Campbell, May 30, 1838, both in Campbell Papers, DU. *Nashville Union,* Apr. 30, June 4, Aug. 8, 1838. *Nashville Republican Banner,* Apr. 25, 1838; Jan. 8, Mar. 2, 1839. *Nashville Whig,* May 13, June 1, 26, July 4, 17, 1839.
75. James Campbell to David Campbell, Oct. 14, 1838, Campbell Papers,

DU; *Nashville Republican Banner,* Jan. 8, Mar. 2, July 25, 1839; *Nashville Whig,* May 13, June 26, July 4, 17, 1839; *Nashville Union,* July 26, 1839.

76. Alexander Anderson to James K. Polk, Aug. 6, 1839, in Weaver et al., *Correspondence of James K. Polk,* 5:179; Andrew Jackson to Francis Preston Blair, Sept. 23, 1839, Jackson Papers, LC.

77. Pearson correlates analyzing the statewide Democratic vote in Tennessee's elections in the 1840s average +.95 and often approach +.99. The average drops only to +.91 during the 1850s. Throughout the era of the party system, the figure never drops below the +.85 of 1857. While these correlates represent a comparison of county returns rather than actual votes of individuals, the consistently high figures strongly indicate persistent party voting among Tennessee's electors after 1839. See Jonathan M. Atkins, "'A Combat for Liberty': Politics and Parties in Jackson's Tennessee, 1832-1851" (Ph.D. diss., Univ. of Michigan, 1991), 449-53.

78. Journal of George W. House, Aug. 1, 1839, Mary Hamilton Thompson Orr Collection, TSLA; *Nashville Union,* Sept. 17, 1840; *Elizabethton Tennessee Whig,* Dec. 26, 1839.

Chapter 4. Federalists and Spoilsmen, Banks and Free Trade: Party Ideologies and Economic Policy

1. See, e.g., James K. Polk to David Burford, Nov. 7, 1840, on p. 5:576-77, and Archibald Wright to Polk, Nov. 13, 1840, on p. 5:582, both in Weaver et al., *Correspondence of James K. Polk*; Felix K. Zollicoffer to Robert L. Caruthers, Jan. 13, 1843, Caruthers Papers, SHC; Caleb C. Norvell to William B. Campbell, May 18, 1843, Campbell Papers, DU.

2. Brownlow, *Political Register,* 12; Jeremiah G. Harris to Adam Ferguson, Dec. 16, 1840, Ferguson Papers, TSLA; *Nashville Whig,* Oct. 18, 1842, and Jan. 14, 1843; *Jonesborough Whig,* July 5, 1843; *Nashville Union,* June 1, 1840; *Knoxville Argus,* June 23, 1840; *Clarksville Jeffersonian,* Nov. 2, 1844; *Memphis Appeal,* Aug. 25, 1843.

3. *Address to the Republican People of Tennessee, by the Central Corresponding Committee of the State* [No. 2] (Nashville: n.p., 1840), 3; *Address to the Republican People of Tennessee, by the Central Corresponding Committee of the State* [No. 1] (Nashville: n.p., 1840), 3; *Clarksville Jeffersonian,* Nov. 2, 1844; *Knoxville Argus,* June 23, 1841; *Nashville Union,* Feb. 13, 1839; June 1, Sept. 17, 1840; John E. Wheeler, *Speech of Mr. Wheeler of the Senate, upon the Instructing Resolutions* (Nashville: n.p., 1839), 6-8.

4. *Knoxville Argus,* June 23, 1840; *Nashville Union,* Mar. 30, 1840; Dec. 2, 1843; *Clarksville Jeffersonian,* Sept. 28, 1844; Wheeler, *Speech of Wheeler upon the Instructing Resolutions,* 6; James K. Polk to William Smith et al., Aug. 31, 1839, in Weaver et al., *Correspondence of James K. Polk,* 5:219.

5. *Nashville Union,* Sept. 17, 1840; Feb. 18, 1841; Dec. 2, 1843. *Clarksville Jeffersonian,* Nov. 2, 1844.

6. *Knoxville Argus,* Aug. 4, 1841; *Address to the Republican People of Tennessee* [No. 1], 4; *Nashville Union,* Dec. 2, 1843.

7. *Nashville Union,* Apr. 16, 1840; Dec. 2, 1843.
8. *Nashville Republican Banner,* Oct. 18, 1839; *Clarksville Jeffersonian,* July 13, 1844; *Nashville Union,* Sept. 2, 1841.
9. *Nashville Union,* Sept. 2, 1841; James K. Polk to Felix Grundy, May 27, 1840, in Weaver et al., *Correspondence of James K. Polk,* 5:470.
10. *Nashville Union,* Sept. 2, 1841; *Knoxville Argus,* Aug. 3, 1842, and May 24, 1843; Robert Armstrong to Andrew Jackson, Sept. 23, 1840, Jackson Papers, LC.
11. *Nashville Republican Banner,* Aug. 21, 1839; Nov. 29, 1843; *Elizabethton Tennessee Whig,* Nov. 21, 1839; Feb. 6, May 14, 1840; *Memphis Enquirer,* July 22, 1837; *Nashville Whig,* Nov. 26, 1841.
12. *Nashville Republican Banner,* July 24, 31, 1839; July 31, 1840; *Jonesborough Whig,* May 6, Oct. 7, 1840; Dec. 15, 1841; John Blair to James K. Polk, Nov. 7, 1839, in Weaver et al., *Correspondence of James K. Polk,* 5:287-88.
13. *Nashville Whig,* Oct. 18, 1842; Jan. 14, 1843; *Jonesborough Whig,* Nov. 2, 1842; *Nashville Republican Banner,* May 18, 1838; Journal of George W. House, Aug. 2, 1839, Orr Collection, TSLA; Brownlow, *Political Register,* 12. On the origin and significance of the term "Locofoco," see Arthur M. Schlesinger, Jr., *The Age of Jackson* (Boston: Little, Brown, 1945), 190-209.
14. *Nashville Whig,* June 2, 1842; *Nashville Republican Banner,* Sept. 16, 1844; William B. Campbell to David Campbell, Feb. 1, 1840, Campbell Papers, DU.
15. *Nashville Republican Banner,* Aug. 1, 1837; July 24, Sept. 14, 1839; *Nashville Whig,* May 8, 1840; Wilson Cage to William B. Campbell, June 2, 1840, Campbell Papers, DU.
16. *Nashville Whig,* Feb. 9, 1843; *Nashville Republican Banner,* Sept. 14, 1839; July 31, 1840; *Elizabethton Tennessee Whig,* Aug. 29, 1839; *Jonesborough Whig,* Mar. 16, 1842; *Memphis Enquirer,* Sept. 2, 1837; [Hall], *Counterfeit Detector,* 48.
17. Wheeler, *Speech of Wheeler upon the Instructing Resolutions,* 10; *Nashville Whig,* Feb. 9, 1843; *Jonesborough Whig,* Sept. 1, 1841; *Nashville Republican Banner,* Jan. 6 and July 31, 1840, and Mar. 31, 1845.
18. *Nashville Whig,* Jan. 9, 1839; *Nashville Union,* Apr. 16, 1840; *Nashville Republican Banner,* Apr. 25 and May 18, 1839; *Elizabethton Tennessee Whig,* July 25, 1839; *Address to the People of Tennessee, by the Whig Convention, Which Assembled at Knoxville, on Monday, the 10th of February, 1840* (Knoxville: n.p., 1840), 6. On the bill to prevent interference in elections, see ch. 3, n. 5, above.
19. The map is based upon the election returns reported in Anne H. Hopkins and William Lyons, *Tennessee Votes: 1799-1976,* Studies in Tennessee Politics, no. 2 (Knoxville: Bureau of Public Administration, Univ. of Tennessee, 1978). A county was classified as either "Whig" or "Democratic" if either party carried the county in at least seven of the ten elections between 1839 and 1851, or if one party carried it in every contest if returns were available for less than seven elections. According to this standard, the only counties

categorized as "contested" were Campbell, DeKalb, Lawrence, and Morgan. No returns were available in the 1840s for Scott County.

20. William Wallace to James K. Polk, June 12, 1840, in Weaver et al., *Correspondence of James K. Polk*, 5:489; *Nashville Republican Banner*, Apr. 6, 1841.

21. *Nashville Union*, Oct. 28, 1837; *Nashville Republican Banner*, July 11, 1840; Samuel H. Laughlin, diary, Oct. 1, 1842, Samuel H. Laughlin Papers, THS; Allen Brown to James K. Polk, Mar. 14, 1834, in Weaver et al., *Correspondence of James K. Polk*, 2:358.

22. *Nashville Union*, Jan. 18, 1841; E. G. Eastman to James K. Polk, Jan. 21, 1841, on pp. 5:619-20, and John C. McLemore to Polk, Feb. 14, 1841, on pp. 5:633-34, both in Weaver et al., *Correspondence of James K. Polk*; Thomas B. Alexander, *Thomas A. R. Nelson of East Tennessee* (Nashville: Tennessee Historical Commission, 1956), 19-20.

23. John W. Childress to James K. Polk, Apr. 9, 1838, in Weaver et al., *Correspondence of James K. Polk*, 4:420; Lowrey, "Tennessee Voters during the Second Two-Party System," 98-99, 106, 107. The conclusion concerning the pattern of party division within counties is based upon the author's observation of voting returns in Davidson, Knox, Lincoln, Madison, McMinn, Montgomery, and Shelby counties, and upon the conclusions for Rutherford and McNairy counties presented in Carroll Van West, "'The Money Our Fathers Were Accustomed To': Banks and Political Culture in Rutherford County, Tennessee, 1800-1850" (Ph.D. diss., College of William and Mary, 1982), 169-203; and Charles L. Lufkin, "Divided Loyalties: Sectionalism in Civil War McNairy County, Tennessee," *THQ* 47 (Fall 1988): 169-77. Concerning economic influences on voting behavior, see Harry L. Watson, *Jacksonian Politics and Community Conflict: The Emergence of the Second American Party System in Cumberland County, North Carolina* (Baton Rouge: Louisiana State Univ. Press, 1981), 198-245; Watson, "Conflict and Collaboration"; and Charles G. Sellers, "Who Were the Southern Whigs?" *American Historical Review* 59 (Jan. 1954): 335-46.

24. *Nashville Republican Banner*, Oct. 19 and 21, 1839; *Nashville Whig*, Oct. 18 and 21, 1839; *Nashville Union*, Aug. 30, Oct. 18 and 21, 1839; *Elizabethton Tennessee Whig*, Dec. 26, 1839; Temin, *Jacksonian Economy*, 148-71; Schweikart, *Banking in the American South*, 73, 77-79; Hammond, *Banks and Politics*, 500-548; Campbell, *Banking in Tennessee*, 108-10.

25. James Hill to Michael Shoffner, Nov. 20, 1841, Michael Shoffner Papers, SHC; *Nashville Republican Banner*, June 3, 1842; *Jonesborough Whig*, Apr. 20, 1842; *Knoxville Argus*, Sept. 9, 1840; Mar. 23, 1842; *Nashville Whig*, Feb. 18, 1843; Edmund Cooper to William F. Cooper, Aug. 6, 1842, Cooper Papers, TSLA.

26. *Elizabethton Tennessee Whig*, Sept. 5, 1839; *Nashville Whig*, Aug. 30, 1839; *Nashville Union*, Apr. 8, 1835; June 28, 1842; *Memphis Enquirer*, Apr. 20, 1836; *Memphis Appeal*, July 7, 1843; John Shoffner to Michael Shoffner, Mar. 29, 1842, Shoffner Papers, SHC; Temin, *Jacksonian Economy*, 148-52; Dunlap, "Report," 17.

27. *Jonesborough Whig,* Dec. 8, 1841, and Sept. 7, 1842; *Nashville Republican Banner,* Oct. 12, 1842; Edmund Cooper to William F. Cooper, Aug. 6, 1842, Cooper Papers, TSLA; Benjamin R. Owen to William B. Campbell, Jan. 28, 1840, and William B. Campbell to David Campbell, Sept. 10, 1842, both in Campbell Papers, DU; Thomas L. Watson to Robert L. Caruthers, May 22, 1842, Caruthers Papers, SHC; John H. Bills to James K. Polk, Dec. 14, 1839, in Weaver et al., *Correspondence of James K. Polk,* 5:342.

28. Thomas L. Bransford to William B. Campbell, June 19, 1842, Campbell Papers, DU.

29. *Nashville Union,* Aug. 30, 1839; Apr. 20, 1840; Sept. 5, 1843. *Knoxville Argus,* Jan. 13, 1841.

30. *Nashville Union,* Oct. 18, Nov. 4, 1839; James Walker to James K. Polk, Oct. 20, 1839, in Weaver et al., *Correspondence of James K. Polk,* 5:267-68; Andrew Jackson to Andrew J. Hutchings, Aug. 12, 1840, Dyas Collection, Coffee Papers, THS.

31. *Address to the Republican People of Tennessee* [No. 2], 15; *Nashville Union,* Feb. 13, 1839; *Clarksville Jeffersonian,* Mar. 25, 1843; *Knoxville Argus,* June 14, 1842.

32. *Nashville Union,* May 24, 1842; *Knoxville Argus,* Feb. 10, 1841; Nov. 16, 1842; Mar. 1, 1843.

33. *Memphis Appeal,* Dec. 20, 1844. *Nashville Union,* Feb. 8, May 17, Aug. 23, 1839; Apr. 16, 1840; Aug. 16, 1842. *Clarksville Jeffersonian,* May 25, 1844.

34. Andrew Jackson to Francis Preston Blair, Feb. 3, 1842, Jackson Papers, LC; *Nashville Union,* Sept. 5, 1843; White and Ash, *Messages of the Governors* 3:287-88; John Catron to James K. Polk, Jan. 2, 1842, on pp. 6:3-5, and James Walker to Polk, Aug. 19, 1837, on pp. 4:211-14, both in Weaver et al., *Correspondence of James K. Polk;* Cave Johnson to Felix Grundy, May 30, 1837, Grundy Papers, SHC; *Knoxville Argus,* Sept. 3, 1839.

35. John Catron to James K. Polk, Jan. 2, 1842, in Weaver et al., *Correspondence of James K. Polk,* 6:5; *Nashville Union,* Mar. 15, 1841.

36. Brownlow, *Political Register,* 120. *Nashville Whig,* Aug. 30, 1839; Feb. 26, Mar. 18, 1840. *Nashville Republican Banner,* Nov. 2, 1839; Feb. 3, 1843; Feb. 5, 1845. *Elizabethton Tennessee Whig,* Mar. 5, 1840. *Jonesborough Whig,* July 8, 1840.

37. *Nashville Whig,* Aug. 20, 1842; *Elizabethton Tennessee Whig,* Oct. 31, 1839; Mar. 5, 1840; *Jonesborough Whig,* July 15, 1840; *Address to the People of Tennessee, by the Whig Convention, 1840,* 7; Matthew D. Cooper to William F. Cooper, Jan. 14, 1840, Cooper Papers, TSLA.

38. *Nashville Republican Banner,* Mar. 5, Apr. 7, and July 31, 1840; Feb. 3, 1843; *Nashville Whig,* Oct. 1, 1841; June 20, 1844; *Jonesborough Whig,* June 30, 1841; Brownlow, *Political Register,* 15, 17-18, 22-24, 132-37; Edmund Dillahunty to Robert L. Caruthers, May 6, 1842, Caruthers Papers, SHC.

39. *Nashville Whig,* Oct. 1, 1841; Feb. 9, 1843; *Nashville Republican Banner,* June 21, 1843.

40. Return J. Meigs to Robert L. Caruthers, May 25, 1841, and James Woods to Caruthers, Mar. 23, 1842, both in Caruthers Papers, SHC; *Jonesborough*

Notes to pages 95-98

Whig, Dec. 8, 1841; *Nashville Whig*, Oct. 1, 1841; *Nashville Republican Banner*, Mar. 24, Aug. 2, 1841; Mar. 29, 1843; *Address to the People of Tennessee, by the Whig Convention, 1840*, 3-4; E. J. Scales to David Campbell, May 22, 1843, Campbell Papers, DU.

41. *Nashville Whig*, Aug. 28, Dec. 20, 1839; Mar. 20, 1840; Mar. 10, Aug. 11, 1842; Mar. 4, 1843. *Jonesborough Whig*, Mar. 3, Nov. 10, 1841.

42. Brownlow, *Political Register*, 29; *Nashville Republican Banner*, July 31, 1840; July 21, 1843; *Nashville Whig*, Aug. 30, 1839; *Nashville Union*, Feb. 11, 1837; Feb. 28, 1842; [Hall], *Counterfeit Detector*, 9-10.

43. Ephraim H. Foster to Robert L. Caruthers, June 22, 1842, and Edmund Dillahunty to Caruthers, May 6, 1842, both in Caruthers Papers, SHC; *Jonesborough Whig*, Jan. 4, 1843; William B. Campbell to David Campbell, June 8 and July 24, 1842, both in Campbell Papers, DU. The lone Whig congressman to vote for the 1842 Tariff Act was Joseph L. Williams of Knoxville. Several Whigs opposed this act, apparently because its final version omitted a proposal to distribute the proceeds from the sale of public lands to the states. Meredith P. Gentry of Williamson County proposed this amendment to an earlier version of the bill, and four Tennessee Whigs voted to pass this version. See *Jonesborough Whig*, Aug. 31 and Sept. 7, 1842; *Congressional Globe*, 27th Congress, 2d sess., 756, 762, 926.

44. Edmund Dillahunty to Robert L. Caruthers, May 6, 1842; Felix K. Zollicoffer to Caruthers, May 17, 1842; and Ephraim H. Foster to Caruthers, June 22, 1842, all in Caruthers Papers, SHC. *Nashville Republican Banner*, Apr. 8, Sept. 28, 1842; Mar. 29, 1843; Oct. 14, 1844. *Nashville Whig*, Dec. 16, 1840; Oct. 15, 20, 1841; May 3, Sept. 20, 1842; June 17, 1843. *Jonesborough Whig*, Apr. 13, May 11, 18, 1842. Brownlow, *Political Register*, 50, 64. Thomas L. Bransford to William B. Campbell, June 19, 1842, Campbell Papers, DU.

45. *Clarksville Jeffersonian*, May 6, 1843; *Nashville Union*, Jan. 31, 1842; *Knoxville Argus*, Mar. 30, July 27, 1842; Aaron V. Brown, *Speeches, Congressional and Political, and Other Writings, of Ex-Governor Aaron V. Brown, of Tennessee* (Nashville: John L. Marling, 1854), 81-86.

46. *Nashville Union*, Mar. 30, 1844; Brown, *Speeches, Congressional and Political*, 95-96, 104-5; *Nashville Union*, Feb. 28, 1842; *Clarksville Jeffersonian*, May 6, 1843; *Memphis Appeal*, Sept. 5, 1845.

47. *Memphis Appeal*, Feb. 2, 1844; *Clarksville Jeffersonian*, Oct. 12, 1844. See also Wayne Cutler, "Jackson, Polk, and Johnson: Defenders of the Moral Economy," *THQ* 54 (Fall 1995): 178-89.

48. *Clarksville Jeffersonian*, Sept. 11, 1847; White and Ash, *Messages of the Governors* 4:408; J. M. Sturtevant, "Fifth Biennial Report of the Institution of the Blind," in *Appendix to the House and Senate Journals* (1853-54), 151.

49. *Nashville Whig*, Apr. 29, 1839; Thomas L. Bransford to William B. Campbell, July 24, 1842, Campbell Papers, DU. For a sophisticated and illuminating discussion of the relationship between local and national issues in the politics of the party system, see Watson, *Jacksonian Politics and Community Conflict*, 151-97.

50. White and Ash, *Messages of the Governors* 3:615-16; John Overton to John S. Claybrooke, Oct. 24, 1842, Claybrooke-Overton Papers, THS; William H. Polk to James K. Polk, Sept. 30, 1842, in Weaver et al., *Correspondence of James K. Polk*, 6:118; *Jonesborough Whig*, Oct. 5, 1842.

51. *Senate Journal* (1842), 56, 110, 114-15, 118, 134, 150; *House Journal* (1842), 91, 97-98, 133, 191-93; *Public Acts* (1842), 14-15, 20-22, 26; John C. Rogers to George W. Jones, 1842, George Washington Jones Papers, SHC; *Nashville Whig*, Oct. 15, Nov. 3, 1842; *Jonesborough Whig*, Oct. 5, 1842; *Nashville Union*, Oct. 11, 1842; *Nashville Republican Banner*, Apr. 22, Oct. 12, 1842.

52. *Nashville American*, Mar. 13, 1851; *Senate Journal* (1841-42), 549-50, 607-8; *Public Acts* (1841-42), 241.

53. Tennessee Constitution, 1834, Art. 11, Sec. 9. Folmsbee, *Sectionalism and Internal Improvements*, 70-147, 162-76, 207-10. *Nashville Union*, May 17, 1837; Dec. 21, 1838; Nov. 25, 1839; Jan. 17, 1844. *Nashville Republican*, Mar. 23, Apr. 1, 1837. *Knoxville Argus*, Jan. 27, July 27, 1841. *Clarksville Jeffersonian*, Nov. 20, 1849. Burton W. Folsom, II, "The Politics of Elites: Prominence and Party in Davidson County, Tennessee, 1835-1861," *Journal of Southern History* 39 (Aug. 1973): 359-78. David L. Eubank, ed., "J. G. M. Ramsey as a Bond Agent: Selections from the Ramsey Papers," East Tennessee Historical Society *Publications* 36 (1964): 81-99.

54. *Nashville Republican Banner*, Oct. 13, 1837.

55. *Public Acts* (1839-40), 33-35, 37-42, 61-63, 134-36, 137-43, 205-6, 225-28, 251-53; *House Journal* (1857-58), 338, 782-83; *Nashville Whig*, Nov. 17, 1841. The index of disagreement is the difference between the proportions of Whigs and Democrats voting in favor of a measure; see Holt, *Political Crisis of the 1850s*, 26-27.

56. For examples of the parties' squabbling over the Bank of Tennessee, see White and Ash, *Messages of the Governors* 3:581-84, 3:631-37, 3:721, 4:291-94, 4:678-85.

57. *Public Acts* (1832), 9, 11-12, and (1833), 38-39, 63-64; *Nashville Union*, Mar. 24, Aug. 1, 1838; Dec. 2, 1839; *Nashville Republican Banner*, Oct. 11, 1837; Nov. 6, 1839; Oct. 12, 1842; *Nashville Whig*, May 18, 1838; Dec. 20, 27, 1839; *Knoxville Argus*, Mar. 30, 1842; Mar. 29, 1843; *House Journal* (1837-38), 533-34, 543.

58. White and Ash, *Messages of the Governors* 3:282; *Nashville Republican Banner*, Nov. 4, 6, 27; Dec. 5, 1839; *Nashville Whig*, Oct. 25, 1839; *Elizabethton Tennessee Whig*, Nov. 28, 1839; *Jonesborough Whig*, Oct. 20, 1841; James Walker to James K. Polk, Dec. 30, 1839, in Weaver et al., *Correspondence of James K. Polk*, 5:360-61; *House Journal* (1839-40), 92, 96-97, 99, 139, 144, 239; *Senate Journal* (1839-40), 305-6, 449-50.

59. *House Journal* (1841-42), 456-57, 552-53, 555-56, 912-15; *Senate Journal* (1841-42), 465, 540, 618-20; *Public Acts* (1841-42), 245-46; *Nashville Whig*, Nov. 2, 12, 1841; Jan. 6, 1842; *Nashville Republican Banner*, Jan. 14, July 1, 29, 1842; *Nashville Union*, Dec. 20, 1841; Jan. 10, July 22, 1842; David Fentress to John H. Bills, Nov. 10, 1841, John Houston Bills Papers, TSLA.

60. *House Journal* (1843-44), 481-82; *Senate Journal* (1843-44), 439.
61. *Public Acts* (1832), 9, and (1833), 38, 63; *Nashville Republican Banner,* Oct. 21, 1842.
62. James K. Polk, "Legislative Message, October 23, 1839," qtd. in White and Ash, *Messages of the Governors* 3:287-88; *Public Acts* (1837-38), 159; *Knoxville Argus,* Jan. 5, 1842; John C. Rogers to George W. Jones, Oct. 19, 1842, Jones Papers, SHC.
63. *Public Acts* (1841-42), 68; (1842, extra sess.), 14-15; (1847-48), 282.
64. *House Journal* (1849-50), 631; *Senate Journal,* (1849-50), 711. On Whig support for state aid for internal improvements, general incorporation and bankruptcy laws, and a reduction of the merchants' tax, see *House Journal* (1849-50), 751, 818-19, 852; *Senate Journal* (1847-48), 600; (1849-50), 417; (1851-52), 360.
65. Andrew Johnson to E. G. Eastman, May 27, 1849, in *The Papers of Andrew Johnson,* ed. Leroy P. Graf and Ralph W. Haskins (Knoxville: Univ. of Tennessee Press, 1967), 1:509; *Nashville Union,* Sept. 27, Nov. 24, 1849; *Memphis Eagle,* June 13, 1849.
66. *Public Acts* (1851-52), 204-15; *House Journal* (1851-52), 643; *Senate Journal* (1851-52), 600.
67. See appendix A of this volume.
68. On the prominence of local issues in other states during the 1850s, see Holt, *Political Crisis of the 1850s,* 101-38; Kruman, *Parties and Politics in North Carolina,* 154-58, 181-96; Ford, *Origins of Southern Radicalism,* 281-337; and William E. Gienapp, *The Origins of the Republican Party, 1852-1856* (New York: Oxford Univ. Press, 1987).
69. The literature on the Market Revolution's influence on the national party system has become extensive and is still growing. For some of the more important works, see Sellers, *The Market Revolution;* Watson, *Liberty and Power;* and Lawrence Frederick Kohl, *The Politics of Individualism: Parties and the American Character in the Jacksonian Era* (New York: Oxford Univ. Press, 1989).
70. Sellers, *Market Revolution,* 363.

Chapter 5. The Politics of Relief: Hard Times and Texas, 1839-1845

1. *Nashville Union,* Aug. 2, 1839; *Knoxville Argus,* Aug. 6, 1839.
2. Andrew Jackson to Francis Preston Blair, Feb. 15, 1840, Jackson Papers, LC; Samuel H. Laughlin to James K. Polk, Aug. 20, 1839, in Weaver et al., *Correspondence of James K. Polk,* 5:195; *Knoxville Argus,* Sept. 17, 1839; *Nashville Union,* Feb. 10, 1840; *Senate Journal* (1839-40), 38-41, 45; *House Journal* (1839-40), 73.
3. *Senate Journal* (1839-40), 76-79, 104-5; *House Journal* (1839-40), 188; *Public Acts* (1839-40), 261-64. James K. Polk to Andrew Jackson, Aug. 12, 1839, on p. 5:185; Cave Johnson to Polk, Sept. 28, [1839], on p. 5:257; Felix Grundy to Polk, Oct. 17, 1839, on pp. 5:264-65; Alexander O. Ander-

son to Polk, Nov. 22, 1839, on pp. 5:308-9; and Grundy to Polk, Jan. 13, 1840, on p. 5:371, all in Weaver et al., *Correspondence of James K. Polk.* Andrew Jackson to Amos Kendall, Oct. 9, 1839, Jackson Papers, LC. William B. Campbell to David Campbell, Oct. 10, 1839, Campbell Papers, DU.

4. Hugh L. White to [Ephraim H. Foster], Nov. 9, 1839, Hugh Lawson White Papers, DU; *Nashville Republican Banner,* Nov. 16, 1839; *Nashville Whig,* Nov. 29, 1839; *House Journal* (1839-40), 189-208, 577-88.

5. Joseph H. Peyton to William B. Campbell, Oct. 26, 1839, Campbell Papers, DU; Allen A. Hall to Henry Clay, Sept. 23, 1839, in Hopkins, *Papers of Henry Clay,* 9:344; *Nashville Whig,* Aug. 9, 1839; *Nashville Republican Banner,* Aug. 12, 16, 1839; *Elizabethton Tennessee Whig,* Aug. 22, 1839.

6. John Bell to William B. Campbell, Aug. 10, 1839, Campbell Papers, DU; William G. Childress to James K. Polk, Aug. 15, 1839, in Weaver et al., *Correspondence of James K. Polk,* 5:188; *Nashville Republican Banner,* Sept. 12, 1839.

7. Ephraim H. Foster to William B. Campbell, Jan. 16, 1840, and William B. Campbell to David Campbell, Dec. 9, 1839, and Jan. 2, 1840, all in Campbell Papers, DU.

8. Thomas D. Arnold to Thomas A. R. Nelson, Jan. 23, 1840, Nelson Papers, McClung; James Campbell to David Campbell, Aug. 7, 1840, Campbell Papers, DU; *Address to the People of Tennessee, by the Whig Convention, 1840,* 7; *Nashville Republican Banner,* Aug. 17, 1839; July 25, 1840; *Nashville Whig,* May 8, 1840.

9. *Nashville Republican Banner,* Dec. 19, 1839; Jan. 6, 1840; *Nashville Whig,* Jan. 17, 1840; *Jonesborough Whig,* June 17, 1840; Wilson Cage to William B. Campbell, June 2, 1840, Campbell Papers, DU.

10. *Nashville Republican Banner,* Feb. 3, 7, 17, 19, 24; Mar. 11, 1840; *Address to the People of Tennessee, by the Whig Convention, 1840,* 5.

11. *Nashville Republican Banner,* Jan. 6, Mar. 5, 1840; *Nashville Whig,* Aug. 30, 1839; Feb. 26, 1840; *Elizabethton Tennessee Whig,* Sept. 5, 1840.

12. *Nashville Republican Banner,* Apr. 14, 1840; *Nashville Whig,* Mar. 11, Mar. 18, Aug. 31, 1840; *Jonesborough Whig,* July 8, 1840; David Campbell of Tennessee to [David Campbell of Virginia], June 15, 1840, Campbell Papers, DU.

13. James Walker to James K. Polk, Mar. 23, 1840, on p. 5:407; James K. Polk to Cave Johnson, Mar. 30, 1840, on p. 5:413; Polk to Felix Grundy, May 27, 1840, on pp. 5:470-71; and A. O. P. Nicholson to Polk, May 29, 1840, on p. 5:474, all in Weaver et al., *Correspondence of James K. Polk. Nashville Union,* Sept. 9, 18, Oct. 21, 23, 1839; July 13, 1840. *Knoxville Argus,* Aug. 27, Sept. 17, 1839; May 28, July 8, 1840.

14. *Knoxville Argus,* Sept. 30, 1840; *Nashville Union,* Dec. 23, 1839; Sept. 28, 1840; *Address to the Republican People of Tennessee* [No. 1], 3-9; *Address to the Republican People of Tennessee* [No. 2], 24.

15. *Nashville Union,* Mar. 4, 1840; Andrew Buchanan to William Buchanan, June 14, 1840, Buchanan-McClellan Papers, SHC; *Knoxville Argus,* May 19, Sept. 30, 1840; *Nashville Union,* July 2, Sept. 24, 1840; *Address to the Republican People of Tennessee* [No. 2], 22-23; Levin H. Coe to James K.

Polk, June 11, 1840, in Weaver et al., *Correspondence of James K. Polk,* 5:487.

16. *Knoxville Argus,* Nov. 11, 1840; Jan. 13, 1841; *Nashville Union,* Nov. 2, 1840; Mar. 18, 1841; A. O. P. Nicholson to James K. Polk, Nov. 15, 1840, in Weaver et al., *Correspondence of James K. Polk,* 5:587.

17. James K. Polk to Samuel H. Laughlin, Mar. 9, 1841, in Weaver et al., *Correspondence of James K. Polk,* 5:653; *Nashville National Banner,* Sept. 9, 1836; *Nashville Republican Banner,* Mar. 5, 6, 24, Apr. 9, June 20, July 17, 1840.

18. William B. Campbell to David Campbell, Apr. 7, 1840, and Abraham Caruthers to William B. Campbell, June 14, 1841, both in Campbell Papers, DU; John Bell to Thomas A. R. Nelson, Nov. 8, 1840, Nelson Papers, McClung.

19. Archibald Wright to James K. Polk, Nov. 13, 1840, in Weaver et al., *Correspondence of James K. Polk,* 5:582; *Nashville Republican Banner,* Mar. 24, Mar. 30, Apr. 5, May 10, May 19, May 24, June 19, 1841; *Jonesborough Whig,* May 5, Aug. 6, 1841; *Nashville Union,* Apr. 22, May 20, May 24, July 5, 1841.

20. *Knoxville Argus,* Jan. 20, Feb. 3, Mar. 3, 1841; *Nashville Union,* May 3, June 14, 24, 1841; James K. Polk, *Address of James K. Polk, to the People of Tennessee* (Nashville: n.p., 1841), 16; Andrew Jackson to Francis Preston Blair, Feb. 19, 1841, Jackson Papers, LC.

21. *Nashville Whig,* Aug. 11, 1841. Because of the extra session of Congress, the state held its congressional elections on May 6, rather than in August, to allow the new representatives to attend the session; see *Nashville Whig,* Mar. 29, 1841.

22. Return J. Meigs to Robert L. Caruthers, May 25, 1841, Caruthers Papers, SHC; *Nashville Republican Banner,* July 17, 1841; *Jonesborough Whig,* Mar. 3 and Aug. 3, 1841; *Knoxville Argus,* Feb. 10, 1841.

23. *Nashville Republican Banner,* Apr. 15, June 9, 1841; Aug. 25, Sept. 18, 1841. *Knoxville Argus,* Sept. 1, 1841. Norma Lois Peterson, *The Presidencies of William Henry Harrison and John Tyler* (Lawrence: Univ. Press of Kansas, 1989), 57-93.

24. *Nashville Republican Banner,* Aug. 26, 27, Sept. 13, 20, 21, 1841; *Nashville Whig,* Aug. 30, Sept. 6, Sept. 20, 1841; *Jonesborough Whig,* Aug. 25, Sept. 1, 1841; Sackfield Maclin to James K. Polk, Aug. 31, 1841, in Weaver et al., *Correspondence of James K. Polk,* 5:743.

25. *Jonesborough Whig,* Sept. 8, 1841; *Nashville Republican Banner,* Apr. 27, 1842.

26. *Nashville Republican Banner,* June 3, July 11, Aug. 3, Aug. 29, 1842; *Nashville Whig,* Apr. 12, Aug. 16, 1842; John Shoffner to Michael Shoffner, Mar. 29, 1842, Shoffner Papers, SHC; *Jonesborough Whig,* Nov. 10, 1841.

27. *Nashville Union,* Aug. 26, Sept. 20, 1841; *Knoxville Argus,* Sept. 1, 8, 1841.

28. *Knoxville Argus,* Jan. 27, July 28, 1841; *Nashville Union,* Sept. 6, 1842; June 27, 1843; Robert B. Reynolds to James K. Polk, Feb. [15], 1841, on p. 5:635, and John F. Gillespie to Polk, [Oct. 1], 1841, on p. 5:768, both in Weaver et al., *Correspondence of James K. Polk.*

29. *Nashville Union,* Apr. 8, 1841; Feb. 7, 1842; Francis B. Fogg to Robert

L. Caruthers, Dec. 4, 1841, and Alexander Allison to Caruthers, Jan. 18, 1842, both in Caruthers Papers, SHC; *Knoxville Argus*, Apr. 7, 1841; Feb. 9, June 29, 1842; Thomas L. Bransford to William B. Campbell, Sept. 4, 1841, Campbell Papers, DU. The *Nashville Whig* and the *Jonesborough Whig* defended the Bankrupt Act, while the *Nashville Republican Banner* maintained that the act passed with members of Congress from both political parties voting for it; see *Nashville Whig*, Sept. 18, 29, 1841; *Jonesborough Whig*, June 16, Nov. 10, 1841; and *Nashville Republican Banner*, Jan. 7, July 15, 1842.

30. *Knoxville Argus*, Oct. 6, 1841.

31. *Nashville Republican Banner*, May 19, 1840; David Hubbard to James K. Polk, Sept. 17, 1841, in Weaver et al., *Correspondence of James K. Polk*, 5:759; William G. Brownlow to Alexander Williams, Oct. 18, 1841, Alexander Williams Papers, DU. Governor Polk appointed A. O. P. Nicholson to serve in Grundy's seat until the next session of the legislature; see *Nashville Union*, Dec. 28, 1840.

32. *Nashville Union*, Nov. 19, 1841; Jan. 7, 1842; White and Ash, *Messages of the Governors* 3:500-576.

33. *Senate Journal* (1841-42), 280. According to the state constitution, two-thirds of both branches of the legislature constituted a quorum in a joint session.

34. White and Ash, *Messages of the Governors* 3:509, 3:511; *Knoxville Argus*, Dec. 15, 1841; *Nashville Union*, Jan. 10, 1842; *Nashville Republican Banner*, Feb. 11, 1842. The interrogatories asked senatorial candidates to give their opinions regarding (1) the Bankrupt Act, (2) distribution of the proceeds from the sales of public lands, (3) an act increasing taxes on salt, food, and clothing, (4) an act authorizing a government loan, (5) the national bank, (6) a donation given by Congress to Harrison's widow, and (7) the legislature's right of instruction.

35. Hopkins L. Turney to James K. Polk, Aug. 24, 1841, on p. 5:734; Jeremiah G. Harris to Polk, Dec. 15, 1841, on p. 5:789; and Polk to Samuel H. Laughlin, Dec. 29, 1841, on p. 5:792, all in Weaver et al., *Correspondence of James K. Polk*; Andrew Johnson to William Lowry, Oct. 24, 1841, in Graf and Haskins, *Papers of Andrew Johnson*, 1:33-34; John R. Nelson to T.A. R. Nelson, Nov. 11, 1841, Nelson Papers, McClung; *Nashville Union*, Dec. 22, 1841; Feb. 14, 1842; *Knoxville Argus*, Nov. 17, 1841; Feb. 16, 28, 1842.

36. William H. Polk to James K. Polk, Jan. 6, 1842, in Weaver et al., *Correspondence of James K. Polk*, 6:9.

37. Foster appears to have been willing to sacrifice Jarnigan to secure his own election, but Democrats refused to accept any offer unless Foster answered the interrogatories; Bell offered to answer interrogatories and exert his influence toward the election of a Democrat, but party leaders refused to deal in any way with Bell because of his role in backing White's presidential candidacy and in establishing Tennessee's Whig party. See Jeremiah G. Harris to James K. Polk, Dec. 13, 1841, on pp. 5:785-85; Hopkins L. Turney to Polk, Dec. 26, 1841, on pp. 5:790-91; James Walker to Polk, Jan. 13, 1842, on pp. 6:12-13; Polk to Sackfield Maclin, Jan. 17, 1842, on p. 6:13; and Maclin to

Polk, Jan. 26, 1842, on p. 6:19, all in Weaver et al., *Correspondence of James K. Polk*.

38. *Nashville Republican Banner,* Nov. 17, 19, 1841; John Catron to James K. Polk, Jan. 2, 1842, in Weaver et al., *Correspondence of James K. Polk*, 6:5.

39. Samuel H. Laughlin to James K. Polk, Nov. 24, 1842, on p. 5:783, and Polk to Sackfield Maclin, Jan. 17, 1842, on p. 6:14, both in Weaver et al., *Correspondence of James K. Polk*; Ephraim H. Foster to Robert L. Caruthers, Feb. 13, 1842, and James C. Jones to Caruthers, Feb. 4, 1842, both in Caruthers Papers, SHC.

40. *Senate Journal* (1841-42), 366-67, 410-12, 692, 709; *Knoxville Argus,* Feb. 16, 1842; *Nashville Union,* Jan. 10, 1842; James Campbell to William B. Campbell, Feb. 13, 1842, Campbell Papers, DU.

41. *Nashville Republican Banner,* Mar. 14, May 2, Aug. 5, Dec. 12, 1842; July 31, 1843; *Jonesborough Whig,* May 18, Sept. 28, 1842. On the Democratic challenge for a general resignation of the state legislature, see White and Ash, *Messages of the Governors* 3:603-13.

42. James K. Polk to Samuel H. Laughlin, May 8, 1843, in Weaver et al., *Correspondence of James K. Polk*, 6:280; *Nashville Republican Banner,* Mar. 8, 20, 27, 29, May 3, June 12, July 14, 28, 1843; *Nashville Whig,* Feb. 9, May 2, June 6, Aug. 22, 1843; *Jonesborough Whig,* Mar. 1, Apr. 12, May 10, Aug. 30, 1843; *Nashville Union,* Mar. 28, Apr. 14, 21, May 16, June 20, 1843.

43. Cave Johnson to James K. Polk, May 10, 1843, in Weaver et al., *Correspondence of James K. Polk*, 6:281.

44. William B. Campbell to David Campbell, Aug. 9, 1843, Campbell Papers, DU; *Nashville Whig,* Aug. 22, Sept. 5, 1843; *House Journal* (1843-44), 766; *Senate Journal* (1843-44), 568; *Public Acts* (1827), 230-37, and (1843-44), 319; *Jonesborough Whig,* Mar. 8, Sept. 13, 1843.

45. *Nashville Republican Banner,* May 10, 1844; *Nashville Whig,* May 14, 1844; *Jonesborough Whig,* May 15, 1844.

46. James K. Polk to Robert Armstrong, Aug. 7, 1843, on p. 6:331, and Polk to Martin Van Buren, Aug. 18, 1843, on p. 6:332, both in Weaver et al., *Correspondence of James K. Polk*; *Nashville Union,* Aug. 8, 18, 1843; Diary of Samuel H. Laughlin, Oct. 2, 1843, 114-15, Laughlin Papers, THS; *Knoxville Argus,* Aug. 16, 1843.

47. James K. Polk to Andrew J. Donelson, Oct. 19, 1843, in Weaver et al., *Correspondence of James K. Polk*, 6:348; *Nashville Union,* Nov. 28, 1843; *Knoxville Argus,* May 24, 1843; *Memphis Appeal,* Sept. 22, Nov. 3, 1843; Jan. 26, 1844.

48. Andrew Johnson to Robert B. Reynolds, Sept. 9, 1843, in Graf and Haskins, *Papers of Andrew Johnson,* 1:121; Aaron V. Brown to James K. Polk, Mar. 22, 1842, in Weaver et al., *Correspondence of James K. Polk*, 6:34. National disillusion with Van Buren's expected nomination is ably discussed in Michael A. Morrison, "Martin Van Buren, the Democracy, and the Partisan Politics of Texas Annexation," *Journal of Southern History* 61 (Nov. 1995): 700-709.

49. Cave Johnson to James K. Polk, Aug. 28, 1842, on p. 6:103; Julius W.

Blackwell to Polk, Oct. 5, 1843, on p. 6:336; David Craighead to Polk, [Nov. 6], 1843, on p. 6:357-58; Johnson to Polk, Nov. 10, 1843, on p. 6:359; Samuel H. Laughlin to Polk, Nov. 17, 1843, on p. 6:360; and Johnson to Polk, Feb. 6, 1844, on pp. 7:54-55, all in Weaver et al., *Correspondence of James K. Polk*. Andrew Jackson to Francis Preston Blair, Jan. 5, 1844, Jackson Papers, LC. *Nashville Union*, Dec. 2, 1843. Sellers, *James K. Polk: Continentalist*, 3-14.

50. James K. Polk to Martin Van Buren, Nov. 30, 1843, on pp. 6:364-65; and Gideon J. Pillow to Polk, May 24, 1844, on p. 7:151, both in Weaver et al., *Correspondence of James K. Polk*. "Address prepared by the Democratic Central Committee at Nashville," Jan. 17, 1844, Laughlin Papers, THS. Andrew Jackson to Cave Johnson, Dec. 11, 1843, Jackson Papers, LC. Andrew Johnson to A. O. P. Nicholson, Feb. 12, 1844, on pp. 1:149-50; and A. Johnson to David T. Patterson, May 13, 1844, on pp. 1:162-63, both in Graf and Haskins, *Papers of Andrew Johnson*.

51. *House Journal* (1837-38), 509, and (1841-42), 948-49; *Senate Journal* (1837-38), 444, and (1841-42), 708-9; *Public Acts* (1837-38), 450, and (1841-42), 235; [Tennessee] Democratic Central Committee, *The Annexation of Texas to the United States Fully and Fairly Discussed; Together with all the Important Documents Connected with the Question* (Nashville: n.p., 1844), 5; Aaron V. Brown to Samuel H. Laughlin, Dec. 8, 1843, Miscellaneous File, THS; Aaron V. Brown to Polk, Dec. 9, 1843, in Weaver et al., *Correspondence of James K. Polk*, 6:370-71; *Nashville National Banner*, Feb. 12, 1836.

52. *Nashville Union*, Apr. 6, 1844; *Clarksville Jeffersonian*, June 1, 1844; [Tennessee] Democratic Central Committee, *Annexation of Texas*, 6.

53. *Nashville Republican Banner*, May 6, 1844; *Nashville Union*, May 9 and 14, 1844; *Memphis Appeal*, May 10, 1844; Robert Armstrong to Andrew Jackson, May 8, 1844, Jackson Papers, LC.

54. Leonard P. Cheatham to James K. Polk, May 7, 1844, on p. 7:124; Polk to Cave Johnson, May 13, 1844, on p. 7:135; and Robert Armstrong to Polk, May 7, [1844], on p. 7:123, all in Weaver et al., *Correspondence of James K. Polk*. Armstrong to Andrew Jackson, June 1, 1844, Jackson Papers, LC. Jackson to Francis Preston Blair, May 7, 1844, John P. Heiss Papers, THS.

55. James K. Polk to Cave Johnson, May 15, 1844, in Weaver et al., *Correspondence of James K. Polk*, 7:139-40; Sellers, *James K. Polk: Continentalist*, 67-107.

56. *Clarksville Jeffersonian*, June 8, 1844; *Knoxville Argus*, June 12, 1844; James K. Polk to William L. Marcy, June 9, 1844, in p. 7:330, and Robert Armstrong to Polk, June 4, [1844], on p. 7:197, both in Weaver et al., *Correspondence of James K. Polk*; A. O. P. Nicholson to Andrew Johnson, July 23, 1844, in Graf and Haskins, *Papers of Andrew Johnson*, 1:173; *Nashville Union*, June 8, July 20, 1844; *Memphis Appeal*, June 14, 1844.

57. Daniel Kenney to James K. Polk, Sept. 18, 1844, James K. Polk Papers, LC; *Nashville Union*, Feb. 10, May 23, June 13, 1844; *Clarksville Jeffersonian*, July 13, Sept. 14, Nov. 2, 1844; *Memphis Appeal*, June 14, 1844.

58. *Nashville Union*, Apr. 20, 1844.

59. Alexander O. Anderson, *The Letter of Alexander Anderson, of Tennessee, in Reply to the Committee of Invitation to Attend a Dinner Given by the Democracy of Maury, Tennessee, on the 13th July to the Delegation from that State to the National Convention* (n.p., 1844), 12; *Nashville Union*, May 28, 1844; *Memphis Appeal*, May 17, 1844. See also Kenneth S. Greenberg, *Masters and Statesmen: The Political Culture of American Slavery* (Baltimore, Md.: Johns Hopkins Univ. Press, 1985), 107-23.

60. *Columbia Tennessee Democrat*, July 24, 1844; *Nashville Union*, May 18, 21, June 20, 1844; *Knoxville Argus*, July 17, 1844; *Memphis Appeal*, May 17, 1844.

61. Andrew J. Donelson to James K. Polk, Nov. 6, 1844, Polk Papers, LC; *Memphis Appeal*, May 24, 1844; *Knoxville Argus*, Oct. 30, 1844.

62. *Columbia Tennessee Democrat*, July 24, 1844.

63. *Clarksville Jeffersonian*, Nov. 30, 1844; Anderson, *Letter of Anderson to Maury Committee*, 23; [Tennessee] Democratic Central Committee, *Annexation of Texas*, 6; *Nashville Union*, May 21, July 20, Nov. 1, 1844; *Knoxville Argus*, July 17, 1844; *Memphis Appeal*, Apr. 5, May 24, Aug. 30, 1844.

64. Anderson, *Letter of Anderson to Maury Committee*, 23.

65. [Tennessee] Democratic Central Committee, *Annexation of Texas*, 6; *Nashville Union*, June 18, July 2, Aug. 6, Sept. 6, 1844; *Columbia Tennessee Democrat*, July 24, 1844.

66. Aaron V. Brown to Samuel H. Laughlin, Dec. 8, 1843, Miscellaneous File, THS; James Campbell to [David Campbell], Dec. 13, 1843, and Ephraim H. Foster to William B. Campbell, Apr. 6, 1844, both in Campbell Papers, DU; William B. Campbell to Adam Ferguson, May 1, 1842, Ferguson Papers, TSLA; *Nashville Republican Banner*, Mar. 29, 1844.

67. *Nashville Whig*, Mar. 28, Apr. 23, 30, 1844; *Nashville Republican Banner*, Mar. 27, 1844; *Jonesborough Whig*, May 1, 1844; James Campbell to William B. Campbell, Apr. 8 and 14, 1844, in Campbell Papers, DU. On the national Whig party's opposition to annexation and expansion, see Michael A. Morrison, "Westward the Curse of Empire: Texas Annexation and the American Whig Party," *Journal of the Early Republic* 10 (Summer 1990): 221-49; and Michael A. Morrison, "'NEW TERRITORY versus NO TERRITORY': The Whig Party and the Politics of Western Expansion, 1846-1848," *Western Historical Quarterly* 23 (Feb. 1992): 25-51.

68. *Nashville Whig*, May 7, June 22, 1844; *Nashville Republican Banner*, Mar. 13, 1844. Whigs bolstered Clay's arguments against annexation by circulating copies of a speech against Tyler's treaty, delivered in the Senate by the Democrat Thomas Hart Benton of Missouri; after the election, Jackson reported that the state's Democratic leaders concluded that this speech "lost us in Tennessee at least 3,000 votes"; Andrew Jackson to Amos Kendall, Nov. 28, 1844, Jackson Papers, LC. See also Adam Huntsman to Samuel H. Laughlin, July 6, 1844, Laughlin Papers, THS.

69. *Nashville Whig*, June 1, 1844.

70. *Jonesborough Whig*, July 3, 10, 1844; *Nashville Republican Banner*, May 8, Oct. 14, 1844; *Nashville Whig*, May 7, June 6, 1844.

71. *Nashville Republican Banner,* June 7, 1844.
72. *Nashville Whig,* June 8, 1844; *Nashville Republican Banner,* June 10, 1844; William G. Brownlow to Thomas A. R. Nelson, Sept. 16, 1844, Nelson Papers, McClung.
73. *Nashville Republican Banner,* June 10, 1844.
74. *Nashville Whig,* Sept. 17, Oct. 17, 1844; *Nashville Republican Banner,* Sept. 6, 1844; *Jonesborough Whig,* June 12, 19, 1844.
75. William B. Campbell to David Campbell, Aug. 14, 1844, Campbell Papers, DU; *Nashville Whig,* June 18, 1844; *Nashville Republican Banner,* June 14, 1844.
76. *Nashville Republican Banner,* July 6, Aug. 5, 1844; *Nashville Whig,* July 16, 20, 1844; *Jonesborough Whig,* June 26, Aug. 7, 1844.
77. *Nashville Whig,* July 16, 1844; *Nashville Republican Banner,* June 26, 28, 1844; *Jonesborough Whig,* June 26, July 10, 1844; William B. Campbell to David Campbell, July 9, 1844, Campbell Papers, DU.
78. *Nashville Whig,* July 2, 9, 1844; *Nashville Republican Banner,* June 26, 1844.
79. *Nashville Whig,* July 16, Sept. 10, 1844; *Nashville Republican Banner,* July 3, 1844.
80. James K. Polk to Andrew J. Donelson, June 26, 1844, on p. 7:286, and Cave Johnson to Polk, June 10, 1844, on p. 7:228, both in Weaver et al., *Correspondence of James K. Polk. Nashville Union,* June 27, 29; July 2, 4, 6, 11, 16; Aug. 17, 19, 1844. *Clarksville Jeffersonian,* Aug. 17, 1844.
81. *Knoxville Argus,* July 17, 1844; *Nashville Union,* June 29, 1844; *Memphis Appeal,* July 30, 1844.
82. *Jonesborough Whig,* June 12, Aug. 21, 28, 1844; *Nashville Republican Banner,* Aug. 2, Sept. 2, 1844; Robert B. Everett, "James K. Polk and the Election of 1844 in Tennessee," West Tennessee Historical Society *Papers* 16 (1962): 5-28.
83. Julius W. Blackwell to James K. Polk, Nov. 19, 1844; Samuel Rhea to Polk, Nov. 21, 1844; and Jeremiah G. Harris to Polk, Dec. 4, 1844, all in Polk Papers, LC. *Nashville Union,* Nov. 19, 1844. The "Coons" alluded to by Blackwell are raccoons, which had become the symbol of the Whig party.
84. *Jonesborough Whig,* Nov. 20, 1844; *Nashville Republican Banner,* Nov. 8, 18, 1844. Wayne Cutler, currently editor of Polk's papers, observes: "Fortunately for the Democrats in 1844, they did not need Tennessee's electoral vote, although the vote count there would have been hotly contested had New York gone Whig"; in Weaver et al., *Correspondence of James K. Polk,* 8:xvi.
85. *Congressional Globe,* 28th Cong., 2d sess., 127-30; *Nashville Republican Banner,* Jan. 31, Feb. 7, May 23, 1845; *Nashville Whig,* Feb. 27, Mar. 30, 1845; *Nashville Union,* Apr. 12, Aug. 3, 1845; *Memphis Appeal,* July 25, 1845. J. H. Thompson to James K. Polk, Mar. 20, 1845, and Austin Miller to Polk, Apr. 15, 1845, both in Polk Papers, LC. William B. Campbell to David Campbell, Jan. 16, 1845; Ephraim H. Foster to David Campbell, Jan. 30, 1845; and Joseph H. Peyton to William B. Campbell, Feb. 16, 1845, all in Campbell

Notes to pages 138-43   313

Papers, DU. William W. Freehling, *The Road to Disunion: Secessionists at Bay, 1776-1854* (New York: Oxford Univ. Press, 1990), 440-48. Foster's and Brown's resolutions called for Texas's admission on the conditions that (1) Texas's boundary would be adjusted before its admission, (2) the United States would not assume Texas's debt, and (3) the status of slavery in any new state formed out of Texas's territory would be determined by extending the Missouri Compromise line through Texas.

86. *Nashville Union*, Jan. 30, Feb. 18, 27, Mar. 18, 22, Aug. 2, 1845; *Memphis Appeal*, Apr. 15, May 2, July 25, 1845; *Clarksville Jeffersonian*, Mar. 29, 1845; *Jonesborough Whig*, Apr. 16, July 16, 1845. Adam Huntsman to James K. Polk, Nov. 17, [1844]; Levin H. Coe to Polk, Apr. 16, 1845; and Alfred Balch to Polk, Apr. 26, 1845, all in Polk Papers, LC. Andrew Jackson to Francis Preston Blair, Mar. 10, 1845, Jackson Papers, LC. Frederick P. Stanton was the Democratic candidate for Congress for the 11th District.

87. John Catron to James K. Polk, May 20, 1845, and Philip B. Glenn to Polk, July 12, 1845, both in Polk Papers, LC; *Nashville Republican Banner*, Oct. 28, 1844; July 28, Aug. 15, 1845; *Nashville Whig*, July 3, Aug. 16, 1845; *Nashville Union*, Aug. 9, 1845; *Knoxville Argus*, Mar. 1, 29, 1843.

88. Alfred Balch to James K. Polk, Sept. 13, 1845; David Craighead to Polk, Aug. 26, 1845; and William Hunter to Polk, Aug. 12, 1845; all in Polk Papers, LC.

Chapter 6. The Politics of Slavery: Abolitionists, Nullifiers, and Compromise, 1846-1851

1. Abraham Caruthers to William B. Campbell, Mar. 18, 1847, Campbell Papers, DU.

2. Adam Ferguson to Duncan and Mrs. McNab, Feb. 20, 1846, Ferguson Papers, TSLA; *Jonesborough Whig*, Feb. 24, 1847; Winters, "Agricultural Ladder in Southern Agriculture," 36-52.

3. Aaron V. Brown to James K. Polk, Oct. 7, 1845; C. Connor to Polk, Oct. 22, 1845; Alfred Balch to Polk, Dec. 14, 1845; and Andrew J. Donelson to Polk, Jan. 27, 1846, all in Polk Papers, LC. *Nashville Union*, Sept. 18, 1845. *Clarksville Jeffersonian*, Sept. 20, 1845.

4. See, e.g., William B. Campbell to David Campbell, Aug. 7, 1848, Campbell Papers, DU; and William H. Polk to James K. Polk, Oct. 3, 1848, Polk Papers, LC.

5. John W. Childress to Sarah C. Polk, July 26, 1846; Aaron V. Brown to James K. Polk, Dec. 15, 1846; and S. H. Laughlin to Polk, Feb. 5, 1847, all in Polk Papers, LC. Andrew Johnson to Blackston McDaniel, July 22, 1846, on pp. 1:331-33, and Johnson to McDaniel, Feb. 16, 1847, on pp. 1:387-88, both in Graf and Haskins, *Papers of Andrew Johnson*. *Clarksville Jeffersonian*, Feb. 27, 1847. Paul H. Bergeron, *The Presidency of James K. Polk* (Lawrence: Univ. Press of Kansas, 1987), 137-70.

6. *Nashville Union*, Oct. 25, 28, Nov. 1, 4, 11, 14, 18, 1845; *Nashville Republican Banner*, Oct. 29, 1845; *Nashville Whig*, Dec. 18, 20, 1845. James

K. Polk to Aaron V. Brown, Sept. 15, 1845; Brown to Polk, Oct. 16 and 27, 1845; [Thomas W. Bradley] to Polk, Oct. 17, 1845; Gideon J. Pillow to Polk, Oct. 23, 1845; Harvey M. Watterson to Polk, Nov. 3, 1845; and Samuel H. Laughlin to Polk, Nov. 11, 1845, and Jan. 2, [1846], all in Polk Papers, LC. Jeptha Fowlkes to A. O. P. Nicholson, Jan. 9, 1848, Alfred Osborne Pope Nicholson Correspondence, NYHS. *House Journal* (1845-46), 95-96; *Senate Journal* (1845-46), 140.

7. Frederick P. Stanton to James K. Polk, Mar. 20, 1847, and James Walker to Polk, June 16, 1847, both in Polk Papers, LC; Cave Johnson to Arthur R. Crozier, July 5, 1847, Arthur R. Crozier Papers, TSLA; *Nashville Union*, Apr. 13, 1847.

8. *Nashville Union*, Feb. 28, June 20, 1846; Alfred Balch to James K. Polk, June [26], 1846, and Alexander O. Anderson to Polk, June 30, 1846, both in Polk Papers, LC.

9. *Clarksville Jeffersonian*, May 16, 1846. *Nashville Union*, May 19, May 21, June 2, 1846; Nov. 23, 1847. James Walker to James K. Polk, May 29, 1846, and Levin H. Coe to Polk, June 16, 1846, both in Polk Papers, LC. On the origins and course of the Mexican War, see K. Jack Bauer, *The Mexican War, 1846-1848* (New York: Macmillan, 1974); Sellers, *James K. Polk: Continentalist*, 398-444; Bergeron, *Presidency of James K. Polk*, 65-111.

10. *Nashville Union*, Jan. 3, 1846; June 3, 30, Nov. 23, 1847; Jan. 15, 1848; Mar. 30, 1849. Blackston McDaniel to Andrew Johnson, Jan. 28, 1848, in Graf and Haskins, *Papers of Andrew Johnson*, 1:409.

11. *Nashville Union*, Apr. 12, May 5, July 7, 1847; *Memphis Appeal*, June 26, 1846; Jan. 8, Mar. 12, and Sept. 2, 1847; *Clarksville Jeffersonian*, May 30, 1846; W. M. Cox to Arthur Crozier, June 30, 1847, Crozier Papers, TSLA.

12. *Nashville Republican Banner*, May 11, 29, 1846; *Nashville Whig*, May 12, 21, 1846; *Memphis Eagle*, May 7, 1846; Jan. 15, 1847; *Jonesborough Whig*, Jan. 13, 1847.

13. *Nashville Republican Banner*, May 22, 1846; Jan. 15, 1847; *Jonesborough Whig*, July 14, Aug. 11, 1847.

14. *Nashville Republican Banner*, Mar. 5, 1847; Samuel M. Fite to William B. Campbell, Dec. 30, 1846, Campbell Papers, DU.

15. *Nashville Republican Banner*, Apr. 6, 1846; May 5, 1847. *Jonesborough Whig*, Sept. 9, 1846. *Memphis Eagle*, July 11, 1846; Apr. 7, 1847; May 17, 1848. Samuel M. Fite to William B. Campbell, Aug. 13, 1846, Campbell Papers, DU. Edmund Cooper to William F. Cooper, Mar. 26, 1847, Cooper Papers, TSLA.

16. *Nashville Republican Banner*, Jan. 8, June 2, Aug. 16, 1847. *Nashville Whig*, Oct. 6 and 10, 1846; Dec. 22, 1846; May 6, 1847. *Memphis Enquirer*, Jan. 26, Feb. 11, 1848.

17. *Athens Post*, Oct. 13, 27, 1848. *Nashville Republican Banner*, Apr. 19, June 7, 21, July 19, Sept. 24, Oct. 13, 1847; Sept. 6, 1848. *Nashville Whig*, Apr. 22, July 10, 1847. *Memphis Eagle*, Sept. 4, 1847. K. Jack Bauer, *Zachary Taylor: Soldier, Planter, Statesman of the Old Southwest* (Baton Rouge: Louisiana State Univ. Press, 1985), 215-55.

18. *Nashville Republican Banner,* Aug. 10, Sept. 2, 1846; Jan. 8, Mar. 8, May 12, July 23, 1847. *Nashville Whig,* June 13, Oct. 28, 1848. *Memphis Eagle,* June 8, 1848.

19. *Nashville Republican Banner,* Aug. 17 and 31, 1846. Benjamin R. Owen to William B. Campbell, Oct. 18, 1846; James Campbell to [David Campbell], Nov. 7, 1846; Meredith P. Gentry to William B. Campbell, Nov. 24, 1846; and William B. Campbell to David Campbell, Jan. 23, 1848, all in Campbell Papers, DU. Daniel Graham to James K. Polk, Apr. 13, 1847, Polk Papers, LC.

20. *Nashville Republican Banner,* June 11, 21, Aug. 16, 1847; *Nashville Whig,* Sept. 2, 1847; *Memphis Eagle,* Apr. 13, May 17, 1847; *Jonesborough Whig,* Aug. 4, 1847; Parks, *John Bell of Tennessee,* 229-33.

21. *House Journal* (1847-48), 449; *Senate Journal* (1847-48), 291; John Bell to William B. Campbell, Dec. 23, 1847, Campbell Papers, DU; Walton, "A Matter of Timing," 141-42; Parks, *John Bell of Tennessee,* 211-16. Senator Spencer Jarnigan lost support among Whigs when he provided the deciding vote in the Senate behind the passage of the Tariff of 1846; at the opening of the legislative session, Jarnigan destroyed any prospect for reelection by Democratic votes, when he stated that he would return to the Senate only if he were elected by Whigs; see *Nashville Republican Banner,* Sept. 13, 1847; *Nashville Union,* Aug. 4, 6, 18, 1846; Sept. 15, 1847; Gustavus A. Henry to Robert L. Caruthers, Sept. 15, 1847, Caruthers Papers, SHC; Aaron V. Brown to James K. Polk, Sept. 17, 1847, Polk Papers, LC.

22. William B. Campbell to David Campbell, Jan. 23 and May 29, 1848; Meredith P. Gentry to William B. Campbell, Apr. 18, 1848; and John Bell to William B. Campbell, May 23, 1848, all in Campbell Papers, DU. Marion Henry to Gustavus A. Henry, Jan. 28, 1848, Gustavus A. Henry Papers, SHC. Henry Cooper to [William F. Cooper], May 28, 1848, Cooper Papers, TSLA. *Nashville Republican Banner,* Jan. 7; Mar. 8, 20, 24, 31; Apr. 10; May 12; July 3; Aug. 9, 1848. *Nashville Whig,* Oct. 21, 1847; Jan. 4, 1848; Feb. 12, 19, 26, 1848; Mar. 18, 25, 30, 1848; Apr. 27, 1848; May 11, 16, 1848. *Memphis Eagle,* Jan. 7 and 13, Feb. 18 and 21, Apr. 29, May 22, June 16, 1848.

23. On Bell's and Gentry's control of Whig patronage in Tennessee, see Balie Peyton to Gustavus A. Henry, Apr. 14, 1849, Henry Papers, SHC; Marcus B. Winchester to John S. Claybrooke, Apr. 18, 1849, Claybrooke-Overton Papers, THS; William G. Brownlow to Thomas A. R. Nelson, Mar. 19, 1849, Nelson Papers, McClung; Andrew Ewing to [Ephraim H. Foster], July 31, 1850, Foster-Woods Papers, TSLA; Parks, *John Bell of Tennessee,* 233-39.

24. Daniel Graham to James K. Polk, May 5, 1847, Polk Papers, LC; *Nashville Republican Banner,* May 17, 1847; *Nashville Union,* Sept. 4, 1847; *Nashville Whig,* May 11, 1847. Aaron Brown also suffered from public dissatisfaction concerning his delay in organizing the state's volunteers for service in the Mexican War, a delay he justified by explaining that it had been necessary to insure the equal participation of East and West Tennesseans along with volunteers from Middle Tennessee. See *Nashville Union,* May 28, June 13, Sept. 19, 1846; *Nashville Republican Banner,* June 12, 1846, Apr. 28, 1847;

Memphis Eagle, June 4 and 12, 1846; *Memphis Appeal,* May 29 and June 19, 1846; Robert J. Nelson to James K. Polk, June 3, 1846, and Aaron V. Brown to Polk, June 10, 1846, both in Polk Papers, LC.

25. R. W. Gardner to James K. Polk, Aug. 14, 1847, and Alfred Balch to Polk, Sept. 3, 1847, both in Polk Papers, LC; Lucien B. Chase to Arthur R. Crozier, Crozier Papers, TSLA; *Nashville Union,* Aug. 13, 1847.

26. *Nashville Union,* Apr. 21 and 27, May 10 and 11, June 14, 1847; June 10, 1848. *Nashville American,* Oct. 12, Nov. 7, 1848. *Clarksville Jeffersonian,* Oct. 23, 1847. *Memphis Appeal,* July 27, Sept. 28, 1847, Aug. 25, 1848.

27. *Nashville American,* Apr. 27, May 30, June 10, Oct. 12, Nov. 7, 1848; *Nashville Union,* May 1 and 29, July 6, 1848; *Memphis Appeal,* June 16, 17, 28, 1848; Alfred Balch to James K. Polk, Oct. 25, 1847, Polk Papers, LC; S. E. Benson to A. O. P. Nicholson, Apr. 15, 1848, Nicholson Papers, NYHS; Andrew Johnson to Blackston McDaniel, Mar. 24, 1848, on p. 1:417, and Johnson to A. O. P. Nicholson, May 14, 1848, on pp. 1:424-26, both in Graf and Haskins, *Papers of Andrew Johnson;* Richard D. Currey to Andrew J. Donelson and Elizabeth Donelson, Jan. 28, 1848, Yeatman-Polk Collection, TSLA; Cave Johnson to James Buchanan, Oct. 14, 1849, James Buchanan Papers, HSP.

28. *Nashville Republican Banner,* Aug. 4, 25; Sept. 1, 6, 27; Nov. 15, 1848. *Memphis Enquirer,* June 10, 24, 1848. *Nashville Whig,* Mar. 7, July 8 and 26, Sept. 28, 1848. *Memphis Eagle,* Feb. 14, May 30, 1848.

29. *Jonesborough Whig,* May 26, 1847; May 10, June 21, 1848. Joseph L. Williams to James K. Polk, Aug. 23, 1847, and Nov. 3 and 14, 1848; and Aaron V. Brown to Polk, Sept. 17, 1847, all in Polk Papers, LC.

30. See, for example: *Nashville Republican Banner,* Jan. 10, 1838; Jan. 3 and July 17, 1839; July 9, 1847; *Nashville Whig,* Sept. 21, 1838; *Nashville Union,* Jan. 17 and Mar. 4, 1837; Dec. 31, 1838; Oct. 6, 1846; *Memphis Appeal,* Oct. 16 and Nov. 13, 1846; A. O. P. Nicholson to James K. Polk, Jan. 31, 1836, in Weaver et al., *Correspondence of James K. Polk,* 3:479.

31. *Memphis Eagle,* Jan. 26, 1847; *Nashville Whig,* Mar. 2, 1847; *Nashville Union,* Mar. 6 and 9, Oct. 6, 1847; *Memphis Appeal,* Apr. 9, 1847; *Nashville Republican Banner,* Aug. 27, 1847.

32. *Nashville Union,* Oct. 6, 1847; Aaron V. Brown, *Speeches, Congressional and Political,* 298; *Nashville Republican Banner,* Feb. 25, 1848; Bergeron, *Presidency of James K. Polk,* 95-106.

33. *Memphis Eagle,* July 22 and 29, 1847; *Memphis Enquirer,* Mar. 7 and May 9, 1849; *Nashville Union,* July 7, 1849; *Memphis Appeal,* Aug. 18 and Sept. 7, 1847.

34. *Nashville Union,* Dec. 2, 1847; May 6, 1848; June 12, 15, 27, 1848; July 17, Aug. 9, Sept. 8, Oct. 18, 1848. *Nashville American,* June 11 and 23, Sept. 9, 1848. *Memphis Appeal,* Sept. 7, 1847; June 13, July 30, Nov. 2, Nov. 12, 1848. *Clarksville Jeffersonian,* Dec. 25, 1847; July 4, 1848.

35. *Nashville Union,* Jan. 15, 21; Mar. 25; May 3; June 1, 2, 5; July 31; Oct. 26, 1848. *Nashville American,* July 1, 1848. *Memphis Appeal,* June 18, 1848.

36. *Nashville Republican Banner,* Aug. 16, 28, Sept. 6, 8, 13, and 18, 1848; *Memphis Eagle,* Sept. 18, 1848. Democrats justified their party's sup-

port for the Oregon bill by arguing that the bill's provisions were "not inconsistent" with the prohibition on slavery contained in the Missouri Compromise of 1820; see *Nashville Union*, Aug. 24, 1848.

37. *Athens Post*, Nov. 3, 1848; *Nashville Republican Banner*, July 5 and Sept. 6 and 15, 1848; *Nashville Whig*, June 1, 3, 10, 17, 27, Sept. 14, 1848; *Memphis Eagle*, June 14, 17, 1848; *Jonesborough Whig*, July 26, Aug. 23, 1848.

38. *Jonesborough Whig*, Oct. 11, 1848; *Nashville Republican Banner*, Oct. 22, Nov. 1, 1847; Mar. 15, July 31, Dec. 1, 1848; *Memphis Eagle*, Aug. 26, June 8, 1848; *Memphis Enquirer*, Jan. 1, 1848.

39. *Jonesborough Whig*, July 5, 1848; *Athens Post*, Nov. 3, 1848; *Memphis Eagle*, July 21, Oct. 25, 1848; *Memphis Enquirer*, June 20 and 22, 1848; *Nashville Whig*, June 15, 1848.

40. David M. Potter, *The Impending Crisis, 1848-1861* (New York: Harper and Row, 1976), 83-86; John Niven, *John C. Calhoun and the Price of Union: A Biography* (Baton Rouge: Louisiana State Univ. Press, 1988), 323-37; Richard K. Crallé, ed., *The Works of John C. Calhoun* (New York: D. Appleton and Co., 1855), 6:290-313.

41. *Nashville Republican Banner*, Dec. 4, 1848; Feb. 7, 1849; *Nashville Whig*, Jan. 30, 1849; *Athens Post*, Dec. 22, 1848; Feb. 9, 1849; *Memphis Eagle*, Feb. 6, 1849; *Clarksville Jeffersonian*, Feb. 13, 1849.

42. Aaron V. Brown to James K. Polk, Sept. 10, 1847, and July 12, 1848; and Joseph L. Williams to Polk, Nov. 14, 1848, all in Polk Papers, LC; Brown to A. O. P. Nicholson, April 5, 1849, Nicholson Papers, NYHS; Brown to Gideon J. Pillow, Jan. 20, 1850, Aaron Venable Brown Papers, TSLA.

43. *Nashville Union*, Jan. 8, Feb. 20 and 28, Mar. 12, Apr. 9 and 21, 1849; *Nashville American*, Feb. 18, Mar. 10 and 31, Apr. 8, 1849; *Clarksville Jeffersonian*, July 3, 1849; *Athens Post*, Apr. 27, 1849; Neill S. Brown to John Bell, Mar. 27, 1849, John Bell Collection, LC. Unfortunately, the issues of the *Memphis Appeal* between Nov. 25, 1848, and Jan. 2, 1851, are not extant; nevertheless, contemporary testimony provides sufficient evidence to conclude that, during that period, it was one of the state's leading Fire-Eater papers; see, e.g., *Nashville American*, Oct. 16, 1850.

44. *Nashville Union*, Apr. 20, 1849.

45. *Nashville Union*, Feb. 16, May 2 and 9, 1849; *Memphis Appeal*, July 27, 1848; *Nashville American*, Oct. 20, 1848; Jan. 19, 1849.

46. *Nashville Union*, May 3, July 12, 1849.

47. *Nashville Union*, Feb. 16, 1849.

48. *Nashville Union*, Apr. 26, May 3, July 18 and 24, Aug. 6, 1849; *Nashville American*, Jan. 19, 1849.

49. *Nashville Union*, Aug. 9, 1848; Jan. 5, Mar. 10, 21, 1849.

50. *Nashville Union*, Feb. 14, Apr. 20, 26, June 9, July 9, 24, Aug. 1, 1849.

51. *Nashville Union*, Apr. 23, May 5, 12, and 19, 1849; *Memphis Appeal*, May 13, 1851; *Nashville True Whig*, May 26, 1849; *Memphis Eagle*, May 15, 1849; *Nashville Republican Banner*, May 9, 1849.

52. *Nashville Union*, Apr. 26, May 21, June 9, July 23, 26, 1849; *Nashville American*, May 30, 1849.

53. *Nashville Union,* Apr. 21, 1849; *Nashville True Whig,* Apr. 21, May 17, 1849; *Nashville American,* May 22, June 7, July 11, Aug. 16, 1849; *Clarksville Jeffersonian,* May 15, July 24, 31, 1849.

54. Cave Johnson to James K. Polk, May 23, 1849, and Polk to Cave Johnson, May 28, 1849, both in Polk Papers, LC; Andrew Johnson to E. G. Eastman, May 27, 1849, in Graf and Haskins, *Papers of Andrew Johnson,* 1:509; Cave Johnson to James Buchanan, June 17, 1849, Buchanan Papers, HSP; *Nashville True Whig,* June 21, 1849.

55. *Nashville Republican Banner,* Jan. 5; Mar. 26; Apr. 24, 25, 28; May 4, 5, 18, 1849. *Nashville True Whig,* June 30, 1849. *Memphis Eagle,* May 26, 1849.

56. *Nashville Republican Banner,* Feb. 23, Apr. 25, 1849; *Nashville True Whig,* July 7, July 24, Oct. 2, 1849; *Memphis Eagle,* Mar. 14, Apr. 26, May 14, 28, June 15, 1849.

57. *Nashville Republican Banner,* Feb. 19, 23, 1849; *Nashville True Whig,* June 5, 1849; *Memphis Eagle,* Jan. 9, 10, 29, Apr. 25, 28, May 14, 1849.

58. *Jonesborough Whig,* Jan. 3, 1849; Edmund Dillahunty to George W. Gordon, July 21, 1849, Gordon and Avery Papers, TSLA; *Nashville Republican Banner,* Feb. 7, Apr. 21, May 12, 1849; *Nashville True Whig,* May 12, 15, June 5, 19, 21, 30, July 31, 1849; *Memphis Eagle,* Apr. 30, May 9, 11, 1849.

59. *Nashville Republican Banner,* Apr. 25, May 22, 1849; *Athens Post,* Jan. 18, July 27, 1849; *Nashville True Whig,* Apr. 26, May 19, 1849; *Memphis Eagle,* Jan. 31, May 26, June 8, 15, July 31, 1849. On the importance of Constitutional Unionism in antebellum political culture, see Peter B. Knupfer, *The Union As It Is: Constitutional Unionism and Sectional Compromise, 1787-1861* (Chapel Hill: Univ. of North Carolina Press, 1991).

60. *Memphis Enquirer,* Mar. 13, 22; Apr. 6, 26, 28; May 3, 4, 8, 9, 17, 19; June 6; July 24, 1849; *Memphis Eagle,* Mar. 12; Apr. 6, 30; June 1, 22, 23, 1849; *Nashville Union,* Mar. 21 and July 6 and 7, 1849; Cave Johnson to James Buchanan, June 17, 1849, Buchanan Papers, HSP. The 10th Congressional District included Dyer, Fayette, Hardeman, Haywood, Lauderdale, McNairy, Shelby, and Tipton counties.

61. *Nashville Republican Banner,* Apr. 26, May 9, 1849; *Nashville Union,* June 2, 7, 15; July 9; Aug. 1, 1849; *Nashville True Whig,* Apr. 28, May 22, 1849.

62. Ebenezer Alexander to Thomas A. R. Nelson, Feb. 1, 1849; John A. Wilds to Nelson, May 25, 1849; James C. Jones to Nelson, July 12, 1849; and William Wales to Nelson, July 12, 1849, all in Nelson Papers, McClung. Washington Barrow to William B. Campbell, Aug. 7, 1849, and William B. Campbell to David Campbell, Aug. 19, 1849, both in Campbell Papers, DU. *Jonesborough Whig,* Jan. 10, 1849; *Athens Post,* Apr. 20, June 22, 1849.

63. *Nashville Union,* Aug. 8, 22, 27; Oct. 12, 1849; *Memphis Enquirer,* Nov. 21, 1849; *Clarksville Jeffersonian,* Aug. 14, 1849; Washington Barrow to William B. Campbell, Aug. 7, 1849, Campbell Papers, DU; Cave Johnson to James Buchanan, Apr. 14, 1850, Buchanan Papers, HSP. In Middle Tennessee, in 16 counties with a slave population of more than 20%, Whig totals declined 11.94% from the 1848 tally, and in the 7 predominantly Whig counties with a

slave population of more than 20%, the total declined 14.23%. In West Tennessee, the total Whig vote declined by 7.64% from the presidential election, and the party's vote declined in every county except Decatur, Dyer, Lauderdale, McNairy, and Obion counties. In each of these categories, the Democratic vote in 1849 remained virtually the same as in 1848.

64. On the Crisis of 1850, see Holman Hamilton, *Prologue to Conflict: The Crisis and Compromise of 1850* (Lexington: Univ. Press of Kentucky, 1964); Potter, *Impending Crisis*, 63-120; Holt, *Political Crisis of the 1850s*, 69-99; Cooper, *South and the Politics of Slavery*, 269-321; and Freehling, *Road to Disunion*, 475-510. On the Nashville Convention and Tennessee's association with that assembly, see Thelma Jennings, *The Nashville Convention: Southern Movement for Unity, 1848-1851* (Memphis, Tenn.: Memphis State Univ. Press, 1980); Thelma Jennings, "Tennessee and the Nashville Conventions of 1850," *THQ* 30 (Spring 1971): 70-82; St. George L. Sioussat, "Tennessee, The Compromise of 1850, and the Nashville Convention," *Tennessee Historical Magazine* 4 (Dec. 1918): 215-47.

65. Cave Johnson to James Buchanan, Apr. 14, 1850, Buchanan Papers, HSP; *Nashville Union*, Dec. 22, 1849; Feb. 16, 1850; *Nashville Republican Banner*, Feb. 21, 1850; *Nashville True Whig*, Oct. 16, 1849; *Memphis Enquirer*, Dec. 18, 1849; Mar. 6, 1850; *Memphis Eagle*, Oct. 12, 1849.

66. *Nashville Union*, Dec. 22, 1849; Jan. 22, 23, and 26; Mar. 25; Apr. 17; May 16, 1850; *Nashville American*, Jan. 6 and 24; Feb. 15; Mar. 7, 1850; Andrew Ewing to Adam Ferguson, Jan. 24, 1850, Ferguson Papers, TSLA.

67. *Clarksville Jeffersonian*, Mar. 5, 1850.

68. William F. Cooper to J. Knox Walker, Apr. 7, 1850, letterbook, Cooper Papers, TSLA; *Memphis Eagle*, Mar. 29, 1850.

69. *Nashville Republican Banner*, Feb. 1, May 23, 1850; Jacob McGavock to Randall McGavock, May 31, 1850, Randall William McGavock Papers, TSLA; William B. Campbell to David Campbell, June 11, 1850, Campbell Papers, DU; *Nashville True Whig*, Feb. 14, 1850; *Nashville Union*, May 24, June 11, 1850; John Bell, *The Compromise Bill: Speech of Hon. John Bell, of Tennessee, in the Senate of the United States, July 3 and 5, 1850, on the Bill for the Admission of California into the Union, the Establishment of Territorial Governments for Utah and New Mexico, and Making Proposals to Texas for the Settlement of Her Northern and Western Boundaries* (Washington, D.C.: Congressional Globe Office, 1850), 9; Hamilton, *Prologue to Conflict*, 43-62.

70. *Nashville Republican Banner*, Feb. 9, 14, 19, 25, 28, and Mar. 2, 7, 1850; *Nashville True Whig*, Feb. 23, Mar. 14, 21, Apr. 20, May 16, 21, 23, 1850; *Memphis Eagle*, Mar. 9, Apr. 16, May 11, 1850; *Knoxville Whig*, Mar. 2, 1850.

71. *Knoxville Whig*, Mar. 16, 1850.

72. *Nashville Republican Banner*, Feb. 11, 20, 22, Mar. 12, Apr. 10, May 22, 28, 1850; *Nashville True Whig*, May 30, 1850; *Memphis Eagle*, Dec. 24, 1849; Feb. 6, Apr. 6, and May 15 and 27, 1850; *Knoxville Whig*, Mar. 2, 23, May 25, 1850; Meredith P. Gentry, *Speech of M. P. Gentry, of Tennessee, on*

the *Admission of California, Delivered in the House of Representatives, U.S., Monday, June 10, 1850* (Washington: Gideon and Co., 1850), 15; Philip Gaspard Stiver Perkins, *Speech of Mr. P. G. Stiver Perkins, of Williamson County, on the Resolutions of the Committee on Federal Relations* (Nashville: B. R. McKennie and Co., 1850), 33-35.

73. *Nashville Republican Banner,* Jan. 28, Feb. 2 and 26, 1850; *Nashville True Whig,* Feb. 14, 1850; *Athens Post,* Feb. 15, Mar. 1, and Nov. 8, 1850.

74. William F. Cooper to J. Knox Walker, Apr. 17, 1850, letterbook, Cooper Papers, TSLA; William B. Campbell to David Campbell, Apr. 10, 1850, Campbell Papers, DU; Cave Johnson to Andrew J. Donelson, May 10, 1850, Andrew Jackson Donelson Papers, LC; Cave Johnson to [James Buchanan], June 6, 1850, Buchanan Papers, HSP; *Nashville Union,* Feb. 19, 20, 22, 28, Mar. 1 and 6, 1850; *Nashville American,* Feb. 20 and 23, Mar. 21, June 19, 1850.

75. *Nashville Republican Banner,* June 3, 7, 10, 11, 15, 17, 25, and July 13, 1850.

76. *House Journal* (1849-50), 788-97; *Senate Journal* (1849-50), 690-91, 758-66; *Nashville Union,* Jan. 9, Feb. 20, Mar. 25, 1850.

77. *Memphis Eagle,* May 17 and 29, 1850; *Nashville Union,* Apr. 6, 8, 13; May 7, 9, 10, 11, 13, 14, 16, 17, 20, 21, 22, 29, 31; and June 4, 1850; *Nashville Republican Banner,* Apr. 5, 12, May 7, 1850; *Nashville True Whig,* Apr. 6, May 4, 7, 9, 1850. Thelma Jennings identified only two Whigs and one "probable Whig" in the state's delegation; see Jennings, *Nashville Convention,* 233-50.

78. *Nashville Republican Banner,* May 14, June 19, July 18, 1850; *Nashville True Whig,* Apr. 18, May 11 and 14, 1850; Cave Johnson to James Buchanan, Jan. 20, 1850, Buchanan Papers, HSP.

79. *Nashville American,* June 7 and 13, 1850; William F. Cooper to David R. Arnell, June 10, 1850, letterbook, Cooper Papers, TSLA; *Nashville Republican Banner,* June 26, 1850; *Nashville Union,* June 13, 1850; Aaron V. Brown, *Speeches, Congressional and Political,* 331-45; Jennings, *Nashville Convention,* 135-66; Eric H. Walther, *The Fire-Eaters* (Baton Rouge: Louisiana State Univ. Press, 1992), 43-46, 138-41.

80. *Memphis Eagle,* June 18 and 19, 1850; *Nashville Republican Banner,* June 17, 1850; *Nashville True Whig,* June 18 and 20, 1850.

81. *Nashville Union,* July 3 and 4, 1850; *Nashville Republican Banner,* July 27, Aug. 5, 1850; *Nashville True Whig,* July 4 and 27, 1850.

82. *Nashville Union,* July 11, 22, 29, Aug. 5, Sept. 2, 1850; Cave Johnson to James Buchanan, Aug. 10, 1850, Buchanan Papers, HSP.

83. *Nashville American,* Aug. 2, 1850; *Nashville Union,* Sept. 6, 9, 28, 1850; Jan. 28, 1851; *Nashville Republican Banner,* July 30, 1850; Sept. 27, 1851; Cave Johnson to [James Buchanan], Sept. 20, 1850, Buchanan Papers, HSP. The division among Democrats was one of emphasis rather than a separation into clearly defined factions. Though contemporaries recognized the different opinions and used several different designations to identify them, they agreed upon no generally accepted labels to distinguish the Democratic wings; for conve-

nience, the following paragraphs will use the terms "Unionist" and "Southern Rights" to distinguish between the two Democratic positions.

84. *Nashville Republican Banner*, Aug. 6 and 22, 1850; *Nashville True Whig*, Aug. 10, 1850; *Nashville Union*, Aug. 29, 1850; *Knoxville Whig*, Aug. 3, 1850.

85. Hamilton, *Prologue to Conflict*, 133-50, 195-200.

86. *Nashville American*, Sept. 13, Oct. 5, 1850; *Nashville Union*, Sept. 17, 1850; *Nashville True Whig*, Sept. 24, 1850; *Nashville Republican Banner*, Sept. 24 and 25, 1850; J. J. Burnett to William B. Campbell, Oct. 14, 1850, Campbell Papers, DU.

87. *Nashville Republican Banner*, Sept. 3, 12, 14, 16; and Oct. 1, 3, 10, 1850; *Nashville True Whig*, Sept. 10; Oct. 5, 15, 19, 22; Dec. 3, 10, and 19, 1850; *Nashville Union*, Sept. 6, Oct. 18, Nov. 27, 1850; *Nashville American*, Sept. 15 and 19, Oct. 15, Nov. 24 and 28, 1850; *Clarksville Jeffersonian*, Oct. 2, 1850; *Knoxville Whig*, Oct. 12 and 20, Nov. 2, 1850; *Memphis Eagle*, Sept. 14 and 20, 1850; Cave Johnson to James Buchanan, Nov. 10 and Dec. 13, 1850, both in Buchanan Papers, HSP.

88. *Nashville Union*, Nov. 15, 19, 20, 1850; *Nashville Republican Banner*, Nov. 19, 1850; *Nashville True Whig*, Nov. 16 and 21, 1850; *Knoxville Whig*, Nov. 30, 1850; Jennings, *Nashville Convention*, 187-209.

89. *Nashville American*, Nov. 19, 20, 21, 1850; *Nashville Union*, Nov. 16 and 20, 1850; *Nashville True Whig*, Nov. 19, Dec. 31, 1850; Jennings, *Nashville Convention*, 196-97. Donelson claimed the right to move for a reconsideration because he had voted in favor of the resolutions, with the intent to move for reconsideration, at a meeting of the Tennessee delegation.

90. *Nashville Union*, Feb. 26, 1851; *Nashville American*, Oct. 6, 1850; Feb. 22, June 22, 1851; *Nashville Republican Banner*, Mar. 7 and 8, 1851; William F. Cooper to A. O. P. Nicholson, Dec. 14, 1850, Nicholson Papers, NYHS; William B. Campbell to David Campbell, Apr. 14, 1851, Campbell Papers, DU.

91. *Nashville Union*, Jan. 15, Feb. 27 and 28, 1851; *Nashville American*, Feb. 27, 1851; *Memphis Appeal*, Feb. 15, May 5, June 17, July 9, 1851.

92. *Nashville American*, Mar. 1; June 13, 22, 27; July 23, 1851; *Clarksville Jeffersonian*, Oct. 23, 1850, and Apr. 2, 1851; *Nashville Union*, Feb. 27; Mar. 10, 21, 26; Apr. 8; June 18; July 12 and 23, 1851; *Memphis Appeal*, Feb. 28; Mar. 13; Apr. 11, 14, 19; July 31, 1851.

93. Andrew Johnson to A. O. P. Nicholson, Apr. 16, 1851, in Graf and Haskins, *Papers of Andrew Johnson*, 1:614.

94. *Nashville Republican Banner*, May 2, 3, 16; July 4, 1851; *Nashville American*, May 29 and June 27, 1851; *Memphis Appeal*, Feb. 8, Mar. 4, June 2, 1851; Felix K. Zollicoffer to William B. Campbell, June 10, 1851, Campbell Papers, DU.

95. "Hugh Preston" to William B. Campbell, May 1, 1851; W. H. Sneed to Campbell, July 6, 1851; and Ebenezer Alexander to Campbell, July 15, 1851, all in Campbell Papers, DU; *Nashville True Whig*, May 29, 1851; *Clarksville Jeffersonian*, Apr. 12 and 30, June 18, 1851.

96. *Nashville American,* Jan. 22, Mar. 4, Apr. 20, May 17, June 17, 1851; *Nashville Republican Banner,* July 29, 1851; Andrew Johnson to A. O. P. Nicholson, May 11, 1851, in Graf and Haskins, *Papers of Andrew Johnson,* 1:615-16; Cave Johnson to [James Buchanan], Mar. 30 and July 21, 1851, both in Buchanan Papers, HSP. The 1st Congressional District included Carter, Cocke, Greene, Hawkins, Johnson, Sullivan, and Washington counties; Giles, Hardin, Hickman, Lawrence, Maury, and Wayne counties made up the 6th District.

97. *Nashville Republican Banner,* Jan. 29; Mar. 14, 17, 21; May 29; June 14, 23; Aug. 7, 1851; *Nashville True Whig,* Jan. 9, Feb. 1, Mar. 8, June 12, 1851; *Athens Post,* Apr. 11, May 30, 1851. John Bell to William B. Campbell, Jan. 25, 1851; Felix K. Zollicoffer to Campbell, Feb. 9, 1851; B. H. Sheppard to Campbell, Feb. 10, 1851; and George W. Gordon to Campbell, Feb. 12, 1851, all in Campbell Papers, DU.

98. *Nashville Republican Banner,* Mar. 10 and 13; Apr. 30; May 10, 21, 24; June 25; July 8, 11, 28; Aug. 7, 1851; *Athens Post,* July 4, Aug. 1, 1851; *Nashville True Whig,* Mar. 7, 17, 19; Apr. 25, 30; May 7; June 11, 1851; *Knoxville Whig,* Apr. 26, 1851; Samuel M. Fite to William B. Campbell, July 28, 1851, Campbell Papers, DU; Alexander, *Thomas A. R. Nelson,* 38-41.

99. *Clarksville Jeffersonian,* July 12, 1851; *Nashville American,* Feb. 27, 1851; *Nashville Union,* Apr. 19; May 1, 8, 9, 16; July 7, 17, 21, 1851; *Memphis Appeal,* Mar. 8; May 5, 6, 7, 10; June 7; July 10, 15, 1851; C. O. Faxon to William Trousdale, May 28, 1851, Trousdale Papers, THS.

100. *Nashville Union,* May 21, 1851.

101. *Nashville Republican Banner,* May 13 and 28, June 5, July 10, 1851; *Nashville True Whig,* Apr. 30; May 10, 12, 23; June 27 and 28; Aug. 5, 1851; *Knoxville Whig,* June 7, 21, July 26, 1851.

102. *Nashville Republican Banner,* Aug. 12, 1851; William B. Campbell to David Campbell, Aug. 9, 1851, Campbell Papers, DU; *Nashville True Whig,* Aug. 21, 1851.

103. Qtd. in *Nashville American,* Sept. 7, 1851; *Nashville Union,* Sept. 5, 1851; *Clarksville Jeffersonian,* Aug. 13, 1851. As in 1849, an incumbent governor's failure to promote assistance for internal improvements damaged his standing in East Tennessee. In his message to the legislature in 1849, Trousdale advocated aid for railroad projects only if Tennessee's credit would not suffer from an increase in the state debt, and he gave no support to a bill appropriating funds to railroads already under construction. Campbell, meanwhile, promised to support "every judicious and practicable means" that would secure the completion of railroads connecting East Tennessee to lines in Virginia and Georgia. *Nashville Republican Banner,* May 22 and 24, July 8, 1851; *Knoxville Whig,* Oct. 27, 1849; Mar. 29, 1851; White and Ash, *Messages of the Governors* 4:298-301; J. G. M. Ramsey to [William Trousdale], May 24, 1851, Trousdale Papers, TSLA. Felix K. Zollicoffer to William B. Campbell, Mar. 22, 1851; Alexander Williams to Campbell, June 17, 1851; and Frederick S. Heiskell to Campbell, June 1851, all in Campbell Papers, DU.

104. *Nashville Union,* Aug. 12 and 19, 1851; *Nashville American,* Aug. 20,

1851; *Athens Post,* Aug. 29, 1851; Cave Johnson to James Buchanan, Sept. 15, 1851, Buchanan Papers, HSP.

105. Potter, *Impending Crisis,* 121-30; Holt, *Political Crisis of the 1850s,* 91-94; Cooper, *South and the Politics of Slavery,* 304-10; Freehling, *Road to Disunion,* 515-35; Thornton, *Politics and Power in a Slave Society,* 186-99.

106. *Nashville Republican Banner,* Jan. 15, 1851; *Nashville Union,* Jan. 23, 1851; Charles Ready to John Bell, Jan. 3, 1851, and Thomas A. R. Nelson to Bell, Jan. 10, 1851, both in Bell Collection, LC.

107. *Nashville Union,* Aug. 15, Sept. 24, Oct. 17, 1850; *Nashville American,* Oct. 5, 26, 1850.

108. Edwin H. Ewing to William B. Campbell, Feb. 10, 1851, Campbell Papers, DU; *Clarksville Jeffersonian,* May 28, 1851.

109. Qtd. in *Nashville Republican Banner,* Aug. 28, 1850; July 2, 1851; Cave Johnson to James Buchanan, Jan. 20, 1850, Buchanan Papers, HSP.

110. *Nashville Republican Banner,* Nov. 2, 1850; Jan. 21, 1851; *Nashville American,* Sept. 1, 1850; Mar. 29, 1851; *Nashville Union,* Dec. 10, 1950; *Memphis Appeal,* Feb. 11, 13, May 14, 27, Aug. 25, 1851.

Chapter 7. The Politics of Union: The Triumph of Democracy, 1852-1857

1. White and Ash, *Messages of the Governors* 4:455-58; *Clarksville Jeffersonian,* Feb. 23, 1852; *Nashville Republican Banner,* May 25, 1853.

2. *Nashville Union,* Jan. 8, 10, Feb. 5, 10, 1852; *Nashville American,* Jan. 22, 25, 27, 1852; Feb. 8, 1853; Alexander Williams to Thomas A. R. Nelson, Oct. 11, 1851, Nelson Papers, McClung.

3. A. O. P. Nicholson to John P. Heiss, Nov. 30, 1851, Heiss Papers, THS; *Nashville Union,* Dec. 5, 1851.

4. Andrew Ewing to Andrew J. Donelson, Nov. 9, 1851, and Jan. 9, 1852; and Alfred Balch to Donelson, Dec. 28, 1851, all in Andrew Jackson Donelson Papers, LC. Cave Johnson to [James Buchanan], Dec. 11, 1851; and Jan. 10 and Nov. 18, 1852, all in Buchanan Papers, HSP. *Nashville Union,* Nov. 17, 1851; *Nashville American,* Nov. 18, 20, Dec. 2, 1851; Jan. 1, 7, Feb. 4, Mar. 4, 1852; Tricamo, "Tennessee Politics," 101-7.

5. Cave Johnson to [James Buchanan], Jan. 10, 1852, Buchanan Papers, HSP; A. O. P. Nicholson to John P. Heiss, Nov. 30, 1851, Heiss Papers, THS; *Nashville Union,* Jan. 12, 13, June 12, 1852; *Nashville American,* Jan. 13, 1852; *Nashville Republican Banner,* Jan. 9, 1852.

6. *Nashville Union,* Apr. 1, 17, June 15, 17, 1852; *Nashville American,* July 1, 16, 1852; *Memphis Appeal,* May 28, June 7, July 31, 1852.

7. Andrew Johnson to Sam Milligan, July 20, 1852, in Graf and Haskins, *Papers of Andrew Johnson,* 2:68; E. G. Eastman to Adam Ferguson, Sept., 1852, Ferguson Papers, TSLA; S. E. Benson to A. O. P. Nicholson, Sept. 2, 1852, Nicholson Papers, NYHS; Cave Johnson to James Buchanan, Nov. 18, 1852, Buchanan Papers, HSP.

8. *Nashville American,* June 3, Aug. 7, Oct. 16, 1852; *Nashville Union,* Dec. 11, 1851; Apr. 10, 23, June 8, 26, July 2, 21, Aug. 2, Oct. 20, 1852; *Clarksville Jeffersonian,* Sept. 1, 1852; *Memphis Appeal,* June 26, 1852.

9. *Nashville American,* July 16; Sept. 11; Aug. 1, 13, 21; Oct. 3, 1852; *Nashville Union,* Feb. 12; Apr. 21, 24, 28; May 4, 7, 10, 25, 31; June 16, 25, 26; July 6, 15; Aug. 27; Oct. 4, 1852; *Memphis Appeal,* June 24, 25, July 10, 1852; *Nashville Republican Banner,* Apr. 28, May 11, 1852.

10. *Nashville Union,* Mar. 27, June 28, 1852; *Nashville American,* May 2, 9, Oct. 6, 1852; *Clarksville Jeffersonian,* Mar. 9, 1852.

11. *Nashville Republican Banner,* Mar. 17; July 13, 16, 22; Aug. 7; Sept. 7, 8, 23, 1852; *Nashville True Whig,* May 28; July 1, 2, 10; Oct. 12, 22, 1852; *Athens Post,* Oct. 15, 1852; *Memphis Eagle and Enquirer,* June 25, 1852; *Nashville American,* Aug. 15, 23, 1852.

12. *Nashville Union,* July 15, 1852; *Nashville American,* Jan. 9, Mar. 26, May 8 and 28, Aug. 5, 1852; *Clarksville Jeffersonian,* July 28, 1852; *Memphis Appeal,* Mar. 2, July 28, 1852.

13. *Nashville American,* Nov. 6 and 10, 1852; *Nashville Union,* Nov. 11 and 14, 1852; *Nashville Republican Banner,* July 27, Aug. 7, Sept. 23, Nov. 8, 1852; Cave Johnson to James Buchanan, Nov. 18, 1852, Buchanan Papers, HSP.

14. *Nashville American,* Oct. 9, 1851; Andrew Johnson to Sam Milligan, July 20, 1852, in Graf and Haskins, *Papers of Andrew Johnson,* 2:69.

15. *Nashville American,* May 17, 1853.

16. *Athens Post,* May 6, 1852; *Nashville Republican Banner,* Apr. 29 and May 4, 1853; *Nashville True Whig,* Apr. 29, 1853; *Nashville Union,* Mar. 28, Apr. 25, 28, 1853; A. O. P. Nicholson to Franklin Pierce, Apr. 12, 1853, Nicholson Papers, NYHS.

17. *Nashville American,* Oct. 1, 1851; Apr. 24, 1852; *Nashville Union,* Sept. 13, 1852; *Clarksville Jeffersonian,* Oct. 9, 1852; *Memphis Appeal,* Oct. 2, 1852.

18. *Nashville American,* Apr. 23, 1853; *Nashville Union,* Apr. 28 and 30, May 3, 4, 11, 12, 1853; *Nashville Union and American,* May 20 and 31, June 3, 1853; *Memphis Appeal,* May 12, 1853; *Nashville Republican Banner,* May 4 and Aug. 3, 1853; S. R. Anderson to A. O. P. Nicholson, Aug. 16, 1853, Nicholson Papers, NYHS.

19. *Nashville Union,* May 10 and 14, 1853; *Nashville Union and American,* June 25, July 1, 6, 13, 1853; *Memphis Appeal,* May 25, June 2, 13, 1853; William B. Campbell to David Campbell, July 4, 1853, Campbell Papers, DU; Andrew Johnson to E. G. Eastman, May 27, 1849, on p. 1:509, and Johnson, "Speech at Shelbyville," on pp. 2:144-60, both in Graf and Haskins, *Papers of Andrew Johnson.*

20. *Clarksville Jeffersonian,* May 18, June 29, July 20, 1853; *Nashville Union,* May 9, 1853; *Nashville Union and American,* May 21, 25; June 3, 15, 18; July 14, 19, 1853.

21. *Nashville Union and American,* July 14, 1853.

22. *Nashville Republican Banner,* June 4, 9, 13, 15, 28, 29; July 6, 8, 9,

11-16, 22, 23, 26, 1853; *Nashville True Whig,* May 9, 17, 24; June 2, 11, 13, 22; July 6, 11, 13, 14, 16, 1853; *Knoxville Whig,* May 14 and July 2, 1853; *Athens Post,* June 17, 1853.

23. William B. Campbell to David Campbell, Mar. 23, 1853, Campbell Papers, DU; *Nashville Republican Banner,* Apr. 4, 14, 19, 25; May 5 and 26; June 3 and 11; July 4, 1853; *Nashville True Whig,* May 5, 10, 26; June 10; July 9, 18, 20, 23, 1853.

24. Each party carried 5 of the 10 congressional seats. Early during the first session of Congress, 1st District Democrat Brookins Campbell died, and the Whig Nathaniel G. Taylor won a special election, giving the Whigs a 6-4 advantage.

25. Andrew Johnson, Inaugural Address, qtd. in White and Ash, *Messages of the Governors* 4:527, 4:531; *Clarksville Jeffersonian,* Oct. 26, 1853; *Nashville True Whig,* Oct. 20, 1853.

26. William B. Campbell to David Campbell, Nov. 1, 1851, Campbell Papers, DU.

27. *Nashville American,* Nov. 21, 1851; *Nashville Republican Banner,* Nov. 24, Dec. 9, 1851; *Clarksville Jeffersonian,* Nov. 19, 1851; Gustavus A. Henry to Marion Henry, Nov. 21, 1851, Henry Papers, SHC; William B. Campbell to David Campbell, Nov. 2 and 20, 1851, both in Campbell Papers, DU; Tricamo, "Tennessee Politics," 88-93; Alexander, *Thomas A. R. Nelson,* 41-45.

28. T. Nixon Van Dyke to William B. Campbell, Dec. 5, 1851, Campbell Papers, DU; Gustavus A. Henry to Thomas A. R. Nelson, Feb. 10, 1852, Nelson Papers, McClung.

29. William B. Campbell to David Campbell, Feb. 15 and May 25, 1852; and Christopher H. Williams to William B. Campbell, Jan. 26, 1852, all in Campbell Papers, DU; Cave Johnson to James Buchanan, May 6, 1852, Buchanan Papers, HSP; *Knoxville Whig,* Mar. 20, 1852.

30. *Nashville Republican Banner,* Jan. 9 and 12; Feb. 3; May 12, 14, 25, 29; June 11, 1852; *Nashville True Whig,* Jan. 19, Feb. 14, May 21, June 1, 1852; *Memphis Eagle and Enquirer,* Feb. 24, Mar. 18 and 31, 1852; *Knoxville Whig,* Dec. 13, 1851; Mar. 20, 1852.

31. *Nashville Republican Banner,* Jan. 10, Feb. 5-7 and 9-12, 1852; *Nashville Union,* Feb. 11 and 12, 1852. Henry accepted and Nelson declined nomination as elector.

32. Christopher H. Williams to William B. Campbell, Feb. 19, 1852, and William Cullom to Campbell, Dec. 29, 1851, both in Campbell Papers, DU; Cullom to Robert L. Caruthers, Mar. 14, 1852, Caruthers Papers, SHC; James C. Jones to William T. Avery, Apr. 4, 1852, Gordon and Avery Papers, TSLA; John Bell to J. N. Clark, Dec. 27, 1851, TSLA; Andrew Johnson to David T. Patterson, Apr. 4, 1852, in Graf and Haskins, *Papers of Andrew Johnson,* 2:31; *Nashville Republican Banner,* Mar. 8, 1852; *Nashville Union,* Mar. 6, 1852.

33. Christopher H. Williams to William B. Campbell, Feb. 19 and Apr. 29, 1852; Meredith P. Gentry to Campbell, Mar. 24, 1852; and William Cullom to Campbell, Feb. 28, 1852, all in Campbell Papers, DU; Gustavus A. Henry to

Thomas A. R. Nelson, Feb. 10, 1852, Nelson Papers, McClung; *Knoxville Whig,* Mar. 13 and Apr. 10, 1852; *Nashville Union,* Apr. 15, 1852.

34. John Bell to William B. Campbell, Sept. 3, 1852, and William B. Campbell to David Campbell, June 2, 1852, both in Campbell Papers, DU; John Bell to [John S.] Russwurm, May 6, 1852, Russwurm Papers, TSLA; *Nashville Republican Banner,* May 26, July 7, 1852; *Nashville Union,* Apr. 22 and 30, July 7, 1852. The *Union* reported the 3 other Tennessee Whig delegates voting for Scott to be Felix Zollicoffer, John Netherland of Hawkins County, and Paulding Anderson of Wilson County.

35. Robert L. Caruthers to William B. Campbell, June 22, 1852; William B. Campbell to William Cullom, June 26, 1852; and William B. Campbell to David Campbell, June 29, 1852, all in Campbell Papers, DU; Marcus B. Winchester to John S. Claybrooke, June 28, 1852, Claybrooke-Overton Papers, THS; *Knoxville Whig,* July 3 and 10, Aug. 14, 1852; *Nashville Republican Banner,* June 23, July 14, 1852; *Nashville Union,* Apr. 10, June 28, 1852; *Nashville American,* June 22, 1852; *Clarksville Jeffersonian,* July 10, 1852; *Memphis Appeal,* Oct. 14, 1852.

36. Meredith P. Gentry, *Speech of Honorable M. P. Gentry, of Tennessee, Delivered in the House of Representatives, June 14, 1852* (Washington, D.C.: n.p., 1852), 4; John Bell to William B. Campbell, [1852], and Robert L. Caruthers to Campbell, Oct. 3, 1852, both in Campbell Papers, DU; Bell to H. C. Yeatman, Jan. 8, 1853, Yeatman-Polk Collection, TSLA; *Nashville Republican Banner,* Aug. 27 and Oct. 25, 1852; *Knoxville Whig,* Apr. 3, June 26, July 31, Aug. 28, 1852; *Nashville American,* Sept. 12 and 19, 1852; *Nashville Union,* Oct. 11, 19, 20, 21, 1852; *Clarksville Jeffersonian,* July 14, 1852.

37. *Nashville Republican Banner,* July 2, 10, 26; Aug. 5 and 11; Oct. 19, 1852; *Knoxville Whig,* Sept. 4, 1852; *Nashville American,* Sept. 15, Oct. 27, 1852.

38. Marcus B. Winchester to John S. Claybrooke, July [22], 1852, Claybrooke-Overton Papers, THS.

39. William G. Brownlow to Thomas A. R. Nelson, Jan. 18, 1853, Nelson Papers, McClung; [Gustavus A. Henry] to William B. Campbell, [Jan.], 1853, Campbell Papers, DU; *Nashville Republican Banner,* Feb. 3 and 26, 1853; *Nashville Union,* Jan. 7, 1853.

40. William B. Campbell to David Campbell, Aug. 17 and July 29, 1852, both in Campbell Papers, DU.

41. William B. Campbell to David Campbell, July 4, 1853; and Gustavus A. Henry to William B. Campbell, Aug. 26, 1853, both in Campbell Papers, DU; Henry to Thomas A. R. Nelson, Aug. 29, 1853, Nelson Papers, McClung; *Nashville Republican Banner,* Jan. 12, Apr. 26, Aug. 18, 1853; *Nashville True Whig,* Apr. 26, 1853; *Clarksville Jeffersonian,* Mar. 16, 1853. The intention of Jones's supporters to oppose Campbell's nomination for a second term probably induced Campbell to retire, although the governor often expressed his intention to serve only one term; see Christopher H. Williams to Campbell, Jan. 4, 1852, Campbell Papers, DU.

42. *House Journal* (1853-54), 98-159; Henry Cooper to Matthew D. Cooper, Oct. 14, 1853, Cooper Papers, TSLA; Marcus B. Winchester to John S.

Claybrooke, Oct. 7, 1853, Claybrooke-Overton Papers, THS; John K. Howard to A. O. P. Nicholson, Sept. 21, 1853, Nicholson Papers, NYHS; John C. Stark to Gustavus A. Henry, Sept. 24, 1853, and Gustavus A. Henry to Marion Henry, Oct. 9, 1853, both in Henry Papers, SHC; Robert L. Caruthers to William B. Campbell, Sept. 30, 1853, and William B. Campbell to David Campbell, Aug. 10, 1853, both in Campbell Papers, DU; *Nashville Republican Banner,* Sept. 15 and 30, Oct. 31, 1853; *Nashville Union and American,* Sept. 27, Oct. 30, 1853. Brownlow noted that Western District Democrats supported Bell "from first to last: because they believed Bell more likely to succeed at getting *Memphis* chosen as the terminus for a planned railroad to the Pacific"; Brownlow to Oliver P. Temple, Oct. 26, 1853, Oliver P. Temple Papers, UT. Possibly, too, western Democrats saw Bell's success as an opportunity to weaken fellow West Tennessean Jones.

43. Robert W. Johannsen, *Stephen A. Douglas* (New York: Oxford Univ. Press, 1973), 374-464; *Nashville Republican Banner,* Apr. 7, 1854.

44. *Nashville Union and American,* May 26, Nov. 11, 1854.

45. *Memphis Appeal,* Jan. 20, Feb. 13, 14, 16, 1854; *Nashville Union and American,* Feb. 12; Mar. 3, 5, 7; May 28, 1854; *Clarksville Jeffersonian,* Feb. 22, 1854.

46. *Nashville Union and American,* June 7, Sept. 30, 1854; *Memphis Appeal,* July 25, 1854.

47. *Congressional Globe,* 33rd Cong., 1st sess., app., 407-15; John Bell, *Speech of Hon. John Bell, of Tennessee, on the Nebraska and Kansas Bill, Delivered in the Senate of the United States, May 24 and 25, 1854* (Washington, D.C.: Congressional Globe Office, 1854), 19; Bell to James McCallum, May 8, 1854, THS; Bell to William B. Campbell, Aug. 10, 1854, Campbell Papers, DU. See also Freehling, *Road to Disunion,* 557.

48. *Nashville Republican Banner,* Mar. 9, 11, 23, 24; Apr. 4; Aug. 2, 1854; William M. Nunn to John Bell, Apr. 24, 1854, and Jane E.Y. Bell to Henry Clay Yeatman, May 21, 1854, both in Yeatman-Polk Collection, TSLA.

49. *Nashville Republican Banner,* Jan. 31, Apr. 29, May 6 and 25, June 6, and July 8 and 28, 1854; Emerson Etheridge, *Speech of Emerson Etheridge, of Tennessee, in the House of Representatives, May 17, 1854* (Washington, D.C.: Buell and Blanchard, 1854).

50. *Nashville Republican Banner,* Feb. 17, 1854.

51. *Nashville True Whig,* Feb. 25, Mar. 10, Apr. 20 and 21, 1854; *Memphis Appeal,* Aug. 4, 1854; Felix K. Zollicoffer, *Speech of Mr. Zollicoffer, of Tennessee, on the Nebraska and Kansas Bill. Delivered in the House of Representatives, May 9, 1854* (Washington, D.C.: n.p., 1854), 13; Charles Ready, *Speech of the Hon. Charles Ready, of Tennessee, on the Nebraska and Kansas Bill. Delivered in the House of Representatives, May 17, 1854* (Washington, D.C.: Towers, 1854), 6; James C. Jones, *Speech of the Hon. James C. Jones, of Tenn. on a Petition for the Repeal of the Fugitive Slave Law, Presented by Mr. Rockwell, from Massachusetts; and on the Recent Address of Certain Members of Congress. In the Senate of the United States, June 26, 1854* (Washington, D.C.: Congressional Globe Office, 1854), 11.

52. *Nashville True Whig,* Mar. 15, May 8, 1854; *Nashville Republican Ban-*

ner, Feb. 6, Apr. 3, 1855; *Nashville Union and American,* Mar. 21; June 6, 7, 20; Nov. 25, 1854; *Memphis Appeal,* Aug. 4, 1854; Charles Ready, *Speech on Nebraska-Kansas Bill, 1854,* p. 2.

53. Holt, *Political Crisis of the 1850s,* 139-56; Gienapp, *Origins of the Republican Party; Athens Post,* June 27, 1856; *Nashville Union and American,* Oct. 2, 1856.

54. Holt, *Political Crisis of the 1850s,* 156-81; Holt, *Political Parties and American Political Development,* 112- 50; Tyler Anbinder, *Nativism and Slavery: The Northern Know-Nothings and the Politics of the 1850s* (New York: Oxford Univ. Press, 1992), 3-102.

55. *Nashville Republican Banner,* Oct. 3 and 4, 1854; *Nashville Gazette,* Oct. 8, 1854; *Nashville Union and American,* Oct. 4, 1854; *Memphis Appeal,* June 30, July 6, 1854; *Clarksville Jeffersonian,* Jan. 10, 1855.

56. J. J. F. Billings to John Bell, Dec. 11, 1854, Polk-Yeatman Collection, SHC; William G. Brownlow to Bell, Jan. 22, 1855, Yeatman-Polk Collection, TSLA; *Knoxville Whig,* Oct. 13, 1855; *Nashville Gazette,* Oct. 2, 1855; [W. N. Bilbo], *The American's Text-Book: Being a Series of Letters, Addressed by "An American," to the Citizens of Tennessee, in Exposition and Vindication of the Principles and Policy of the American Party* (Nashville: n.p., 1855), 30.

57. *Nashville Republican Banner,* Jan. 21, Mar. 3 and 4, 1855; John Bell, *Speech of the Hon. John Bell, Delivered at a Mass Meeting of the American Party, held at Knoxville, Tenn., Sept. 22, 1855* (N.p., 1855), 6.

58. Smith P. Bankhead to William B. Campbell, Jan. 18, 1856, and James Woods, L. M. Temple, and J. C. Thompson to Campbell, Apr. 11, 1855, both in Campbell Papers, DU; Benjamin F. Allen to William Trousdale, Apr. 30, 1855, Trousdale Papers, THS; *Nashville Republican Banner,* June 16 and 24, 1855.

59. William G. Brownlow, *Americanism Contrasted with Foreignism, Romanism, and Bogus Democracy, in the Light of Reason, History, and Scripture, in Which Certain Demagogues in Tennessee, and Elsewhere, Are Shown Up in Their True Colors* (Nashville: n.p., 1856), 14; Christopher H. Williams to William B. Campbell, Mar. 11, 1852, Campbell Papers, DU; *Nashville Gazette,* Feb. 5, May 18, 1856; *Athens Post,* Jan. 27, 1860.

60. [Bilbo], *American's Text-Book,* 21-22, 35; Felix K. Zollicoffer, *Speech of F. K. Zollicoffer, Delivered at Nashville, June 16, 1855* (Nashville: n.p., 1855), 7; *Nashville True Whig,* Apr. 26, July 3, 1855; *Athens Post,* Jan. 12, 1855; *Nashville Gazette,* Nov. 30, 1855. For an excellent discussion of southern Know-Nothingism and republican ideology, see Gregg Cantrell, *Kenneth and John B. Rayner and the Limits of Southern Dissent* (Urbana: Univ. of Illinois Press, 1993), 82-99. See also Anbinder, *Nativism and Slavery,* 103-26.

61. *Nashville Republican Banner,* May 10 and 18, June 30, 1855; *Nashville Gazette,* Mar. 25; Apr. 3, 5, 25; May 6; July 25, 1855; *Nashville True Whig,* May 23, Aug. 15, June 1, 1855; *Nashville Patriot,* Dec. 1, 1855; Brownlow, *Americanism Contrasted with Foreignism,* 7; [Bilbo], *American's Text-Book,* 5-9.

62. *Athens Post,* June 23, 1854, and June 1, 1855; [Bilbo], *American's Text-*

Book, 31; *Nashville Republican Banner,* Mar. 31, 1855; *Clarksville Jeffersonian,* Dec. 19, 1855.

63. Bell, *Speech of Bell at Knoxville, 1855,* 5; [Bilbo], *American's Text-Book,* 3, 31; *Knoxville Whig,* Apr. 28, 1855; *Athens Post,* Oct. 6, 1854; *Nashville Gazette,* Mar. 11 and 29, 1855; *Clarksville Jeffersonian,* June 13, 1855; *Nashville Republican Banner,* Sept. 11, 1855; *Nashville True Whig,* Apr. 15 and 20, 1855.

64. *Nashville Republican Banner,* Oct. 9, 1854; May 30, 1855; *Nashville True Whig,* May 11 and 15, 1855; *Nashville Gazette,* May 31; June 2; July 4, 18, and 29, 1855; *Clarksville Jeffersonian,* July 5, 1855; Brownlow, *Americanism Contrasted with Foreignism,* 58-59.

65. *Nashville Republican Banner,* May 25, July 4 and 8, Dec. 6, 1855. Andrew J. Donelson to Andrew J. Donelson, Jr., May 12 and June 22, 1852; Andrew J. Donelson to Elizabeth Donelson, July 23, 1855; and Andrew J. Donelson to H. V. M. Miller, July 17, 1856, all in Andrew Jackson Donelson Papers, LC.

66. *Nashville Republican Banner,* June 26, 1855.

67. Brownlow, *Americanism Contrasted with Foreignism,* 7, 115; *Athens Post,* June 23, 1854; *Knoxville Whig,* Oct. 14, 1854, and Feb. 17, 1855.

68. Brownlow, *Americanism Contrasted with Foreignism,* 3-4.

69. *Nashville Republican Banner,* May 10 and 26, June 9 and 24, July 6 and 28, Aug. 26, 1855; *Nashville Gazette,* Mar. 20 and 25, Apr. 25, June 14 and 16, 1855; *Nashville True Whig,* Apr. 16 and 20, May 8, July 18, 1855; *Nashville Patriot,* Dec. 1, 1855; *Athens Post,* July 6, 1855; *Memphis Whig,* June 28, 1855; Brownlow, *Americanism Contrasted with Foreignism,* 10; W. H. Sneed to Oliver P. Temple, Dec. 10, 1855, Temple Papers, UT.

70. Bell, *Speech of Bell at Knoxville, 1855,* 18.

71. *Nashville Republican Banner,* Feb. 1 and 15, 1855; *Nashville True Whig,* Feb. 15 and May 11, 1855; *Nashville Gazette,* May 3 and 4, 1855; *Athens Post,* Dec. 8, 1854; Jan. 1, 1855; *Knoxville Whig,* Dec. 2 and 16, 1854; William B. Campbell to David Campbell, Oct. 25, 1854, Campbell Papers, DU; William G. Brownlow to [John Bell], Nov. 14, 1854, and Jan. 22, 1855, both in Yeatman-Polk Collection, TSLA.

72. *Knoxville Whig,* Oct. 28, Dec. 2, 1854; Mar. 5, Apr. 21, May 12, 1855; *Nashville Republican Banner,* Jan. 17, 23; Feb. 11, 13, 15, 23; Mar. 31; May 1, 17; June 1, 27; and July 11, 1855; *Nashville Union and American,* Jan. 10, Apr. 28, and May 4, 1855; *Clarksville Jeffersonian,* July 18, 1855; William B. Campbell to David Campbell, Oct. 25, 1854, Campbell Papers, DU; R. W. Humphreys to Randall McGavock, May 15, 1855, McGavock Papers, SHC; [John S. Claybrooke] to Meredith P. Gentry, June 12, 1855, Claybrooke-Overton Papers, THS. The State Temperance Convention advocated a Maine Liquor Law prohibiting the sale of all alcoholic liquors; in 1853, both gubernatorial candidates had refused to endorse this position, and in 1855 Johnson again refused to approve a prohibitory law; see White and Ash, *Messages of the Governors* 4:617-20.

73. William B. Campbell to David Campbell, July 25 and Aug. 2, 1855, both in Campbell Papers, DU; *Nashville True Whig,* Feb. 23, Apr. 28, 1855.

74. *Nashville Union and American,* June 15, Sept. 24, Dec. 23, 1854; Jan. 27, Feb. 8, Apr. 25, May 5 and 27, June 1 and 13, and July 1 and 13, 1855; *Memphis Appeal,* Mar. 24, June 17, July 22 and 24, 1855; *Clarksville Jeffersonian,* July 5, 1854; May 30, 1855; Aaron V. Brown, *Speeches, Congressional and Political,* 616-19.

75. *Nashville Union and American,* Sept. 16, 1854; Jan. 23; Feb. 1, 16, 24; Mar. 17, 21; Apr. 17; May 8, 10; Nov. 29, 1855; *Memphis Appeal,* Feb. 9, May 2, 16, 1855; *Clarksville Jeffersonian,* Nov. 11, 1854; Jan. 10, 1855; *Athens Post,* June 15, 1855.

76. *Nashville Union and American,* Jan. 24, 26, 27; Feb. 8, 21; May 4, 6, 12; Aug. 21, 1855; [Adam Ferguson] to *Sumner County Flag,* June 1855, Ferguson Family Papers, TSLA; Aaron V. Brown, *Speeches, Congressional and Political,* 623-29.

77. *Nashville Union and American,* Jan. 5, Mar. 9, Apr. 3, July 4 and 29, 1855; *Memphis Appeal,* June 7, 1855.

78. *Nashville Union and American,* Apr. 3, 1855.

79. Andrew Johnson, "Speech at Murfreesboro," on pp. 2:280 and 2:292, and his "Speech at Pulaski," on pp. 304-5, both in Graf and Haskins, *Papers of Andrew Johnson; Nashville Union and American,* Mar. 28, 1855. Johnson also recognized a dissatisfaction among voters caused by a slight economic downturn in consequence of the Crimean War; see Andrew Johnson to David T. Patterson, Feb. 17, 1854, on p. 2:258; and Johnson to William M. Lowry, Feb. 24, 1855, on p. 2:261, both in Graf and Haskins, *Papers of Andrew Johnson.*

80. Andrew Johnson, "Speech at Murfreesboro," on p. 2:293; and his "Speech at Pulaski," on p. 2:304, both in Graf and Haskins, *Papers of Andrew Johnson.*

81. Andrew Johnson, "Speech at Murfreesboro," in Graf and Haskins, *Papers of Andrew Johnson,* 2:281; *Nashville Republican Banner,* May 2, June 29, 1855; *Nashville Union and American,* July 28, 1855; *Athens Post,* May 11, 1855.

82. *Nashville Union and American,* May 29; June 15, 20, 22, 29; July 25, 1855; *Nashville Republican Banner,* June 14, 20, 1855; *Nashville True Whig,* June 20, 1855; *Athens Post,* June 29, 1855; Holt, *Political Parties and American Political Development,* 132; Anbinder, *Nativism and Slavery,* 162-74.

83. *Athens Post,* Dec. 8, 1854; *Nashville Union and American,* Mar. 22, May 6, 1855; *Memphis Whig,* Feb. 28, Mar. 6 and 8, July 12, 1855.

84. *Nashville Republican Banner,* June 6, July 17, 1855; *Nashville Union and American,* June 7, 1855.

85. *Nashville Republican Banner,* July 17, 1855; *Nashville True Whig,* June 6, 1855; *Nashville Union and American,* June 9, 1855; *Memphis Whig,* June 29, 1855.

86. Felix K. Zollicoffer to William B. Campbell, June 13, 1855, and John H. Callender to Campbell, June 21, 1855, both in Campbell Papers, DU; *Nashville True Whig,* Apr. 23, 1855.

87. *Nashville Union and American,* Aug. 9 and 11, 1855; *Athens Post,*

Notes to pages 205-8 331

Aug. 17, 1855; William B. Campbell to David Campbell, Aug. 4, 1855, Campbell Papers, DU.

88. *Knoxville Whig,* Aug. 18, 1855; *Nashville Union and American,* Aug. 14, Sept. 25, 1855; *Athens Post,* Aug. 17, 1855.

89. William H. Sneed to [Oliver P. Temple], Jan. 25, 1856, Temple Papers, UT; Charles Ready to William B. Campbell, May 12, 1856, Campbell Papers, DU; John S. Brien to Thomas A. R. Nelson, Jan. 20, 1856, Nelson Papers, McClung; *Nashville Union and American,* Oct. 12, 1855.

90. *Nashville Republican Banner,* Feb. 13, 1856.

91. Thomas F. Henry to [Susan Henry], Mar. 2, 1856, Henry Papers, SHC; William B. Campbell to David Campbell, Mar. 7 and Apr. 6, 1856, both in Campbell Papers, DU; *Athens Post,* June 27, 1856.

92. *Knoxville Whig,* Mar. 1, Oct. 18, 1856; *Athens Post,* Nov. 23, 1855; Mar. 14, 1856; *Nashville Republican Banner,* Feb. 28, 1856; *Nashville Patriot,* Feb. 28, Mar. 8, 1856; *Nashville Gazette,* Feb. 24, 28, 1856.

93. Potter, *Impending Crisis,* 199-266.

94. *Nashville Union and American,* Feb. 16, Mar. 7, May 7, Sept. 17, Oct. 3, 1856; *Nashville Republican Banner,* Apr. 2, May 31, Aug. 31, Oct. 3, 1856; *Memphis Appeal,* Sept. 6, 1856; William B. Campbell to David Campbell, Oct. 5, 1856, Campbell Papers, DU.

95. *Nashville Union and American,* Jan. 10, Oct. 25, 1856; Andrew Johnson to William M. Lowry, June 26, 1856, in Graf and Haskins, *Papers of Andrew Johnson,* 2:386; Tricamo, "Tennessee Politics," 156-59.

96. Andrew Johnson to Robert E. Johnson, June 28, 1856, in Graf and Haskins, *Papers of Andrew Johnson,* 2:391; S. R. Anderson to A. O. P. Nicholson, Nov. 21, 1855, and Mar. 15, 1856, both in Nicholson Papers, NYHS; *Nashville Union and American,* Sept. 14, 1855.

97. *Nashville Union and American,* Feb. 28, Mar. 22 and 28, Apr. 1, July 12 and 26, 1856; *Memphis Appeal,* Feb. 29, July 8 and 16, 1856; *Clarksville Jeffersonian,* Mar. 19, 1856.

98. *Memphis Appeal,* Mar. 12, May 24, June 8 and 20, July 8 and 22, Aug. 16 and 21, 1856; *Clarksville Jeffersonian,* Sept. 26, Nov. 7, 1855; *Nashville Union and American,* Dec. 11, 1855; Jan. 10; Feb. 23; Mar. 22; Apr. 6, 13; May 1, 7, 11, 13; June 10, 15, 21; Oct. 2, 8, 16, 1856; Thomas R. Childress to Andrew Johnson, July 23, 1856, in Graf and Haskins, *Papers of Andrew Johnson,* 2:437; William W. Ferguson to Adam Ferguson, Oct. 8, 1856, Ferguson Family Papers, TSLA.

99. *Nashville Republican Banner,* June 14 and 25; July 10 and 26; Aug. 8, 9, 10, 17; Oct. 3, 1856; *Nashville Patriot,* June 7, 9, 10, 11, 26; Aug. 16, 1856; *Nashville Gazette,* June 10 and 15, 1856; *Athens Post,* June 20 and 27, 1856; Brownlow, *Americanism Contrasted with Foreignism,* 162-63; Andrew J. Donelson to Andrew J. Donelson, Jr., Sept. 27, 1856, Andrew Jackson Donelson Papers, LC.

100. *Nashville Republican Banner,* Jan. 2 and 5; Mar. 27; Apr. 24 and 27; May 4; June 4, 8, 11, 19; July 2; Oct. 30, 1856; *Nashville Patriot,* Jan. 12; May 8, 15, 20; July 30; Aug. 9, 1856; *Nashville Gazette,* July 20 and 22, 1856.

101. *Nashville Patriot,* Feb. 29, Mar. 11 and 27, 1856; *Nashville Republican Banner,* Feb. 24, 1856.
102. *Knoxville Whig,* May 10, Oct. 25, 1856; *Nashville Republican Banner,* Nov. 15, 1855; Feb. 16; Oct. 1, 3, and 5, 1856; *Nashville Patriot,* Sept. 4, 5, 27, 1856; *Athens Post,* Apr. 11, May 30, July 18, Oct. 24, 1856; Brownlow, *Americanism Contrasted with Foreignism,* 180-81.
103. *Nashville Republican Banner,* Apr. 2 and 22, June 19, July 29, Aug. 5 and 16, Sept. 16, Oct. 22, 1856; *Nashville Patriot,* July 7, Aug. 21, 1856; *Nashville Gazette,* Apr. 5, July 9, 1856; *Knoxville Whig,* July 19, Oct. 11 and 25, Nov. 1, 1856; *Athens Post,* Sept. 12, 1856.
104. *Nashville Republican Banner,* Feb. 26 and Mar. 1, 1856; *Nashville Union and American,* Mar. 2 and 20, 1856; *Memphis Appeal,* Feb. 26, 1856; Holt, *Political Parties and American Political Development,* 140-41; Anbinder, *Nativism and Slavery,* 206-9.
105. *Nashville Republican Banner,* Apr. 25, June 28, Aug. 31, 1856; [James Williams], *Reflections and Suggestions on the Present State of Parties, by an Old Clay Whig* (Nashville: G. C. Torbett & Co., 1856), 41-42, 85; *Nashville Union and American,* Jan. 8, Apr. 22, June 26, July 1, 6, Aug. 21, Sept. 13, 1856; *Nashville Patriot,* Apr. 18, 1856; *Memphis Appeal,* Mar. 12, June 17, Aug. 12, 1856; *Memphis Whig,* Mar. 8, 1856; *Clarksville Jeffersonian,* Jan. 23, 1856; *Knoxville Whig,* May 3, Aug. 2, 1856; Brownlow, *Americanism Contrasted with Foreignism,* 184-91; W. P. Bond to William T. Avery, Mar. 29, 1856, and Avery to [Bond], 1856, both in Gordon and Avery Papers, TSLA; Cave Johnson to James Buchanan, Aug. 24, 1856, Buchanan Papers, HSP; Daniel Shoffner to Michael Shoffner, Aug. 25, 1856, Shoffner Papers, SHC; Milton H. Haynes to William B. Campbell, Jan. 19, 1856, Campbell Papers, DU; James C. Jones, *Speech of the Hon. James C. Jones, in the United States Senate, Aug., 1856* (Washington, D.C.: n.p., 1856), 14.
106. *Clarksville Jeffersonian,* Sept. 17 and 24, 1856.
107. James McCallum to John Bell, June 1856, Bell Collection, LC; McCallum to Bell, July 17, 1856, Polk-Yeatman Papers, SHC.
108. William B. Campbell to David Campbell, Sept. 22, 1856; Felix K. Zollicoffer to William B. Campbell, Aug. 7, 1856; and John Bell to William B. Campbell, Sept. 10, 1856, all in Campbell Papers, DU; Henry March to John Bell, July 28, 1856, Polk-Yeatman Papers, SHC; Cave Johnson to Wilson W. Candless, Sept. 16, 1856, Buchanan Papers, HSP; *Nashville Republican Banner,* Sept. 23, 1856; *Nashville Union and American,* Sept. 7 and 26, 1856.
109. Andrew Johnson to A. O. P. Nicholson, Oct. 28, 1856, in Graf and Haskins, *Papers of Andrew Johnson,* 2:446; Andrew J. Donelson to [unknown], Oct. 27, 1856 [fragment], Andrew Jackson Donelson Papers, LC; William F. Cooper to Matthew D. Cooper, Oct. 12, 1856, Cooper Papers, TSLA; William B. Campbell to David Campbell, Oct. 26, 1856, Campbell Papers, DU; *Nashville Union and American,* Oct. 16, 1856; *Memphis Appeal,* Oct. 3 and 11, 1856.
110. William F. Cooper to Matthew D. Cooper, Nov. 14, 1856, Cooper Papers, TSLA; *Memphis Appeal,* Nov. 6, 1856; *Nashville Union and American,* Nov. 12, 1856.

111. Lucius J. Polk to Mary B. P. Yeatman, Nov. 19, 1856, Yeatman-Polk Collection, TSLA.
112. *Clarksville Jeffersonian,* May 6, 1857; William B. Campbell to David Campbell, July 2 and Aug. 16, 1857, both in Campbell Papers, DU; R. Love to Oliver P. Temple, May 9, 1857, Temple Papers, UT; *Athens Post,* July 24 and Aug. 21, 1857; Bergeron, *Antebellum Politics in Tennessee,* 127-30; Tricamo, "Tennessee Politics," 167-75.
113. William B. Campbell to David Campbell, Apr. 23, 1857, Campbell Papers, DU; *Knoxville Whig,* Nov. 15, 1856; *Nashville Republican Banner,* Nov. 13, 1856.

Chapter 8. The Politics of Revolution: Tennessee in the Crisis of Union, 1858-1861

1. *Nashville Republican Banner,* Mar. 28, 29; May 2; June 19; July 7, 8, 25, 26; Aug. 4, 1857; *Nashville Union and American,* Apr. 3; July 25, 26, 28, 1857; *Knoxville Whig,* May 16, 1857; *Athens Post,* June 26, 1857; Tricamo, "Tennessee Politics," 165-75.
2. *Nashville Republican Banner,* Dec. 22, 1857.
3. *Nashville Republican Banner,* Mar. 2, 17, 29, 30; Apr. 24; May 3, 11; June 21; July 5, 31; Aug. 3, 1859; James L. Huston, *The Panic of 1857 and the Coming of the Civil War* (Baton Rouge: Louisiana State Univ. Press, 1987), 14-34; Charles W. Calomiris and Larry Schweikart, "The Panic of 1857: Origins, Transmission, and Containment," *Journal of Economic History* 51 (Dec. 1991): 807-34; Schweikart, *Banking in the American South,* 183-85; Claude A. Campbell, *Banking in Tennessee,* 133-55.
4. *Athens Post,* Aug. 12, 1859; *Nashville Patriot,* Aug. 9, 1859; Tricamo, "Tennessee Politics," 189-98.
5. *Nashville Union and American,* Apr. 25, 1858; Aug. 10, 1859; William B. Campbell to David Campbell, Mar. 4, 1858, Campbell Papers, DU; Duncan B. Frierson to Matthew D. Cooper, Feb. 6, 1858, Cooper Family Papers, TSLA; Claude A. Campbell, *Banking in Tennessee,* 145-46.
6. [Tennessee] Democratic Central Committee, "The Currency and Other Questions: The Views of the Democracy Contrasted with Those of the Opposition!" (Nashville: n.p., 1859), 2, 6, 7, 11; *Nashville Union and American,* Mar. 11, 24; May 4, 6, 13, 18, 25; June 2, 10, 18; July 1, 1859; *Clarksville Jeffersonian,* June 22, Aug. 3, 1859.
7. Potter, *Impending Crisis,* 267-327; Don E. Fehrenbacher, *Slavery, Law, and Politics: The Dred Scott Case in Historical Perspective* (New York: Oxford Univ. Press, 1981).
8. [Tennessee] Democratic Central Committee, "The Currency and Other Questions," 16-17, 19, 21. Andrew Johnson, "Speech at Bristol," May 21, 1859, in Graf and Haskins, *Papers of Andrew Johnson,* 3:277-79. *Nashville Union and American,* Nov. 5, 1858; and Feb. 13; Apr. 20; May 3, 4, 27; July 2, 1859; Jan. 7, 1860. *Athens Post,* July 15, 1859.
9. Potter, *Impending Crisis,* 297-327; Johannsen, *Stephen A. Douglas,* 576-613.

10. *Nashville Union and American,* Dec. 19 and 30, 1857; Jan. 20, Feb. 7 and 11, Apr. 3 and 24, May 6, 1858; *Memphis Appeal,* Dec. 16, 17, 22, 23, 1857; Jan. 17, Feb. 2, 6, 12, 13, Nov. 10, 1858; *Clarksville Jeffersonian,* Apr. 7, 1858.

11. Johannsen, *Stephen A. Douglas,* 614-714; Andrew Johnson to A. O. P. Nicholson, Nov. 22, 1858, in Graf and Haskins, *Papers of Andrew Johnson,* 3:196; *Nashville Patriot,* Sept. 1, 1859.

12. George B. Peters to John Houston Bills, Oct. 27, 1859, TSLA; Sam Milligan to Andrew Johnson, Feb. 8, 1860, on pp. 3:419-420, and Robert D. Powel to Johnson, Mar. 24, 1860, on pp. 3:487-88, both in Graf and Haskins, *Papers of Andrew Johnson; Nashville Republican Banner,* July 13, 1858; *Nashville Union and American,* June 24, Oct. 3, 1858; Sept. 14, 1859; *Clarksville Jeffersonian,* Dec. 8, 1858.

13. *Nashville Union and American,* Feb. 3, 1860; *Nashville Republican Banner,* July 11, Oct. 26, 1858; *Nashville Patriot,* Sept. 11, 1858; Mar. 22, Apr. 6, 1859; Andrew Johnson to Robert Johnson, Jan. 23, 1858, on pp. 3:7-8; Andrew Johnson to A. O. P. Nicholson, Nov. 22, 1858, on p. 3:196; and David M. Currin to Andrew Johnson, Feb. 21, 1860, on p. 3:440, all in Graf and Haskins, *Papers of Andrew Johnson.*

14. *Memphis Appeal,* July 3, July 23, Aug. 12, Aug. 31, Sept. 7, Sept. 9, Oct. 24, Nov. 12, Nov. 19, Nov. 30, Dec. 1, 1858; June 16, Sept. 1, Sept. 8, Sept. 10, Oct. 26, 1859; Apr. 17, 1860; *Nashville Union and American,* Mar. 22, 1860; *Nashville Republican Banner,* Mar. 30, 1860; Robert Johnson to Andrew Johnson, Oct. 14, 1859, in Graf and Haskins, *Papers of Andrew Johnson,* 3:294.

15. *Nashville Republican Banner,* Dec. 3, 1858; June 18, 21, Nov. 1, 1859; *Memphis Appeal,* July 14, 20, 1860; *Athens Post,* Oct. 1, 1858.

16. Holt, *Political Crisis of the 1850s,* 183-217.

17. *Nashville Union and American,* Oct. 21, 23, 26, Dec. 7, 1859; *Memphis Appeal,* Oct. 20 and 21, 1859; *Nashville Republican Banner,* Oct. 24, 1859; *Nashville Patriot,* Oct. 20 and 27, 1859; *Athens Post,* Oct. 28, 1859.

18. Cave Johnson to Andrew Johnson, Jan. 8, 1860, on p. 3:370; Andrew Johnson to Robert Johnson, Jan. 12, 1860, on p. 3:380, both in Graf and Haskins, *Papers of Andrew Johnson;* William G. Brownlow to [John Bell], Jan. 17, 1859, Yeatman-Polk Papers, TSLA.

19. *Nashville Republican Banner,* Jan. 19, 20, 25, 27, 1860; *Nashville Union and American,* Jan. 19 and 21, 1860; *Nashville Patriot,* Jan. 19, 1860; *Memphis Appeal,* Jan. 21, 1860; William M. Lowry to Andrew Johnson, Jan. 27, 1860, in Graf and Haskins, *Papers of Andrew Johnson,* 3:401-2; William W. Ferguson to Adam Ferguson, Jan. 21, 1860, Ferguson Family Papers, TSLA.

20. *Nashville Union and American,* Jan. 19 and 20, 1860; *Memphis Appeal,* Jan. 22, 1860; Washington C. Whitthorne to Andrew Johnson, Jan. 19, 1860, on p. 3:388; Robert Johnson to Andrew Johnson, Jan. 22, 1860, on p. 3:392; William Henry Maxwell to Andrew Johnson, Feb. 2, 1860, on pp. 3:410-11; John K. Howard to Andrew Johnson, Feb. 5, 1860, on pp. 3:413-14; Frank C. Dunnington to Andrew Johnson, Feb. 13, 1860, on pp. 3:425-

26; Hu Douglas to Andrew Johnson, Mar. 19, 1860, on pp. 3:474-75; Sam Milligan to Andrew Johnson, Mar. 20, 1860, on pp. 3:477-79; Andrew Johnson to Robert Johnson, Apr. 8, 1860, on pp. 3:517-18; and Hu Douglas to Andrew Johnson, Dec. 30, 1860, on pp. 4:103-4, all in Graf and Haskins, *Papers of Andrew Johnson*.

21. Andrew Johnson to Robert Johnson, Apr. 22, 1860, in Graf and Haskins, *Papers of Andrew Johnson*, 3:573.

22. *Nashville Union and American*, May 6, 1860; Sam Milligan to Andrew Johnson, May 7, 1860, on pp. 3:586-88; Washington C. Whitthorne to Johnson, May 8, 1860, on pp. 3:590-92; and William E. A. Jones to Johnson, May 15, 1860, on p. 3:599, all in Graf and Haskins, *Papers of Andrew Johnson*; Potter, *Impending Crisis*, 407-12; Roy F. Nichols, *The Disruption of the American Democracy* (New York: Macmillan, 1948), 292-309.

23. *Nashville Union and American*, May 10, July 1 and 6, 1860; *Nashville Patriot*, June 15, 1860; Hu Douglas to Andrew Johnson, Apr. 26, 1860, in Graf and Haskins, *Papers of Andrew Johnson*, 3:575-76.

24. Robert Johnson to Andrew Johnson, May 8, 1860, on p. 3:589, and Tazewell W. Newman to Andrew Johnson, [May] 15, 1860, on pp. 3:600-601, both in Graf and Haskins, *Papers of Andrew Johnson*; *Clarksville Jeffersonian*, May 23, 1860; *Nashville Union and American*, May 22, 1860; *Nashville Republican Banner*, May 25 and June 2, 1860; *Memphis Appeal*, June 15, 1860.

25. *Nashville Union and American*, May 8 and 15, June 8, 1860; *Memphis Appeal*, May 5, June 2 and 10, 1860; *Nashville Republican Banner*, May 26, June 5, 1860; *Nashville Patriot*, May 10, June 13, 1860. Washington C. Whitthorne to Andrew Johnson, May 8, 1860, on p. 3:592; Tazewell W. Newman to Johnson, [May] 15, 1860, on pp. 3:600-601; William M. Lowry to Johnson, May 19, 1860, on p. 3:602; Albert S. Graham to Johnson, May 23, 1860, on p. 3:605; Lowry to Johnson, May 29, 1860, on pp. 3:610-11; and Whitthorne to Johnson, June 5, 1860, on p. 3:615, all in Graf and Haskins, *Papers of Andrew Johnson*.

26. *Nashville Union and American*, July 1 and 28, 1860; Nichols, *Disruption of the American Democracy*, 314-20.

27. *Nashville Union and American*, June 23, July 1 and 24, 1860; *Nashville Patriot*, Sept. 1, 1860. Tennessee sent no formal delegation to the Richmond convention, which endorsed Breckinridge's nomination, though the *Nashville Union and American*, June 17, 1860, reported that two Knoxville residents, George W. Bradfield and William T. Helms, attended and acted for the state.

28. *Nashville Union and American*, June 28; July 1, 18, 20, 25; Aug. 7, 24, 30; Sept. 1, 12, 18; Oct. 14, 17, 20, 1860. John C. Burch to Andrew Johnson, [July] 12, 1860, on p. 3:645, and Washington C. Whitthorne to Johnson, July 24, 1860, on p. 3:650, in Graf and Haskins, *Papers of Andrew Johnson*.

29. *Memphis Appeal*, May 9, July 21 and 24, 1860; *Nashville Republican Banner*, July 8, 21, 29, 1860; *Nashville Patriot*, July 30, 1860; *Nashville Union*, June 12, 1860; *Knoxville Whig*, July 14, 1860.

30. *Nashville Union and American,* July 6, Aug. 12, Sept. 2, 1860; *Memphis Appeal,* May 10, 11, 18, 19, 20; June 24; July 8 and 14; Aug. 15, 16, 30; Sept. 5, 20, 25, 27, 29, 1860; George W. Jones to Andrew Johnson, Aug. 15, 1860, in Graf and Haskins, *Papers of Andrew Johnson,* 3:656.

31. John Bell to William B. Campbell, Jan. 19, 1857, and William B. Campbell to David Campbell, Dec. 19, 1858, both in Campbell Papers, DU; *Nashville Republican Banner,* May 4, 1859; *Nashville Union and American,* Aug. 18, Sept. 18, 1859.

32. *Athens Post,* Sept. 4, 1857; *Nashville Republican Banner,* Dec. 23, 1858; May 27, 1859; *Nashville Patriot,* Jan. 14, 1860; Neill S. Brown to John Bell, Aug. 10, 1858, Bell Papers, LC; John C. Gant to Thomas A. R. Nelson, Jan. 11, 1860, Nelson Papers, McClung.

33. John Bell, *Speech of Hon. John Bell, of Tennessee, on the Admission of Kansas under the Lecompton Constitution, Delivered in the Senate of the United States, Mar. 18, 1858* (Washington, D.C.: Buell and Blanchard, 1858), 16; Parks, *John Bell of Tennessee,* 326-38. Bell also emphasized that the fraudulent circumstances behind the Lecompton Constitution's composition revealed that it did not embody the will of the people of Kansas.

34. *Nashville Republican Banner,* Jan. 16, 24; Feb. 3, 10, 12, 17, 20, 24; Apr. 22, 23, 1858; *Nashville Union and American,* Apr. 17, 1857; Feb. 24, 1858; Apr. 2, 1859; *Knoxville Whig,* May 8, 1858. On Opposition support for Kansas and Lecompton, see *Nashville Patriot,* Nov. 30, Dec. 9 and 16, 1857; Jan. 12, 13, 21, 26; Feb. 10; Apr. 17, 1858.

35. *Nashville Republican Banner,* Nov. 26, 1859; Jan. 5, 12, 13; Feb. 12, 23, 24; May 11, 12, 16, 1860; *Nashville Patriot,* Sept. 5, 1859, Jan. 6, Jan. 12, Feb. 23, May 11, 15, 16, 1860; *Nashville Union and American,* Jan. 14, 1857, Jan. 13, 1860; *Knoxville Whig,* Feb. 11, 1860; William G. Brownlow to [John Bell], Jan. 17, 1859, Yeatman-Polk Papers, TSLA; Parks, *John Bell of Tennessee,* 339-60.

36. *Nashville Republican Banner,* May 19, June 17, July 13, Sept. 19, 1860; *Nashville Patriot,* May 4 and 16, June 26, 1860; *Athens Post,* May 4, 1860; *Knoxville Whig,* June 30, 1860.

37. *Knoxville Whig,* July 14, Aug. 18 and 25, 1860; *Nashville Republican Banner,* Feb. 1; Mar. 22; June 8; July 4, 17, 22; Aug. 2, 8, 9, 30; Sept. 14; Oct. 21, 25, 30, 1860; *Nashville Patriot,* May 9, 26, 28; July 2, 4, 12, 18; Aug. 2, 3; Oct. 11, 20, 1860; *Athens Post,* Aug. 24, Sept. 14, 1860.

38. *Knoxville Whig,* Mar. 3, June 30, July 14 and 21, 1860; *Nashville Republican Banner,* Jan. 21; Feb. 9, 26; Mar. 8, 29; Apr. 3, 10; May 19; June 8, 15, 20, 26, 28; July 26; Sept. 7, 18, 19, 29; Oct. 16, 18, 20, 21; Nov. 1 and 3, 1860; *Nashville Patriot,* May 2, 12, 24; June 5; July 16, 25; Aug. 8; Oct. 22, 1860; *Nashville Union and American,* Aug. 30, 1860.

39. John C. Gant to Thomas A. R. Nelson, Aug. 11, 1860, Nelson Papers, McClung; John S. Brien to Oliver P. Temple, June 29, 1860, and Jacob S. Matthews to Temple and Samuel R. Rodgers, July 25, 1860, both in Temple Papers, UT; *Nashville Union and American,* June 29, July 20, Sept. 2, 1860; *Clarksville Jeffersonian,* July 11, 1860; *Knoxville Whig,* Aug. 16, 1860.

40. *Nashville Republican Banner,* June 8, Sept. 5, 14, 23, and 27, 1860; *Knoxville Whig,* Aug. 16, 18, 1860; *Nashville Patriot,* Sept. 1, 1860; *Nashville Union and American,* June 27, 28; July 8; Aug. 12, 19; Sept. 2, 20, 27; Oct. 4, 1860; *Athens Post,* Aug. 17, Oct. 5, Nov. 2, 1860; *Memphis Appeal,* Aug. 16, Sept. 25, 26, 27, 1860; *Clarksville Jeffersonian,* Sept. 12, 1860; John S. Brien to Oliver P. Temple, July 7, 1860, Temple Papers, UT; Democratic Central Committee to Samuel Powel, Sept. 6, 1860, Powel III Papers, DU.

41. *Nashville Republican Banner,* Sept. 18, 20, 25; Oct. 17, 27, 28; Nov. 4, 1860; *Nashville Patriot,* Sept. 24, Oct. 2, 4, 12, 13, 17, 18, 1860; *Nashville Union and American,* Aug. 22, 25, 28; Oct. 11, 12, 13, 16, 23, 24, 25, 27, 30, 1860; *Memphis Appeal,* June 24; Sept. 27; Oct. 4, 13, 17, 20, 24, 1860; *Clarksville Jeffersonian,* Oct. 31, 1860; *Knoxville Whig,* Sept. 22 and 29, Oct. 13, 1860; F. C. Gallaher to Oliver P. Temple, Sept. 7, 1860, Temple Papers, UT.

42. J. H. C. Basham to Andrew Johnson, Dec. 1, 1860, in Graf and Haskins, *Papers of Andrew Johnson,* 3:680; A. W. Howard to Thomas A. R. Nelson, Nov. 23, 1860, Nelson Papers, McClung; *Nashville Union and American,* Aug. 21, 1860; Feb. 21, Mar. 5 and 8, 1861; *Memphis Appeal,* Mar. 10, 1861.

43. W. Y. C. Humes to Oliver P. Temple, Feb. 27, 1861, Temple Papers, UT; *Nashville Union and American,* Dec. 1, 1860; *Nashville Patriot,* Jan. 12, 1861.

44. *Nashville Republican Banner,* Sept. 17, 1857; Jan. 22, 1861; John F. Henry to Marion Henry, Jan. 5, 1861, Henry Papers, SHC; George W. Jones to [torn], Nov. 20, 1860, Jones Papers, SHC; Samuel Milligan to Samuel Powel, Jan. 25, 1861, Powel III Papers, DU; Matthew D. Cooper to Duncan B. Frierson, Feb. 10, 1861, Cooper Family Papers, TSLA.

45. Andrew Johnson, *The Constitutionality and Rightfulness of Secession: Speech of Hon. Andrew Johnson, of Tennessee, in the Senate of the United States, On Tuesday and Wednesday, Dec. 18 and 19, 1860* (Washington, D.C.: n.p., 1860); Cave Johnson to Andrew Johnson, Jan. 2, 1861, on pp. 4:121-23, and Harvey M. Watterson to Andrew Johnson, Jan. 4, 1861, on pp. 4:125-26, both in Graf and Haskins, *Papers of Andrew Johnson;* [William H. Polk] to [unknown], Dec. 17, 1860, William H. Polk Papers, NCDAH; *Nashville Republican Banner,* Jan. 26, 1861.

46. George W. Jones to [torn], Nov. 20, 1860, Jones Papers, SHC; John Houston Bills Diary (typescript), 35, 39, John Houston Bills Papers, TSLA; *Nashville Republican Banner,* Nov. 7, 10, 17, 21, 23, 24, 25, Dec. 8 and 13, 1860; Jan. 22, Feb. 1, 1861; *Nashville Patriot,* Nov. 13 and Dec. 18, 1860; Jan. 22 and 28, 1861; *Knoxville Whig,* Nov. 24, 1860.

47. William B. Campbell to A. C. Beard, Mar. 15, 1861, Campbell Papers, DU; William H. Polk to [unknown], Jan. 19, 1861, Polk Papers, NCDAH; Andrew Johnson, *Constitutionality and Rightfulness of Secession,* 17; Emerson Etheridge, *Speech of the Hon. Emerson Etheridge, of Tennessee, Delivered in the House of Representatives, Jan. 23, 1861* (Washington, D.C.: Henry Polkinhorn, 1861), 5, 6; *Nashville Republican Banner,* Nov. 9, 23, Dec. 2, 1860; Jan. 19, 24, 26, 1861; *Nashville Patriot,* Dec. 25, 1860; Jan. 12 and 26, 1861; *Knoxville Whig,* Dec. 15, 1860.

48. *Knoxville Whig,* Nov. 17, 1860, Jan. 26, 1861; *Nashville Republican Banner,* Nov. 21 and 28, Dec. 4, 6, 13, 14, 15, and 29, 1860; Jan. 4, 6, 31; Feb. 1, 3, 6, 23, 24; Mar. 5, 1861; *Nashville Patriot,* Dec. 13 and 20, 1860; Jan. 2, Mar. 6, Apr. 3, 1861; Andrew Johnson, *Constitutionality and Rightfulness of Secession,* 20; William H. Polk to [unknown], Dec. 17, 1860, Polk Papers, NCDAH; Andrew Johnson to Sam Milligan, Jan. 13, [1861], in Graf and Haskins, *Papers of Andrew Johnson,* 4:160-61; Robert Hatton to William B. Campbell, Jan. 31, 1861, Campbell Papers, DU; William R. Sevier to Thomas A. R. Nelson, Dec. 11, 1860, and D. H. Kelly to Nelson, Dec. 30, 1860, both in Nelson Papers, McClung.

49. *Nashville Republican Banner,* Nov. 25 and 27, Dec. 8, 11, 13, 28, 1860; *Clarksville Jeffersonian,* Dec. 19, 1860; Feb. 6, 1861; *Nashville Patriot,* Nov. 8, 13, 29; Dec. 3 and 18, 1860; Jan. 11, 1861; Andrew Johnson, *Constitutionality and Rightfulness of Secession,* 22; O. N. Chapin to Andrew Johnson, Dec. 20, 1861, on p. 4:58; John Lellyett to Johnson, Dec. 20, 1860, on p. 4:62; and John C. McGaughey to Johnson, Feb. 21, 1861, on pp. 4:324-25, all in Graf and Haskins, *Papers of Andrew Johnson;* Adam Ferguson to William B. Stokes, Jan. 29, 1861, Ferguson Family Papers, TSLA.

50. George W. Jones to [torn], Nov. 20, 1860, Jones Papers, SHC.

51. *Clarksville Jeffersonian,* Nov. 14, 1860; Jan. 16, 1861; *Nashville Republican Banner,* Dec. 13, 1860; Jan. 20, 1861; *Nashville Patriot,* Nov. 22, 1860; Jan. 4; Feb. 2 and 5; Apr. 12, 1861; Lucius J. Polk to Emily Polk, Feb. 1, 1861, Polk-Yeatman Papers, SHC; A. Waldo Putnam to Andrew Johnson, Feb. 18, 1861, in Graf and Haskins, *Papers of Andrew Johnson,* 4:310-11.

52. *Nashville Republican Banner,* Dec. 22, 1860; Jan. 11, 12, 19, 25; Feb. 8; Apr. 3, 1861; *Nashville Patriot,* Dec. 21, 1860; Jan. 22 and Feb. 2, 1861; *Athens Post,* Dec. 14, 1860. On Crittenden's proposals and the other prominent compromise plans before Congress, see Crofts, *Reluctant Confederates,* 195-214.

53. Henry G. Smith to Andrew Johnson, Dec. 23, 1860, on p. 4:79, and Robert Johnson to Andrew Johnson, Jan. 17, [1861], on p. 4:178, both in Graf and Haskins, *Papers of Andrew Johnson;* Robert Hatton to William B. Campbell, Jan. 24, 1861, Campbell Papers, DU; William H. Polk to [unknown], Jan. 8, 1861, Polk Papers, NCDAH; *Nashville Republican Banner,* Nov. 16, 1860; Feb. 6 and 10, 1861.

54. *Nashville Union and American,* Nov. 8, 9, 17, 18, 20, 21, 25, 27; Dec. 1, 2, 7, 14, 19, 1860; Jan. 8, 9, 13, 19, 22, 23; Feb. 5, 6, 27, 1861; *Memphis Appeal,* Dec. 5, 8, 11, 13, 18, 21, 1860; Jan. 12, 13, 1861; C. R. Barteau, *A Brief Review: What Has Been Done in Tennessee* (Hartsville, Tenn.: Plaindealer Book and Job Printing Office, 1861), 5-8.

55. *Nashville Union and American,* Dec. 6, 7, 25, 28, 29, 1860; Jan. 2, 3, 20, 22; Feb. 12, 14, 26, 1861; *Memphis Appeal,* Dec. 14, 1860; Jan. 9, 11, 23; Feb. 3, 14; Mar. 8, 15, 21, 1861.

56. *Nashville Union and American,* Jan. 8, 13, 24; Feb. 16; and Mar. 3, 1861; *Memphis Appeal,* Jan. 22, 1861.

57. *Nashville Union and American,* Dec. 28 and 29, 1860; Jan. 15, 1861.

Notes to pages 235-39

58. *Nashville Republican Banner,* Dec. 9, 1860; *Nashville Patriot,* Jan. 1, 1861; *Nashville Union and American,* Dec. 8, 1860; *Clarksville Jeffersonian,* Nov. 28, 1860; *Athens Post,* Dec. 14, 1860; Jan. 25, 1861.

59. Cave Johnson to William B. Campbell, Jan. 6, 1861, Campbell Papers, DU; Robert McCorkle to Thomas A. R. Nelson, Jan. 30, 1861, Nelson Papers, McClung.

60. Isham G. Harris, "Legislative Message, January 7, 1861," White and Ash, *Messages of the Governors* 5:255. The five amendments proposed by Harris would have established a line "upon the Northern boundary of the present Slave States" dividing the territories into permanently free and permanently slave regions; required states failing to deliver fugitives to pay double the value of the slaves to their owners; protected slave property while in transit through any state; expressly prohibited Congress from abolishing slavery "in the District of Columbia, in any dock yard, navy yard, arsenal, or district of any character, within the limit of any slave State"; and prohibited any of the preceding amendments from being changed, "except by consent of all the slave States"; see White and Ash, *Messages of the Governors* 5:263-64.

61. Ibid., 5:265.

62. *Senate Journal* (1861, 1st extra sess.), 31; *Nashville Union and American,* Jan. 10, 1861.

63. *House Journal* (1861, 1st extra sess.), 24-29, 58, 62-66; *Senate Journal* (1861, 1st extra sess.), 43-44, 52-55, 67; Michael Burns to Andrew Johnson, Jan. 13, 1861, in Graf and Haskins, *Papers of Andrew Johnson,* 4:156; *Nashville Republican Banner,* Jan. 9, 1861.

64. *House Journal* (1861, 1st extra sess.), 61-62; *Senate Journal* (1861, 1st extra sess.), 37, 51; *Public Acts* (1861, 1st extra sess.), 15-17; Roderick R. Butler to Andrew Johnson, Jan. 15, 1861, on p. 4:169, and John W. Richardson to Johnson, Feb. 8, 1861, on p. 4:266, both in Graf and Haskins, *Papers of Andrew Johnson.* See appendix B below for party votes during this session.

65. *House Journal* (1861, 1st extra sess.), 131, 181, 217-18; *Senate Journal* (1861, 1st extra sess.), 63, 92, 117.

66. Return J. Meigs to Andrew Johnson, Feb. 7, 1861, in Graf and Haskins, *Papers of Andrew Johnson,* 4:263-64; S. D. Morgan to John Bell, Jan. 22, 1861, Polk-Yeatman Papers, SHC.

67. *Public Acts* (1861, 1st extra sess.), 27, 45-47.

68. Ibid., 49-54.

69. *House Journal* (1861, 1st extra sess.), 18, 159-69, 202; *Senate Journal* (1861, 1st extra sess.), 98-107, 150-51; *Public Acts* (1861, 1st extra sess.), 54. On the Washington Peace Conference, see Robert Gray Gunderson, *Old Gentlemen's Convention: The Washington Peace Conference of 1861* (Madison: Univ. of Wisconsin Press, 1961).

70. Jordan Stokes to William B. Campbell, Jan. 7, 1861, Campbell Papers, DU; William H. Carroll to Andrew Johnson, Jan. 2, [1861], on p. 4:117, and Jackson B. White to Johnson, Feb. 22, 1861, on p. 4:330, both in Graf and Haskins, *Papers of Andrew Johnson;* A. A. Kyle to Thomas A. R. Nelson, Jan.

14, 1861, Nelson Papers, McClung; William H. Polk to [unknown], Jan. 29, 1861, Polk Papers, NCDAH; *Nashville Republican Banner,* Jan. 15 and 31, 1861.

71. *Nashville Union and American,* Jan. 15, 19, 20, 29; Feb. 1, 2, 3, 6, 9, 12, 1861; *Memphis Appeal,* Jan. 22, 25, 27; Feb. 1, 5, 7, 1861.

72. *Nashville Republican Banner,* Jan. 17, 22, 24, 26, 27, 31, 1861; *Clarksville Jeffersonian,* Jan. 30, Feb. 6, 1861; *Nashville Patriot,* Jan. 21 and 25; Feb. 2, 7, 8, 1861; *Knoxville Whig,* Feb. 2, 1861; Harvey M. Watterson to Andrew Johnson, Feb. 12, 1861, in Graf and Haskins, *Papers of Andrew Johnson,* 4:287.

73. Reuben F. Alexander to Andrew Johnson, Dec. 25, 1860, on p. 4:88; William R. Hurley to Johnson, Jan. 14, 1861, on p. 4:167; and John P. White to Johnson, Feb. 16, 1861, on p. 4:298, all in Graf and Haskins, *Papers of Andrew Johnson;* W. H. Johnson to Thomas A. R. Nelson, Jan. 19, 1861, Nelson Papers, McClung; *Nashville Republican Banner,* Jan. 2, 1861; *Nashville Patriot,* Jan. 30, 1861; *Nashville Union and American,* Jan. 27, 1861; Crofts, *Reluctant Confederates,* 132.

74. C. H. Mills to Andrew Johnson, Feb. 10, 1861, on p. 4:268; John W. Richardson to Johnson, Feb. 8, 1861, on p. 4:266; Charles O. Faxon to Johnson, Jan. 15, 1861, on p. 4:171; and William H. Morrow to Johnson, Feb. 22, 1861, on p. 4:328-29, all in Graf and Haskins, *Papers of Andrew Johnson;* Samuel Milligan to Samuel Powel, Jan. 25, 1861, Powel III Papers, DU; *Nashville Republican Banner,* Feb. 13, 1861; *Nashville Patriot,* Feb. 15, 1861.

75. Crofts, *Reluctant Confederates,* 144-53, 164-94, 371.

76. John McGaughey to Andrew Johnson, Feb. 13, 1861, on p. 4:288; Richard M. Edwards to Johnson, Feb. 11, 1861, on p. 4:273; and Blackston McDaniel to Johnson, Feb. 16, 1861, on p. 4:295, all in Graf and Haskins, *Papers of Andrew Johnson; Nashville Republican Banner,* Feb. 19, 1861.

77. *Nashville Union and American,* Feb. 12, 13, 20, 22; Mar. 7, 12, 15, 24, 28, 30, 31; Apr. 3, 10, 11, 12, 13, 1861; *Memphis Appeal,* Feb. 10, 12, 13, 16, 19, 20, 22; Mar. 10, 17, 27; Apr. 2, 7, 1861; Barteau, *Brief Review,* 1.

78. C. H. Mills to Andrew Johnson, Feb. 10, 1861, on p. 4:268; William Lellyett to Johnson, Feb. 12, 1861, on pp. 4:281-82; Neill S. Brown to Johnson, Feb. 17, 1861, on p. 4:301; Joseph S. Fowler to Johnson, Feb. 21, 1861, on p. 4:323; Pitser Miller to Johnson, Feb. 27, 1861, on p. 3:341; and C. O. Faxon to Johnson, Mar. 20, 1861, on p. 4:414, all in Graf and Haskins, *Papers of Andrew Johnson;* Jacob Peck to Thomas A. R. Nelson, Feb. 14, 1861, Nelson Papers, McClung; John L. Hopkins to [William H. Polk], Mar. 9, 1861, Polk Papers, NCDAH.

79. *Nashville Union and American,* Feb. 19; Mar. 5, 6, 12, 30; Apr. 4, 1861; *Memphis Appeal,* Feb. 15, 16, 21; Mar. 5, 6, 7, 19, 1861; Potter, *Impending Crisis,* 555-77.

80. Jeptha Fowlkes to Andrew Johnson, Mar. 23, 1861, in Graf and Haskins, *Papers of Andrew Johnson,* 4:425.

81. Thomas J. Campbell to William B. Campbell, Mar. 17, 1861, Campbell Papers, DU; Jeptha Fowlkes to Andrew Johnson, Mar. 17, 1861, on p. 4:401;

Cave Johnson to Andrew Johnson, Mar. 21, 1861, on p. 4:424; Samuel Williams to Andrew Johnson, Mar. 25, 1861, on p. 4:430, all in Graf and Haskins, *Papers of Andrew Johnson*; John L. Hopkins to [William H. Polk], Mar. 9, 1861, Polk Papers, NCDAH; *Nashville Republican Banner*, Feb. 27; Mar. 6, 7, 13, 14, 17, 19, 21, 22, 23, 26; Apr. 4, 9, 15, 1861; *Nashville Patriot*, Mar. 6, 7,13, 15, 26; Apr. 4, 1861; *Knoxville Whig*, Feb. 23 and Mar. 9, 1861; *Clarksville Jeffersonian*, Mar. 13, 1861.

82. James M. McPherson, *Battle Cry of Freedom: The Civil War Era* (New York: Oxford Univ. Press, 1988), 264-75.

83. John Houston Bills diary (typescript), 39, Bills Papers, TSLA; William F. Cooper to Edmund Cooper and Henry Cooper, May 21, 1861, Cooper Family Papers, TSLA; B. J. Shoffner to Michael Shoffner, June 24, 1861, Shoffner Papers, SHC; Andrew J. Donelson to Mary Donelson Wilcox, May 24, 1861, Andrew Jackson Donelson Papers, LC; *Nashville Republican Banner*, Apr. 17, May 12 and 25, June 7, 1861; *Nashville Patriot*, Apr. 19, 20, 24; May 4, 5, 12, 1861; *Athens Post*, Apr. 19, 1861.

84. Felix K. Zollicoffer to William B. Campbell, May 15, 1861, Campbell Papers, DU.

85. *Clarksville Jeffersonian*, Apr. 17, 1861; *Nashville Republican Banner*, Apr. 16, 18, 19, 21, 24, 27; May 7, 9, 10, 11; June 2, 1861; *Nashville Patriot*, Apr. 14, 16, 17, 19, 24; May 7 and 16, 1861; *Nashville Union and American*, Apr. 14 and 21, 1861; A. Hilman to William B. Campbell, Apr. 21, 1861, Campbell Papers, DU; Parks, *John Bell of Tennessee*, 396-400.

86. *Nashville Union and American*, Apr. 16, 17, 19, 20, 23; May 14, 19, 26; June 2, 1861; *Memphis Appeal*, Apr. 13, 14, and 16, 1861.

87. *Nashville Union and American*, Apr. 14, 18, 25; May 1, 18, 29; June 8, 1861; *Memphis Appeal*, Apr. 16 and 18, 1861; *Nashville Republican Banner*, Apr. 19, 1861.

88. *House Journal* (1861, 2d extra sess.), 32, 57, 79; *Senate Journal* (1861, 2d extra sess.), 32-33, 55, 68-69; White and Ash, *Messages of the Governors* 5:285.

89. See appendix C below for party votes in this session.

90. F. W. Gordon to William B. Campbell, May 4, 1861; Emerson Etheridge to Campbell, May 9, 1861; A. S. Lindsley to Campbell, Apr. 16, 1861; and B. F. C. Smith to Campbell, June 2, 1861, all in Campbell Papers, DU; *Nashville Patriot*, June 5, 1861; *Nashville Union and American*, May 17, 1861; *Knoxville Whig*, May 25, 1861.

91. Crofts, *Reluctant Confederates*, 341-45, 371.

92. The Pearson correlate of East Tennessee's vote for Bell in the 1860 presidential election and support for Union in the June referendum is +.67. A good discussion of the reasons for the persistence of Unionism in Tennessee can be found in Noel Charles Fisher, "'War at Every Man's Door': The Struggle for East Tennessee, 1860-1869" (Ph.D. diss., Ohio State Univ., 1993), 69-128; see also Oliver P. Temple, *East Tennesseans and the Civil War* (Cincinnati, Ohio: Robert Clarke Co., 1899), 544-64; and Eric Russell Lacy, *Vanquished Volunteers: East Tennessee Sectionalism from*

Statehood to Secession (Johnson City, Tenn.: East Tennessee State Univ. Press, 1965), 183-91. John C. Inscoe suggests that East Tennessee's Unionism, in contrast to western North Carolina's support for secession, despite the two regions' social and economic similarities, was attributable to East Tennessee's "long-nurtured inferiority complex" and western North Carolinians' belief that they lived in "a region on the rise"; see Inscoe, "Mountain Unionism, Secession, and Regional Self-Image: The Contrasting Cases of Western North Carolina and East Tennessee," in *Looking South: Chapters in the Story of an American Region,* ed. Winifred B. Moore, Jr., and Joseph F. Tripp, 115-29 (New York: Greenwood, 1989). Also, slavery appears to have played a different role in East Tennessee society than Inscoe describes in western North Carolina; see John C. Inscoe, *Mountain Masters, Slavery, and the Sectional Crisis in Western North Carolina* (Knoxville: Univ. of Tennessee Press, 1989), 211-57, and the text below.

93. Crofts, *Reluctant Confederates,* 273, 326-38, 445-46; Andrew Johnson, *Constitutionality and Rightfulness of Secession;* J. Milton Henry, "The Revolution in Tennessee, February, 1861, to June, 1861," *THQ* 18 (June 1959): 99-119; James L. Baumgardner, "Abraham Lincoln, Andrew Johnson, and the Federal Patronage: An Attempt to Save Tennessee for the Union," East Tennessee Historical Society *Publications* 45 (1973): 51-60. Although Crofts severely criticizes the arguments in Henry's and Baumgardner's articles, they provide detailed accounts of the maneuvering over the decision concerning the distribution of Tennessee's patronage. On the importance of Unionist leadership, see Temple, *East Tennesseans and the Civil War,* 561-64; and Lacy, *Vanquished Volunteers,* 187-88.

94. *Nashville Union and American,* June 14, 1859; Dec. 8, 1860; and Jan. 19, 1861.

95. *Athens Post,* June 28, 1861; Sam Milligan to Andrew Johnson, Jan. 8, 1861, in Graf and Haskins, *Papers of Andrew Johnson,* 4:148; C. Stuart McGehee, "'The Property and Faith of the City:' Secession in Chattanooga," East Tennessee Historical Society *Publications* 60 (1988): 23-38; Peter Wallenstein, "Which Side Are You On? The Social Origins of White Union Troops from Civil War Tennessee," *Journal of East Tennessee History* 63 (1991): 72-103.

96. *Knoxville Whig,* May 4, 11, 18, and 25, and July 6, 1861; *Nashville Union and American,* May 15, 1861; Thomas N. Frazier to Oliver P. Temple, May 18, 1861, Temple Papers, UT; James Henry to Thomas A. R. Nelson, June 29, 1861, Nelson Papers, McClung; Andrew Johnson, *Constitutionality and Rightfulness of Secession,* 6; Charles Johnson to Andrew Johnson, Jan. 1, 1861, in Graf and Haskins, *Papers of Andrew Johnson,* 4:111.

97. *Knoxville Whig,* May 25, and June 8, 15, and 25, 1861; Charles F. Bryan, Jr., "A Gathering of Tories: The East Tennessee Convention of 1861," *THQ* 39 (Spring 1980): 37, 39-44.

98. Reply of Joint Select Committee on Greeneville Resolutions, qtd. in White and Ash, *Messages of the Governors* 5:314; *Nashville Union and American,* June 23, 27, 28, and 29, and July 26, 1861; *Clarksville Jeffersonian,* July 2, 1861; Isham G. Harris to Leroy Pope Walker, May 25, 1861, Isham

G. Harris Papers, TSLA; *The War of the Rebellion: A Compilation of the Official Records of the Union and Confederate Armies* (Washington, D.C.: Government Printing Office, 1898), ser. 1, vol. 52, pt. 2, p. 123.

99. *Public Acts* (1861, 2d extra sess.), 75; John Houston Bills diary (transcript), 41, Bills Family Papers, TSLA; John Lellyett to William B. Campbell, May 16, 1861, and W. R. Hunley to Campbell, May 20, 1861, both in Campbell Papers, DU; Isaac Sampson to William H. Polk, May 24, 1861, Polk Papers, NCDAH; Roderick R. Butler to Andrew Johnson, July 1, 1861, in Graf and Haskins, *Papers of Andrew Johnson*, 4:529-30. Harris offered the service of the provisional army to the Confederate States shortly after the passage of the assembly's resolutions; see Isham G. Harris to Jefferson Davis, July 2, 1861, Harris Papers, TSLA.

100. *Nashville Republican Banner*, May 3, 1861; Neill S. Brown, Balie Peyton, John S. Brien, and John Bell to William B. Campbell, May 3, 1861; W. B. Lewis to Campbell, May 2, 1861; William G. Brownlow to Campbell, May 6, 1861; Robertson Topp to Campbell, May 29, 1861; and Rolfe S. Saunders to Campbell, May 31, 1861, all in Campbell Papers, DU.

101. *Nashville Republican Banner*, June 29 and 30, and July 2 and 5, 1861.

102. *Nashville Republican Banner*, July 10, 11, 14, 16, 20, 23, 25, 1861; Robert H. McEwen to Oliver P. Temple, July 12, 1861, Temple Papers, UT. The state constitution prohibited sitting senators and representatives from eligibility "to any office or place of trust, the appointment of which is vested in the Executive or the General Assembly, except to the office of Trustee of a literary institution."

103. *Nashville Republican Banner*, June 23; July 18, 20, 23, 25, 26, 31; and Aug. 2, 1861.

104. *Knoxville Whig*, July 13 and 20, 1861; *Nashville Republican Banner*, July 16, 1861; Robert A. Crawford to Thomas A. R. Nelson, July 18, 1861, Nelson Papers, McClung; George W. Bridges to William H. Polk, July 17, 1861, Polk Papers, NCDAH; Alexander, *Thomas A. R. Nelson*, 87.

105. William H. Polk to Thomas A. R. Nelson, July 13, 1861, and George W. Bridges to Nelson, July 16, 1861, both in Nelson Papers, McClung; *Knoxville Whig*, July 20, 1861.

106. *Athens Post*, June 28, 1861; *Clarksville Jeffersonian*, July 30, 1861; *Nashville Union and American*, July 26 and 30, 1861; *Nashville Patriot*, July 3, 13, 18, 19, and 27, 1861; *Nashville Republican Banner*, July 5, 1861.

107. *Nashville Union and American*, May 12, and July 4, 5, 7, 13, 14, and 31, 1861; *Memphis Appeal*, June 25, and July 9, 12, 17, and 26, 1861; *Nashville Patriot*, July 3, 6, 16, and 19, 1861; Isham G. Harris to Jefferson Davis, July 13, 1861, Harris Papers, TSLA.

108. *Nashville Patriot*, Aug. 6, 1861.

109. *Nashville Union and American*, Aug. 2, 3, and 7, 1861; Isham G. Harris to Felix K. Zollicoffer, Aug. 4, 1861, and Harris to Leroy Pope Walker, Aug. 16, 1861, both in Harris Papers, TSLA. On the Confederacy's efforts to control Unionism in East Tennessee, see Noel Fisher, "'The Leniency Shown Them

Has Been Unavailing': The Confederate Occupation of East Tennessee," *Civil War History* 40 (Dec. 1994): 275-91; and Charles F. Bryan, Jr., "'Tories' Amidst Rebels: Confederate Occupation of East Tennessee, 1861-1863," East Tennessee Historical Society *Publications* 60 (1988): 3-22.

110. White and Ash, *Messages of the Governors* 5:364-72.

111. Charles R. Mott, ed., "War Journal of a Confederate Officer," *THQ* 5 (Sept. 1946): 237.

Bibliography

I. Primary Sources

A. Manuscripts

Burrow Library, Rhodes College, Memphis
    Topp, Robertson, Papers
Historical Society of Pennsylvania, Philadelphia
    Buchanan, James, Papers
James D. Hoskins Library, Univ. of Tennessee, Knoxville
    Donelson, Andrew Jackson, Letters
    Park Family Papers
    Temple, Oliver P., Papers
Library of Congress, Washington, D.C.
    Bell, John, Collection
    Donelson, Andrew Jackson, Papers
    Jackson, Andrew, Papers
    Polk, James K., Papers
McClung Collection, East Tennessee Historical Center, Knoxville
    Nelson, Thomas Amis Rogers, Papers
New York Historical Society, New York City
    Nicholson, Alfred Osborne Pope, Correspondence
North Carolina Dept. of Archives and History, Raleigh
    Polk, William H., Papers
William R. Perkins Library, Duke Univ.
    Campbell, David, Papers
    Hodgson, William Brown, Papers
    Powel, Samuel III, Papers
    White, Hugh Lawson, Papers
    Williams, Alexander, Papers
Southern Historical Collection, Univ. of North Carolina, Chapel Hill
    Buchanan-McClellan Papers
    Caruthers, Robert Looney, Papers
    Grundy, Felix, Papers
    Henry, Gustavus A., Papers

Jones, George Washington, Papers
McGavock Family Papers
Polk-Yeatman Collection
Shoffner, Michael, Papers
Tennessee Historical Society, Nashville
   Claybrooke-Overton Papers
   Donelson, Andrew Jackson, Papers
   Donelson, Bettie M., Papers
   Dyas Collection, John Coffee Papers
   Heiss, John P., Papers
   Laughlin, Samuel H., Papers
   Miscellaneous Files
   Murdock Collection-Overton Papers
   Trousdale, William, Papers
Tennessee State Library and Archives, Nashville
   Bills, John Houston, Papers
   Brown, Aaron Venable, Papers
   Cooper Family Papers
   Crozier, Arthur R., Papers
   Ferguson Family Papers
   Foster-Woods Papers
   Gordon and Avery Papers
   Grundy, Felix, Papers
   Harris, Isham G., Papers
   Horn, Stanley, Collection, Andrew Jackson Papers
   McEwen, Robert Houston, Papers
   McGavock, Randall William, Papers
   Orr, Mary Hamilton Thompson, Collection
   Russwurm Papers
   Trousdale, William, Papers
   Yeatman-Polk Collection

B. Newspapers

Athens (Tenn.) Post
Clarksville (Tenn.) Jeffersonian
Columbia (Tenn.) Observer
Columbia (Tenn.) Tennessee Democrat
Elizabethton (Tenn.) Tennessee Whig
Jackson (Tenn.) Southern Statesman
Jonesborough (Tenn.) Whig
Knoxville Argus
Knoxville Register
Knoxville Whig
Memphis Appeal
Memphis Eagle

Memphis Eagle and Enquirer
Memphis Enquirer
Nashville American
Nashville Gazette
Nashville National Banner
Nashville Patriot
Nashville Republican
Nashville Republican Banner
Nashville True Whig
Nashville Union
Nashville Union and American
Nashville Whig

C. Government Documents

Dunlap, James T. "Report of James T. Dunlap, Comptroller of the Treasury, to the General Assembly of Tennessee, October, 1859." In Tennessee General Assembly. *Appendix to House and Senate Journals.* Nashville.

Journal of the Convention of the State of Tennessee; Convened for the Purpose of Revising and Amending the Constitution Thereof. Nashville: n.p., 1834.

Journal of the Proceedings of a Convention Begun and Held at Knoxville, January 11, 1796. Knoxville, Tenn., 1796; reprinted Nashville: n.p., 1852.

Sturtevant, J. M. "Fifth Biennial Report of the Institution of the Blind." Tennessee General Assembly. *Appendix to House and Senate Journals.* Nashville, 1853-54.

Tennessee General Assembly. *Journal of the House of Representatives of the State of Tennessee.* 1832-61. Nashville.

———. *Journal of the Senate of the State of Tennessee.* 1832-61. Nashville.

———. *Public Acts of the State of Tennessee.* 1827-61. Nashville.

U.S. Census Office. *Agriculture of the United States in 1860; Compiled from the Original Returns of the Eighth Census, Under the Direction of the Secretary of the Interior, by Joseph C. G. Kennedy, Superintendent of Census.* Washington, D.C.: Government Printing Office, 1864.

———. Manuscripts. Fifth Census, 1830; Sixth Census, 1840; Seventh Census, 1850; Eighth Census, 1860.

———. *Population of the United States in 1860: Compiled from the Original Returns of the Eighth Census, Under the Direction of the Secretary of the Interior, by Joseph C. G. Kennedy.* Washington, D.C.: Government Printing Office, 1864.

———. *Preliminary Report on the Eighth Census of the United States; 1860.* Washington, D.C.: Government Printing Office, 1862.

———. *Seventh Census of the United States: 1850.* Washington, D.C.: R. Armstrong, 1853.

———. *Sixth Census of Enumeration of the Inhabitants of the United States.* Washington, D.C.: Blair and Rives, 1841.

U.S. Congress. *Congressional Globe*. Washington, D.C., 1835-55.
The War of the Rebellion: A Compilation of the Official Records of the Union and Confederate Armies. Washington: Government Printing Office, 1898.

D. Published

Address to the People of Tennessee by the Whig Convention, Which Assembled at Knoxville, on Monday, the 10th of February, 1840. Knoxville: n.p., 1840.
Address to the Republican People of Tennessee by the Central Corresponding Committee of the State [No. 1]. Nashville: n.p., 1840.
Address to the Republican People of Tennessee by the Central Corresponding Committee of the State [No. 2]. Nashville: n.p., 1840.
Anderson, Alexander O. *The Letter of Alexander Anderson, of Tennessee, in Reply to the Committee of Invitation to Attend a Dinner Given by the Democracy of Maury, Tennessee, On the 13th July to the Delegation from That State to the National Convention.* N.p., 1844.
Bassett, John Spencer, ed. *Correspondence of Andrew Jackson*. 7 vols. Washington, D.C.: Carnegie Institute, 1926-35.
Barteau, C. R. *A Brief Review: What Has Been Done in Tennessee*. Hartsville, Tenn.: *Plaindealer* Book and Job Printing Office, 1861.
Bell, John. *The Compromise Bill, Speech of Hon. John Bell, of Tennessee, in the Senate of the United States, July 3 and 5, 1850, On the Bill for the Admission of California into the Union, the Establishment of Territorial Governments for Utah and New Mexico, and Making Proposals to Texas for the Settlement of Her Northern and Western Boundaries.* Washington, D.C.: Congressional Globe Office, 1850.

———. *Speech of the Hon. John Bell, Delivered at a Mass Meeting of the American Party Held at Knoxville, Tennessee, September 22, 1855.* N.p., 1855.

———. *Speech of the Hon. John Bell, Delivered at Vauxhall Garden, Nashville, on the 23rd of May, 1835.* Nashville: W. Hasell Hunt, 1835.

———. *Speech of the Hon. John Bell, of Tennessee, on the Admission of Kansas Under the Lecompton Constitution, Delivered in the Senate of the United States, March 18, 1858.* Washington, D.C.: Buell and Blanchard, 1858.

———. *Speech of Hon. John Bell, of Tennessee on the Nebraska and Kansas Bill, Delivered in the Senate of the United States. May 24 and 25, 1854.* Washington, D.C.: Congressional Globe Office, 1854.

———. *Speech of Mr. Bell, of Tennessee, on the Bill to Secure the Freedom of Elections, Delivered in the House of Representatives, January, 1837.* Washington, D.C.: William W. Moore, 1837.
[Bilbo, W. N.] *The American's Text-Book, Being a Series of Letters, Addressed by "An American," to the Citizens of Tennessee, in Exposition and Vindication of the Principles and Policy of the American Party.* Nashville: n.p., 1855.

Brown, Aaron V. *Speeches, Congressional and Political, and Other writings, of Ex-Governor Aaron V. Brown, of Tennessee.* Nashville: John L. Marling and Co., 1854.

Brownlow, William G. *Americanism Contrasted with Foreignism, Romanism, and Bogus Democracy, in the Light of Reason, History, and Scripture; in which Certain Demagogues in Tennessee, and Elsewhere, Are Shown Up in Their True Colors.* Nashville: n.p., 1856.

———. *A Political Register, Setting Forth the Principles of the Whig and Locofoco Parties in the United States, with the Life and Public Services of Henry Clay. Also an Appendix Personal to the Author; and a General Index.* Jonesborough, Tenn.: n.p., 1844.

Crallé, Richard K., ed. *The Works of John C. Calhoun.* 6 vols. New York: D. Appleton and Co., 1854-56.

Etheridge, Emerson. *Speech of the Hon. Emerson Etheridge, of Tennessee, Delivered in the House of Representatives, January 23, 1861.* Washington, D.C.: Henry Polkinhorn, 1861.

———. *Speech of Emerson Etheridge, of Tennessee, in the House of Representatives, May 17, 1854.* Washington, D.C.: Buell and Blanchard, 1854.

Eubank, David L., ed., "J. G. M. Ramsey as a Bond Agent: Selections from the Ramsey Papers." East Tennessee Historical Society *Publications* 36 (1964): 81-99.

Gentry, Meredith P. *Speech of Honorable M. P. Gentry, of Tennessee, Delivered in the House of Representatives, June 14, 1852.* Washington, D.C.: n.p., 1852.

———. *Speech of M. P. Gentry, of Tennessee, on the Admission of California, Delivered in the House of Representatives, U.S., Monday, June 10, 1850.* Washington, D.C.: Gideon and Co., 1850.

Graf, Leroy P., and Ralph W. Haskins, et al., eds. *The Papers of Andrew Johnson.* 11 vols. Knoxville: Univ. of Tennessee Press, 1967- .

Guild, Josephus C. *Old Times in Tennessee.* Nashville: Tavel, Eastman, and Howell, 1878.

[Hall, Allen A.] *The Counterfeit Detector, or, The Leaders of 'The Party' Exposed.* Nashville: n.p., 1839.

Hopkins, Anne H., and William Lyons. *Tennessee Votes: 1799-1976.* Studies in Tennessee Politics, no. 2. Knoxville: Bureau of Public Administration, Univ. of Tennessee, 1978.

Hopkins, James F., et al., eds. *The Papers of Henry Clay.* 11 vols. Lexington: Univ. of Kentucky Press, 1959-92.

Johnson, Andrew. *The Constitutionality and Rightfulness of Secession; Speech of Hon. Andrew Johnson, of Tennessee, in the Senate of the United States, on Tuesday and Wednesday, December 18 and 19, 1860.* Washington, D.C.: n.p., 1860.

Jones, James C. *Speech of the Hon. James C. Jones, in the United States Senate, Aug., 1856.* Washington, D.C.: n.p., 1856.

———. *Speech of the Hon. James C. Jones of Tennessee on a Petition for the Repeal of the Fugitive Slave Law, Presented by Mr. Rockwell, from Mas-*

sachusetts; and on the Recent Address of Certain Members of Congress. In the Senate of the United States, June 26, 1854. Washington, D.C.: Congressional Globe Office, 1854.

Mott, Charles R., ed. "War Journal of a Confederate Officer." *Tennessee Historical Quarterly* 5 (Sept. 1946): 237.

Perkins, Philip Gaspard Stiver. *Speech of Mr. P. G. Stiver Perkins, of Williamson County, on the Resolutions of the Committee on Federal Relations. Delivered in the House of Representatives, February 6, 1850.* Nashville: B. R. McKenzie and Co., 1850.

Polk, James K. *Address of James K. Polk, to the People of Tennessee.* Nashville: n.p., 1841.

———. *Speech of the Hon. James K. Polk, Delivered at a Public Dinner at Mooresville, Maury County, Tennessee, on the 22nd Day of October, 1835.* Nashville: n.p., 1835.

Ready, Charles. *Speech of the Hon. Charles Ready, of Tennessee, on the Nebraska and Kansas Bill. Delivered in the House of Representatives, May 17, 1854.* Washington, D.C.: Towers, 1854.

Richardson, James D. *A Compilation of the Messages and Papers of the Presidents.* 20 vols. New York: Bureau of National Literature, 1897-1911.

Scott, Nancy N., ed. *A Memoir of Hugh Lawson White.* Philadelphia: J. B. Lippincott, 1856.

Temple, Oliver P. *East Tennessee and the Civil War.* Cincinnati, Ohio: Robert Clark Co., 1899.

[Tennessee] Democratic Central Committee. *The Annexation of Texas to the United States Fully and Fairly Discussed; Together with All Important Documents Connected with the Question.* Nashville: n.p., 1844.

———. *The Currency and Other Questions. The Views of the Democracy Contrasted with Those of the Opposition!* Nashville: n.p., 1859.

Weaver, Herbert, et al., eds. *Correspondence of James K. Polk.* 8 vols. Knoxville: Univ. of Tennessee Press, 1969- .

Wheeler, John E. *Speech of Mr. Wheeler of the Senate, Upon the Instructing Resolutions.* Nashville: n.p., 1839.

White, Robert H., and Stephen V. Ash, eds. *Messages of the Governors of Tennessee.* 11 vols. Nashville: Tennessee Historical Commission, 1952- .

[Williams, James]. *Reflections and Suggestions on the Present State of Parties, by an Old Clay Whig.* Nashville: G. C. Torbett and Co., 1856.

Williams, Samuel C., ed. "Journal of Events (1825-1873) of David Anderson Deadrick." East Tennessee Historical Society *Publications* 8 (1936): 130.

Zollicoffer, Felix K. *Speech of F. K. Zollicoffer, Delivered at Nashville, June 16, 1855.* Nashville: n.p., 1855.

———. *Speech of Mr. Zollicoffer, of Tennessee, on the Nebraska and Kansas Bill. Delivered in the House of Representatives, May 9, 1854.* Washington, D.C.: n.p., 1854.

II. Secondary Sources

A. Articles

Abernethy, Thomas Perkins. "The Early Development of Commerce and Banking in Tennessee." *Mississippi Valley Historical Review* 14 (Dec. 1927): 311-25.

———. "The Origin of the Whig Party in Tennessee." *Mississippi Valley Historical Review* 12 (Mar. 1926): 504-22.

Bacon, H. Phillip. "Nashville's Trade at the Beginning of the Nineteenth Century." *Tennessee Historical Quarterly* 15 (Mar. 1956): 30-36.

Baker, Steve. "Agriculture, Race, and Free Blacks in West Tennessee." West Tennessee Historical Society *Papers* 48 (Dec. 1994): 107-17.

Baumgardner, James L. "Abraham Lincoln, Andrew Johnson, and the Federal Patronage: An Attempt to Save Tennessee for the Union." East Tennessee Historical Society *Publications* 45 (1973): 51-60.

Bergeron, Paul H. "James K. Polk and the Jacksonian Press in Tennessee." *Tennessee Historical Quarterly* 41 (Fall 1982): 257-77.

———. "Tennessee's Response to the Nullification Crisis." *Journal of Southern History* 39 (Feb. 1973): 23-44.

Brown, Richard H. "The Missouri Crisis, Slavery, and the Politics of Jacksonianism." *South Atlantic Quarterly* 65 (Winter 1966): 55-72.

Brown, Thomas. "From Old Hickory to Sly Fox: The Routinization of Charisma in the Early Democratic Party." *Journal of the Early Republic* 11 (Fall 1991): 339-69.

Bryan, Charles F., Jr. "A Gathering of Tories: The East Tennessee Convention of 1861." *Tennessee Historical Quarterly* 39 (Spring 1980): 27-48.

———. "'Tories' Amidst Rebels: Confederate Occupation of East Tennessee, 1861-1863." East Tennessee Historical Society *Publications* 60 (1988): 3-22.

Calomiris, Charles W., and Larry Schweikart. "The Panic of 1857: Origins, Transmission, and Containment." *Journal of Economic History* 51 (Dec. 1991): 807-34.

Cutler, Wayne. "Jackson, Polk, and Johnson: Defenders of the Moral Economy." *Tennessee Historical Quarterly* 54 (Fall 1995): 178-89.

De Fiore, Jayne Crumpler. "Come, and Bring the Ladies: Tennessee Women and the Politics of Opportunity during the Presidential Campaigns of 1840 and 1844." *Tennessee Historical Quarterly* 51 (Winter 1992): 197-212.

Everett, Robert B. "James K. Polk and the Election of 1844 in Tennessee." West Tennessee Historical Society *Papers* 16 (1962): 5-28.

Fisher, Noel. "'The Leniency Shown Them Has Been Unavailing': The Confederate Occupation of East Tennessee." *Civil War History* 40 (Dec. 1994): 275-91.

Folsom, Burton W., II. "The Politics of Elites: Prominence and Party in Davidson County, Tennessee, 1835-1861." *Journal of Southern History* 39 (Aug. 1973): 359-78.

Gatell, Frank Otto. "Spoils of the Bank War: Political Bias in the Selection of Pet Banks." *American Historical Review* 70 (Oct. 1964): 35-58.

Goodheart, Lawrence B. "Tennessee's Antislavery Movement Reconsidered: The Example of Elihu Embree." *Tennessee Historical Quarterly* 41 (Fall 1982): 224-38.

Goodheart, Lawrence B., Neil Hanks, and Elizabeth Johnson. "'An Act for the Relief of Females . . .': Divorce and Changing the Legal Status of Women in Tennessee, 1796-1860." 2 parts. *Tennessee Historical Quarterly* 44 (Fall 1985): 318-39, and 44 (Winter 1985): 402-16.

Henry, J. Milton. "The Revolution in Tennessee, February, 1861, to June, 1861." *Tennessee Historical Quarterly* 18 (June 1959): 99-119.

Howington, Arthur F. "'Not in the Condition of a Horse or an Ox': Ford v. Ford, the Law of Testamentary Manumission, and the Tennessee Court's Recognition of Slave Humanity." *Tennessee Historical Quarterly* 34 (Fall 1975): 249-68.

Inscoe, John C. "Mountain Unionism, Secession, and Regional Self-Image: The Contrasting Cases of Western North Carolina and East Tennessee." In *Looking South: Chapters in the Story of an American Region*, edited by Winifred B. Moore, Jr., and Joseph F. Tripp. 115-29. New York: Greenwood, 1989.

Jennings, Thelma. "Tennessee and the Nashville Conventions of 1850." *Tennessee Historical Quarterly* 30 (Spring 1971): 70-82.

Kruman, Marc W. "The Second American Party System and the Transformation of Revolutionary Republicanism." *Journal of the Early Republic* 12 (Winter 1992): 509-37.

Latner, Richard B. "The Eaton Affair Reconsidered." *Tennessee Historical Quarterly* 36 (Fall 1977): 330-51.

———. "The Nullification Crisis and Republican Subversion." *Journal of Southern History* 43 (Feb. 1971): 19-38.

Lufkin, Charles L. "Divided Loyalties: Sectionalism in Civil War McNairy County, Tennessee." *Tennessee Historical Quarterly* 47 (Fall 1988): 169-77.

———. "Secession and Coercion in Tennessee: The Spring of 1861." *Tennessee Historical Quarterly* 50 (Summer 1991): 98-109.

McCormick, Richard P. "Was There a 'Whig Strategy' in 1836?" *Journal of the Early Republic* 4 (Spring 1984): 47-70.

McGehee, C. Stuart. "'The Property and Faith of the City': Secession in Chattanooga." East Tennessee Historical Society *Publications* 60 (1988): 23-38.

Moore, Powell. "The Revolt Against Jackson in Tennessee, 1835-1836." *Journal of Southern History* 2 (Aug. 1936): 335-59.

Morrison, Michael A. "Martin Van Buren, the Democracy, and the Partisan Politics of Texas Annexation." *Journal of Southern History* 61 (Nov. 1995): 696-724.

———. "'New Territory versus No Territory': The Whig Party and the Politics of Western Expansion, 1846-1848." *Western Historical Quarterly* 23 (Feb. 1992): 25-51.

———. "Westward the Curse of Empire: Texas Annexation and the American Whig Party." *Journal of the Early Republic* 10 (Summer 1990): 221-49.

Rodgers, Daniel T. "Republicanism: The Career of a Concept." *Journal of American History* 79 (June 1992): 11-38.
Schweikart, Larry. "Tennessee Banks in the Antebellum Period." *Tennessee Historical Quarterly* 45 (Summer 1986): 119-32.
Sellers, Charles G. "Banking and Politics in Jackson's Tennessee, 1817-1827." *Mississippi Valley Historical Review* 41 (June 1954): 61-84.
―――. "Jackson Men with Feet of Clay." *American Historical Review* 62 (Apr. 1957): 537-51.
―――. "Who Were the Southern Whigs?" *American Historical Review* 59 (Jan. 1954): 335-46.
Shalhope, Robert E. "Republicanism and Early American Historiography." *William and Mary Quarterly* 39 (Apr. 1982): 334-56.
―――. "Toward a Republican Synthesis: The Emergence of an Understanding of Republicanism in American Historiography." *William and Mary Quarterly* 29 (Jan. 1972): 49-80.
Silbey, Joel H. "Election of 1836." In *History of American Presidential Elections, 1789-1968*, edited by Arthur M. Schlesinger, Jr. New York: McGraw-Hill, 1971.
Sioussat, St. George L. "Tennessee, the Compromise of 1850, and the Nashville Convention." *Tennessee Historical Magazine* 4 (Dec. 1918): 215-247.
Soltow, Lee. "Land Inequality on the Frontier: The Distribution of Land in East Tennessee at the Beginning of the Nineteenth Century." *Social Science Historian* 5 (Summer 1981): 275-91.
Thornton, J. Mills, III. "The Ethic of Subsistence and the Origins of Southern Secession." *Tennessee Historical Quarterly* 48 (Summer 1989): 67-85.
Timberlake, Richard H. "The Specie Circular and Distribution of the Surplus." *Journal of Political Economy* 68 (Apr. 1960): 109-17.
Varon, Elizabeth R. "Tippecanoe and the Ladies, Too: White Women and Party Politics in Antebellum Virginia." *Journal of American History* 82 (Sept. 1995): 494-521.
Wallenstein, Peter. "Which Side Are You On? The Social Origins of White Union Troops from Civil War Tennessee." *Journal of East Tennessee History* 63 (1991): 72-103.
Walton, Brian G. "A Matter of Timing: Elections to the United States Senate in Tennessee before the Civil War." *Tennessee Historical Quarterly* 31 (Summer 1972): 129-48.
Watson, Harry L. "Conflict and Collaboration: Yeoman, Slaveholders, and Politics in the Antebellum South." *Social History* 10 (Oct. 1985): 273-98.
Wilson, Major L. "The 'Country' versus the 'Court': A Republican Consensus and Party Debate in the Bank War." *Journal of the Early Republic* 15 (Winter 1995): 619-47.
―――. "Republicanism and the Idea of Party in the Jacksonian Period." *Journal of the Early Republic* 8 (Winter 1988): 419-42.
Winters, Donald L. "The Agricultural Ladder in Southern Agriculture: Tennessee, 1850-1870." *Agricultural History* 61 (Summer 1987): 36-52.
―――. "'Plain Folk' of the Old South Reexamined: Economic Democracy in Tennessee." *Journal of Southern History* 53 (Nov. 1987): 565-86.

B. Books

Abernethy, Thomas Perkins. *From Frontier to Plantation in Tennessee: A Study in Frontier Democracy.* Chapel Hill: Univ. of North Carolina Press, 1932.
Alexander, Thomas B. *Thomas A. R. Nelson of East Tennessee.* Nashville: Tennessee Historical Commission, 1956.
Anbinder, Tyler. *Nativism and Slavery: The Northern Know-Nothings and the Politics of the 1850s.* New York: Oxford Univ. Press, 1992.
Ash, Stephen V. *Middle Tennessee Society Transformed, 1860-1870: War and Peace in the Upper South.* Baton Rouge: Louisiana State Univ. Press, 1988.
Bailyn, Bernard. *The Ideological Origins of the American Revolution.* Cambridge, Mass.: Belknap Press of Harvard Univ. Press, 1967.
Banning, Lance. *The Jeffersonian Persuasion: Evolution of a Party Ideology.* Ithaca, N.Y.: Cornell Univ. Press, 1978.
Bauer, K. Jack. *The Mexican War, 1846-1848.* New York: Macmillan Publishing Co., 1974.
———. *Zachary Taylor: Soldier, Planter, Statesman of the Old Southwest.* Baton Rouge: Louisiana State Univ. Press, 1985.
Bergeron, Paul H. *Antebellum Politics in Tennessee.* Lexington: Univ. of Kentucky Press, 1982.
———. *The Presidency of James K. Polk.* Lawrence: Univ. Press of Kansas, 1987.
Brown, Thomas. *Politics and Statesmanship: Essays on the American Whig Party.* New York: Columbia Univ. Press, 1985.
Campbell, Claude A. *The Development of Banking in Tennessee.* Nashville: n.p., 1932.
Campbell, Mary E. R. *The Attitude of Tennesseans Toward the Union, 1847-1861.* New York: Vantage Press, 1961.
Cantrell, Greg. *Kenneth and John B. Rayner and the Limits of Southern Dissent.* Urbana: Univ. of Illinois Press, 1993.
Cimprich, John. *Slavery's End in Tennessee, 1861-1865.* University: Univ. of Alabama Press, 1985.
Clark, Blanche Henry. *The Tennessee Yeoman, 1840-1860.* Nashville: Vanderbilt Univ. Press, 1942.
Cole, Donald B. *Martin Van Buren and the American Political System.* Princeton, N.J.: Princeton Univ. Press, 1984.
———. *The Presidency of Andrew Jackson.* Lawrence: Univ. Press of Kansas, 1993.
Cooper, William J., Jr. *The South and the Politics of Slavery, 1828-1856.* Baton Rouge: Louisiana State Univ. Press, 1978.
Crofts, Daniel W. *Reluctant Confederates: Upper South Unionists in the Secession Crisis.* Chapel Hill: Univ. of North Carolina Press, 1989.
Ellis, Richard E. *The Union at Risk: Jacksonian Democracy, States' Rights and the Nullification Crisis.* New York: Oxford Univ. Press, 1987.
Fehrenbacher, Don E. *Slavery, Law and Politics: The Dred Scott Case in Historical Perspective.* New York: Oxford Univ. Press, 1981.

Folmsbee, Stanley John. *Sectionalism and Internal Improvements in Tennessee, 1796-1845.* Knoxville: East Tennessee Historical Society, 1939.
Ford, Lacy K. *Origins of Southern Radicalism: The South Carolina Upcountry, 1800-1860.* New York: Oxford Univ. Press, 1988.
Fredrickson, George M. *The Black Image in the White Mind.* Middleton, Conn.: Wesleyan Univ. Press, 1971.
Freehling, William W. *Prelude to Civil War: The Nullification Controversy in South Carolina, 1816-1836.* New York: Harper and Row, 1965.
———. *The Road to Disunion: Secessionists at Bay, 1776-1854.* New York: Oxford Univ. Press, 1990.
Gienapp, William E. *The Origins of the Republican Party, 1852-1856.* New York: Oxford Univ. Press, 1987.
Goodstein, Anita Shafer. *Nashville, 1780-1860: From Frontier to City.* Gainesville: Univ. of Florida Press, 1989.
Greenberg, Kenneth S. *Masters and Statesmen: The Political Culture of American Slavery.* Baltimore, Md.: Johns Hopkins Univ. Press, 1985.
Gunderson, Robert Gray. *Old Gentleman's Convention: The Washington Peace Conference of 1861.* Madison: Univ. of Wisconsin Press, 1961.
Hamilton, Holman. *Prologue to Conflict: The Crisis and Compromise of 1850.* Lexington: Univ. Press of Kentucky, 1964.
Hammond, Bray. *Banks and Politics in America from the Revolution to the Civil War.* Princeton, N.J.: Princeton Univ. Press, 1957.
Hofstadter, Richard. *The Idea of a Party System: The Rise of Legitimate Opposition in the United States, 1780-1840.* Berkeley: Univ. of California Press, 1969.
Holt, Michael F. *The Political Crisis of the 1850s.* New York: Norton, 1978.
———. *Political Parties and American Political Development from the Age of Jackson to the Age of Lincoln.* Baton Rouge: Louisiana State Univ. Press, 1992.
Howington, Arthur F. *What Sayeth the Law: The Treatment of Slaves and Free Blacks in the State and Local Courts of Tennessee.* New York: Garland, 1986.
Huston, James L. *The Panic of 1857 and the Coming of the Civil War.* Baton Rouge: Louisiana State Univ. Press, 1987.
Inscoe, John C. *Mountain Masters, Slavery, and the Sectional Crisis in Western North Carolina.* Knoxville: Univ. of Tennessee Press, 1989.
Jennings, Thelma. *The Nashville Convention: Southern Movement for Unity, 1848-1851.* Memphis: Memphis State Univ. Press, 1980.
Johannsen, Robert W. *Stephen A. Douglas.* New York: Oxford Univ. Press, 1973.
Jordan, Winthrop D. *White Over Black: American Attitudes Toward the Negro, 1550-1812.* Chapel Hill: Univ. of North Carolina Press, 1968.
Ketcham, Ralph. *Presidents Above Party: The First American Presidency, 1789-1829.* Chapel Hill: Univ. of North Carolina Press, 1984.
Klein, Milton M., Richard D. Brown, and John B. Hench, eds. *The Republican Synthesis Revisited: Essays in Honor of George Athan Billias.* Worcester, Mass.: American Antiquarian Society, 1992.

Knupfer, Peter B. *The Union As It Is: Constitutional Unionism and Sectional Compromise, 1787-1861*. Chapel Hill: Univ. of North Carolina Press, 1991.

Kohl, Lawrence Frederick. *The Politics of Individualism: Parties and the American Character in the Jacksonian Era*. New York: Oxford Univ. Press, 1989.

Kruman, Marc W. *Parties and Politics in North Carolina, 1836-1865*. Baton Rouge: Louisiana State Univ. Press, 1983.

Lacy, Eric Russell. *Vanquished Volunteers: East Tennessee Sectionalism from Statehood to Secession*. Johnson City: East Tennessee State Univ. Press, 1965.

Latner, Richard B. *The Presidency of Andrew Jackson: White House Politics, 1829-1837*. Athens: Univ. of Georgia Press, 1979.

Masterson, William H. *William Blount*. Baton Rouge: Louisiana State Univ. Press, 1954.

McBride, Robert M., and Dan M. Robison, eds. *Biographical Directory of the Tennessee General Assembly*. 3 vols. Nashville: Tennessee State Library and Archives and the Tennessee Historical Commission, 1975.

McClure, Wallace M. *State Constitution-Making, with Especial Reference to Tennessee*. Nashville: Marshall and Bruce Co., 1915.

McCormick, Richard P. *The Second American Party System: Party Formation in the Jackson Era*. New York: Norton, 1966.

McFaul, John M. *The Politics of Jacksonian Finance*. Ithaca, N.Y.: Cornell Univ. Press, 1972.

McKenzie, Robert Tracy. *One South or Many? Plantation Belt and Upcountry in Civil War Era Tennessee*. Cambridge, England: Cambridge Univ. Press, 1994.

McPherson, James M. *Battle Cry of Freedom: The Civil War Era*. New York: Oxford Univ. Press, 1988.

———. *What They Fought For, 1861-1865*. Baton Rouge: Louisiana State Univ. Press, 1994.

Morgan, Edmund S. *American Slavery, American Freedom: The Ordeal of Colonial Virginia*. New York: Norton, 1975.

Mooney, Chase C. *Slavery in Tennessee*. Bloomington: Indiana Univ. Press, 1957.

Nichols, Roy F. *The Disruption of the American Democracy*. New York: Macmillan, 1948.

Niven, John. *John C. Calhoun and the Price of Union: A Biography*. Baton Rouge: Louisiana State Univ. Press, 1988.

Oakes, James. *The Ruling Race: A History of American Slaveholders*. New York: Vintage Books, 1982.

Parks, Joseph Howard. *Felix Grundy: Champion of Democracy*. Baton Rouge: Louisiana State Univ. Press, 1940.

———. *John Bell of Tennessee*. Baton Rouge: Louisiana State Univ. Press, 1950.

Patton, James W. *Unionism and Reconstruction in Tennessee, 1860-1869*. Chapel Hill: Univ. of North Carolina Press, 1934.

Peterson, Norma Lois. *The Presidencies of William Henry Harrison and John Tyler.* Lawrence: Univ. Press of Kansas, 1989.
Phillips, U. B. *Life and Labor in the Old South.* Boston: Little, Brown, 1963.
Potter, David M. *The Impending Crisis, 1848-1861.* New York: Harper and Row, 1976.
Rable, George C. *The Confederate Republic: A Revolution Against Politics.* Chapel Hill: Univ. of North Carolina Press, 1994.
Schlesinger, Arthur M., Jr. *The Age of Jackson.* Boston: Little, Brown, 1945.
Schweikart, Larry. *Banking in the American South from the Age of Jackson to Reconstruction.* Baton Rouge: Louisiana State Univ. Press, 1987.
Sellers, Charles G. *James K. Polk: Continentalist, 1843-1846.* Princeton, N.J.: Princeton Univ. Press, 1966.
——. *James K. Polk: Jacksonian, 1795-1843.* Princeton, N.J.: Princeton Univ. Press, 1957.
——. *The Market Revolution: Jacksonian America, 1815-1846.* New York: Oxford Univ. Press, 1991.
Temin, Peter. *The Jacksonian Economy.* New York: Norton, 1969.
Thornton, J. Mills, III. *Politics and Power in a Slave Society: Alabama, 1800-1860.* Baton Rouge: Louisiana State Univ. Press, 1978.
Walther, Eric H. *The Fire-Eaters.* Baton Rouge: Louisiana State Univ. Press, 1992.
Ward, John William. *Andrew Jackson: Symbol for an Age.* New York: Oxford Univ. Press, 1955.
Watson Harry L. *Jacksonian Politics and Community Conflict: The Emergence of the Second American Party System in Cumberland County, North Carolina.* Baton Rouge: Louisiana State Univ. Press, 1981.
——. *Liberty and Power: The Politics of Jacksonian America.* New York: Noonday Press, 1990.
Winters, Donald L. *Tennessee Farming, Tennessee Farmers: Antebellum Agriculture in the Upper South.* Knoxville: Univ. of Tennessee Press, 1994.
Wood, Gordon S. *The Creation of the American Republic, 1776-1787.* Chapel Hill: Univ. of North Carolina Press, 1969.
Wooster, Ralph A. *Politicians, Planters, and Plain Folk: Courthouse and Statehouse in the Upper South: 1850-1860.* Knoxville: Univ. of Tennessee Press, 1975.
Wright, Gavin. *The Political Economy of the Cotton South: Households, Markets, and Wealth in the Nineteenth Century.* New York: Norton, 1978.

C. Dissertations

Atkins, Jonathan M. "'A Combat for Liberty': Politics and Parties in Jackson's Tennessee, 1832-1851." Ph.D. diss., Univ. of Michigan, 1991.
Fisher, Noel Charles. "'War at Every Man's Door': The Struggle for East Tennessee, 1860-1869." Ph.D. diss., Ohio State Univ., 1993.
Lowrey, Frank Mitchell. "Tennessee Voters During the Second Two-Party System, 1836-1860: A Study in Voter Constancy and in Socio-Economic and Demographic Distinctions." Ph.D. diss., Univ. of Alabama, 1973.

Tilly, Bette Baird. "Aspects of Social and Economic Life in West Tennessee before the Civil War." Ph.D. diss., Memphis State Univ., 1974.
Tricamo, John Edgar. "Tennessee Politics, 1845-1861." Ph.D. diss., Columbia Univ., 1965.
Van West, Carroll. "'The Money Our Fathers Were Accustomed To': Banks and Political Culture in Rutherford County, Tennessee, 1800-1850." Ph.D. diss., College of William and Mary, 1982.

Index

abolition, 18, 20, 137, 152, 156, 157, 161, 172, 173, 201, 203, 210, 227, 233, 234, 250
abolitionists, 53, 115, 129-31, 136, 139, 149-51, 158, 163, 166, 175, 178-80, 183, 184, 186, 187, 190, 197, 213, 259, 279n6; *see also* Republican party
Adams, John, 74, 115, 129, 187, 202, 260
Adams, John Quincy, 23, 73, 115, 125, 130, 137, 186
Alabama, 15, 17, 39, 89, 135, 222, 236
Alexandria, Tenn., 260
amendments, constitutional, federal, 86, 233, 235-36, 238, 271-73, 339n60; state, 106, 108, 264, 265, 268
American Party, 195-213, 215-16, 225, 259; conventions, 206, 209
American System, 34, 71, 74
Anderson, Alexander, 78, 113, 120, 129, 131
Anderson, Paulding, 326n34
Arkansas, xii, 19
Arledge, Jesse, 177
Armstrong, Robert, 63-65, 128
army, state, 236-39, 247, 252-54, 257, 260, 271-72, 274, 275, 343n99

Arnell, David R., 168
Arnold, Thomas D., 284-85n52
Athens, Tenn., 189, 248
Athens Post, 195, 209, 216, 225
Avery, William T., 210, 233

Balch, Alfred, 1, 47, 148
Baltimore, Md., 15, 40-45, 52, 210, 222, 224, 290n53
bank, national, 38, 48, 52, 53, 60, 66, 68, 71, 75, 97, 111, 156, 157, 289n34, 308n34; *see also* Bank of the United States, Second; Whig party
Bank of Alabama, 89
Bank of East Tennessee, 104, 106, 266-68
Bank of England, 61
Bank of Tennessee, Knoxville, 33
Bank of Tennessee, Nashville, 66, 77, 102, 105, 106, 304n56
Bank of the United States, Second, 24, 37, 39-40, 44, 60-62, 67, 73, 82, 89, 91-93, 100
Bank War, 26, 32-35, 48-58, 118
Bankrupt Act (1841), 118, 120, 308n29, 308n34
bankruptcy, 106, 305n64
banks, 5, 21, 42, 88, 178, 255
banks, state, 22, 58, 59, 77, 86, 90, 99, 102-6, 112, 142, 217, 293n10; roll call votes on, 263-68; *see also* Bank of East

banks, *cont.*
    Tennessee; Bank of Tennessee, Knoxville; Bank of Tennessee, Nashville; Farmers and Merchants Bank of Memphis; Planters' Bank of Nashville; Union Bank of Nashville; free banking
Barrow, Washington, 247
Bedford County, Tenn., 3
Bell, John, 30, 31, 41, 55, 56, 63-66, 68-70, 76, 113, 116, 161, 162, 194, 212, 293n5, 336n33; American party and, 196, 200, 210, 215-16; elected to Senate, 147-48; "Immortal Thirteen" and, 120-22, 308n37; presidential candidate (1860), xi, 225-27, 341n92; re-elected to Senate, 191-92, 327n42; rivalry with Jones, 188-92, 203, 213; secession crisis and, 245, 247, 249; White presidential candidacy and, 35-38, 42-44, 48
Benton, Thomas Hart, 48, 311n68
Biddle, Nicholas, 61, 62, 89
Bilbo, W. N., 196-97
Billings, J. J. F., 196
Bills, John Houston, 63, 65
Blackwell, Julius W., 137, 312n83
Blair, Francis Preston, 78
Bledsoe County, Tenn., 14, 250
Blount, William, 22
Bolivar Democrat, 177
Bradfield, George W., 335n27
Bransford, Thomas L., 90, 136
Breckinridge, John C., 223-28, 335n27
Brien, John S., 245
Britton, James, 226-27
Brown, Aaron V., 49, 68, 126, 133, 153, 155, 158, 168, 172, 173, 182, 185, 207, 212, 220; gubernatorial candidate, 138-39, 147-48, 315n24
Brown, John, 220
Brown, John S., 50

Brown, Milton, 138, 189, 313n85
Brown, Neill S., 66, 147, 159-61, 196-97, 245
Brown, Thomas, 123
Brownlow, William G., 80, 119, 125, 133, 142, 149, 165, 191, 196-97, 199, 205, 214, 231, 252, 256, 327n42
Buchanan, Andrew, 2
Buchanan, James, 182, 207-12, 214, 217-20, 225

Calhoun, John C., 22, 26-30, 56, 57, 65, 66, 126, 136, 153, 155, 160, 161, 164, 168, 179
California, 144, 145, 150, 156, 163, 164, 170
Cameron, Simon, 246
Campbell, Brookins, 325n24
Campbell, James, 55, 77, 123, 133
Campbell, Thomas J., 244
Campbell, William B., 24, 31, 51, 53, 56, 57, 90, 116, 135, 164, 178, 196-97, 212, 214, 245; as governor, 189, 192, 326n41; gubernatorial candidate (1851), 174-76, 322n103; nominated for governor (1861), 254-55
Campbell County, Tenn., 301n19
Cannon, Newton, 12, 63-65, 72, 75-80, 116
Cannon County, Tenn., 167, 248
Carroll, William, 1, 2, 6, 12, 14, 22, 28, 30, 33, 35, 43, 44, 63, 72, 286-87n11
Carroll, William H., 219, 224, 230
Carroll County, Tenn., 17
Carter County, Tenn., 322n96
Carthage, Tenn., 190
Caruthers, Abraham, 142
Caruthers, Robert L., 28, 70, 94, 123
Cass, Lewis, 126-27, 149, 151, 152, 157, 169, 182
Catron, John, 58, 63, 92, 139
Charleston, S.C., xi, 168, 218, 220, 221, 222, 244

Chattanooga, Tenn., 87, 248, 253
Cheatham, Leonard P., 128
Cherokee Indians, 15
Chickasaw Indians, 15, 17
Childress, John W., 65, 88
Cincinnati, Ohio, 221
Cincinnati Signal, 151, 153
Civil War, xi, xiv, 3, 19, 142
Claiborne, Thomas, 11
Clarksville, Tenn., 44, 173, 181, 196, 210
Clarksville Jeffersonian, 82, 97, 131, 148, 159, 163, 169, 173, 178, 193, 212, 256
Clay, Henry, 23, 26, 28, 34, 39, 48, 56, 98, 164, 188, 199, 208; presidential candidate, 22, 43, 57, 65, 189; (1840), 60, 68-76, 78-79, 113; (1844), 119-20, 124-26, 128-30, 133, 135-39, 147, 311n68
Cleveland, Tenn., 244
Cocke, William M., 206
Cocke County, Tenn., 322n96
Coe, Levin, 62, 158
coercion, 232-34, 237, 239, 240, 243, 246, 249
Columbia, Tenn., 35, 72, 94, 137, 223
compromise, 95, 122, 123, 147, 152, 157-58, 231, 235, 239, 240, 243-45, 338n52
Compromise of 1833, 28
Compromise of 1850, 170-80, 182-85, 189-91, 193; *see also* Crisis of 1850
Confederate States of America, xi-xiii, 19, 228, 229, 243, 246-48, 250, 254-57, 274, 275, 343n99
constitution, 163
constitution, Confederate, 243, 257, 275
constitution, Tennessee, 3-5, 279n6; (1796), 18; (1834), 13, 20, 43, 99, 254, 308n33, 343n102; *see also* amendments, constitutional

constitution, United States, 2, 5, 23, 34, 70, 74, 82, 85, 96, 113, 119, 121, 135, 136, 146, 174, 200, 202, 203, 209, 214, 226; in secession crisis, xi, 229-34, 238, 240, 244, 245, 252, 259; slavery and, 150-52, 157, 158, 165, 201, 228; *see also* amendments, constitutional; strict construction
Constitutional Union party, xi, 226-27, 229
convention, 48, 50, 137, 173, 200, 201, 224, 238, 239, 243, 246, 271, 272, 335n27; proposed (1861), xi, 235-37, 239-41, 270-72; secessionist (1861), 242, 256; *see also* American party; Democratic party; Opposition; Union party; Whig party
convention, constitutional (1796), 3; (1834), 4, 18, 37, 123, 280
Cooper, William F., 166-68, 211
corn, 16, 17, 58, 89, 90, 142, 249
corporations, 83, 84, 108, 216-17, 263, 264, 265, 268; legislative control over, 100-102
"corrupt bargain," 23, 125, 129, 208
cotton, 6, 7, 15-17, 19, 28, 33, 53, 58, 88, 89, 96, 116, 156, 157, 189, 231, 232, 234, 240, 249, 250
Craighead, David, 139
Crawford, William H., 22, 42
Crimean War, 330n79
Crisis of 1850, 163-72, 177, 185, 213; *see also* Compromise of 1850
Crisp, Elihu C., 72
Crittenden, John J., 232, 240, 338n52
Crockett, David, 285n52
Cullom, William, 190, 191
Currin, David M., 219

Dallas, George M., 128-29
Darnell, Nicholas, 65-66
Davidson County, Tenn., 6, 11, 129, 147, 167, 301n23
Davis, Jefferson, 247, 253, 257
Decatur County, Tenn., 248, 319n63
Declaration of Independence, Tennessee (1861), 246, 274, 275
DeKalb County, Tenn., 260, 301n19
Democratic Party, xii-xiii, 24-26, 54, 55, 60, 81, 94, 95, 111, 119, 124, 212-14, 236-39, 247-49, 254, 258, 259; constituency of, 87, 88; divisions within, 142-43, 158-59, 168-69, 172, 173, 182, 184-85, 218-19, 224, 226-27, 320-21n83; economic policies of, 91-92, 96-97; ideology of, 82-84, 86-87, 90-91, 177-78; local issues and, 98-109; national conventions, 24, 40-46, 52, 70, 72-73, 127, 128, 148-49, 182-85, 207, 218-19, 220-23, 290n53; Panic of 1837 and, 61-62; slavery and, 149-61, 177-80, 316-17n36; state conventions, 83, 126, 155, 157, 158, 172, 182, 185, 202, 220-24; *see also* crisis of 1850; elections; "Immortal Thirteen"; Kansas-Nebraska Act; Mexican War; slavery; southern rights; Texas, annexation of
Deposit Act (1836), 59
Dick, N. and J. Company, 57
"dictation," 56, 143, 158; *see also* elections, freedom of; Jackson, Andrew
Dillahunty, Edmund, 28, 94, 160
distribution, 71, 117, 118, 133, 216, 303n43, 308n34
Distribution Act (1836), 66
District of Columbia, 109, 170, 289n34, 339n60; *see also* Washington, D.C.

disunion, xi-xii, xv, 28, 29, 135-37, 158, 160, 165, 166, 170, 173-75, 183, 184, 189-90, 209, 212, 214, 227, 230, 233, 239, 241, 244, 248, 250; *see also* secession
Donelson, Andrew Jackson, 46, 130, 171, 198-99, 206, 209, 321n89
Douglas, Stephen A., 169, 182, 192-93, 233; presidential candidate (1860), 218-24, 226-28
Dred Scott v. Sandford, 217, 218, 221
Dyer County, Tenn., 318n60, 319n63

East Tennessee, 13-15, 37, 39, 50, 53, 55, 89, 123, 137, 174, 185, 221, 233, 267, 315n24; antislavery in, 19-20; election results in, 52, 78, 176, 241; internal improvements and, 16, 66, 77, 99-100, 162, 322n103; legislators from, 9-10; slavery in, 19-21, 179, 249-50; unionism in, xii, 215, 241, 244, 247-48, 250-56, 258, 259, 341n92; United States senators and, 17, 121, 147, 189; voting patterns in, 87
East Tennessee Convention (1861), 252, 253, 257
Eastman, E. G., 125, 155, 156, 158, 159, 162, 167, 169-71, 185, 187, 209
Eaton, John H., 29-31, 37-38
elections, xiv, 3, 11, 13, 14, 21, 24, 31, 32, 47, 65, 86, 186, 195, 219, 284-85n52, 287n11; freedom of, 54, 56, 64, 86, 293n5
elections, presidential 6; (1824), 22-23; (1828), 23, 85; (1832), xiii, 1, 24, 25, 52; (1836), 36-55, 57, 73; (1840), 76, 112-17, 150; (1844), 126-40, 150; (1848), 148-49, 159; (1852), 181-85, 189-91; (1856), 206-11, 213; (1860), xi, 81, 215,

Index

217-28, 341n92
elections, state, 6, 21, 114, 150, 307n21; (1821), 8, 22; (1835), 12, 43; (1837), 63-65, 74, 76; (1839), 72-81, 112; (1841), 116-18; (1843), 120, 124-25, 137-38; (1845), 138-39; (1847), 147-48, 150; (1849), 155-62, 318-19n63; (1851), 172-77, 180-82, 322n103; (1853), 185-88, 191-92, 329n72; (1855), 200-205, 207, 329n72; (1857), 55, 212, 216; (1859), 108-9, 216-17; (1861), xiii, 242-44, 253-59
elections, state referenda, 1861, February, xi, 239-43, 270; June, 246-48, 252, 256, 341n92
elections, United States senator, 17, 56, 111, 284n52, 292n3; (1831-33), 29-32; (1837), 65; (1839), 112-13; (1845), 143; (1847), 147-48, 315n21; (1851), 17-18, 173-74, 188-89; (1857), 212; *see also* "Immortal Thirteen"
Elizabethton, Tenn., 29
Elizabethton Tennessee Whig, 76
Emancipator, The, 20
Embree, Elihu, 20
England. *See* Great Britain
Ewing, Andrew, 158, 182, 185, 245
Ewing, Edwin H., 68, 178, 245
expansion, territorial, 140, 144; *see also* slavery, expansion of; Texas, annexation of
expunging resolutions, 48-50, 75

farmers, 6-8, 15-17, 28, 33, 34, 89, 96, 97, 131, 142, 234, 241, 250, 281n16
Farmers and Merchants Bank of Memphis, 33, 57
Faxon, Charles, 82
Fayette County, Tenn., 62, 161, 318n60
federalist, 23, 44, 50, 53, 73, 74, 76,
78-80, 82, 83, 86, 96, 98, 111, 112, 115, 120, 129, 131, 137, 139, 148, 186, 187, 202, 208, 213, 259
Federalist party, 6, 71, 73, 84, 118, 148
Fentress County, Tenn., 90, 248
Ferguson, Adam, 142
Fillmore, Millard, 151, 169, 174-76, 183, 188-90; presidential candidate (1856), 206, 208-11, 216, 227
"fire eaters," 167, 168, 170, 171, 177, 213, 220, 228, 230, 231, 259, 317n43
Fitzgerald, William, 285n52
Florida, 24, 63, 243
Fogg, Francis B., 35, 120
Foote, Henry S., 219, 233, 247
Force Bill (1833), 27-28, 35; (1861), 243
Fort Donelson, 258
Fort Henry, 258
Fort Pickens, 243
Fort Sumter, xi-xii, 215, 243, 244, 251, 253, 278
Foster, Ephraim H., 29-32, 55-56, 63-65, 96, 114, 116, 133, 147, 189, 313n85; gubernatorial candidate (1845), 138-39, 147; "Immortal Thirteen" controversy and, 120-23, 125, 308n37; "instructed" out of senate, 112-13; White presidential candidacy and, 35-38, 44
Fowlkes, Jeptha, 243
France, 96
Franklin, Tenn., 119
Franklin County, Tenn., 143, 177
free banking, 106-8
free blacks, 19, 279n6
Free Soil party, 152
Frelinghuysen, Theodore, 125
Fremont, John C., 206, 209-11
Fugitive Slave Law (1850), 170, 172, 173, 175, 179, 183, 228, 230

Gainesboro, Tenn., 90
Gallatin, Tenn., 19, 119, 155
General Assembly, Tennessee, 3, 5-6, 19, 21, 23, 33, 37, 43, 56, 77, 81, 97-108, 111, 112, 118, 125, 139, 157, 162, 173, 176, 177, 212, 257, 258, 292n3; roll-call votes in, 100, 101, 103, 105, 107, 263-75
General Assembly, Tennessee, sessions (1835-36), 48-49; (1837-38), 65-66, 102, 127; (1839-40), 101-3, 105, 112; (1841-42), 104-6, 120-24, 127; (1842 extra), 98-99, 106; (1843-44), 106; (1845-46), 106, 142-43; (1847-48), 107, 147, 162; (1849-50), 106, 166-67; (1851-52), 106, 108, 181; (1861 first extra), 234-39; (1861 second extra), 246-47; *see also* elections, United States senator; General Assembly, Tennessee; "Immortal Thirteen"
general incorporation, 106, 305n64
Gentry, Meredith P., 148, 162, 170, 174, 190, 191, 303n43; gubernatorial candidate (1855), 201-3, 205, 210
Georgia, 22, 52, 87, 167, 170, 241, 322n103
Gibson County, Tenn., 17, 244
Giles County, Tenn., 15, 66, 322n96
Gordon, George W., 160
Graham, Daniel, 148
Grand Divisions. *See* East Tennessee; Middle Tennessee; Tennessee, state sectionalism; West Tennessee
Great Britain, 2, 40, 96, 129-32, 143-44
Greene County, Tenn., 20, 52, 322n96
Greeneville, Tenn., 126, 252
Grundy, Felix, 29-31, 33-37, 43-45, 48, 55-56, 63, 65, 66, 68, 72, 112-14, 120, 308n31

Guadalupe-Hidalgo, Treaty of, 150
Guild, Josephus C., 48, 49, 65
Guthrie, James L., 221
Gwin, James, 44, 51
Gwin Letters, 45-46

Hall, Allen A., 34, 54, 68
Hamilton, Alexander, 74, 82
Hamilton County, Tenn., 248
Hardeman County, Tenn., 318n60
Hardin County, Tenn., 248, 322n96
Harper's Ferry, Va., 220
Harris, Isham G., xiii, 109, 181, 185, 212, 216, 220, 221, 223; in secession crisis, 233-39, 241, 242, 245-47, 251-59, 339n60, 343n99
Harris, Jeremiah G., 80
Harrison, William Henry, 48, 52, 53, 57, 65, 73, 117-18, 120, 125; presidential candidate, (1840), 113-15
Hatton, Robert S., 212, 216
Hawkins County, Tenn., 322n96, 326n34
Haynes, Landon C., 174, 233, 242
Haywood County, Tenn., 318n60
Heiskell, Frederick S., 23, 24
Helms, William T., 335n27
Henderson County, Tenn., 65, 248
Henry, Gustavus Adolphus, 189, 190, 192, 247, 325n31; *see also* "Henrymander"
Henry, John F., 229
Henry County, Tenn., 17
"Henrymander," 181, 186, 187, 205, 212, 216
Hickman County, Tenn., 322n96
Hill, H. R. W. and Company, 57
House, George W., 80
House, John F., 247
House of Representatives, United States, 23, 34-36, 41, 43, 48, 52, 150, 194, 207
Howard, John K., 222
Hunt, W. Hasell, 34

Index

Hunter, William, 139
Huntsman, Adam, 285n52

Illinois, 169, 182, 218, 219, 222, 224, 228
"Immortal Thirteen," 120-25, 139, 187
Independent Treasury, 65, 67-69, 74-76, 91-93, 95, 97, 112, 113, 116-18
index of disagreement, 304n55
Indian removal, 24, 35, 54, 73
Indiana, 210
individual liability, 100-102, 268
instructing resolutions, 48-49, 65, 112, 121
internal improvements, federal, 5, 73, 115, 116; state, 16, 17, 21, 64, 66, 71, 77, 98-100, 102, 106, 108, 143, 188, 263, 267, 269, 305n64, 322n103
interrogatories, 121-23, 308n34
Ireland, 142

Jackson, Andrew, xii, xiii, xv, 1, 2, 6, 15, 17, 36-43, 55-57, 61, 63, 67, 73, 74, 78, 82-85, 94, 95, 115, 126, 138, 139, 186, 187, 198, 199, 207, 208, 212, 213, 258, 284n52; Bank War and, 32-35; and 1836 presidential election, 43-54; fiscal policies, 58-60, 92-94; interference and "dictation" of, 31-32, 45-46, 50-51, 85-87, 134; Nullification and, 26-32, 135-36, 140, 179, 213, 229; as republican leader, 22-25; Texas annexation and, 128, 134
Jackson, Tenn., 138
Jackson County, Tenn., 90
Jarnigan, Spencer, 121-23, 125, 147, 308n37, 315n21
Jefferson, Thomas, 6, 23, 41, 74, 82, 147, 186, 187, 260
Johnson, Andrew, xii, 126, 129, 143, 149, 159, 174, 177, 181, 198, 207, 212, 213, 221, 222, 243, 244, 258; gubernatorial candidate (1853), 185-88, 192; (1855), 201-3, 205, 211, 329n72, 330n79; in secession crisis, 230-32, 236, 237, 239, 241, 249, 252
Johnson, Cave, 44, 52, 92, 114, 128, 159, 182, 184, 229, 245, 288n31
Johnson, Richard M., 36-37, 72, 114, 290n53
Johnson, Robert, 222, 232
Johnson County, Tenn., 322n96
Jones, George Washington, 143, 230, 231
Jones, James C., 18, 96, 137-38, 147, 181, 211, 219; as governor, 98; gubernatorial candidate (1841), 116-18; (1843), 124-25; as senator, 188-92, 194, 196-97, 203-5, 209, 210, 212-13, 326n41, 327n42
Jonesborough, Tenn., 20
Jonesborough Whig, 20, 95, 119, 124, 125
judicial system, Tennessee, 3-4, 11, 99, 159, 280n9

Kansas, 217-19, 225, 336n33
Kansas-Nebraska Act (1854), 192-95, 200, 202, 203, 206, 217, 218, 219
Kentucky, 22, 28, 36, 56, 68, 71, 75, 76, 88, 104, 113, 119, 147, 186, 221, 222, 232, 247, 258, 293n5
Kincaid, Joseph, 3
Kingston, Tenn., 253, 257
"know-nothings." *See* American party
Knox County, Tenn., 82, 252, 301n23
Knoxville, Tenn., 15, 20, 51, 68, 87, 113, 114, 248, 255, 284n52, 303n43, 335n27

Knoxville Argus, 77, 115, 120, 125, 137
Knoxville Register, 20, 23, 60, 194
Knoxville Whig, 165, 175, 191, 198, 209, 214, 230, 255

Lane, Joseph, 220, 223, 224
"last extremity," 155, 157-60, 179, 184-86, 188, 238
Lauderdale County, Tenn., 318n60, 319n63
Laughlin, Samuel H., 50, 112, 125
Lawrence County, Tenn., 301n19, 322n96
Lea, Luke, 285n52
Lea, Pryor, 284-85n52
Lebanon, Tenn., 50, 51
Lecompton Constitution, 217-19, 225, 336n33
legislators, characteristics of, 7-10
Liberia, 19
Lincoln, Abraham, xii, xiii, 215, 218, 225, 227-28, 258; secession crisis and, 229-33, 239, 243-45, 249, 252, 254, 259
Lincoln County, Tenn., 15, 167, 301n23
liquor, regulation of, 21, 201; *see also* temperance; tippling houses
Locofoco, 85-86, 88, 93, 124, 135, 146, 181, 300n13
Louisiana, 104, 153, 160, 192-93
Louisiana Territory, 167, 192-93, 206

Macon County, Tenn., 248
Madison, James, 74
Madison County, Tenn., 138, 301n23
Manassas, first battle of, 256
Marion County, Tenn., 14, 248
market revolution, 109, 304n69
Martin, Andrew L., 66
Martin, William, 51
Maryland, 211
Massachusetts, 48, 151
Maury County, Tenn., 6, 16, 47, 167, 322n96

Maynard, Horace, 255, 256
Maysville Turnpike bill, 24, 54
McCullum, James, 210
McDowell, James P., 252
McGaughey, John, 242
McGavock, Jacob, 164
McMinn County, Tenn., 121, 248, 301n23
McNairy, Boyd, 191
McNairy County, Tenn., 301n23, 318n60, 319n63
Meigs, Return J., 237
Meigs County, Tenn., 248
Memphis, Tenn., 89, 150, 151, 153, 158, 161, 188, 196, 205, 219, 226, 232, 243, 258, 327n42
Memphis and Charleston Railroad Company, 188-89
Memphis Appeal, 138, 155, 158, 159, 169, 193, 208, 211, 219, 233, 234, 242, 317n43
Memphis Avalanche, 220
Memphis Bulletin, 256
Memphis Eagle, 147, 165, 167
Memphis Enquirer, 57, 60, 62, 68, 146, 161
Mexican Cession, 160, 164, 167, 168
Mexican War, 141, 144-47, 149, 150, 315n24
Mexico, 127, 132, 133, 155, 178
Michigan, 126, 149
Middle Tennessee, 7, 10, 14-18, 28, 65, 76, 89, 121, 167, 174, 179, 252, 254, 255, 258, 315n24; election results in, 52, 78, 162, 176, 177, 211, 256-57, 318-19n63; internal improvements and, 66, 99; slavery in, 19-20, 249-50; support for disunion in, xii, 215, 248-50, 253, 259; voting patterns in, 53, 87-88
Military League (1861), 247, 274, 275
Mills, C. H., 241
Mississippi, 17, 163, 219, 236

Index

Missouri, 13
Missouri Compromise, 167-69, 193, 194, 206, 209, 313n85, 317n36
"money power," 32, 44, 52, 79, 82-84, 88, 91, 92, 115, 185, 217
Monroe County, Tenn., 248
Monterrey, battle of, 174
Montgomery, Ala., 238, 239, 243, 271, 272
Montgomery County, Tenn., 301n23
Mooresville, Tenn., 47
Morgan County, Tenn., 14, 301n19
Mott, William H., 260-61
Murfreesborough, Tenn., 72-75, 116, 119, 258, 261

Nashville, Tenn., 11, 15, 16, 29, 31, 33-36, 52, 57, 68, 81, 88, 89, 104, 113, 114, 120, 121, 128, 133, 136, 137, 150, 185, 191, 196, 224, 238-40, 245, 258, 271; *see also* Nashville Convention
Nashville American, 159, 169, 170, 172, 174, 179, 184, 189, 191
Nashville Bridge Company, 58
Nashville Convention (1850), 163-72, 174, 184
Nashville Gazette, 197, 198, 200
Nashville National Banner, 34, 46, 50, 53, 54, 60, 64, 66, 69
Nashville Patriot, 232, 257
Nashville Republican, 23, 39, 40, 42, 46, 51, 53, 57, 58, 60
Nashville Republican Banner, xi-xii, 68, 69, 71, 76, 77, 84, 85, 94, 100, 102-4, 119, 124, 133-36, 138, 145, 152, 159, 160, 164-69, 176, 179, 183, 193, 216, 220, 229-31, 234, 240, 254-56
Nashville True Whig, 165, 170, 187, 194, 198, 200, 203
Nashville Union, 44, 49, 50, 53, 57, 61, 65, 66, 73, 74, 77-78, 80, 92, 115, 119, 128, 129, 132, 137, 144, 148, 152, 155-59, 162, 169, 171, 172, 174, 175, 183
Nashville Union and American, 185, 187, 193, 202, 205, 208, 209, 219, 234, 240, 242, 246, 335n27
Nashville Whig, 68-70, 75, 85, 86, 101, 104, 114, 119, 133-36, 139, 147
National Republican party, 26, 82
Nelson, Thomas A. R., 18, 174, 181, 189, 190, 192, 199, 252, 255-57, 325n31
Netherland, John, 189, 216, 217, 252, 326n34
New Hampshire, 182
New Jersey, 125
New Mexico, 144, 150, 156, 163, 170
New Orleans, La., 16, 22, 57, 89, 130, 135
New York, 57, 77, 137, 199, 222, 237, 270, 272, 312n84
Nicholson, Alfred O. P., 66, 68, 116, 126, 129, 143, 149, 151, 168, 173, 182, 185, 212, 308n31
nonintervention, 151-52, 169, 170, 178, 193, 208, 212, 214, 217-19, 221, 223, 224
North Carolina, xii, 18, 278, 342n92
Norvell, Caleb C., 68, 86, 94
Nullification, 24, 26-31, 53, 95, 136, 199, 233, 285n52
"nullifier," 29, 45, 135-37, 155, 160, 164, 165, 178, 182, 184, 185, 200, 209, 216, 259

Obion County, Tenn., 319n63
Ohio, 15, 114, 115
Old Line Whigs, 204-7, 209-13, 219, 228
Opposition, 109, 216-17, 230, 236-37, 239, 247, 259, 336n33; conventions, 225-26
Order of the Star-Spangled Banner, 195

Oregon, 143-44, 152, 159, 220, 317n36
Overton, John, 22
Overton County, Tenn., 90

Panic, financial, of 1819, 13, 22, 33, 90; of 1837, 13, 57-63, 79, 80; of 1839, 88-91; of 1857, 216-17, 259
participation, voter, 1, 6, 52, 78, 79, 115, 143, 183, 184, 191, 216, 247, 299n77
party, political, xii, xiii, 1, 23, 50, 64, 76, 207, 289n45; local issues and, 21, 98-108; opposition to, 40-42, 44, 51, 56, 59-61, 67, 115; organization, xiii, 81, 113; *see also* American party; Democratic party; Opposition; Whig party
patronage, 17, 46, 54, 56, 57, 60, 69, 75, 85, 86, 126, 143, 145, 149, 190, 249, 254, 342n93
Pennsylvania, 48, 61, 70, 89, 150, 182, 199, 207, 210
Peyton, Balie, 56, 57, 64, 245
Philadelphia, Pa., 15, 57, 197, 203, 206
Pierce, Franklin, 182-84, 187, 191, 193, 199, 207
Pillow, Gideon J., 128, 130, 171, 182
planters. *See* farmers
Planters' Bank of Nashville, 13, 33, 57-58, 109, 216
Poinsett, Joel R., 113
Polk, James K., xii, 41, 52, 58, 62, 63, 65, 67-68, 83, 88, 111, 123, 125, 138, 150, 155, 159, 188, 198, 199, 213, 219; Bank War and, 33-36; as governor, 92, 103, 105, 308n31; gubernatorial candidate (1839), 72-80, 98; (1841), 116-18; (1843), 124-25; as president, 97, 143-49, 152; presidential candidate (1844), 128-29, 134-37; presidential election

of 1836 and, 37, 43, 44, 47, 51; vice-presidential hopes, 112, 114-15, 126-27
Polk, Lucius J., 211
Polk, William H., 122, 167, 174, 177, 182, 219, 224, 229-30; gubernatorial candidate (1861), 254-59
Polk County, Tenn., 248
popular sovereignty. *See* nonintervention
post notes, 99
Powel, Samuel, 55
Pulaski, Tenn., 147, 210

railroads, 16, 100, 106, 107, 234, 253, 255, 266, 322n103, 327n42
Raleigh, N.C., 128, 133
Raleigh, Tenn., 161
Republican party, 195, 196, 200, 206-8, 210, 211, 213, 217, 218, 225, 258, 259; presidential election of 1860 and, 217, 220, 223, 225-27; secession crisis and, 228-36, 239-40, 242-44, 249, 250, 254
republicanism, xiv-xvi, 1-6, 14, 21, 23-25, 39, 46, 54, 61, 79, 82, 86, 139, 167, 179, 202, 260
revolution, right of, xii, 179-80, 232, 245
Reynolds, Robert B., 126
Rhea County, Tenn., 12, 248
Rhett, Robert Barnwell, 168
Richmond, Va., 15, 222, 238, 253, 335n27
Roane County, Tenn., 253
Robb, Alfred, 210
Rucker, Edmund, 290n53
Rucker, William, 63
Rutherford County, Tenn., 301n23

Scott, Winfield, 175, 181-82, 183, 184, 190-92, 196, 203, 211, 326n34

Index

Scott County, Tenn., 14, 250, 301n19
secession, xi, xii, 21, 27, 28, 170, 171, 173, 174, 179, 180, 200, 207, 209, 215, 220, 229, 231, 232, 244, 259; in Tennessee, 233-43, 246-49, 255, 342n92
Seminole War, 24, 63-64, 155
Senate, United States, 40, 48-49, 55, 123, 124, 132, 150, 190, 192, 249
Sequatchie County, Tenn., 248
Shelby County, Tenn., 161, 301n23, 318n60
Shiloh, battle of, 258
slave rebellion, 18, 19, 220, 229
slave trade, 170, 202, 284-85n52
slavery, xiv, 18-22, 25, 42, 53, 88, 115, 129-30, 132, 137, 138, 182, 183, 187, 193, 200, 201, 209, 212-13, 219, 221-23, 259, 260, 318-19n63, 339n60, 342n92; expansion of, xv, 21-22, 109, 140, 149-55, 177-79, 195, 206-8, 214, 217-18, 224, 226, 313n85, 317n36; federal protection of, 220-23; in secession crisis, 228-31, 233-35, 242, 247-50; *see also* Crisis of 1850; Democratic party; Kansas-Nebraska Act; nonintervention; Whig party
slaves, 3, 13, 16, 58, 89, 142, 161, 281; ownership of, xiii, 7-10, 19, 282
small notes, 99, 104-6, 294n12
Smith, Henry G., 232
Smith, Samuel G., 33, 39
Smith County, Tenn., 50
Somerville, Tenn., 161
South Carolina, 22, 24, 26-28, 56, 135, 160, 167, 168, 170, 175, 178, 179, 184, 228, 243
southern rights, xi, 21, 151, 152, 155, 159-61, 166, 168, 172, 173, 177, 179, 183, 186, 188, 193, 204, 206-9, 212, 217, 220, 224, 227, 229-33, 235, 239, 244, 251, 255
Sparta, Tenn., 77, 164
"spoils party," 75, 76, 84, 85, 94, 111, 113, 114, 199
"spoilsmen," xv, 53, 71, 86, 148, 208, 259
squatter sovereignty, 194, 197, 208, 218, 223
Standifer, James, 37
Stanton, Frederick P., 138, 153, 161, 181, 313n86
state rights, xiii, 53, 224, 239, 240
Stewart County, Tenn., 19, 145
Stones River, battle of, 258
strict construction, 83, 91, 92, 94, 178, 193-94, 213
Sturtevant, J. M., 97
"submission," 134, 162, 175, 178, 237, 239, 240
subtreasury. *See* Independent Treasury
Sullivan County, Tenn., 52, 248, 322n96
Sumner County, Tenn., 48, 155

Talbot, Joseph H., 65
Taney, Roger B., 32
tariff, 27, 28, 35, 71, 73, 82, 95-97, 115, 124, 129, 133, 143, 149, 178, 202, 231, 243, 303n43, 315n21
taxation, 13, 33, 96, 97, 99, 106, 108, 231, 244, 247, 252, 254, 263, 264, 266, 267, 282n24, 305n64, 308n34
Taylor, Nathaniel G., 325n24
Taylor, Zachary, 146-49, 151, 153, 155, 157, 160, 164, 169, 188-89
Temperance, 201, 329n72
Temple, Oliver P., 252
Tennessee, economic conditions in, xiii, 57-58, 77-79, 88-90, 111, 138-39, 142, 330n79
Tennessee, state sectionalism in, xiv,

Tennessee, state sectionalism in, *cont.*
  14-18, 21, 25, 87-88, 98, 99, 189
Tennessee Manumission Society, 20
Tennessee Platform, 174, 222
Tennessee School for the Blind, 97, 266, 269
Texas, 170; annexation of, 111, 127-40, 142, 144, 147, 150, 313n85
Thomas, James H., 174
Thompson, James L., 233
Timberlake (Eaton), Peggy O'Neal, 30
Tippling houses, 98
Tipton County, 318n60
tobacco, 6, 7, 15-17, 19, 58, 90, 96, 249
Topp, Robertson, 151, 161
Totten, A. O. W., 247
treasury bank, 59, 92
Treasury Circular, 59
Trenton, Tenn., 244
Trigg, Connally F., 255
Trousdale, William, 155-57, 159, 162, 163, 166, 172, 173, 175, 177, 182, 183, 322n103
Turner, Nat, 18
Turney, Hopkins L., 123, 143, 153, 173-74, 177, 181
Turney, Samuel, 121
Tyler, John, 118-20, 124, 126, 127, 132-34, 138, 311n68

union, xi-xiii, xv, 21, 136-37, 140, 179-80, 207, 213, 217, 225, 244, 245; *see also* American party; Democratic party; Union party; Whig party
Union Bank of Nashville, 13, 33, 57-58, 101, 109, 216
Union party, 177, 229-32, 240-47, 249, 251, 253-54; *see also* elections, state (1861)
Utah, 170

Van Buren, Martin, 24, 26, 32, 55, 56, 61, 63, 64, 66, 67, 74, 85, 91, 92, 125, 152; Panic of 1837 and, 59-60, 62, 67-68; presidential candidate (1836), 36-38, 40-54, 290n53; (1840), 68-69, 75, 76, 112; (1844), 126-28, 134
Van Dyke, T. Nixon, 189
Van Pelt, Henry, 155
Vernon, Miles, 12-13
veto, 4, 5; presidential, 24, 32-34, 54, 84, 86, 92-93, 118-19, 124, 146, 149, 151, 160
Virginia, xii, 6, 8, 18, 222, 252, 253, 257, 278n2, 322n103

Walker, James, 62, 66, 67, 77, 92
Walker, Joseph Knox, 166, 182, 219, 221
Walker, Leroy Pope, 236, 257
War of 1812, 15, 16, 155
Ward, Edward, 8, 22
Warren County, Tenn., 2
Washington, George, 23, 179, 225, 260
Washington, D.C., 42, 51, 72, 73, 83, 118, 147, 165, 178, 190, 191, 243, 257; *see also* District of Columbia
Washington County, Tenn., 18, 20, 52, 248, 322n96
Washington Globe, 54
Washington Peace Conference, 239, 271, 339n69
Washington Union, 198
Watterson, Harvey M., 169, 219, 224, 230
Wayne County, Tenn., 248, 322n96
Weakly County, Tenn., 17, 248
Webster, Daniel, 37, 47, 48, 57, 65, 73, 118, 130, 191, 202
West Tennessee, 10, 14, 16-18, 28, 62, 76, 147, 189, 233, 254, 255, 258; election results in,

Index

52, 78, 162, 176, 205, 211, 228, 241, 256-57; internal improvements and, 66, 77, 99, 327n42; slavery in, 19-20, 155, 161, 249-50; support for disunion in, xii, 179, 215, 248-50, 253, 259; voting patterns in, 53, 87-88
Western and Atlantic Railroad, 87, 267
Wharton, Thomas, 236
wheat, 15, 58, 142
Whig party, xii-xiii, 25, 44, 52-53, 55-57, 65-66, 81, 91, 111, 118, 212-13, 218, 236, 248-49, 254, 259, 293n5, 308n37, 312n83; constituency of, 87-88; divisions within, 142, 188-92, 194-95; economic policies of, 91-96, 303n43, 305n64; ideology of, 84-87, 90-91, 177-78; local issues and, 98-109; national bank and, 114-18, 120, 124, 125, 129, 132, 137-39, 148, 149; national conventions, 70-71, 80, 113, 125, 147-48, 183, 190, 210; opposition to "party," 60-61, 69-70, 74, 134; Panic of 1837 and, 60-62, 66-67; slavery and, 149-50, 152-53, 159-62, 177-80; state conventions, 97, 114, 116, 125, 160-61, 174, 190; unionism of, 160-62, 165-66, 174, 178-79; *see also* American party; crisis of 1850; elections; "Immortal Thirteen"; Kansas-Nebraska Act; Mexican War; Opposition; slavery; southern rights; Texas
White, Hugh Lawson, 33, 55, 56, 63-66, 68-69, 70, 75, 83, 87, 114, 115, 120, 121, 124, 289n34; "instructed" out of senate, 112-13, 116; presidential candidate (1836), 37-40, 42-54
White County, Tenn., 164
Whitthorne, W. C., 223
Williams, Alexander, 181
Williams, Christopher, 191
Williams, James, 209
Williams, John, 284
Williams, Joseph L., 149, 303n43
Williams, Samuel, 244
Williamson County, Tenn., 303n43
Wilmot, David, 150, 152
Wilmot Proviso, 150-53, 155-63, 178
Wilson County, Tenn., 50, 116, 222, 326n34
Winchester Independent, 179

Yancey, William L., 222, 224
Yeatman, Woods and Company, 57, 58
yeomen. *See* farmers
Yerger, Jacob S., 57
Young, John, 51

Zollicoffer, Felix K., 197, 205, 245, 326n34

www.ingramcontent.com/pod-product-compliance
Lightning Source LLC
Chambersburg PA
CBHW030300080526
44584CB00012B/383